CUISINES OF
EUROPE

CUISINES OF EUROPE

by Tony Schmaeling

EXETER BOOKS • NEW YORK

First published in USA 1983
by Exeter Books
Distributed by Bookthrift
Exeter is a trademark of Simon & Schuster, Inc.
Bookthrift is a registered trademark of Simon & Schuster, Inc.
New York, New York

ISBN 0-671-06440-1

Printed in Singapore by Toppan Printing Co.

CONTENTS

INTRODUCTION

One of the great joys of travelling through Europe is the experience of trying out the cooking of each country. For such a comparatively small area, Europe has a large and diverse range of cooking styles. Travelling through Europe, as I did, over two 5-month periods, one can see what influence one country had on another, how the climate and conditions of a particular area determined its cooking and how the cuisines of each country evolved.

I visited many restaurants during my travels, from 3-star establishments to modest roadside inns, sampling and taking photographs of the food, talking to the owners and chefs, trying to obtain a true and balanced picture of the type of food available in Europe today.

There were some disappointments along the way: the country pubs and restaurants of Ireland serve 'International' food and it was difficult to find authentic Irish dishes. The same was true of many countries, particularly in the 'tourist' areas. The prosperity and industrialisation of the last hundred years has played havoc with traditional cooking. Countries like France, those of southern Europe and the Mediterranean seem to have fared better than others in preserving their traditional cuisines.

Appropriately my travels began in Rome, where you can find the cooking of all the regions of Italy. My journey to the south was full of surprises: vegetable dishes had a richness of flavour to equal the most elaborate meat cooking of the north. But the north was enjoyable too. In Florence I sampled some of the most flavoursome meat I have ever tasted. And I would gladly spend the rest of my life in Venice, eating the best seafood in the world.

After a restful journey across the Adriatic, I arrived in one of my favourite towns, Dubrovnik, which became the starting point of my fascinating tour of Yugoslavia. The country is an interesting mixture of people and food styles: the south has been influenced by 500 years of Turkish rule and its food is Middle Eastern in character. By contrast the food of the north is Central European.

I crossed the border into Hungary and my next stop was Budapest, one of the most elegant and sophisticated cities in Europe and the capital of a country which has developed its own characteristic food style. How could one mistake one of their most famous dishes, Goulash, for anything but Hungarian? In its time, as part of the empire of Austria-Hungary, it exerted an influence over the cooking of a large part of central Europe.

Vienna, which was the hub of this empire has many claims to European culinary fame. In the past its cooking style, which could best be described as sophisticated home-style, was adopted by the prosperous households of its neighbouring countries. Its pastries, together with those of France, are considered to be the finest in the world.

My journey from Austria, on my way to Switzerland, took me through some of the most picturesque parts of Europe. The main attraction of Switzerland is not its traditional food yet the plain, hearty, nutritious farm-style cooking that was offered was welcome and appealing.

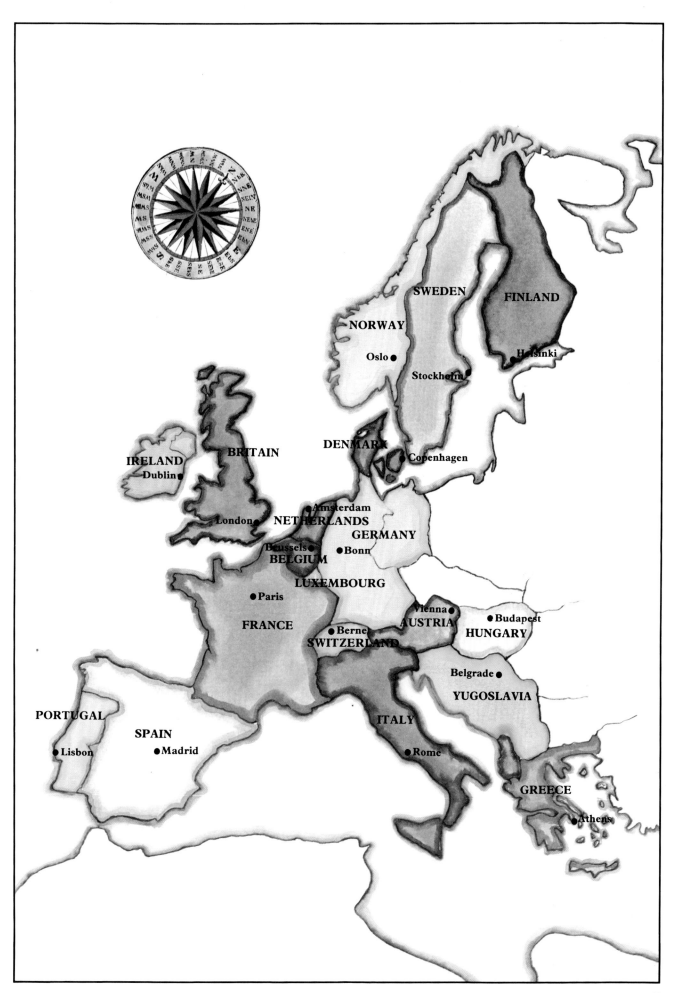

Germany is an interesting example of the dilemma suffered by many countries in recent years where new eating habits have developed at the expense of traditional cooking. That is not to say that traditional cooking is not to be found in Germany: looking for it is part of the fun of travelling through that country.

Of all the countries in Europe, France has been most successful in preserving its traditional cooking styles. One of the main attractions of travelling through France is the food. Each province has retained its individual style and without knowing where one is, it would be possible to guess the province just by tasting the food. Each part of France uses particular ingredients and cooking methods which makes it possible to identify its origin. The availability of wines of exceptional quality throughout the country has greatly contributed to the development of fine food.

Across the Channel in Britain, the picture is quite different. Over the last few years there has been a revival of interest in past eating traditions. It is now possible to travel through the counties of England, Wales and Scotland and to find restaurants, hotels and inns where local traditional dishes are being prepared. I foresee a bright future where once more, throughout the cities and counties of Britain, traditional food will play an important part in the daily lives of the people.

In Ireland the situation is similar. The availability of first class vegetables, fish, fruit and meat is a good start to resurrecting lost food traditions.

The following year my first stop was the four Scandinavian countries. While each individual country has developed separate cooking traditions, the main attractions are the elements which they have in common. Fish and seafood are undoubtedly the best features of Scandinavian food: the fresh fish from the seas, lakes and rivers and the immense range of smoked, dried and pickled fish. They all find their way on to the Smorgasbord, the most typical form of presenting food in Scandinavia. In fact everything that is the best in Scandinavian food is presented on the Smorgasbord: meat, salads, bread, cheese and other dairy products.

The traditional food of the three Benelux countries — Belgium, Netherlands and Luxembourg — is basically that of the farmer and fisherman. The Flemish cooking of northern Belgium and that of Holland are similar: their fishermen bring home the same catch, but there are differences in their preparation. The thrifty Dutch prepare their fish in a simple way while the more exuberant Belgians add a characteristic flair. The Dutch are famous for their cheeses, while the Belgians make some of the finest chocolates in the world. The food of south Belgium, where French is spoken, is in many ways related to provincial French cooking. Belgium and Luxembourg share the Ardenne mountains, famous for its game and pig breeding. The well-known Ardenne ham, pork meat and charcuteries form an important part of Luxembourg cooking. Mountain streams yield trout and pike and the grapes along the Moselle River are made into the excellent wines of Luxembourg.

After months in northern Europe I was now looking forward to the climate and the food of the south. Spain provided a fascinating contrast in all respects and I enjoyed exploring the regional food. The whole trip is filled with pleasant memories: the roast meats of central Spain, the seafood of Barcelona, the paellas of Valencia, the exuberance of the south.

In Portugal, where no part is far from the sea, the seafood is abundant and delicious. Wherever I went fresh seafood was on the menu. The Portuguese are very fond of egg yolks too and use them extensively in their desserts. And there is no better way of finishing a Portuguese meal than with a glass of Port.

Appropriately my last stop in Europe was Greece where European food stops and Middle Eastern cooking begins. Four hundred years of Turkish domination has influenced the cooking of Greece in a profound way. The way they cook their meat, which is mainly lamb, their vegetables such as eggplant and okra, their desserts: baklava, halva, loukoumia, all reflect Middle Eastern traditions.

All flour is plain (all-purpose) flour unless otherwise specified.

ACKNOWLEDGEMENTS

I would like to thank all the chefs and restaurateurs, members of the national and regional tourist offices and all those who made this collection of European recipes possible. Lack of space precludes my mentioning everyone but I would like to particularly thank the following people:

France: Madame Andrieux (Paris)

Italy: Giuliana Bartelletti (Rome); Maureen Campbell (Sydney)

Germany: Uwe Woggon (Frankfurt); Manfred Staeuber (Sydney)

U.K.: Peter Ffrench-Hodges, Catherine Althouse (London); Pip Stuart (Sydney)

Ireland: Dorothy Payten (Sydney); Tim Magennis (Dublin)

Spain: Juan Sanchez Lorenzo (Madrid); Roberto Cunad (Sydney)

Portugal: Miss Fatima (Lisbon)

Greece: Mr Josephopoulos, Miss Pollatos, Mrs Greenberg, Miss Paliadow Lia (Athens)

Austria: Dr Sonja Jordan (Vienna); Mr Noe-Nordberg (Sydney)

Hungary: Judit Mándi (Budapest)

Denmark: Kurt Neilsen (Copenhagen); Stephen Langhorn (Sydney)

Sweden: Katarina Appelkvist, Evelyn Stenberg, Christina Guggenberg (Stockholm)

Finland: Kaarina Pelkonen (Helsinki); Charles Lloyd Jones, Commander Warren Brash (Sydney)

Norway: Elisabeth Heyerdahl (Oslo)

Belgium: Jean Gyory, Katia de Diesbach (Brussels)

The Netherlands: Augusta van Berckel, Cecile Laugenberg (The Hague); Els Wamsteeker (Amsterdam)

Luxembourg: The National Tourist Office, Luxembourg

Yugoslavia: Caslar Krasic (Sydney); Desa Kostic, Milo Domancic (Dubrovnik); Predrag Djordyevic (Belgrade)

Switzerland: Peter Kuehler (Berne); Henry Mendleson (Sydney)

The Publishers would like to thank the following people for lending props and preparing food for the front cover: David Prentice of the Accoutrement Cook Shop, Mosman; Mowbray English Pork Pies, Balgowlah; The Paris Cake Shop, Bondi; The Croissant D'Or Cake Shop, Potts Point; Handler Double Bay Butchery.

FRANCE

France is made up of many provinces which in the past, in one way or another, have led their own existence as independent countries or dukedoms or even as sovereign kingdoms.

That is why, when we speak of French food, we think of the food of the different provinces: Alsace with its foie gras, Normandy its dairy products and apples etc. Even haute cuisine, refined through the ages by the chefs of the aristocracy, has provincial origins. For me, the most interesting aspect of French cooking is that it is a living and ever-growing thing. During my travels through France, having done a great deal of reading on French food, I would arrive at my destination in any province where I was to collect recipes and take photographs of regional dishes, expecting some typical examples which would best represent the region.

But this was not to be, because for the chef to present just a standard rendition of a local dish would be considered an insult to his culinary *genius*. Every cook, every chef, be it at home or in a public eating place, makes his or her own contribution to the ever-changing and growing cuisine of the country. At every stop I made in France I saw examples of that personal touch and the proud announcement of it on the menus. *Fait à la maison, à la façon du chef, préparé par le chef,* or proclaiming the name of its creator: *la Truite Soufflée Celine, Rognon de Veau Flambés 'Lasserre'* and countless others.

There is hardly another country where travelling by one's stomach is more fun. There is always the element of pleasant surprise and discovery, and for the connoisseur, there's the satisfaction of finding yet another 'gem' of provincial food.

Many of the recipes included here were collected during my gastronomic tour through the provinces of France. Some of them were selected because they are representative of the food from that province, but most of them are here because they are interesting, fun to prepare and great to eat. A large number of these recipes was very kindly and unstintingly given to me by the chefs or owners of the many restaurants I visited. They also prepared the fine food which I photographed and which I hope in some way conveys the different feelings and atmospheres of their establishments.

I didn't spend nearly as long in France as I would have liked, but despite my hurried progress, I was able to take in what I consider to be the very essence and spirit of French cooking: the rich diversity of the dishes, the ability of French cooks to get the best out of local ingredients, and, even in the most modest dishes, the evidence of an attitude to cooking which few people in other countries possess.

Right: The Dordogne Valley

FIRST COURSES

Leek Tart
Flamiche aux Poireaux

Serves 6

500 g (1 lb) leeks, cleaned
90 g (3 oz) butter
3–4 tablespoons water
4 tablespoons thick cream
salt and freshly ground black pepper
500 g (1 lb) puff pastry (see p. 331)
1 egg yolk, mixed with a little water

1. Preheat the oven to 200°C (400°F/Gas 6).
2. Chop the leeks finely, using all the white part and
very little of the green. **3.** Melt half the butter in a
heavy pan and stew the leeks gently, gradually adding the rest of the butter as they are cooking.
4. Moisten with the water, cover and cook gently
until the leeks are quite soft and all the liquid has
been absorbed. **5.** Add the cream and season well.
6. Prepare the pastry and divide it into two. **7.** Roll
out half into a thin round and place it on a damp
baking sheet. **8.** Place the leek mixture in the
middle, leaving a border of 3 cm (1½ in) all round.
9. Brush the border with water. **10.** Roll out the rest
of the pastry in the same way and place on top of
the leek mixture. **11.** Press the edges firmly together
so that they are well sealed. **12.** To help the
pastry to rise, feather the edges with a sharp knife.
13. Glaze the surface by brushing with diluted egg
yolk, and make a trellis pattern with the point of a
knife. **14.** Cook the tart for 10 minutes. **15.** Reduce
the heat to 180°C (350°F/Gas 4) and cook for a
further 20–25 minutes until the surface of the pastry
is golden. **16.** The tart should be served very hot,
but it may be cooked in advance and reheated.

Pike Quenelles in Financière Sauce
Quenelles de Brochet Vesaul

Serves 4–6

1.85 kg (3¾ lb) boneless pike meat
(any firm white-fleshed fish may be
substituted)
185 g (6 oz) butter
3 eggs
salt and freshly ground black pepper

Financière Sauce:
2 cups (16 fl oz) Béchamel Sauce
(see p. 329)
125 g (4 oz) mushrooms, finely chopped
2 tablespoons lemon juice
½ cup (4 fl oz) Madeira

1. Pound the fish in a mortar, adding the butter bit
by bit until it forms a smooth paste, or use a food
mill, electric blender, or food processor. **2.** Add the
eggs, one by one. **3.** Season to taste with salt and
pepper. **4.** Leave for 3 or 4 hours in a cool place,
or in the refrigerator. **5.** Preheat the oven to 210°C
(425°F/Gas 7). **6.** Form the mixture into small
sausage-shaped quenelles. **7.** Bring a large saucepan
of salted water to the boil. **8.** Poach the quenelles in
the water for about 20 minutes. **9.** Drain them well,
and arrange on a flameproof serving dish. **10.** Prepare the sauce by making 2 cups of Béchamel.
11. Place the chopped mushrooms into a small
saucepan with the lemon juice and 1 tablespoon of
water and cook for 5 minutes. **12.** Add the drained
mushrooms to the Béchamel sauce. **13.** Add the
Madeira to the sauce and cook a few minutes longer.
14. Cover the quenelles with the sauce. **15.** Cook in
the oven for about 15 minutes. The quenelles should
treble in size. **16.** Serve immediately.

Salted Cod with Aioli Sauce
Aioli Garni

This dish, very popular in Provence, is composed of vegetables, eggs, and fish, decoratively arranged and served with Aioli Sauce.

Serves 6

500 g (1 lb) salt codfish
12 small new potatoes in their jackets
6 small sweet potatoes in their jackets
6 zucchinis (courgettes)
500 g (1 lb) small carrots
500 g (1 lb) green beans
6 eggs
6 ripe tomatoes, peeled and cut into wedges
lettuce
fresh herbs such as parsley, basil, to garnish

Aioli Sauce:
4 cloves garlic per person
1 egg yolk per two persons
olive oil
salt and freshly ground black pepper
lemon juice

1. Soak the codfish overnight in cold water. **2.** Simmer the fish in fresh water for about 10 minutes until cooked. Drain well. **3.** Steam all the vegetables separately until they are cooked, but still quite firm; on no account should they be overcooked. **4.** Hardboil the eggs and cut in half. **5.** Take a large round serving dish and place the fish in the centre, surrounded by the hot vegetables, hard-boiled eggs and raw tomatoes, decorated with lettuce and sprigs of fresh herbs. Serve with Aioli Sauce, from which this famous dish gets its name.

Aioli Sauce: 1. Take 4 cloves of garlic per person and 1 egg yolk for each two persons. **2.** Crush the garlic to a smooth paste in a mortar with a little salt, or use a food processor. **3.** Blend in the egg yolks until the mixture is a smooth homogeneous mass. **4.** Whisk the olive oil into the egg mixture, at first drop by drop, then in a thin trickle, as you would for a mayonnaise. **5.** The aioli will thicken gradually until it reaches the proper stiff, firm consistency. (The exact quantity of oil is determined by the number of egg yolks used, but the sauce should resemble a firm mayonnaise.) **6.** Season to taste with salt, freshly ground black pepper and lemon juice. The sauce is served chilled.

Scrambled Eggs with Ham, Tomatoes and Peppers
Piperade

Serves 4-6

30 g (1 oz) butter
4 tablespoons oil
375 g (12 oz) onions, finely sliced
500 g (1 lb) green peppers (capsicums), cored, seeded, and coarsely chopped
1 kg (2 lb) tomatoes, peeled, seeded and chopped
3 cloves garlic, crushed
bouquet garni
salt and freshly ground black pepper
4-6 thin slices raw ham
8-10 eggs, separated
chopped parsley to garnish

1. Heat the butter and half the oil in a large frying pan. **2.** Sauté the onions until they begin to soften. **3.** Add the peppers and cook for 2 to 3 minutes. **4.** Stir in the tomatoes, garlic, bouquet garni, salt and pepper. **5.** Simmer gently for 30 minutes. **6.** Fry the ham in the remaining oil until tender. Keep warm. **7.** Remove the vegetables from the heat and discard the bouquet garni. **8.** Beat the egg whites until stiff. **9.** Mix with the egg yolks and add to the cooked vegetable mixture. **10.** Stir quickly with a wooden spoon over a moderate heat until the mixture thickens and is blended, with a light and foamy mousse-like consistency. **11.** Place the slices of ham on top. **12.** Garnish with parsley and serve immediately.

Savoury Meat Rolls

Friands Parisiens

Makes approximately 2 dozen friands

500 g (1 lb) best available pork sausage meat
2 tablespoons finely chopped parsley
1 tablespoon finely chopped sage
salt and pepper
1 teaspoon lemon juice
250 g (8 oz) puff pastry (see page 331)
1 egg, beaten

1. Preheat the oven to 190°C (375°F/Gas 5).
2. Mash the sausage meat with the chopped parsley,
sage, salt, pepper and lemon juice until all the ingredients are well blended. **3.** Roll out the puff
pastry and cut it into strips about 7.5 cm (3 in) wide.
4. Place a spoonful of the stuffing on the end of one
strip of pastry, roll it over once and cut across the
pastry. **5.** Dampen the edges with water before
pressing together. **6.** Brush with beaten egg and
place on a baking tray. **7.** Continue in the same way,
until you have used all the meat. **8.** Bake the savoury
rolls for 20 minutes.

Potted Pork Rillettes

Rillettes de Tours

*This recipe comes from Restaurant Le Calandre
in Le Mans.*

Serves 6–8

1 kg (2 lb) pork neck
90 g (3 oz) finest lard
¼ cup (2 fl oz) water
salt and pepper
1 teaspoon mixed spice

1. Cut up the fresh pork neck into small pieces.
2. Melt 30 g of the lard in a heavy pan with a lid.
3. Add the pork pieces and cook lightly, turning
often. **4.** Add the water, and cook gently with the lid
on the pan, for 3 hours, stirring frequently to make
sure the meat does not stick to the bottom of the
pan. The mixture is ready when the meat flakes into
pieces under the pressure of a fork. **5.** Drain the
pieces of pork and reserve any liquid. **6.** Skim the
fat off the liquid and add to the pork. **7.** Season with
salt, pepper and mixed spice, and pound the mixture
finely. **8.** Pour this mixture into small individual
pots. **9.** In a clean saucepan, melt the remaining 60 g
of lard. **10.** Cover each pot with a thin layer of lard,
and chill well.

Duck and Orange Terrine

Terrine de Canard a l'Orange

*This recipe comes from the Hôtel Terminus in
Niort.*

Serves 12

1 kg (2 lb) duck meat, boned and chopped
1 kg (2 lb) minced pork
4 eggs
finely grated rind of 2 oranges
salt and freshly ground black pepper
pinch of allspice
½ cup (4 fl oz) rum

1. Preheat the oven to 180°C (350°F/Gas 4).
2. Blend the duck meat, pork, eggs, orange rind,
salt, pepper, allspice and rum until they are all well
mixed. **3.** Transfer to a well-buttered terrine dish
and cover. **4.** Stand the terrine in a dish of simmering water, and cook in the oven for 1½ hours.
5. Allow to cool, and chill well before serving.

Mushroom Rolls

Croûtes aux Champignons de Montargis

Serves 6–8

250 g (8 oz) mushrooms, sliced
90 g (3 oz) butter
¼ cup (1 oz) flour
1 cup (8 fl oz) milk
salt and pepper
6–8 round bread rolls

1. Simmer the sliced mushrooms in 60 g of the butter for 5 minutes. **2.** Melt the remaining butter in
a saucepan, add the flour and make a roux. **3.** Add
the milk, salt and pepper, and stir briskly with a
wire whisk until the sauce is thick. **4.** Add the mushrooms and their liquid to the sauce and cook
together gently for a few minutes. **5.** Warm the rolls
in the oven. When they are crisp, slice them open
and remove the soft centre. **6.** Butter the hollowed
out rolls lightly and heat again. **7.** Spoon the mushroom mixture into the hollowed out rolls and serve.

***Right:** Duck and Orange Terrine (above) as prepared at the
Hôtel Terminus in Niort, Poitou. Poitou is not one of the
better known gastronomic areas of France and its cuisine is
characterised by its simplicity. The Terminus serves wholesome, bourgeois food which makes the most of the good quality
local produce, especially poultry and pork.*

SOUPS

Vegetable Soup with Pistou

Soupe au Pistou

Pistou is a sauce made with tomatoes, garlic, basil, olive oil and Parmesan cheese — hence the name of this popular soup.

Serves 6–8

125 g (4 oz) dried haricot beans
125 g (4 oz) dried kidney beans
250 g (8 oz) green beans, chopped in half
1 large onion, chopped
250 g (8 oz) carrots, chopped
250 g (8 oz) zucchinis (courgettes), chopped
250 g (8 oz) tomatoes, peeled and chopped
250 g (8 oz) small noodles
2 cloves garlic
1½ tablespoons fresh basil
2 tablespoons olive oil
salt

1. Soak the white haricot beans and red kidney beans in water for 2 to 3 hours. Drain. **2.** Place the chopped beans, onion, carrots, zucchinis and tomatoes in a large saucepan. **3.** Add the dried beans and cover with plenty of salted water. **4.** Bring to the boil, and simmer for 1½ hours. **5.** Add the noodles to the simmering stock and continue cooking for a further 5 to 10 minutes. **6.** While the soup is cooking, crush the garlic in a mortar with plenty of green basil leaves. **7.** Add the olive oil to the mortar and mix to a paste. **8.** When the vegetables are cooked, add a scoop of the hot soup to the garlic, basil and oil paste. Mix well, and return to the soup. **9.** Bring to the boil, and serve, accompanied by rounds of French bread, olive oil and some grated cheese.

Fish Chowder

La Bouillabaisse

There is no general agreement on the ingredients for this dish, each locality varies and the final choice depends upon the catch of the day.

Serves 6–8

Soup:
6 tablespoons olive oil
2 medium onions, finely chopped
1 leek, chopped
½ stalk fennel, chopped
2 medium tomatoes, peeled, seeded and chopped
3 cloves garlic, crushed
generous sprig of thyme
1 bay leaf
1 celery stalk, chopped
1.75 kg (3½ lb) coarse-fleshed fish, such as cod, mullet, mackerel etc.
12 cups (3 litres) white wine fish fumet (see p. 328)
salt and freshly ground black pepper
1 teaspoon powdered saffron
1.75 kg (3½ lb) fine-fleshed fish, such as snapper, whiting, sole, John Dory etc.
garlic-flavoured croûtons

Rouille:
2 cloves garlic, crushed
2 small green peppers (capsicums)
2 egg yolks
6 tablespoons olive oil

Soup: 1. Heat 4 tablespoons of the olive oil in a large fireproof casserole dish or fish kettle. **2.** Add the onions, leek and fennel and cook them gently over a very low heat until the onion is tender, but not browned. **3.** Add the tomatoes, garlic, thyme, bay leaf and celery, and cook for a few minutes longer. **4.** Remove the heads from the fish, clean and trim them. **5.** Add the coarse-fleshed fish and the fish stock to the vegetables. **6.** Season with salt and freshly ground black pepper and the saffron. **7.** Bring to the boil and cook over a brisk heat for 6 minutes. **8.** Add the rest of the fish and continue cooking over a brisk heat for another 6 minutes, or until all the fish is cooked. Take great care not to overcook the fish. **9.** Lift out the fish with a slotted spoon and put into a large warmed serving bowl. Sprinkle with the remaining 2 tablespoons of oil. **10.** Pour the stock into a soup tureen, and put the garlic croûtons in a separate bowl.

Rouille: 1. Crush the garlic with the green peppers in a mortar, or food processor. **2.** Add the egg yolks, and beat in the oil as for a mayonnaise. **3.** Season to taste with salt and freshly ground black pepper. **4.** Finish with a tablespoon of the hot fish broth, beaten in with a wire whisk. **5.** Serve in a sauceboat with the rest of the bouillabaisse. Serve the fish separately.

Cabbage Soup with Bacon
Bréjauda

Serves 8

500 g (1 lb) stewing lamb, diced
125 g (4 oz) lean bacon, diced
10 cups (2.5 litres) water
125 g (4 oz) carrots, finely sliced
4 medium onions, sliced
1 parsnip, sliced
1 leek, washed and sliced
500 g firm cabbage, cut into 8 pieces
4 medium potatoes, quartered
salt and freshly ground black pepper

1. Bring the diced meat and bacon to the boil in the water in a large pot. **2.** Skim the pot well. **3.** Add the vegetables, except for the cabbage and the potatoes. Season well with salt and pepper. **4.** Simmer for 1 hour, or until the meat is cooked. **5.** Add the potatoes and cabbage to the pot and simmer for a further 20 minutes, or until the potatoes and cabbage are cooked. **6.** Serve in deep soup bowls.

Leek and Potato Soup
Soupe à la Bonne Femme

Serves 6-8

4 leeks, the white parts only, finely shredded
125 g (4 oz) butter
8 cups (2 litres) chicken stock (see p. 328)
375 g (12 oz) potatoes, cut in thin slices
salt and pepper
1 tablespoon chopped fresh chervil leaves

1. Cook the leeks in a covered saucepan in half the butter, without allowing the leeks to colour. **2.** When the leeks are cooked and quite soft, add the stock and bring to the boil. **3.** Add the potatoes. **4.** Bring to the boil, reduce the heat and simmer gently. Check the seasoning. **5.** At the last moment, when the potatoes are just cooked through, remove the saucepan from the heat and add the rest of the butter and the chervil leaves.

Bacon and Vegetable Soup
Garbure

A magnificent broth which makes not only a very savoury soup, but also a delicious stew. Garbure is one of the classic dishes of the Béarn district.

Serves 6-8

500 g (1 lb) white beans, dried
2 bay leaves
2 sprigs thyme
4 sprigs parsley
250 g (8 oz) potatoes, peeled and quartered
500 g (1 lb) green beans, cut
1.5 kg (3 lb) confit d'oie (preserved goose) or salt pork
freshly ground black pepper
4 tablespoons goose fat or olive oil
2 carrots, thickly sliced
2 turnips, thickly sliced
4 leeks, sliced
1 onion, sliced
2 cups (8 oz) cabbage, coarsely chopped
croûtons

1. Soak the beans in cold water for several hours. **2.** Drain and rinse them. **3.** Put the beans into a large flameproof casserole with the bay leaves, thyme and parsley. **4.** Add the potatoes, green beans, preserved goose or pork and enough water to cover. **5.** Season to taste with pepper, but add very little if any salt as the preserved goose, or salt pork, is highly salted. **6.** Cook, covered, for 1½ hours, adding more water from time to time if necessary. **7.** Heat the goose fat or olive oil in a heavy frying pan, and sauté the carrots, turnips, leeks and onion without letting them take on any colour. **8.** Add these vegetables to the soup. **9.** Continue cooking at a gentle simmer for another ½ hour. **10.** Remove the goose or salt pork, and keep warm. **11.** Add the cabbage and continue cooking for a further 45 minutes. **12.** The soup, which should by now be very thick, is ready to be served, accompanied by croûtons of French bread. **13.** The meat is served separately, accompanied by steamed potatoes, and whole baby carrots and turnips, which can be added to the soup during the final half hour of cooking.

Fish Soup with Vermicelli

Soupe de Poisson au Vermicelle à la Marseillaise

Serves 6–8

Soup:
6 tablespoons olive oil
2 onions, finely chopped
4–5 cloves garlic, crushed
1 kg (2 lb) small rockfish, cleaned, or selection
of fish heads and trimmings
2 tablespoons tomato paste
10 cups (2.5 litres) water
bouquet garni
salt and freshly ground black pepper
2 potatoes, peeled and chopped
pinch of powdered saffron
60 g (2 oz) broken spaghetti, or vermicelli

Rouille:
2 cloves garlic
2 egg yolks
6 tablespoons olive oil
½ teaspoon powdered saffron
salt and freshly ground black pepper

To serve:
French bread, sliced in rounds and lightly
toasted grated Gruyère or Cheddar

Soup: 1. Heat the oil in a large saucepan, and sauté the onions and garlic until soft and transparent. **2.** Add the fish and the tomato paste, and cook, stirring for 2 minutes. **3.** Pour in the water and bring to the boil. Add the bouquet garni, salt, freshly ground black pepper and potatoes. Simmer for 30 minutes. **4.** Strain the soup into another pan, pressing as much fish as possible through the sieve. **5.** Add the saffron and check the seasoning, adding more salt if necessary. **6.** Bring to the boil, stir in the spaghetti and simmer for 10 minutes. **7.** While the soup is simmering, make the rouille.

Rouille: 1. Beat together the garlic and the egg yolks. **2.** Whisk in the oil, drop by drop as for a mayonnaise. **3.** Add the saffron, and season with salt and pepper.

To Serve:
1. Spread the toast generously with the rouille, and sprinkle some grated cheese on top. **2.** Ladle the soup into dishes and garnish with the toast.

Onion Soup

Tourin

Serves 6–8

60 g (2 oz) pork dripping or fat
750 g (1½ lb) onions, finely sliced
7½ cups (2 litres) chicken stock (see p. 328)
salt and freshly ground black pepper
2 cloves garlic, crushed
4 egg yolks
6–8 rounds of French bread

1. Melt the pork fat in a large, heavy saucepan, and gently fry the onions until they are soft and just beginning to turn brown. **2.** Add the stock, bring to the boil and simmer for 15 to 20 minutes. **3.** Season with salt, freshly ground pepper and the crushed garlic. **4.** Mix the egg yolks together in a large bowl. **5.** Slowly whisk in the hot soup, a little at a time. **6.** The mixture will thicken as the eggs cook. **7.** Return the thickened soup to the saucepan, and stir over a gentle heat for five minutes. **8.** Take great care not to let the soup boil. **9.** Serve with rounds of bread roasted in the oven in a baking dish with a few drops of oil.

Cream of Prawn Soup

Potage Velouté de Crevettes à la Normande

Serves 6

500 g (1 lb) cooked school prawns (shrimps),
shelled
5 cups (1.25 litres) fish fumet (see p. 328)
90 g (3 oz) butter
¾ cup (3 oz) flour
3 egg yolks
½ cup (4 fl oz) cream
12 oysters
salt and pepper

1. Prepare the fish fumet, using the prawn shells. Strain. **2.** In a large saucepan, melt the butter and add the flour to make a roux. **3.** Whisking well all the time, add the fish fumet to the roux to make a Velouté sauce. Season well. **4.** Pound ¾ of the prawns in a mortar, or process them lightly in a food processor. **5.** Add the pounded prawns to the fish Velouté, and simmer gently for 5 minutes. **6.** In a bowl, whisk the egg yolks and the cream together. **8.** Return this mixture to the saucepan. **9.** Add the rest of the prawns and the oysters to the soup. **10.** Heat the soup through, stirring well, taking care not to let it boil, and serve.

Right: Chef Lucien Fleury from the Restaurant Le Champenoise in Audresselles with the ingredients for his speciality — seafood fondue. It is made with pieces of fish, scallops, prawns, mussels and cuttlefish, cooked at the table in hot oil and then dipped into a choice of 3 delicious sauces: Sauce l'Américaine (fish stock, tomatoes and wine); Sauce l'Audressellaise (cream and tomato); and Sauce la Champenoise (fish stock, Champagne and cream).

VEGETABLES

Apples with Bacon
Pommes au Lard

From the Restaurant Ar Milin in Châteaubourg.

Serves 4

4 apples, peeled
4 slices streaky bacon, thinly sliced

1. Preheat the oven to 180°C (350°F/Gas 4).
2. Poach the peeled apples gently in water until they are only just cooked, and still firm. **3.** Wrap each apple in a slice of bacon, securing with a toothpick, and place them in an ovenproof dish. **4.** Cook them in the oven, without butter, until they are golden-brown. **5.** Serve the apples, very hot, as an accompaniment to Fricassée of Rabbit (see p. 33).

Savoury Onion Tart
Pissaladière

Serves 6-8

250 g (8 oz) short crust pastry (see p. 331)
2 tablespoons olive oil
3 large onions, finely sliced
12 black olives
60 g (2 oz) anchovy fillets
125 g (4 oz) grated cheese (Gruyère or Cheddar)

1. Preheat the oven to 210°C (420°F/Gas 7).
2. Prepare the short crust pastry. **3.** Heat the oil in a heavy-bottomed frying pan, and cook the finely sliced onions gently until they are soft but still transparent. **4.** Roll out the pastry and line a 30 cm (12 in) shallow pie tin. **5.** Top the pastry with the cooked onions. **6.** Decorate with anchovies and olives. **7.** Sprinkle the cheese over the whole tart. **8.** Bake until the pastry is cooked and the tart is golden on top (about 20 minutes). **9.** Serve hot.

Baked Mushrooms with 'Snail Butter'
Champignons avec Beurre d'Escargot

The mushrooms of the Touraine are big field mushrooms. They are served inverted on slices of toasted French bread, brimming with snail butter, and form an accompaniment to the roasts for which this region is famous.

Serves 6-8

12-16 large mushroom caps
185 g (6 oz) butter, softened
2 tablespoons finely chopped spring onions (scallions)
1 large clove garlic, crushed
1 tablespoon chopped parsley
salt and pepper
12-16 slices of French bread, toasted

1. Preheat the oven to 200°C (400°F/Gas 6).
2. Wash and dry the mushrooms. **3.** Place the butter, spring onions, garlic and parsley in a bowl. Season with salt and freshly ground black pepper and blend well. **4.** Lightly toast the rounds of French bread. **5.** Arrange the toasted rounds of French bread on a baking tray. Place one mushroom, hollow side up, on each round of bread. **6.** Place a generous teaspoon of the butter mixture in each mushroom cap. **7.** Cook the mushrooms in the oven for 5 to 7 minutes, or until the butter is melted, and the mushrooms are just cooked. **8.** Serve immediately.

Sautéed Mushrooms with Breadcrumbs
Cèpes à la Bordelaise

Serves 6

500 g (1 lb) button mushrooms
90 g (3 oz) butter
juice of half a lemon
2 tablespoons oil
1 tablespoon chopped spring onions (scallions)
2 heaped tablespoons fresh breadcrumbs
1 clove garlic, finely chopped
1 tablespoon finely chopped parsley

1. Trim and wash the mushroom caps, reserving the stalks. **2.** Melt the butter with the lemon juice in a heavy pan and simmer the mushroom caps for a few minutes. Drain them. **3.** Heat the oil in a clean pan and sauté the mushrooms, until they brown slightly. **4.** Chop up the mushroom stalks and combine with the spring onions, breadcrumbs, garlic and parsley. **5.** Add this combination to the mushrooms and cook for five minutes, stirring regularly. **6.** Arrange the mushrooms on a dish, sprinkle with a little lemon juice and chopped parsley, and serve.

Stuffed Eggplants au Gratin

Aubergine au Gratin à la Catalan

Serves 6

3 eggplants (aubergines) (allow one half per
person)
salt
4 tablespoons oil
2 onions, finely chopped
3 hard-boiled eggs, chopped
3 tablespoons fresh breadcrumbs
1 tablespoon parsley, finely chopped
2 cloves garlic, crushed
salt and freshly ground black pepper
butter

1. Cut the eggplants in half lengthways. **2.** Make a
few shallow incisions in the pulp, sprinkle with salt
and leave in a dish to 'sweat' for 1 hour. **3.** Heat the
oil in a heavy frying pan. **4.** Pat the eggplants dry
and fry in the oil, turning from time to time, until
the centres are soft. **5.** Drain and allow to cool a
little. **6.** Carefully scoop out the pulp without damaging the outside skin. **7.** Fry the onions gently in
the oil remaining in the pan until they are cooked
through. **8.** Mix the chopped eggplant pulp with the
onions, hard-boiled eggs, breadcrumbs, parsley and
garlic. **9.** Season to taste with salt and freshly
ground black pepper, and mix well. **10.** Fill the eggplant halves with this mixture, and put into a buttered, ovenproof dish. **11.** Sprinkle with a few
breadcrumbs and dot with butter. **12.** Brown the top
of the eggplants under the grill, and serve.

French-style Fresh Garden Peas

Petits Pois à la Française

Serves 4

500 g (1 lb) shelled or frozen peas
1 lettuce heart, shredded
12 small onions, peeled
bouquet garni
90 g (3 oz) + 3 teaspoons butter
1 teaspoon salt
2 teaspoons sugar
3 tablespoons cold water

1. Choose a deep saucepan, and place in it the peas,
lettuce heart, onions, bouquet garni, 90 g of the butter, salt and sugar and stir to mix all the ingredients.
2. Add the water and bring to the boil. **3.** Simmer
gently with the lid on until the peas are cooked
(about 15 minutes). **4.** At the last moment, when the
peas are cooked, remove the bouquet garni, take the
saucepan off the heat, stir in the remaining 3 teaspoons of butter, and serve.

Vegetable Ragoût

Ratatouille Provençale

*A delicious ragoût of summer vegetables,
flavoured with herbs and garlic, which may be
served either hot or cold. It will go equally well
with a roast or casserole dish, or served with
poached eggs on top. Left-over ratatouille makes
a good filling for an omelette.*

Serves 8–10

olive oil
1 kg (2 lb) eggplant (aubergine) peeled, seeded
and chopped
500 g (1 lb) zucchinis (courgettes), chopped
500 g (1 lb) green peppers (capsicums), diced
3 onions, thinly sliced
750 g (1½ lb) tomatoes, peeled, seeded and
crushed
bouquet garni
large sprig of thyme
1 whole head of garlic, with the cloves skinned
and crushed
salt and freshly ground black pepper
3 tablespoons fresh tarragon, finely chopped

1. Pour a thin layer of oil into a heavy frying pan.
2. Lightly fry the eggplant, zucchinis and green peppers, one after the other, transferring them to a dish
as they are done. **3.** Pour off the cooking oil and
wipe the pan. **4.** Pour in a thin layer of fresh olive
oil. **5.** Return the vegetables to the pan, adding the
onions, tomatoes, bouquet garni, thyme and crushed
garlic. **6.** Season with salt and freshly ground black
pepper. **7.** Cover the pan and cook over a low heat
for 1 hour, stirring from time to time. **8.** Add another 1 or 2 tablespoons of oil if necessary, and 2 or
3 tablespoons of boiling water, but take care not to
make the mixture too watery. **9.** Half-way through
the cooking, stir in the chopped tarragon. **10.** Serve
hot or cold in a deep dish.

Potato Hot Pot
Trouffade

Many variations of this dish appear all over the Massif Central. This recipe uses a local Cantal cheese called Tomme, which is soft and creamy in texture, but any soft creamy cheese may be substituted. Alternatively a hard cheese such as a Cheddar or Gruyère, coarsely grated, may be used.

Serves 6

125 g (4 oz) streaky bacon or speck, cut into chunky pieces
500 g (1 lb) potatoes, thinly sliced
250 g (8 oz) Tomme or alternative cheese, coarsely grated
salt and freshly ground black pepper

1. Heat the bacon or speck in a heavy-bottomed frying pan over a moderate heat until the fat runs out. **2.** Add the potatoes and cook for 5–6 minutes, turning constantly to brown them on all sides. **3.** Stir in the cheese, taking care not to break up the potato slices. **4.** Season with salt and pepper. **5.** Leave over a gentle heat for 15 minutes until the base is crisp and brown, watching carefully to make sure that it does not catch. **6.** Invert on to a warmed serving plate, and serve.

Potatoes and Cheese au Gratin
Gratin Dauphinois

Serves 4-6

1 clove garlic
1 kg (2 lb) potatoes, peeled and finely sliced
salt and freshly ground black pepper
250 g (8 oz) grated cheese
1 cup (8 fl oz) milk
1 egg
pinch of nutmeg
knob of butter

1. Preheat the oven to 180°C (350°F/Gas 4). **2.** Rub a deep ovenproof dish with a clove of garlic. **3.** Butter the dish well. **4.** Line the bottom with a layer of potatoes. **5.** Add some salt, pepper and a sprinkling of cheese. **6.** Repeat the layers, potatoes, salt, pepper and cheese. **7.** Pour in the milk, which has been beaten with the egg. **8.** The potatoes should not be quite covered with milk. **9.** Finish with grated nutmeg and cheese and dot with butter. **10.** Bake for about 1 hour, or until the potatoes are cooked and the top is golden, and serve.

Artichoke Hearts, Sweetbreads and Goose Livers
Des Culs d'Artichauts Violets, Ris de Veau et Foie d'Oie

This recipe comes from Le Petit Nice in Marseilles.

Serves 4

4–8 artichokes, depending on size
½ teaspoon salt
water sufficient to cover artichokes
1 lemon
2 sweetbreads
1 cup (8 fl oz) dry white wine
2 tablespoons fresh cream
2-3 goose livers, depending on size (or 350 g (11 oz) chicken livers)
2 tablespoons butter
salt
freshly ground pepper

1. Trim the artichokes and remove the tough external leaves, cut the top of the leaves flat and remove the stalk. **2.** Boil the artichoke hearts in salted water to which the juice of the lemon has been added. Cook for 10 minutes. **3.** In another pan of water blanch the sweetbreads for 5–8 minutes. Remove and save the water. **4.** Rinse the sweetbreads under cold running water and remove the external skin. **5.** Chop the sweetbreads finely. **6.** To the water in which the sweetbreads were cooked add the white wine and cook until it has been reduced to about one quarter of its volume, enough sauce for four people. Add the cream. **7.** Clean the goose livers, cut them into thin slices and trim them into pieces approximately 4 cm (1½ in) square. **8.** In a frying pan, melt the butter and very briefly sauté the goose livers in it. Season with pepper and salt. **9.** To assemble, spread the leaves of the artichoke, if necessary remove the choke, and in between the leaves place the chopped sweetbreads. **10.** To serve, arrange the goose liver squares on a plate, place the artichokes on top of the livers and mask the artichokes with the sauce. Serve immediately.

Note: If fresh artichokes are not available, use canned artichoke hearts. In this case, blanch the sweetbreads in the water from the can.

Right: Artichoke Hearts, Sweetbreads and Goose Livers (above) as prepared at Le Petit Nice in Marseilles. Overlooking the Bay of Marseilles and Château d'If, the fortress prison made famous by Dumas in his story of the Count of Monte Cristo, Le Petit Nice is a place of comfort, refinement and good food. As you would expect in Marseilles, the best dishes on the menu are seafood. Chef Jean Paul Passedat has an original touch, and while he uses purely local ingredients, he comes up with some very unusual combinations.

FISH

Turbot Fillets with Red Butter Sauce

Filet de Turbot au Beurre Rouge

Where turbot is not available, fillets of flounder may be substituted. This recipe comes from the Restaurant Capucin Gourmand in Nancy.

Serves 4

1 bottle of Burgundy (red)
1.5 kg (3 lb) turbot fillets (or flounder)
125 g (4 oz) butter, chilled
¼ cup (2 fl oz) cream, whipped
salt and freshly ground black pepper
cayenne pepper

1. Pour the wine into a saucepan and reduce over a high flame until it is about one-quarter of the original volume. **2.** Steam the fish fillets for about 10 minutes, or until just cooked, but still very firm. Remove them and keep them warm. **3.** Cut the hard butter into small pieces and, using a wire whisk, whip it into the reduced wine over a high heat. The butter should stay creamy. **4.** Just before it reaches the boil whisk in the whipped cream. **5.** Season with salt and freshly ground black pepper. **6.** Serve the fish fillets with this sauce poured over the top, sprinkled with a little cayenne pepper.

Salmon with Sorrel Sauce

Saumon à l'Oseille

If salmon is unobtainable, use a large trout. This recipe comes from the Restaurant Noël in Realmont.

Serves 4

800 g (1 lb 9 oz) salmon, cut into escalopes
2½ cups (20 fl oz) white wine
1 bunch sorrel, finely chopped
1¼ cups (10 fl oz) cream
salt and freshly ground black pepper

1. Poach the escalopes of salmon in the white wine. **2.** When they are cooked, remove from the liquid and keep warm. **3.** Cook the sorrel in this liquid. **4.** When cooked, add the cream and bring to the boil. **5.** Check the seasoning. **6.** Cover the salmon with this sauce and serve very hot.

Crayfish Salad

Salade de Queues d'Écrevisses

This recipe comes from the Restaurant Nandron in Lyon. King prawns may also be used for this dish.

Serves 4

1.5 kg (3 lb) crayfish (yabbies) or king prawns
6 cups (1.5 litres) fish stock
500 g (1 lb) string beans
4 artichoke hearts
1 tomato, peeled and cut into quarters
2 hard-boiled eggs, cut into quarters
6 cos lettuce leaves
½ cup (4 fl oz) cream, whipped
1 teaspoon finely chopped fresh tarragon
1 cup (8 fl oz) mayonnaise

1. Boil the crayfish or king prawns in the fish stock for 3 minutes. **2.** Remove them from the stock and peel the tails. **3.** Top and tail the beans and without cutting them steam or boil them until they are cooked but still firm (not more than 5 minutes). **4.** If using fresh artichokes, boil them for 15 minutes in salted water. When cooked remove the leaves and the choke, using only the artichoke bottom. **5.** To assemble the salad, arrange the tails, beans, artichoke hearts, tomatoes, hard-boiled eggs and lettuce leaves on a serving dish. Mix the whipped cream and tarragon leaves into the mayonnaise and spoon it over the salad.

Crayfish Tails in Bouillon

Les Écrevisses Pattes Rouge à la Nage

This recipe comes from the Capucin Gourmand in Nancy.

Serves 4

3 cups (24 fl oz) Chablis or any good quality dry white wine
6 spring onions (scallions), chopped
4 carrots, sliced
½ stick celery, cut into 2.5 cm (1 in) lengths
1 tablespoon tarragon, chopped
1 fennel bulb, chopped into small pieces
½ small hot red pepper
12 peppercorns
½ teaspoon salt
8 crayfish or king prawns

1. Combine all the ingredients except the crayfish and gently simmer for half an hour. **2.** Add the crayfish and simmer for about 3 minutes. **3.** Remove the tails and peel them. **4.** Arrange two per person in the bottom of a soup bowl. Taste the bouillon and if necessary add more salt and pepper. **5.** To serve, pour the bouillon over the crayfish.

Tuna in White Wine Sauce

Thon à la Provençale

Serves 6

Marinade:
3 tablespoons olive oil
1 tablespoon lemon juice
salt and freshly ground black pepper

6 tuna steaks
3 anchovy fillets
3 tablespoons olive oil
1 onion, finely chopped
3 large tomatoes, peeled, seeded and chopped
1 clove garlic, crushed
bouquet garni
¾ cup (6 fl oz) dry white wine
30 g (1 oz) butter, soft
1 tablespoon flour
1 teaspoon capers

1. Mix the oil, lemon juice, salt and freshly ground black pepper together to make a marinade. 2. Stud each tuna steak with half an anchovy fillet, cut in small pieces. 3. Place the tuna steaks in the marinade for at least an hour. 4. Preheat the oven to 150°C (300°F/Gas 2). 5. Heat the rest of the oil in a large ovenproof dish. 6. Soften the chopped onion in the oil. 7. Add the drained fish and cook it for a couple of minutes, allowing it to colour a little on both sides. 8. Add the tomatoes, garlic and bouquet garni. 9. Season with salt and freshly ground black pepper. 10. Pour the wine over the fish. 11. Transfer the pan to the oven, cover it and cook for about 15–20 minutes, or until the tuna is cooked. 12. Remove the fish from the pan, drain, and set on a warmed serving dish. Keep warm. 13. Blend the butter and flour together to make a beurre manié. 14. Whisk this into the sauce to thicken it. 15. Add the capers and simmer the sauce gently for a couple of minutes. 16. Pour the sauce carefully over the tuna steaks, and serve immediately.

Eel Stuffed with Puréed Fish

Anguille Savoyarde

If you can't buy eel, use any firm-fleshed white fish.

Serves 6

Forcemeat:
1 cup (8 fl oz) milk
3 cups (6 oz) soft breadcrumbs
500 g (1 lb) boned skinned pike (or similar white fish)
salt and pepper
pinch of nutmeg
185 g (6 oz) butter, softened
2 whole eggs
4 egg yolks

1 eel or similar fish (have the fishmonger skin the fish and remove the backbone)
salt and pepper
250 g (8 oz) bacon slices
1 onion, chopped
1 carrot, chopped
125 g (4 oz) butter
bouquet garni
2 cups (16 fl oz) dry white wine
250 g (8 oz) button mushrooms
½ cup (2 oz) flour
1 cup (8 fl oz) cream

1. Prepare the forcemeat by soaking the breadcrumbs in the milk. 2. Blend the pike flesh, salt, pepper and nutmeg in an electric blender, then add the breadcrumbs. 3. Add the butter, the whole eggs and the egg yolks, blending well. 4. Lay the eel flat and season it with salt and pepper. 5. Spread the pike forcemeat on the inside. 6. Re-shape the eel and wrap it in slices of bacon, securing with toothpicks where necessary to ensure it keeps its shape. 7. Twist the eel into a ring shape. 8. In a large frying pan, fry the onion and carrot in 30 g of the butter. 9. Carefully place the eel on top of these vegetables. 10. Add a bouquet garni and pour in the wine, to almost cover the fish. 11. Bring to the boil and simmer gently without a lid for 30 minutes, removing any scum which may form. 12. In a separate pan, toss the mushrooms in 30 g of the butter. 13. Drain the eel and place it carefully into another dish, arranging the mushrooms around it. 14. In a clean saucepan, melt the remaining butter, add the flour and stir to make a roux. 15. Add the strained fish stock, blending well. 16. When the sauce has thickened, add the cream. Heat through, pour over the eel and serve.

Fish in White Wine and Cream Sauce

Pauchouse

In Burgundy only freshwater fish are used to make Pauchouse, but a similar dish could be made from a mixture of fish from the sea.

Serves 6–8

2 kg (4 lb) mixed fish
2 carrots, chopped
2 onions, chopped
salt and pepper
bouquet garni
2 cups (16 fl oz) white wine
90 g (3 oz) butter
½ cup (2 oz) flour
½ cup (4 fl oz) cream
125 g (4 oz) streaky (fat) bacon, chopped
90 g (3 oz) mushrooms, chopped
parsley
croûtons

1. Clean the fish and cut off the heads. **2.** Oil a large pot, and line it with the chopped carrots and onions. **3.** Add salt, freshly ground black pepper and the bouquet garni. **4.** Cut the fish into chunks and arrange them on the vegetables. **5.** Cover with the white wine, or a mixture of white wine and water. **6.** Simmer gently for about 20 minutes, or until the fish is just cooked. **7.** Drain the fish and place it in a deep serving dish. **8.** Strain the stock through a fine sieve and return it to the pan. **9.** Mix 60 g of the butter with the flour to make a beurre manié. **10.** Stir this butter mixture into the stock while heating, whisking all the time so that the sauce thickens smoothly. **11.** Add the cream and correct the seasoning. **12.** Pour this hot sauce over the fish and keep warm. **13.** Toss the chopped bacon and mushrooms in the remaining butter. **14.** Sprinkle these over the top of the fish and decorate with parsley. **15.** Serve with croûtons.

Pike Quenelles 'Gérard Nandron'

Quenelles de Brochet 'Gérard Nandron'

From the Restaurant Nandron in Lyon. There are two recipes for pike quenelles in this book but as Gérard Nandron's quenelles were exceptionally good when I tasted them I include his own method as it differs from the other recipe. Snapper, gemfish or jewfish may be used instead of pike but the result may not be quite as good.

Serves 6

1 kg (2 lb) fish fillets, chilled
4 cups (1 litre) fresh cream
½ teaspoon salt
cayenne pepper
125 g (4 oz) melted clarified butter
3 whole eggs
1½ cups (12 fl oz) Mornay Sauce

1. In a food processor, process the fish until very fine. If you haven't got a food processor, rub the finely chopped flesh through a sieve. **2.** Place it into a bowl set over ice and slowly incorporate the cream, beating it firmly with a wooden spoon. If an electric mixer is available, this can be done using a paddle attachment. The resulting mixture should have the consistency of a heavy mayonnaise. **3.** Add the salt and pepper and slowly incorporate the butter and the eggs. **4.** Refrigerate the mixture for 24 hours. **5.** Form the quenelles, one large or two smaller ones per person, by rolling them into shape on a floured board. **6.** Gently poach them in simmering salted water for about 5 minutes. **7.** To serve, pour some of the Mornay Sauce over each quenelle. Place them under a grill and serve when the sauce browns a little.

***Right:** Pike Quenelles Gérard Nandron (above). Gérard Nandron at his restaurant in Lyon prepares some of the best food in the city, a great credit to him, as Lyon, by reputation, is the gastronomic capital of France and has attracted some of the greatest chefs in the country.*

Crumbed Mussels and Bacon Kebabs

Brochettes de Moules, Sauce Provençale

Serves 4

1 kg (2 lb) mussels
4 slices bacon, cut into 4 squares
1 egg yolk, beaten with 1 tablespoon milk
fresh breadcrumbs
sprig of fresh thyme
olive oil
salt and freshly ground black pepper
1 lemon, cut into quarters

Provençale Sauce:
1 kg (2 lb) tomatoes, peeled, seeded and chopped
3 tablespoons olive oil
bouquet garni
1 clove garlic, crushed
salt and freshly ground black pepper

1. Scrub the mussels, and put them in a deep cast-iron saucepan over a high heat without adding any liquid. **2.** Cover the pan. **3.** As soon as the shells open, remove the mussels from the shells. **4.** Thread them on a skewer, two at a time, inserting a piece of bacon between each pair. **5.** Each skewer should consist of 4 pieces of bacon and 10 mussels. **6.** Dip the skewers in the diluted egg yolks. **7.** Roll the skewers in the breadcrumbs, and set aside. **8.** To make the sauce, cook the tomatoes in the olive oil with the bouquet garni for 35 to 40 minutes. **9.** When cooked, add the garlic, and season with salt and pepper. **10.** To cook the mussels, brush the skewers with a sprig of thyme, dipped in olive oil. **11.** Place under a very hot grill, turning to cook evenly. **12.** Do not let the mussels blacken. They should be dry and well browned. **13.** Transfer the skewers to a heated dish, and garnish with lemon quarters. Serve the sauce separately.

Stuffed Bream

Brème Farcie

Local gourmets maintain that the River Indre, one of the tributaries of the Loire, provides the best carp and bream in the district. Stuffed bream is a popular way of serving this fish.

Serves 6–8

1 bream per person
2 medium-sized onions, finely chopped
2 tablespoons oil
250 g (8 oz) mushrooms, chopped
1 garlic clove, crushed
3 tablespoons fine fresh breadcrumbs
1 tablespoon chopped chives
1 tablespoon chopped parsley
milk
salt and pepper
bouquet garni
1½ cups (12 fl oz) dry white wine
30 g (1 oz) butter

1. Preheat the oven to 190°C (375°F/Gas 5). **2.** Clean and scale the bream. **3.** Fry the onions in the oil until they are transparent. **4.** Add the mushrooms and garlic, and cook for five minutes, stirring often. **5.** Remove the pan from the heat. Add the breadcrumbs, chives and parsley. **6.** Moisten and bind the stuffing mixture with a little milk. **7.** Add salt and pepper to taste. **8.** Stuff each fish with the mixture. **9.** Place the fish in an ovenproof dish. Add the bouquet garni and wine, and dot with butter. **10.** Cook in the oven until tender, basting frequently with the juice. This will take about 15 minutes. **11.** Drain the fish and place on a warm serving dish. **12.** Reduce the liquid over a hot stove to make a light sauce.

POULTRY & GAME

Roast Goose with Braised Sauerkraut
Oie à l'Alsacienne

Serves 6–8

1 goose 4–5 kg (8–10 lb) ready for the oven
flour
1 tablespoon of butter, cut into pieces

Stuffing:
250 g (8 oz) sausage meat
2 tablespoons finely chopped parsley
1 tablespoon chopped fresh thyme

Braised Sauerkraut:
1 onion, finely chopped
250 g (8 oz) bacon and ham, chopped and mixed
750 g (1½ lb) sauerkraut
salt and freshly ground black pepper
500 g (1 lb) Strasbourg sausage (optional)

1. Preheat the oven to 210°C (425°F/Gas 7). **2.** Mix the sausage meat with the parsley and thyme. **3.** Sprinkle the back of the goose with a little flour, and the pieces of butter. **4.** Stuff the goose with the stuffing mixture. **5.** Roast the goose for 15 minutes, then reduce the oven temperature to 180°C (350°F/Gas 4) and continue roasting until the goose is tender (about 25 minutes per 500 g). **6.** From time to time drain off and reserve some of the fat. **7.** Using 2 tablespoons of goose fat in a heavy pan, cook the onion until it is soft and transparent. **8.** Add the bacon and ham and continue to cook gently. **9.** Drain the sauerkraut and rinse it well in fresh water. Drain it again. **10.** Place the washed sauerkraut on top of the onions, bacon and ham and mix all the ingredients together, seasoning well. **11.** Moisten with 1 cup of water, cover the pan and leave to cook very gently for 1 hour. **12.** 10 minutes before serving, add the Strasbourg sausages to the sauerkraut. **13.** Serve the goose on a bed of braised sauerkraut, with the diluted pan juices poured over the top.

Poached Chicken in Half-Mourning
Poularde Pochée Demi-Deuil

Serves 6

60 g (2 oz) truffles, finely sliced
2 chickens, each weighing about 1.2 kg (2¼ lb)
6 leeks, white part only
8 small carrots, scraped
2 turnips, peeled
2 stalks celery
60 g (2 oz) bacon, diced
185 g (6 oz) butter
salt and freshly ground black pepper

1. Insert the slices of truffles under the breast skin of the chickens and truss the birds. **2.** Put the leeks, carrots, turnips, celery and bacon into a large casserole. **3.** Add about 8 cups (2 litres) of water. **4.** Add salt and pepper to taste, and simmer gently for 1 hour. **5.** Add the chickens to the casserole, making sure that there is enough liquid to cover them. **6.** Cover the casserole and simmer gently for 25 minutes. **7.** Remove the vegetables from the stock, but leave the chickens in the casserole covered, with the heat turned off but still on the stove, for another 20 minutes. **8.** In a heavy frying pan melt 125 g of the butter. **9.** Gently stew the vegetables in the butter. They are served as an accompaniment to the chicken. **10.** Drain the chickens and arrange them on a serving dish and keep warm. **11.** Remove the fat from the stock, pour about 4 cups of it into a small heavy saucepan, and boil over a high heat until it is reduced by half. **12.** Whisk in the remaining butter until the sauce is light and fluffy. **13.** Pour the sauce over the chickens and serve.

Chicken in Red Wine

Le Coq au Vin du Pays

From La Rôtisserie du Chambertin in Gevrey-Chambertin.

Serves 4

1.5 kg (3 lb) chicken
30 g (1 oz) butter
½ cup (4 fl oz) Marc de Bourgogne or brandy
giblets
½ cup (2 oz) flour
salt
freshly ground black pepper

Marinade:
2 onions, roughly chopped
2 carrots, sliced
2 stalks celery, cut in 1.25 cm (½ in) lengths
2 spring onions (scallions), roughly chopped
1 clove garlic, chopped
2 sprigs thyme, chopped
2 bay leaves
4 sprigs parsley, chopped
2 cloves
3 cups (24 fl oz) dry, Burgundy-style red wine
½ cup (4 fl oz) wine vinegar
¼ cup (2 fl oz) olive oil

1. Cut the chicken into pieces, place them into a large container and add all the marinade ingredients. Marinate overnight. **2.** Take out the chicken pieces and brown them lightly in the butter. **3.** Add the Marc or brandy and flame it. **4.** Transfer the chicken pieces, the marinade, including all its ingredients, and the giblets into a flameproof casserole dish. **5.** Cover and simmer for approximately 1½ hours, checking the chicken to see if it is tender. **6.** Strain the cooking liquid into a saucepan and add the chicken pieces. **7.** Mix the flour with some water and pour it into the cooking liquid. **8.** Slowly boil the liquid, stirring constantly until it thickens. **9.** Season and serve with sautéed button mushrooms and small onions.

Tarragon Chicken

La Poularde de Bresse Braisée à la Crème d'Estragon

Corn is cultivated intensively around Bresse, to be fed to the famous poultry of the region, which gourmets consider to be the best in France and which is recognised by its distinctive yellow colour. This recipe comes from the Restaurant Auberge du Père Bise in Talloires.

Serves 4

1 chicken, weighing 1.5 kg (3 lb)
salt and freshly ground black pepper
1 bunch fresh tarragon
100 g (3½ oz) butter
the chicken giblets
4 tablespoons chicken stock
4 tablespoons cream

1. Season the inside of the chicken with salt and pepper and stuff it with the bunch of fresh tarragon. **2.** Melt the butter in a heavy flameproof casserole dish, and gently cook the chicken until it is golden on all sides. **3.** Add the giblets to the casserole dish. **4.** Add the chicken stock, cover and cook very gently for about 40 minutes, or until the chicken is cooked through. **5.** Remove the chicken from the casserole and keep warm. **6.** Remove the bunch of tarragon from the chicken, return it to the casserole and continue cooking for a few minutes. **7.** Add the cream, blend well and heat gently without allowing it to boil. **8.** Strain the sauce through a fine sieve and correct the seasoning. It should be smooth, creamy and rather thin. **9.** Cut the chicken into 4 serving pieces, coat each piece with the sauce and serve.

***Right:** Rabbit Fricassée (see page 33) and Apples with Bacon (see page 20) from the Restaurant Ar Milin in Châteaubourg, Brittany. Ar Milin is in a delightful old watermill set over the old mill stream and surrounded by a park. While the guests enjoy their food, swans glide majestically by on the pond. Chef Michel Burel's menu changes with the seasons. He uses only the best and freshest of local products and serves them in interesting traditional and regional dishes.*

Provençale Chicken Fricassée

Fricassée Provençale

A typically Provençale chicken fricassée in which the chicken is combined with a mixture of garlic, almonds and bread soaked in vinegar and the sauce is thickened with a strongly lemon flavoured mayonnaise.

Serves 4

Provençale base:
4 tablespoons olive oil
1 head garlic, each clove peeled
60 g (2 oz) almonds, blanched
75 g (2½ oz) white bread, in one piece, soaked in white wine vinegar and squeezed dry
salt and freshly ground black pepper
½ bay leaf

1 chicken, about 1.5 to 2 kg (3–4 lb), jointed
1 cup (8 fl oz) chicken stock
¾ cup (6 fl oz) mayonnaise, well flavoured with lemon
finely chopped parsley

1. Heat the olive oil in a heavy-bottomed pan, and gently cook the garlic cloves, almonds, bread and bay leaf for 2 to 3 minutes, until they start to take on a little colour. **2.** Remove all these ingredients from the oil, draining them to leave as much oil in the pan as possible. **3.** Dry the chicken pieces, put them in the oil and cook them for about 15 minutes, turning them from time to time so that they become an even colour. **4.** Using a mortar, or a food processor, reduce the base to a paste. **5.** In a small saucepan, reduce the chicken stock over a brisk heat until ½ cup remains. **6.** Thin the Provençale paste with the concentrated chicken stock, and add this sauce to the chicken pieces in the frying pan. **7.** Cover the pan and finish cooking over a moderate heat for 20 to 25 minutes. **8.** Remove the chicken pieces from the pan and keep warm. **9.** Remove the pan from the fire and thicken the sauce by beating in the mayonnaise with a wire whisk, a little at a time. **10.** Return the chicken pieces to the sauce, and keep warm by standing the pan in a dish of boiling water. **11.** The sauce must not boil, or it will curdle. **12.** Transfer the chicken and the sauce to a deep serving dish, and serve sprinkled with freshly chopped parsley.

Fried Chicken with Vegetables

Poulet Sauté à la Basquaise

Serves 4

1 chicken, about 1.5 kg (3 lb), quartered
salt and freshly ground black pepper
flour
6–7 tablespoons oil
4 onions, thinly sliced
4 red peppers (capsicums), finely chopped
4 cloves garlic, crushed
10 tomatoes, skinned, seeded and chopped
2 tablespoons tomato paste
2 teaspoons sugar
1 bouquet garni
small ham bone or piece of ham weighing about 200 g (7 oz)
pinch cayenne pepper
½ cup (4 fl oz) water
1 tablespoon parsley, finely chopped

1. Dust the chicken pieces with salt and flour. **2.** Heat 4 tablespoons of oil in a heavy frying pan until sizzling. **3.** Sauté the chicken pieces over a high heat until they are lightly browned all over. **4.** Reduce the heat, cover the pan and leave to simmer for 10 minutes. **5.** Remove the chicken pieces. **6.** Add 2 tablespoons of oil to the pan, and cook the onions for 3 minutes, until just coloured. **7.** Add another tablespoon of oil if necessary, and put in the peppers. **8.** Add the garlic, tomatoes, tomato paste, sugar, bouquet garni and ham. **9.** Season to taste with salt, freshly ground black pepper and cayenne pepper. **10.** Moisten with the water, adding a little more if necessary. **11.** Cover, and cook the sauce for 15 minutes. **12.** Return the chicken to the pan, cover and leave to simmer over a gentle heat for about 30 minutes, or until the chicken is tender. **13.** Serve in a deep serving dish, sprinkled with finely chopped parsley, and accompanied by a rice pilaf.

Roast Pigeon Madame Raymonde

Pigeonneau de Madame Raymonde

From the Restaurant Le Chapon Fin in Bordeaux.

Serves 6

6 pigeons + their livers
60 g (2 oz) foie gras
butter
400 g (12 oz) mushrooms, finely chopped and sautéed in butter
50 g (2 oz) beans, cooked and finely chopped
50 g (2 oz) truffles (optional)
50 g (2 oz) asparagus tips, cooked
salt and freshly ground black pepper
¼ cup (2 fl oz) brandy
¼ cup (2 fl oz) vermouth
300 g (9 oz) butter

1. Preheat the oven to 180°C (350°F/Gas 4). **2.** Bone the pigeons, cutting down the backbone, and leaving the skin as intact as possible, in order to make a pocket for the stuffing. **3.** Sauté the pigeon livers with the foie gras in a little butter. Mash them with a fork. **4.** Make a stuffing by combining the mushrooms, beans, truffles, asparagus tips, liver mixture and salt and pepper to taste. **5.** Stuff the pigeons with this mixture, and sew up the opening securely with twine. **6.** Place the pigeons in the oven with a little butter on the top and roast for 30–40 minutes, or until cooked. **7.** Remove the pigeons from the dish and keep warm. **8.** Degrease the pan with the brandy and vermouth, scraping well to incorporate all the pieces of pigeon left in the pan. **9.** Allow the sauce to reduce a little, and beat in the butter slowly with a wire whisk. **10.** Correct the seasoning and strain the sauce. **11.** Arrange the pigeons on a serving dish, garnish with carrots and asparagus tips if desired, and serve with the sauce.

Duckling with Green Peppercorns

Canard au Poivre Vert

From the Hôtel D'Étape in Saint-Flour.

Serves 4

2 tablespoons olive oil
100 g (3½ oz) butter
1 duckling — about 2.5 kg (5 lb)
1¼ cups (10 fl oz) demi-glace sauce (see p. 329)
½ cup (4 fl oz) cream
1½ tablespoons green peppercorns
salt

1. Preheat the oven to 220°C (425°F/Gas 7). **2.** In a heavy casserole dish heat the oil and butter. **3.** Brown the duckling on all sides, and cook, uncovered, in the hot oven for ¾ hour. **4.** Remove the dish from the oven, and set the duckling aside. **5.** Add the demi-glace sauce and the cream to the pan juices, and blend well with a wire whisk. **6.** Add the green peppercorns, and blend well. Correct the seasoning. **7.** Carve the duckling into serving pieces and return to the casserole dish. **8.** Cover the dish, and allow the duckling to simmer in the sauce until tender (approximately 45 minutes). **9.** When the duckling is ready to serve, transfer it to a clean serving dish, and cover with the sauce. **10.** The duckling should be accompanied by green vegetables.

Rabbit Fricassée

Fricassée de Lapereau à l'Ail Doux

From the Restaurant Ar Milin in Châteaubourg.

Serves 4

125 g (4 oz) butter
2 rabbits, boned. Only the saddle and thighs are used. The rest of the meat can be used in a ragoût, or in a pâté.
salt and freshly ground black pepper
2 cloves garlic, crushed
½ cup (4 fl oz) cream
1 bunch of chives, chopped

1. Preheat the oven to 180°C (350°F/Gas 4). **2.** Melt half the butter in a heavy-bottomed pan and brown the rabbit pieces. **3.** Season with salt and pepper, and add the crushed garlic. **4.** Cover the pan, and put it in the oven, allowing the rabbit to cook gently in its own steam for 1–1¼ hours. (It may be necessary to reduce the oven temperature after 15 minutes.) **5.** When the rabbit is cooked, melt the remaining butter in a saucepan. **6.** Add the juice from the rabbit casserole, the cream and the chives. **7.** Carve the saddle of rabbit into escalopes lengthwise. **8.** Just before serving, cover the rabbit pieces with the sauce. **9.** Serve with Pommes au Lard (see p. 20).

MEAT

Braised Beef à la Béarnaise
Daube de Boeuf à la Béarnaise

Serves 6–8

2 kg (4 lb) lean beef, cut in 2.5 cm (1 in) cubes
2 onions, sliced
2 carrots, sliced
1 bouquet garni
salt and freshly ground black pepper
1¼ cups (10 fl oz) red wine
4 tablespoons brandy
4 tablespoons oil
250 g (8 oz) bacon, diced
1 large onion, cut in quarters
4 cloves garlic, chopped
1¼ cups (10 fl oz) beef stock or hot water
3 tablespoons flour mixed with 1 tablespoon
water for paste

1. Place the meat in a large bowl, or earthenware casserole, with the onions, carrots, bouquet garni, salt and freshly ground black pepper. 2. Add the red wine and brandy and marinate for 5 to 6 hours, stirring occasionally. 3. Preheat the oven to 120°C (250°F/Gas ½). 4. Heat the oil in a frying pan and cook the diced bacon for a few minutes. 5. Add the onion and brown. 6. Drain the meat and reserve the marinade. 7. Sauté the meat with the bacon bits and the onion, until browned, shaking the pan from time to time. 8. Add the garlic and transfer to a casserole dish. 9. In a small saucepan, heat the marinade and allow it to reduce to half the original quantity over a brisk heat. 10. Add the marinade to the meat, and then pour over the hot stock. 11. Make a paste with the flour and water. 12. Spread this paste around the rim of the casserole dish and press the lid down on top to make an air-tight seal. Alternatively, cover the top of the casserole dish with a sheet of greaseproof paper, and then place the lid on top. 13. Transfer the casserole dish to the preheated oven, and cook very slowly for 3 to 4 hours. 14. When ready to serve, remove the dish from the oven. 15. Skim the fat from the surface and correct the seasoning. **16.** Serve straight from the dish.

Veal Chops with Ham and Parsley Dressing
Côtes de Veau à l'Ardennaise

Serves 6

125 g (4 oz) butter
2 onions, finely chopped
1 carrot, finely chopped
10 juniper berries
½ teaspoon dried basil
½ teaspoon salt
freshly ground black pepper
6 veal chops
3 tablespoons oil
1 cup (8 fl oz) dry white wine
½ cup (4 fl oz) chicken stock (see p. 328)
¾ cup (1½ oz) fresh white breadcrumbs
1 tablespoon finely chopped ham
2 tablespoons parsley, finely chopped
1 teaspoon lemon juice

1. Preheat the oven to 180°C (350°F/Gas 4). 2. Take a large shallow flameproof casserole with a lid (one that is large enough to take the chops in one layer) and melt 30 g of the butter in it. 3. Cook the chopped onions and carrot for 5 minutes until they are slightly coloured. Set aside. 4. With a mortar and pestle, crush the juniper berries, the basil, salt and pepper. 5. Press this seasoning into both sides of the chops, forcing it into the meat as much as possible. 6. In a heavy frying pan, melt 30 g of butter and the oil. 7. Brown the chops on both sides, turning carefully only once, so as not to dislodge the seasoning. Transfer the chops to the casserole. 8. Pour off almost all the fat from the frying pan, and add the wine. Boil briskly, scraping the pan well, until the wine is reduced to ½ a cup. 9. Stir in the stock and pour the mixture round the chops carefully. 10. In a clean frying pan, melt all but 1 tablespoon of the remaining butter and cook the breadcrumbs until they are lightly browned. Remove from the heat. 11. Stir in the ham, parsley and lemon juice. 12. Spoon a portion of the mixture on to each chop and dot the topping with the remaining butter. 13. Bring the casserole to a boil on top of the stove, cover tightly and bake for approximately 30 minutes. 14. When the chops are cooked, transfer them to a heated dish. 15. Strain the contents of the casserole into a small saucepan, pressing the vegetables hard with the back of a spoon. 16. Boil down the liquid over a high heat until it is reduced to about ½ a cup. 17. Correct the seasoning, pour around the chops and serve.

Right: Veal with Maize Flour Pancakes (see page 36) and Mixed Seafood Salad from the Restaurant Joignant in Caen, Normandy.

Veal with Maize Flour Pancakes

Grenadins de Veau des Bords de la Dives

From the Restaurant Joignant in Caen.

Serves 4

4 veal escalopes, trimmed
flour
butter
1 onion, finely chopped
¼ cup (2 fl oz) sherry
1¼ cups (10 fl oz) fresh cream
2 eggs
200 g (6 oz) maize flour
salt and freshly ground black pepper

1. Dust the veal escalopes with a little flour. **2.** Melt a knob of butter in a heavy-bottomed pan, and brown the escalopes on both sides. Remove and keep warm. **3.** Melt a little more butter in the pan, and cook the onion gently until it is soft and golden. **4.** Add the sherry, and stir well. **5.** Allow to cool a little, before adding half the cream. **6.** Adjust the seasoning, adding salt and pepper as necessary. **7.** Meanwhile, in a bowl, beat together the eggs and remaining cream. **8.** Slowly add the maize flour and a little salt, beating well to make a batter. **9.** Take a pancake pan and moisten with a little butter. **10.** Proceed to make small pancakes with the batter in the usual way. **11.** Heat the sauce through, and serve each escalope with a little sauce over the top, accompanied by a pancake.

Parslied Leg of Lamb

Gigot D'Agneau Persillé

Serves 6

1 leg of lamb, about 2.5 kg (5 lb)
1 clove garlic, slivered
sprigs of thyme
2 tablespoons finely chopped parsley
3 tablespoons fresh breadcrumbs

1. Preheat the oven to 200°C (400°F/Gas 6). **2.** Trim off any excess fat from the lamb. **3.** Insert slivers of garlic and small sprigs of thyme into slits in the lamb. **4.** Roast the leg of lamb in the preheated oven for about 1 hour, with a little water in the roasting pan to prevent it from catching. **5.** Mix the parsley with the breadcrumbs in a bowl. **6.** About 10 to 15 minutes before the leg is cooked, coat the leg with the breadcrumb and parsley mixture, taking care to press the mixture well into the fatty surface of the meat so that it adheres. **7.** Return the meat to the oven and roast until the surface turns to a golden crust. **8.** Arrange on a serving dish, garnished with watercress and lemon quarters.

Roast Lamb Bretonne

Gigot de Mouton à la Bretonne

Serves 6

1 leg of mutton or lamb, weighing about 2.5 kg (5 lb)
2 cloves garlic, slivered
sprig of thyme
bay leaves
500 g (1 lb) dried white haricot beans, or red kidney beans, soaked overnight
bouquet garni
1 onion, studded with 3 cloves
salt and pepper
30 g (1 oz) butter
6 small onions, cut in rounds
2 tablespoons consommé
1 teaspoon sugar
2 tablespoons cream
2 tablespoons Calvados (optional)

1. Preheat the oven to 200°C (400°F/Gas 6). **2.** Trim the leg of mutton of any superfluous fat. **3.** Make a few slits in the meat to hold the slivers of garlic. **4.** Place the sprig of thyme and several bay leaves on top of the leg. **5.** Bake in the hot oven, allowing 20 minutes per 500 g in order to have the mutton slightly pink near the bone. **6.** While the meat is cooking, place the beans in a saucepan of cold water with a bouquet garni, and the onion studded with cloves. Season well. **7.** Bring the beans to the boil and allow them to simmer gently until cooked (about 1¼ hours). **8.** Melt the butter in a heavy pan, and gently fry the onion rings, without letting them take on any colour. **9.** Add the consommé, and bring to the boil. Simmer for 5 minutes. **10.** Remove the pan from the heat and add the sugar and cream. **11.** When the beans are cooked, drain them well. **12.** Pour the sauce over the beans, stir gently and place in a warmed serving dish. **13.** Just before serving the mutton, pour the 2 tablespoons of Calvados over the meat, and serve the beans separately.

Sautéed Lamb with Red Peppers

Sauté d'Agneau à la Navarraise

A recipe that is typical of the south-west region of France.

Serves 6

1 leg of lamb, boned and cut in 2.5 cm (1 in) cubes
salt and freshly ground black pepper
60 g (2 oz) unsalted butter
5 tablespoons oil
2 onions, peeled and thinly sliced
1 tablespoon vinegar
6 sweet red peppers (capsicums), seeded and diced
1 clove garlic, crushed
1 teaspoon paprika
dash of powdered cayenne pepper, or 1 small hot pimento

1. Season the lamb cubes with salt and pepper. **2.** Heat the butter and 2 tablespoons of the oil in a heavy frying pan. **3.** Sauté the pieces of lamb until they are golden brown at the edges. **4.** Add the onions, cover the pan and cook for 5 minutes, stirring from time to time. **5.** Add the vinegar, stir, and leave covered, off the heat. **6.** Heat the remaining oil in another frying pan. **7.** Sauté the red peppers gently, stirring often. **8.** Stir in the garlic and paprika and cook gently for 7 to 8 minutes. **9.** Add the peppers to the meat. **10.** Add the cayenne pepper. **11.** Taste, and correct the seasoning. **12.** Simmer very gently for about 5 minutes. **13.** Arrange the sautéed lamb on a warmed serving dish, sprinkle with the parsley and serve.

Lamb Rissoles

Ballotines d'Agneau

Serves 6-8

750 g (1½ lb) minced lamb
2 medium onions, finely chopped
2 cloves garlic, crushed
1½ tablespoons parsley, finely chopped
1½ teaspoons thyme
3 eggs, separated
flour
1½ cups (6 oz) dried breadcrumbs
oil

1. Mix the meat with the finely chopped onions, garlic and herbs. **2.** Add the egg yolks to the meat mixture and blend well. **3.** Make the meat into small ball shapes and dust with flour. **4.** Beat the egg whites until they are stiff and white. **5.** Coat the meatballs with the egg white. **6.** Then coat them in breadcrumbs. **7.** In a large frying pan pour in oil to a depth of 1 cm (½ in) and heat it to sizzling point. **8.** Gently fry the meatballs in the hot oil, turning regularly so that they become cooked on all sides and golden in colour. **9.** Drain and serve.

Pork Fillets with Prunes and Cream Sauce

Noisettes de Porc aux Pruneaux

Serves 6-8

approximately 3 dozen large dried prunes, pitted
1½ cups (12 fl oz) dry white wine
4-6 pork fillets, trimmed and sliced 3.5 cm (1½ in) thick
salt and pepper
flour
80 g (2½ oz) butter
2 tablespoons oil
1 cup (8 fl oz) chicken stock (see p. 328)
1¼ cups (10 fl oz) cream
1 tablespoon redcurrant jelly
1 teaspoon lemon juice

1. Marinate the prunes in the white wine at room temperature for several hours, or overnight if possible. **2.** Cook the prunes and the wine over a moderate heat for 10 minutes. **3.** Drain, and put the prunes and wine aside separately. **4.** Season the noisettes of pork with salt and pepper, and dust with flour. **5.** Melt the butter with the oil in a heavy pan, and sauté the noisettes for about 3 minutes on each side until they are browned. Transfer them from the pan to a plate. **6.** Pour off almost all the fat from the pan. Add the wine in which the prunes have been cooked, and boil it briskly until it has reduced to 1 tablespoon. **7.** Pour in the chicken stock and bring the liquid to the boil again. **8.** Return the noisettes to the pan, cover, and simmer very gently over a low heat for about 15–20 minutes, or until the noisettes are tender. **9.** Transfer the noisettes from the pan to a serving dish, and keep warm. **10.** Thoroughly degrease the stock remaining in the pan. Pour in the cream and bring it to the boil, stirring and scraping in any brown bits. **11.** Boil the sauce briskly, stirring constantly, until it is thick enough to coat the back of a spoon. **12.** Stir in the prunes, redcurrant jelly and lemon juice and cook until the jelly is dissolved and the prunes heated through. **13.** Taste and correct the seasoning. **14.** Arrange the prunes around the noisettes, spoon the sauce over the top and serve at once.

Pork Chops Avesnes Style

Côtes de Porc Avesnoise

Serves 6

60 g (2 oz) butter
6 pork chops
salt and freshly ground black pepper
125 g (4 oz) grated Gruyère cheese
4 tablespoons cream
4 tablespoons mustard
2 tablespoons Calvados

1. Heat the butter in a heavy-bottomed pan, and fry the chops on both sides until they are done (15–20 minutes). **2.** Remove the chops to an ovenproof dish, season with salt and pepper and keep them warm. **3.** Mix together the Gruyère cheese, 2 tablespoons of the cream, and the mustard. **4.** Spread the mixture on the chops, and place under the grill until they are richly coloured. **5.** Keep the chops warm while preparing the sauce. **6.** Pour the Calvados into the frying pan and add the remaining two tablespoons of cream. **7.** Reduce over a brisk flame until the sauce is thick. **8.** Correct the seasoning, pour over the chops and serve.

Ham in Parsley Jelly

Jambon Persillé de Bourgogne

From the Restaurant Chez Pauline in Paris.

Serves 6–8

1 ham, or piece of ham
1 veal knuckle
2 calves' feet
bouquet garni
fresh chervil
fresh tarragon
5–6 spring onions (scallions), chopped
2 bottles of white wine
6 tablespoons parsley, finely chopped
1 teaspoon vinegar
¼ cup (2 fl oz) white wine
salt and freshly ground black pepper

1. Soak the ham overnight. Drain. **2.** Cover with fresh, cold water, bring to the boil. **3.** Cook for 1 hour. Drain the ham and rinse in clean water. **4.** Return the ham to the pan, and add the veal knuckle, calves' feet, bouquet garni, chervil, tarragon, spring onions and the two bottles of white wine. **5.** Simmer gently until the ham is cooked. **6.** Remove the ham from the liquid. **7.** Remove the skin, and crush the meat with a fork, mixing the fat and the lean meat. **8.** Press this mixture into a salad bowl. **9.** Strain the cooking liquid, and clarify it, checking the seasoning to obtain a good colour. **10.** When the liquid begins to set, add the chopped parsley, vinegar and the ¼ cup of white wine. Mix well. **11.** Pour this mixture over the ham and chill. **12.** The ham is usually served directly from the salad bowl.

Tripe Casserole

Tripes à la Mode de Caen

Tripe as prepared in Caen is one of the most famous of all Normandy dishes, the secret of which is very long, slow cooking in a tightly sealed heavy casserole dish.

Serves 4–6

1 kg (2 lb) tripe
1 calf's foot
125 g (4 oz) fat bacon
2 medium carrots, chopped in rounds
2 medium onions, coarsely chopped
bouquet garni
cloves
salt and pepper
pinch of cayenne pepper
4 cups (1 litre) cider

1. Heat the oven to 160°C (325°F/Gas 3). **2.** Simmer the tripe in salted water for ½ hour, drain. Cut it into large squares. **3.** Bone the calf's foot, and dice the meat from it. **4.** Line a heavy casserole dish with a well fitting lid with slices of fat bacon. **5.** Place the chopped vegetables on top of the bacon, then the bones of the calf's foot, and all the seasoning. **6.** Lay the tripe and meat from the calf's foot on top and cover with the cider. **7.** Cook in the oven for ½ hour. **8.** Reduce the oven temperature to 120°C (250°F/Gas ½), and cook for about 7½ hours, reducing the oven temperature still further if the casserole dish appears to steam. **9.** Serve the tripe with the liquid in deep plates, such as old fashioned soup plates.

Right: A selection of dishes from the Hôtel d'Étape in Saint-Flour. Bottom left: Duckling with Green Peppercorns (see page 33); centre: Crayfish a l'armouricaine; bottom right: Galantine of pork; top right: Goose Liver Pâté. Hôtel d'Etape is an example of a family-run French country hotel and restaurant. Here the fine products of the region — pork, duck and freshwater crayfish — are carefully and skilfully prepared. In addition to running the restaurant Victor Roux and his wife breed ducks, geese and guinea fowl and have a cannery where they preserve a fine range of 'Conserves Maison': foie gras, confit of duck, tripe, civet of rabbit, mushrooms and other local products.

Kidneys in Mustard Sauce

Rognons de Veau Gasconne

Serves 6

3-4 veal kidneys
salt and freshly ground black pepper
90 g (3 oz) butter
4 tablespoons oil
125 g (4 oz) button mushrooms
squeeze of lemon juice
½ cup (4 fl oz) Armagnac
1 tablespoon finely chopped spring onion
(scallion)
½ cup (4 fl oz) dry white wine
½ cup (4 fl oz) cream
1 tablespoon strong French mustard

1. Remove any fat from the kidneys and chop into cubes. **2.** Grind a little pepper over them, but not salt as this will make them tough during cooking. **3.** Melt half the butter in a small frying pan and add 1 tablespoon of oil. **4.** Gently cook the mushrooms for a few minutes, without letting them brown. **5.** Season them with salt and pepper and a squeeze of lemon. **6.** Heat the rest of the oil in a separate frying pan, and quickly sauté the kidneys for 3 to 4 minutes. **7.** Drain off the oil, pour in the Armagnac and ignite. **8.** When the flame has died out, remove the kidneys from the pan and keep warm. **9.** Add the rest of the butter to the pan, and the spring onion. **10.** Cook for 1 minute. **11.** Pour in the wine, bring to the boil and let it reduce over a high heat for 2 minutes. **12.** Remove the pan from the heat and add the cream and mustard. **13.** Return the pan to the heat to thicken. **14.** Add the mushrooms and their cooking liquid. **15.** When the sauce has warmed through, put the kidneys in to reheat. **16.** Adjust the seasoning if necessary. **17.** Arrange the kidneys on a serving dish and cover with the sauce.

Veal Kidneys in Red Wine and Mustard Sauce

Rognons de Veau Sauté Vallée de Cousse

Serves 6–8

6-8 veal kidneys
100 g (3½ oz) butter
125 g (4 oz) bacon, finely diced
2 onions, finely chopped
250 g (8 oz) button mushrooms
salt and pepper
1 clove garlic, crushed
pinch of dried tarragon
1¼ cups (10 fl oz) red wine
1 tablespoon French mustard
2 tablespoons cream
finely chopped fresh parsley

1. Trim all the fat and sinew from the kidneys, and slice them. **2.** Melt the butter in a heavy pan, and fry the kidneys over a brisk heat for 3 to 4 minutes, turning them once. **3.** Remove the kidneys with a slotted spoon from the pan to a serving dish and keep them warm. **4.** Sauté the bacon, onions and mushrooms in the same pan until lightly browned. **5.** Add the salt, pepper, garlic, and tarragon, and cook gently. **6.** Stir in the red wine, and simmer to reduce the sauce slightly. **7.** Add the mustard, and then the cream. Blend the sauce well, but do not allow it to boil. **8.** When the sauce is heated through, pour it over the kidneys, sprinkle with chopped parsley and serve immediately.

DESSERTS & CAKES

Apple Tart
Tarte Alsacienne

Serves 6

250 g (8 oz) short pastry (see p. 331)
4 large cooking apples, peeled, cored and thinly sliced
4 tablespoons sugar
2 eggs
1 tablespoon flour
½ cup (4 fl oz) milk or cream
Kirsch or brandy

1. Preheat the oven to 210°C (425°F/Gas 7). **2.** Prepare the pastry. Roll out the pastry and line a 23 cm (9 in) tart tin. **3.** Arrange the slices of apple on the pastry in circles. **4.** Sprinkle with 1 tablespoon of the sugar. **5.** Bake for 10 minutes. **6.** In a mixing bowl, whisk the eggs. **7.** Mix in the flour. **8.** Add the milk or cream, whisking all the time, and then the remaining sugar. **9.** Sprinkle into this mixture a little Kirsch or brandy. **10.** Pour on to the hot partly cooked tart. **11.** Bake the tart for a further 20 minutes in the hot oven, until the top is cooked and the pastry golden brown. (This tart can also be made with stoned plums or cherries.)

Commercy Madeleines
Les Madeleines de Commercy

These are delicate little cakes, baked in shell-shaped madeleine moulds. Makes approximately 30 madeleines.

¾ cup (6 oz) caster (powdered) sugar
1¼ cups (5 oz) flour, sieved
3 eggs
½ teaspoon bicarbonate of soda (baking soda)
grated rind of ½ a lemon
pinch of salt
75 g (2½ oz) butter, melted

1. Preheat the oven to 160°C (325°F/Gas 3). **2.** Mix the sugar, flour, eggs, bicarbonate of soda, lemon rind and salt in a bowl, until the mixture is very smooth. This may be done in a food processor or electric mixer. **3.** Add the melted butter and mix well. **4.** Butter a tray of special madeleine moulds, or indented baking tray. **5.** Fill the moulds two-thirds full of the mixture. **6.** Bake in the preheated oven, for 15–20 minutes. **7.** Turn on to a wire rack to cool.

Green Figs in Wine and Honey
Figues de Marseilles au Miel

Serves 6–8

1 kg (2 lb) fresh green figs
white wine to cover
1 cup (12 oz) honey
fresh cream, whipped

1. Wash the figs, and place them in a saucepan with enough white wine to just cover them. **2.** Bring the pan gently to the boil. **3.** Add the honey. **4.** Simmer for about 15 minutes, or until the figs are tender but still firm. **5.** Chill the figs well in the liquid. **6.** Serve very cold with whipped cream.

Strawberry and Peach Soufflé
Soufflé aux Fruits Frais de Provence

Serves 4

2 large ripe peaches
400 g (13 oz) small strawberries
½ cup (4 fl oz) Grand Marnier
4 egg yolks
100 g (3⅓ oz) caster (powdered) sugar
4 egg whites
pinch of salt
icing (confectioners') sugar

1. Preheat oven to 200°C (400°F/Gas 6). **2.** Pour boiling water over the peaches then peel them. Cut them in halves, remove the stones and chop the flesh into small dice. **3.** In a bowl, combine the diced peaches, the strawberries and the Grand Marnier and marinate for 2–3 hours. (If small strawberries are not available, cut large ones in halves or quarters.) **4.** In a mixing bowl, cream the egg yolks and the sugar until they are pale and creamy. **5.** Mix the fruit and liquid into the yolk mixture. **6.** Beat the egg whites with a pinch of salt until they are stiff. **7.** Gently fold the egg whites into the yolk-fruit mixture. **8.** Butter four small soufflé dishes and sprinkle the inside with sugar. **9.** Fill the dishes and bake for approximately 15 minutes or until they have risen and are golden brown on top. **10.** Serve immediately sprinkled with icing sugar.

Chilled Fresh Raspberry Soufflé

Soufflé Glacé aux Framboises Fraîches

A recipe from Restaurant Capucin Gourmand in Nancy.

Serves 4

500 g (1 lb) raspberries
1¼ cups (10 fl oz) cream, whipped
½ cup (4 oz) caster (powdered) sugar

1. Set a few raspberries aside for decoration, and crush the rest. **2.** Add the whipped cream and the sugar, and mix together. **3.** Take a soufflé dish and make a collar with greaseproof paper. **4.** Pour in the soufflé mixture, and place in the coldest part of the refrigerator. **5.** When ready to serve, remove the soufflé from the refrigerator and remove the paper collar. **6.** Decorate the top with the remaining raspberries and a little icing sugar and serve.

Baked Cherry Pancake

Clafoutis aux Cerises

This is an easily prepared, homely dish from Limousin.

Serves 6

750 g (1½ lb) black cherries, stoned
4 eggs
pinch of salt
½ cup (4 oz) sugar
½ cup (2 oz) flour
60 g (2 oz) butter
1 cup (8 fl oz) milk
caster (powdered) sugar for sprinkling

1. Preheat the oven to 200°C (400°F/Gas 6). **2.** Butter a wide shallow ovenproof dish generously. **3.** Put the stoned cherries in the dish. **4.** Beat the eggs lightly in a bowl. **5.** Whisk in the salt and the sugar. **6.** Blend in the flour. **7.** Melt half of the butter, and beat into the batter. **8.** Pour in the milk, beating well. **9.** Pour this batter over the cherries. **10.** Dot with the remaining butter. **11.** Bake for 35–40 minutes, until the batter has set. **12.** Sprinkle with sugar and serve either hot or cold, accompanied by whipped cream.

Fruit Loaf with Raspberry Sauce

Le Pain de Fruits au Coulis de Framboises

From the Restaurant Le Chapon Fin in Bordeaux.

Serves 10

4 egg yolks
½ cup (4 oz) caster (powdered) sugar
1¼ cups (10 fl oz) milk
1 teaspoon vanilla essence
2 teaspoons gelatine
1¼ cups (10 fl oz) cream
125 g (4 oz) strawberries
125 g (4 oz) blackberries
4 peaches, peeled, halved and stoned

Sauce:
125 g (4 oz) raspberries
¾ cup (6 oz) caster (powdered) sugar

1. Beat the egg yolks and the sugar together until they are fluffy. **2.** Heat the milk and the vanilla essence. **3.** Beating constantly, pour the hot milk on to the egg and sugar mixture, and cook in a double saucepan until the custard thickens a little. **4.** Soften the gelatine in a little milk and beat into the custard until dissolved. **5.** Strain the custard and allow to cool to room temperature. **6.** The custard should be cold, but not set. **7.** Whip the cream until it is firm. **8.** Gently blend the whipped cream into the custard. **9.** Add the whole strawberries, blackberries, and peach halves. **10.** Take great care not to crush the fruit while mixing them into the custard. **11.** Pour this mixture into a gelatine mould, or a bread tin. **12.** Transfer to the refrigerator for 2 to 3 hours.

Sauce: 1. Blend the raspberries and the caster sugar in a food processor, or a food mill. **2.** To serve, unmould the 'loaf' and cut in slices. **3.** Surround each slice with the raspberry sauce and serve.

Right: Chilled Fresh Raspberry Soufflé (above) as served at the Capucin Gourmand in Nancy. In France there seems to be a very fine line between a one-star and a two-star restaurant. Capucin Gourmand with its one star justifiably enjoys the reputation of being the top restaurant in Nancy. The food there was equal to, or better than, many higher rating restaurants. Even the humble Quiche Lorraine, when prepared by chef Gerard Veissière appears as a gourmet creation.

Pithiviers Almond Cake

Gâteau de Pithiviers

Pithiviers is famous for its almond-flavoured pastry and cakes, and this recipe is typical of this region.

Makes one 20 cm (8 in) cake

2 eggs, separated
¾ cup (6 oz) sugar
1 teaspoon vanilla essence
90 g (3 oz) butter, softened
1⅔ cups (6 oz) ground almonds

Icing:
¾ cup (4 oz) icing (confectioners') sugar
1 egg white
glazed fruit peel

1. Preheat the oven to 160°C (325°F/Gas 3). **2.** Beat the egg yolks, sugar and vanilla essence together. **3.** In another bowl, mix the butter with the ground almonds. **4.** Combine all these ingredients together. **5.** Whip the egg whites until stiff, and fold into the cake mixture. **6.** Grease a 20 cm (8 in) cake tin and fill with the mixture. **7.** Bake for 20 minutes.

Icing: 1. When the cake is cool, make an icing by stirring the icing sugar into a lightly beaten egg white, to make a spreading mixture. **2.** Spread the top of the cake with the icing mixture. **3.** Sprinkle the cake with glazed fruit peel.

Caramelised Apple Tart

Tarte aux Pommes Caramelisées

From the Restaurant Ar Milin in Châteaubourg.

Serves 4

Filling:
30 g (1 oz) butter
⅓ cup (3 oz) sugar
5 apples, peeled, cored, and sliced in rounds

Pastry:
155 g (5 oz) butter
2 cups (8 oz) flour
pinch of salt
1 egg

1. Preheat the oven to 180°C (350°F/Gas 4). **2.** Butter the bottom of a teflon coated pie dish. **3.** Sprinkle with the sugar. **4.** Arrange the apples on the sugar, overlapping them slightly. **5.** Prepare the pastry by rubbing the butter into the flour and salt. **6.** Bind with the egg, and a little cold water if necessary. **7.** Roll out thinly and cut a round to cover the pie dish. **8.** Place the pie in the oven for approximately 25 minutes. **9.** When the tart is cooked, place the pie on a hot plate until the apples are well caramelised. **10.** Allow the pie to cool. **11.** Turn the pie out on to a serving dish. **12.** Serve with whipped cream.

Apple Soufflé

Soufflé Normande

This is flavoured with Calvados, and stuffed with macaroons and pieces of cooked apples.

Serves 4–6

60 g (2 oz) butter
½ cup (2 oz) flour
1¼ cups (10 fl oz) hot milk
pinch of salt
5 egg yolks
½ cup (4 oz) sugar
½ teaspoon vanilla essence
3 tablespoons Calvados
½ large apple, peeled, chopped into small pieces and cooked in water until tender
6 egg whites
6 macaroons

1. Preheat the oven to 180°C (350°F/Gas 4). **2.** Melt the butter in the top of a double saucepan. **3.** Add the flour and cook, stirring, until well blended. **4.** Add the hot milk, and salt. **5.** Cook the sauce, stirring constantly, until smooth and thick. **6.** Let the sauce cool slightly. **7.** Beat the egg yolks with the sugar and the vanilla essence, and mix well with the cooled sauce. **8.** Stir in 2 tablespoons Calvados and the cooked apple pieces. **9.** Line a buttered soufflé dish with the macaroons. **10.** Sprinkle them with the remaining tablespoon of Calvados. **11.** Beat the egg whites until stiff, but not dry. **12.** Fold the egg whites into the cooled sauce mixture. **13.** Pour into the prepared soufflé dish. **14.** Bake in the centre of the oven for 35 minutes, or until the soufflé is puffed and golden. **15.** Serve immediately.

Baked Cheesecake

Tourteau Fromage

This cheesecake is typical of the Loire Valley region. In Poitou it is made from goat's cheese, but where this is unobtainable, fresh cream cheese may be substituted.

Makes one 22 cm (9 in) tart

250 g (8 oz) short crust pastry (see p. 331)
185 g (6 oz) fresh cream cheese
3 eggs
½ cup (4 oz) sugar
2 tablespoons cream
2 tablespoons chopped angelica

1. Preheat oven to 150°C (300°F/Gas 2). **2.** Prepare the short crust pastry. **3.** Mix together the cream cheese, eggs, sugar, cream and angelica until the ingredients are well blended. **4.** Line the tart dish with the rolled out pastry. **5.** Fill with the cheese mixture. **6.** Bake the tart for about 40 minutes. **7.** Allow the tart to cool before serving.

Apples Cooked in a Crust

Bourdelots Normands

Serves 6

750 g (1½ lb) flaky pastry
6 tart apples
⅓ cup (2 oz) raisins
cinnamon
⅓ cup (2 oz) brown sugar
mixed spice
milk
caster (powdered) sugar

1. Heat the oven to 160°C (325°F/Gas 3). **2.** Prepare the pastry. **3.** Core the apples. **4.** Roll out the pastry until quite thin. **5.** Place an apple on the pastry, well in from the edge. **6.** Mix the raisins, cinnamon, sugar and a pinch of mixed spice, and stuff the apple with this mixture. **7.** Cut round the apple, leaving a margin of pastry to fold over. **8.** Fold the pastry over the top of the fruit, dampen the edges with milk and press together. **9.** Repeat this process with each apple. **10.** Brush the pastry with a little milk. **11.** Place on a buttered dish and bake in the oven for 30 minutes, or until the pastry is cooked. **12.** Dust with caster sugar and serve either hot or cold.

Almond Cake

Gâteau aux Amandes

This may be served for afternoon tea or as a dessert to accompany vanilla ice cream or chocolate cream.

1 cake, about 22 cm (9 in) in diameter, for 10–12 people

20 very fresh egg whites
pinch of salt
3¾ cups (24 oz) caster (powdered) sugar
250 g (8 oz) unsalted butter, softened
3¼ cups (13 oz) flour
a few drops lemon essence, or the finely grated rind of 1 lemon
½ cup (2 oz) slivered almonds

1. Preheat the oven to 190°C (375°F/Gas 5). **2.** Beat the egg whites with a good pinch of salt until stiff. **3.** Carefully add the sugar, bit by bit, whisking constantly. (The mixture will change consistency, becoming creamier, but firm.) **4.** Add, all together, the well-softened butter, the sifted flour and the lemon essence or rind. **5.** Mix carefully so that the egg whites remain stiff. **6.** Pour the mixture into a well-buttered cake tin, 22 cm (9 in) in diameter. **7.** Sprinkle the top generously with almonds. **8.** Bake for about 45 minutes. **9.** Test with the point of a trussing needle to see whether it is cooked. The needle should come out damp but clean. **10.** Turn out the cake and allow to become cold before slicing.

Breton Cake

Gâteau Breton

This is a thick galette flavoured with rum.

Serves 10

2¼ cups (9 oz) flour
1 cup (7 oz) sugar
pinch of salt
250 g (8 oz) unsalted butter, softened
6 egg yolks
2 tablespoons rum

1. Preheat the oven to 180°C (350°F/Gas 4). **2.** Place 1¾ cups flour in a bowl and make a well in the centre. **3.** Put into the well the sugar, salt, butter, 5 egg yolks and the rum. **4.** Mix and then work well together as if for short crust pastry. **5.** Add the rest of the flour. **6.** Form the dough into a ball with your hands. **7.** Butter a 23 cm (9 in) cake tin. **8.** Roll out the dough to a thickness of about 3 cm (1¼ in). **9.** Line the tin with the dough. **10.** Dilute the remaining egg yolk with a drop of water, and brush over the cake. **11.** Make a criss-cross pattern on the top of the cake with a fork. **12.** Bake for about 20 minutes, or until it is golden.

Macaroons

Macarons

The Touraine is renowned for its cookies and barley sugars, but the particular speciality of the small town of Ligueil is macaroons.

Approximately 3 dozen small macaroons

250 g (8 oz) ground almonds
250 g (8 oz) sugar
2 egg whites, beaten
1 teaspoon vanilla essence
oil

1. Preheat the oven to 180°C (350°F/Gas 4). **2.** Mix the ground almonds with the sugar. **3.** Beat the egg whites until they are stiff. **4.** Stir the egg whites into the sugar and almond mixture and flavour with the vanilla essence. **5.** Line a baking sheet with greaseproof paper and oil lightly. **6.** Make small balls of the mixture with oiled teaspoons and drop on to the baking tray. **7.** Bake for 20 minutes. When removed from the oven, the macaroons will appear to be soft, but they will harden when cooled. **8.** Turn over the paper with the macaroons attached, and peel off gently. If it sticks, moisten the paper with a clean sponge until the macaroons slip off.

ITALY

The cooking of Italy has been developed over the centuries by a people with an immense love of life.

The huge variety in Italian food stems from the geography of the land and from the backgrounds of all the different people who have lived there.

Added to that are the many external cultural influences that the country has been exposed to in the almost three thousand years of its legendary and recorded history. The Etruscans, Greeks, Romans, Byzantines, Saracens, Africans, even the Chinese have all left their mark.

And in turn, Italy has left her mark. In the 16th century, Maria and Catherine dei Medici married French kings. They brought with them from Florence their own cooks who exercised culinary skills not known to the French and they introduced the Court to new ingredients, especially vegetables and fruit. This new knowledge became the basis upon which the haute cuisine of France later developed.

To me, Bernard Shaw's saying "no love is more sincere than the love of food" applies more aptly to Italians than to any other people. They are colourful exuberant people who produce food of such enchanting simplicity that it has become one of the most popular and best loved cuisines in the world.

In my travels through 'la bella Italia', the country so attractive and varied and so dear to my heart (and stomach), I have tried to collect a selection of recipes which will best show the regional diversity of the food.

There is a popular misconception that the same kind of pasta is eaten throughout the country. This is not so. In the southern half of Italy the traditional pasta is the extruded machine-made dried type such as spaghetti and macaroni, usually served with a tomato-based sauce. In the north, especially in Bologna, fresh hand-made flat egg pasta such as fettucini is the most common type eaten. Further north, in the Po Valley and surrounding districts, very little pasta is served and rice is the staple food.

One other important difference between north and south is in the amount of meat eaten. In the prosperous north, many local dishes are based on meat. By contrast, in the south where some of the best vegetables are grown, meat plays a less significant part in regional cooking.

One thing the most regions have in common is good fresh seafood. Italy's long coastline and the fact that nowhere is too far from the sea means that fresh fish and seafood is in abundance.

Wherever you go in Italy, north or south, local cooks succeed in giving their dishes a flavour and character that is unmistakably Italian.

Right: The gardens of the Carthusian Monastery the Certosa di Pavia in Lombardy.

SOUPS

Neapolitan Clam Soup
Zuppa di Vongole

Serves 4

48 clams (pippies, mussels or cockles may be used)
2 cups (16 fl oz) dry white wine
1 leek (the white part only), chopped
1 onion, chopped
1 clove garlic, crushed
2 tablespoons olive oil
4 cups (1 litre) fish stock (see p. 328)
1 large tomato, peeled and chopped
1 teaspoon fresh chopped marjoram
3-4 leaves of celery, chopped
4 large croûtons, fried in butter

1. Place the clams in a saucepan, pour in the wine and gently cook until the clams open. **2.** Drain, save the liquid and remove the shells. **3.** Sauté the leek, onion and garlic in the oil, add the liquid from the clams and the fish stock. **4.** Stir in the tomato, marjoram and celery leaves. **5.** Simmer for 10 minutes, stir in the clams and serve hot, poured over the croûtons.

Onion Soup
Zuppa di Cipolle

Serves 6

750 g (1½ lb) onions, sliced
¼ cup (2 fl oz) olive oil
salt
freshly ground black pepper
6 cups (1.5 litres) beef stock (see p. 328)
250 g (8 oz) potatoes, peeled and cut into small cubes
6 slices bread, toasted and broken into chunks
grated pecorino cheese

1. In a heavy-bottomed saucepan, lightly sauté the onions in the oil. Add salt, pepper, beef stock, and potatoes. **2.** Cover and simmer for 45 minutes. **3.** Serve it hot with the bread and sprinkled with the cheese.

Capri Fish Soup
Zuppa di Pesce Caprese

Serves 4–6

3 tablespoons olive oil
2 onions, thinly sliced
3 stalks celery, chopped
2 cloves garlic, crushed
1 teaspoon each fresh marjoram, thyme and basil
1 kg (2 lb) tomatoes, peeled and chopped
1 teaspoon grated lemon rind
freshly ground black pepper
1 cup (8 fl oz) dry white wine
1 cup (8 fl oz) water
250 g (8 oz) octopus, chopped
1 kg (2 lb) mussels, scrubbed
8 prawns (shrimps), uncooked
12 thick slices fresh tuna, or any fish steaks
4-6 slices bread, fried in butter

1. In a saucepan, heat the oil and add the onions, celery and garlic. Sauté for 5 minutes. Add the herbs, tomatoes, lemon rind and black pepper. Cook for a few minutes. **2.** Add the wine and simmer, covered, until the tomatoes are reduced to a pulp. Add the water and simmer for a further 3 minutes. **3.** Add the octopus and cook on a low flame for 20 to 30 minutes or until it is tender. **4.** Add the mussels and cook until the shells open. **5.** Add the prawns, cook for 3 to 5 minutes, peel and reserve them. **6.** Add the fish, cook for 5 minutes then return the prawns to the pan. **7.** Season and serve with slices of fried bread.

'Little Rags'
Stracciatella

A Roman speciality, now popular throughout Italy, it is a consommé into which a thin batter of eggs, semolina or flour, grated lemon peel and cheese is poured.

Serves 4

2 eggs
2 tablespoons semolina
½ teaspoon grated lemon peel
2 tablespoons grated Parmesan cheese
5 cups (1.25 litres) chicken consommé
salt

1. In a mixing bowl, beat the eggs and add the semolina, lemon peel and cheese. **2.** Add 1 cup of consommé and stir it to a smooth cream. Add a little salt. **3.** Heat the remaining consommé and when it is nearly boiling, pour in the egg mixture stirring constantly with a fork for 3 to 4 minutes. **4.** Bring the soup to the boil and serve immediately; the mixture should have formed into 'little rags'.

Soup with Poached Eggs
Zuppa Pavese

Serves 4

1 loaf French bread
2 tablespoons butter
¼ cup (2 fl oz) olive oil
4 cups (1 litre) chicken or beef consommé
4 eggs
4 tablespoons grated Parmesan cheese

1. Cut the bread into 2.5 cm (1 in) slices and fry them in the butter-oil mixture. **2.** Boil the consommé, turn down the heat and while simmering it lightly, break the eggs one at a time, into a saucer and gently slide them into the consommé. **3.** When the eggs are poached, place the toasted bread in the soup bowl, place the egg on top of the toast, gently pour the consommé over and sprinkle with Parmesan.

Chicken Soup
Zuppa di Pollo

Serves 6

1 chicken, about 1.5 kg (3 lb)
3 bay leaves
2 tablespoons finely chopped herbs (fresh thyme, oregano or marjoram)
salt
freshly ground black pepper
2 tablespoons butter
3 carrots, chopped
½ bunch celery, chopped
3 potatoes, diced
2 leeks (white part only), thinly sliced
300 g (10 oz) fresh or frozen peas
6 slices toasted croûtons
½ cup (2 oz) grated Parmesan cheese

1. Put the chicken into a saucepan with enough water to cover. Add the bay leaves, herbs, salt and pepper. **2.** Bring it slowly to the boil and simmer for 1 hour. Skim the surface. **3.** In the butter sauté all the vegetables except the peas and add them to the saucepan with the chicken. Simmer for a further ½ hour then add the peas. (If raw, simmer for 10 minutes; if deep-frozen, cook for 3 minutes only.) **4.** Remove the chicken, take the meat off the bone, keeping it in fairly large pieces. **5.** Return the meat to the saucepan. Heat gently and serve with the toasted croûtons and grated cheese.

Tuscan Bean Soup
Zuppa di Fagioli alla Toscana

Serves 4

500 g (1 lb) white dried beans
6 cups (1.5 litres) water or beef stock
salt
freshly ground black pepper
2 tablespoons olive oil
1-2 cloves garlic, crushed
¼ cup chopped parsley

1. Wash the dried beans and soak them in the water or stock overnight. **2.** Gently simmer the beans in the same water or stock for approximately 3 hours, or until they are soft. **3.** When cooked, put half the beans in a food processor and purée them until they are fine in texture. If a processor is not available rub them through a sieve. Return the puréed beans to the saucepan and season. **4.** In the olive oil lightly fry the garlic and the parsley. **5.** Stir this mixture into the soup and serve hot with crusty bread.
Note: The traditional recipe calls for fresh oil to be poured into the soup before serving.

Milanese Thick Vegetable Soup
Minestrone alla Milanese

Milanese minestrone is distinguished by the use of rice, while those in other parts of Italy use pasta.

Serves 4

30 g (1 oz) butter
4 slices bacon, finely chopped
1 cup chopped parsley
1 clove garlic, crushed
1 stalk celery, chopped
2 potatoes, diced
2 carrots, chopped
2 zucchinis (courgettes), sliced
125 g (4 oz) green beans, cut into 1.5 cm (½ in) long pieces
1 cup (6 oz) dried beans, previously soaked for 12 hours
3 tomatoes, peeled and chopped
salt
freshly ground black pepper
110 g (3½ oz) cabbage, coarsely chopped
1 cup (6 oz) rice
4 tablespoons Parmesan cheese (optional)

1. Melt the butter in a saucepan, add the bacon, parsley, garlic and celery. Sauté for 5 minutes. **2.** Add the potatoes, carrots, zucchinis, green and dried beans and tomatoes. Season and cover with water. Cover the pan and simmer for half an hour. **3.** Add the cabbage and the rice and simmer for a further half hour. Make sure the rice is not overcooked. **4.** Serve it, if desired, with a sprinkling of Parmesan.

PASTA & PIZZA

Spaghetti Roman Style

Spaghetti alla Prestinara, alla Carbonara, a Cacio e Pepe

Three Roman ways of preparing spaghetti. The sauce recipe may be used for rigatoni (short, thick, ribbed macaroni).

Serves 4

375–500 g (12–16 oz) spaghetti
water
salt

1. Boil the water, add the salt and cook the spaghetti for 4 to 8 minutes depending on the degree of softness desired. Most Italians cook it briefly and serve it 'al dente' (firm).

(1) 'alla prestinara'
A poor man's spaghetti for those who love garlic.
1 cup (8 fl oz) olive oil (for this dish the best quality should be used)
3–4 cloves garlic, chopped
salt
freshly ground black pepper
1 cup (4 oz) grated Parmesan cheese

1. When the spaghetti is cooked, heat the oil in a small saucepan, add the garlic and let it stand for a few minutes without frying it. **2.** Pour the oil over the spaghetti and sprinkle it with the grated cheese.

(2) 'alla carbonara'
125 g (4 oz) prosciutto, smoked ham or bacon, chopped
2 tablespoons butter
2 eggs, beaten
salt
freshly ground black pepper
1 cup (4 oz) grated Parmesan cheese

1. Lightly fry the prosciutto, ham or bacon in the butter. **2.** Add the beaten eggs and briefly cook them until they are just about to turn into scrambled eggs. **3.** Pour the mixture over the cooked spaghetti, season, and stir in half of the Parmesan. **4.** Serve with the remaining cheese sprinkled over it.

(3) 'a cacio e pepe'
salt
lots of freshly ground black pepper
1 cup (4 oz) grated pecorino cheese

1. Add the salt and pepper to the cooked spaghetti. **2.** Sprinkle with the cheese and add some of the hot cooking water from the spaghetti. **3.** Mix well and serve very hot.

Neapolitan Pizza

Pizza alla Napoletana

From Chez Black in Positano.

Serves 4

Dough:
4 cups (1 lb) flour
1 teaspoon salt
1 tablespoon sugar
1½ teaspoons dry yeast
½–¾ cup (4–6 fl oz) lukewarm water

Filling:
1 kg (2 lb) tomatoes, peeled and chopped
⅓ cup (2½ oz) olive oil
½ teaspoon salt
1 teaspoon sugar
1 clove garlic, crushed
90 g (3 oz) mozzarella cheese, sliced
2 teaspoons chopped oregano or basil

Dough: 1. Place the flour on a board, make a well in the centre and add the salt and sugar. Dissolve the yeast in a little of the water and stir it into the flour, adding enough water to make a soft dough. **2.** Beat and pummel the dough until it becomes smooth. Lift the ball of dough and hit it against the board until it is smooth and elastic. **3.** Divide the dough into 4 parts, form them into balls and allow them to rise for 2 to 2½ hours.

Filling: 1. Preheat the oven to 200°C (400°F/Gas 6). **2.** Cook the tomatoes with half the olive oil, the salt, sugar and garlic for 30 minutes.

Preparation of Pizza: 1. Roll out the balls of dough into rounds about 6 mm (¼ in) thick and place them on a greased baking tray. **2.** Spread the cooked tomatoes over the rounds and place the slices of cheese on top of the tomatoes. Sprinkle with the oregano or basil and pour over the remaining olive oil. **3.** Place the baking tray in the preheated oven and bake for about 30 minutes. Serve hot.

Right: *The chef at Chez Black in Positano preparing to cook one of his famous Neapolitan Pizzas (above).*

Turnover Pizza

Calzone

Serves 6

**½ of the dough recipe for Neapolitan Pizza
(see p. 50)
6 slices prosciutto or smoked, cooked ham
6 slices mozzarella or Bel Paese
2 tablespoons olive oil
salt
freshly ground black pepper**

1. Preheat the oven to 200°C (400°F/Gas 6).
2. Prepare the dough as described for Neapolitan
Pizza, roll it out very thinly and, with a teacup, cut
out rounds of dough. **3.** On one side of each round
lay a piece of ham and a slice of cheese, sprinkle it
with oil, salt and pepper. **4.** Fold over to form a half-
moon shape and press the edges together to enclose
the ham and cheese. **5.** Grease a baking tray, arrange
the calzone on the tray and bake in the preheated
oven for 20 to 30 minutes. (The calzone may also be
deep-fried in very hot oil.)

Spaghetti with Tomatoes, Cheese and Bacon

Spaghetti alla Napoletana

Serves 4

**1 medium-sized onion, cut in half and sliced
1 stalk celery, finely sliced
1 small carrot, finely chopped
1 clove garlic, crushed
¼ cup (2 fl oz) olive oil
2 slices bacon, cut into fine strips
⅔ cup (5½ fl oz) dry white wine
4 ripe fresh tomatoes or canned tomatoes,
finely chopped
1 tablespoon tomato purée
salt
freshly ground black pepper
375 g (12 oz) spaghetti
155 g (5 oz) pecorino cheese, grated
200 g (6½ oz) mozzarella or fresh ricotta
cheese, diced or crumbled
1 teaspoon dried oregano**

1. Lightly brown the vegetables in the oil together
with the bacon. **2.** Add the wine and cook until it
has almost evaporated. **3.** Add the tomatoes, tomato
purée, and season it with salt and pepper. **4.** Cook
this mixture until it is thick, stirring occasionally.
5. Cook the spaghetti in lots of boiling water until
cooked but still firm. **6.** Drain the spaghetti and add
the vegetable mixture and one tablespoon of
pecorino. **7.** To serve, place the spaghetti in a bowl
and sprinkle it with mozzarella or ricotta and
oregano. Serve the rest of the pecorino separately.

Spaghetti with Anchovies and Tomatoes

Spaghetti alla Sangiovanniello

Serves 4

**5–7 tinned peeled tomatoes
3 anchovy fillets, coarsely chopped
4 tablespoons olive oil
1 clove garlic, crushed
3 basil leaves, chopped
1 small piece hot chilli pepper, chopped
salt
3 tablespoons parsley, chopped
1 tablespoon capers, chopped
12 black olives, pitted**

1. Purée the tomatoes. **2.** With the back of a fork,
mash the anchovies in the heated oil. **3.** Add the
garlic, basil and chilli and simmer until the sauce is
thick but not dry. Remove the chilli when the sauce
is hot enough for your taste. If the sauce is too thick,
add a little of the spaghetti cooking water. **4.** Just
before serving, add the parsley, capers and olives.
Mix the sauce into the previously cooked spaghetti.

Spaghetti with Asparagus Tips

Spaghetti con Punte d'Asparagi

Serves 4

**1 kg (2 lb) fresh asparagus or 300 g (10 oz)
canned asparagus tips
2½ tablespoons olive oil
400 g (13 oz) fresh tomatoes, peeled and
chopped
salt
freshly ground black pepper
350 g (11 oz) spaghetti
4 tablespoons grated Parmesan cheese**

1. If using fresh asparagus, boil it in plenty of salted
water or steam it for 10 minutes. **2.** Cut off the tips
about 4 cm (1½ in) long. Use the rest of the asparagus to make a cream of asparagus soup. **3.** In a heavy
casserole heat the oil, add the asparagus tips, tomatoes, pepper and salt. **4.** Cook over low heat for 5
minutes. **5.** Cook the spaghetti to taste in boiling
salted water and serve with the sauce poured over it.
Sprinkle with the grated cheese.

Spaghetti with Broccoli
Spaghetti con i Broccoli

Serves 4

4 anchovy fillets
750 g (1½ lb) broccoli flowerets, trimmed
salt
375 g (12 oz) spaghetti
4 tablespoons olive oil
1 clove garlic, crushed

1. Chop the anchovies coarsely. **2.** Steam or boil the broccoli in salted water but do not overcook it. (If boiling, keep the water for the spaghetti.) **3.** Cook the spaghetti 'al dente'. **4.** While the spaghetti is cooking, heat the oil in a frying pan and add the chopped anchovies and the garlic. With the back of a fork, mash the anchovies into a thick sauce. **5.** Mix the broccoli with the anchovy sauce and pour it over the spaghetti. Serve immediately.

Spaghetti with Anchovy Sauce and Breadcrumbs
Spaghetti Ammollicato

Serves 6

1¼ cups (10 fl oz) olive oil
10 anchovy fillets, cut into small pieces
1¼ cups (5 oz) fine dry breadcrumbs
pinch of cayenne pepper
625 g (1¼ lb) spaghetti

1. Use half the olive oil and fry the anchovies; during the cooking time use the back of a fork to mash the anchovy fillets into a paste. **2.** Separately, in the rest of the oil, fry the breadcrumbs until crisp and golden. **3.** Sprinkle them with the cayenne pepper. **4.** Boil the spaghetti in a saucepan of boiling salted water until soft but firm. **5.** Drain the spaghetti and mix in the anchovy sauce. **6.** Serve it hot with the breadcrumbs sprinkled on top.

Macaroni with Fennel
Maccheroni con Finocchio

Serves 6

3 fennel bulbs
salt
juice of ½ lemon
750 g (1½ lb) macaroni
¼ cup (2 fl oz) olive oil
freshly ground black pepper
grated pecorino cheese

1. Blanch the fennel in salted water, to which the lemon juice has been added, for approximately 15 minutes. **2.** Remove the fennel, cool it and cut it into thin strips. **3.** In the fennel water, cook the macaroni until tender but still firm. **4.** Drain the water. **5.** Add the olive oil, fennel, salt and pepper and serve it sprinkled generously with grated cheese.

Calabrian Macaroni
Maccheroni alla Calabrese

Serves 6

¾ cup (6 fl oz) olive oil
1 clove garlic, crushed
1 small hot chilli (optional)
1 onion, finely chopped
155 g (5 oz) prosciutto ham, finely chopped
1.25 kg (2½ lb) tomatoes, peeled, seeded and roughly chopped
salt
pepper
625 g (1¼ lb) macaroni
125 g (4 oz) Caciocavallo (or Cheddar) cheese, grated

1. In ½ cup of the oil sauté the garlic and chilli. When the garlic is brown, discard it. **2.** Add the onion, and cook until golden-brown. **3.** Add the ham and cook for a further 5 minutes. Add the tomatoes, season with salt and pepper and cook on a medium heat for 35 to 40 minutes. **4.** Cook the macaroni in salted water to the 'al dente' stage. **5.** Drain the water, pour the remaining olive oil into the macaroni and mix it well. **6.** In an ovenproof dish arrange a layer of macaroni, sprinkle it with grated cheese and pour over some of the sauce. Place a further layer of macaroni, and more cheese sauce in the dish, alternating until all the macaroni, cheese and sauce are used up. Finish up with a layer of cheese. **7.** Place the dish under a hot grill, brown the cheese and serve while hot.

Macaroni with Clams or Mussels
Maccheroni con Vongole o Cozze

Serves 4

1 kg (2 lb) clams or mussels
2 cloves garlic
3 tablespoons olive oil
1 red chilli, chopped
345 g (11 oz) macaroni
¼ cup chopped parsley

1. Wash the clams or mussels carefully. **2.** Place them in a large heavy-bottomed pan. Cover and heat them, without water, until they open. **3.** Keep the liquid from the clams but discard that of the mussels. **4.** Remove and discard the shells. Fry the garlic in the oil and when it has coloured lightly, add the chilli. Cook for a few minutes then add the clams and their liquid, or the mussels, and heat through. **5.** Separately, in lots of boiling salted water, cook the macaroni until it is 'al dente'. **6.** To serve, place the macaroni in a bowl, add the shellfish and sauce and sprinkle with chopped parsley.

Calabrian Lasagna
Lasagna alla Calabrese

Serves 6

Tomato Sauce:
4 tablespoons olive oil
125 g (4 oz) fresh Italian sausage, peeled and chopped
125 g (4 oz) fresh Italian hot sausage, peeled and chopped
2 teaspoons fresh basil, chopped
2 cloves garlic, crushed
salt
freshly ground pepper
4 tablespoons tomato paste
4 cups (1 litre) tomato purée

Noodles:
500 g (1 lb) lasagna noodles
salt
boiling water

Filling:
2 cups (1 lb) ricotta or cottage cheese, crumbled
1½ cups (7 oz) roughly grated mozzarella cheese
375 g (12 oz) fresh mushrooms, sliced
4 tablespoons butter
¼ cup (1 oz) grated Parmesan or Romano cheese

1. To make the tomato sauce, heat the oil in a saucepan, add the two types of sausage, the basil, garlic, salt and pepper. **2.** Sauté for 3 to 5 minutes, then add the tomato paste and tomato purée. Simmer the sauce until it is fairly thick. **3.** Boil the lasagna in a large saucepan of salted water a few at a time to prevent sticking. Remove the cooked pieces and plunge them into cold water. **4.** Preheat the oven to 200°C (400°F/Gas 6). **5.** Oil a baking dish, place a layer of lasagna in the dish, then a layer of ricotta mixed with the mozzarella and then a layer of mushrooms which have been previously sautéed in the butter. Over the mushrooms pour a layer of tomato sauce. **6.** Repeat the layers, finishing with a layer of tomato sauce. Sprinkle the top with grated cheese and bake in the preheated oven for 30 minutes. Serve very hot.

Lasagna Ferrara Style
Lasagna all Ferrarese

Serves 4

1 onion, chopped
1 carrot, chopped
1 stick celery, chopped
3 tablespoons butter
1 cup (5 oz) prosciutto, chopped
250 g (8 oz) beef, minced
1 cup (8 fl oz) dry white wine
2½ cups (1¼ lb) tinned peeled tomatoes, chopped
salt
freshly ground black pepper
375 g (12 oz) lasagna noodles
1½ cups (6 oz) grated Parmesan cheese

Béchamel Sauce:
2 tablespoons butter
2 tablespoons flour
1½–2 cups (12–16 fl oz) hot milk
¼ teaspoon nutmeg

1. Sauté the onion, carrot and celery in the butter, add the prosciutto and cook for 6 minutes. **2.** Add the minced beef and brown, stirring constantly. **3.** Add the wine and cook until it has almost completely evaporated. **4.** Add the tomatoes, season, lower the heat and simmer for 1 hour. If too much of the liquid evaporates add some water. **5.** Cook the lasagna in plenty of salted water; when still quite firm, remove it from the heat and rinse it in cold water. **6.** Preheat the oven to 200°C (400°F/Gas 6). **7.** Make the Béchamel: In a saucepan melt the butter, add the flour and, stirring constantly, cook for 5 minutes. Add the hot milk and cook for 10 to 15 minutes, stirring occasionally. Season and add the nutmeg. **8.** Grease an ovenproof dish and arrange alternate layers of lasagna, meat sauce and Béchamel, sprinkled with some of the Parmesan. Finish off with a layer of Béchamel sprinkled with the rest of the cheese. **9.** Bake in the preheated oven for 30 to 45 minutes.

Right: Lasagne Ferrara Style (above) from the restaurant Al Catunzein in Bologna. I had a wonderful meal at Al Catunzein, starting with an antipasto of Bologna's most famous product: the mortadella. Then came tiny servings of different types of home-made pasta: green stricchetti with prosciutto, butter and Parmesan; tortelloni stuffed with ricotta and parsley and served in a cream and prosciutto sauce; garganelli with mushrooms; lasagne made with minced beef and prosciutto and best of all, tortellini stuffed with Parmesan, turkey meat, veal, mortadella and nutmeg. And this was only the first course.

Rich Lasagna
Vincisgrassi

An elaborate dish created in 1799 in honour of Prince Windischgrätz of Austria.

Serves 4

6 sheets ready-made lasagna
water
salt
2 calves' brains
2 calves' sweetbreads
3 tablespoons lard or bacon fat
1 onion, chopped
1 carrot, chopped
250 g (8 oz) chicken giblets
1 cup (8 fl oz) dry white wine
1 tablespoon concentrated tomato purée
½ cup (4 fl oz) chicken stock or water
salt
pepper

Béchamel Sauce:
2 tablespoons butter
2 tablespoons flour
1 cup (8 fl oz) hot milk
½ teaspoon nutmeg
1 cup (4 oz) grated Parmesan cheese
melted butter

1. Preheat the oven to 190°C (375°F/Gas 5).
2. Cook the lasagna in boiling salted water for 5 to 8 minutes. **3.** In another pan of boiling salted water blanch the brains and the sweetbreads for 5 minutes. **4.** Melt the fat and sauté the onion and carrot, add the chopped chicken giblets and the wine. **5.** Cook until the wine has almost evaporated, add the tomato purée and the chicken stock or water. **6.** Season, cover and cook gently for 1 hour. Stir occasionally. **7.** Fifteen minutes before it is cooked, add the diced brains and sweetbreads. **8.** Make a Béchamel sauce by melting the butter in a pan over a low heat. Add the flour and cook until golden. **9.** Stir in the hot milk, and cook on a low heat stirring constantly for 5 minutes. Season, add the nutmeg and continue cooking for a further 10 minutes. **10.** Grease an ovenproof dish and arrange alternate layers of pasta, Béchamel sauce, cheese and the meat sauce, finishing up with a layer of Béchamel. **11.** Bake in the preheated oven for 30 to 40 minutes. Pour some melted butter on top and serve piping hot sprinkled with cheese.

Ravioli Stuffed with Fish and Ricotta Cheese
Ravioli di Magro

Serves 6

Stuffing:
500 g (1 lb) white, firm non-fatty fish, grilled
1 bunch borage
1 small bunch fresh herbs such as oregano or marjoram, finely chopped
100 g (3½ oz) ricotta cheese
1 cup (4 oz) grated Parmesan cheese
2 whole eggs
¼ teaspoon salt
freshly ground black pepper

Pasta:
600 g (1 lb 3½ oz) flour
¾ cup (6 fl oz) water
½ cup (2 oz) grated Parmesan cheese

1. Remove all bones from the fish and mince it very finely. **2.** Wash the borage and the herbs, remove the leaves and cook them in a little water for 3 to 4 minutes. Drain thoroughly, squeeze out all excess water and mince the leaves very finely. **3.** In a bowl, combine the minced fish and borage and herbs. Add the rest of the stuffing ingredients and mix together thoroughly until the texture is that of a very fine paste. A food processor is ideal for preparing this stuffing. **4.** To make the pasta, place the flour on a wooden board and form a well. Add the salt to the lukewarm water and carefully combine with the flour to make a flexible dough. **5.** Work the pasta vigorously for approximately 15 minutes. **6.** Divide the pasta into 2 or 3 parts and roll one of them into a thin sheet. With a pastry wheel cut the sheet into 7 cm (3 in) wide strips. **7.** With a teaspoon, place the stuffing approximately one finger's width apart on the lower half of the strip. Fold the upper half of the strip over the lower and firmly press it down so that it fuses with the lower. With the pastry wheel cut the strip into individual ravioli. Repeat the above with the remaining pasta. **8.** In a large saucepan boil a generous amount of salted water and add the ravioli, a few at a time. Boil for approximately 15 minutes. **9.** Serve sprinkled with grated Parmesan cheese.

VEGETABLES

Artichokes Jewish Style
Carciofi alla Giudia

This recipe comes from Sabatini in Rome. This is an ancient recipe for artichokes as prepared in the Jewish quarter in Rome.

Serves 4

16 small artichokes (in Rome they are known as 'cimaroli')
1 lemon
water
salt
freshly ground pepper
approximately 4 cups (1 litre) olive oil

1. Remove the tough outer leaves of the artichokes and cut off the stems leaving approximately 4 cm (1½ in) of stalk. **2.** With a very sharp knife, trim the leaves, shaping each artichoke so that it takes a round shape. **3.** As each artichoke is completed, immerse it in a bowl of water into which you have squeezed the juice of the lemon. This will prevent the artichokes from turning black. **4.** When all the artichokes are shaped, take them out of the water, drain them well and dry them. Holding the artichoke by the stalk, beat the head of each one against the table so that the leaves flatten out. **5.** Sprinkle with salt and pepper. **6.** In a deep cast-iron casserole, heat enough oil to completely cover the artichokes. Add the artichokes and cook them for approximately 10 minutes, turning them occasionally so that they are cooked on all sides. **7.** Turn up the heat and continue cooking for a further 10 minutes. **8.** Remove the artichokes from the oil, drain them and place them on absorbent paper. **9.** Arrange them on a serving plate and serve immediately.

Artichokes, Calabrian Style
Carciofi Gallico Marina

Serves 4

½ cup finely chopped parsley
4 fresh mint leaves, finely chopped
1 clove garlic, finely chopped
salt
freshly ground pepper
2–4 cups (16–32 fl oz) water
8 artichokes
1–2 cups (8–16 fl oz) water

1. Preheat the oven to 160°C (325°F/Gas 3). **2.** Place the parsley, mint leaves and garlic in a cup with salt, pepper and two to three tablespoons of oil. **3.** Trim off the external tough leaves of the artichokes and leave approximately 4 cm (1½ in) of stalk. **4.** With a spoon open up the leaves and in between them place some of the above mixture. Press the leaves together and arrange the artichokes in an oven dish with high sides. **5.** Add salt, pepper and the water and oil, making sure that the artichokes are completely covered. If necessary add more water and oil. **6.** Cover the casserole and place it in the preheated oven for approximately 30 minutes. **7.** When cooked, drain the artichokes and serve. They may also be served cold as an hors d'oeuvre.

Stuffed Eggplants
Melanzane Ripiene

Serves 4

4 large eggplants (aubergines)
125 g (4 oz) white bread, without crusts
1 cup (8 fl oz) milk
8 anchovy fillets, chopped
12 black olives, seeded and chopped
¼ cup parsley, chopped
2 cloves garlic, crushed
1 tablespoon capers
1 tablespoon fresh marjoram, chopped
salt
freshly ground black pepper
¼ cup (2 fl oz) olive oil

1. Preheat the oven to 180°C (350°F/Gas 4). **2.** Cut the eggplants in half and scoop out most of the flesh from each, leaving a thin layer attached to the skin. **3.** Soak the bread in the milk, then squeeze it dry in your hands. **4.** Chop the eggplant flesh and mix it with the remaining ingredients except the oil. **5.** Taste before adding salt, as the anchovy may make the mixture sufficiently salty. **6.** Put the stuffing back into the eggplants and arrange them on a baking tray. **7.** Pour a little oil over each eggplant, cover the dish and cook in the oven for approximately 30 to 40 minutes.

Sauté of Eggplant
Melanzane al Funghetto

The term 'al funghetto' applies to certain vegetables fried in small pieces with their skins on.

Serves 4

3-4 unpeeled eggplants (aubergines), diced
salt
½ cup (4 fl oz) olive oil
2 cloves garlic, chopped
4 tablespoons parsley, chopped

1. Cut the unpeeled eggplant into small dice. Put them into a bowl and sprinkle them with salt. Leave them to drain for 1 hour. **2.** Heat the oil in a large frying pan and gently fry the eggplant for about 15 minutes. **3.** About 5 minutes before they have finished cooking, add the garlic and, just before serving, the parsley. **4.** If the eggplant has not absorbed all the oil, drain it before serving. **5.** The eggplant thus prepared can be served as a vegetable with meat or chicken dishes or by itself as a separate vegetable.

Sweet-and-Sour Onions
Cipolline in Agrodolce

Serves 4

500 g (1 lb) small pickling-type onions
2 tablespoons olive oil
¼ cup (2 fl oz) white wine vinegar
½ cup (4 fl oz) water
1 tablespoon sugar or 2 tablespoons honey
2 cloves
1 bay leaf
1 teaspoon salt

1. Cook the unpeeled onions in water for 10 minutes. When they have cooled, peel them and put them in a clean saucepan with the olive oil. Sauté them lightly for 5 minutes. **2.** Add all the remaining ingredients and simmer gently for 30 minutes. **3.** Drain and serve hot or cold as part of an antipasto or as a separate vegetable course.

Casserole of Peppers (Capsicums)
Peperoni alla Calabrese

From Fata Morgana in Reggio Calabria. This dish may be served as a cold hors d'oeuvre or hot as a vegetable with a main course.

Serves 4

4 large peppers (capsicums)
4 tablespoons olive oil
3 large onions, sliced
315 g (10 oz) tomatoes, cut into four and seeded
2 tablespoons white wine vinegar
salt
60 g (2 oz) green olives, stoned and sliced

1. Cut the peppers into four and remove the seeds. **2.** In a frying pan, heat the oil and brown the onions, then add the tomatoes and the peppers. **3.** When all the vegetables have browned, sprinkle with the vinegar. Add salt and after cooking it for about 10 minutes, add the olives. **4.** Mix well and when the peppers are cooked, but not too soft, transfer to a serving plate.

Marinated Zucchini
Zucchini in Marinata

From Ai Portici in Martina Franca.

Serves 4

8 firm and large zucchinis (courgettes), sliced
1 cup (8 fl oz) olive oil
2-4 cups (16-32 fl oz) vinegar
salt
1 tablespoon finely chopped red chilli

1. Brown the zucchinis a few at a time in the oil. **2.** Place the fried zucchinis in a dish (not aluminium). **3.** Heat sufficient vinegar to cover the zucchinis, add salt and the chilli to taste. **4.** When the vinegar boils, pour it over the zucchinis. **5.** Allow to cool, place in a glass jar and preserve for serving.

Right: *Marinated Zucchini (above) from the restaurant Ai Portici in Martina Franca. Martina Franca is a fine jewel among the many beautiful towns of Italy. Splendidly preserved and immaculately maintained, it is one of the prettiest towns I have ever visited. Ai Portici has a modest entrance off one of the elegant baroque squares. Its basement location gives it a cosy atmosphere.*

Salad of Beans and Tuna

Insalata Conti

From Conti in Reggio Calabria.

Serves 6

3 medium-sized potatoes, boiled and sliced
½ cup (3 oz) dried white beans (first soaked
then boiled until tender)
½ cup (2½ oz) black olives, pitted and cut in
quarters
1 clove garlic, crushed
2 tablespoons parsley, chopped
2 teaspoons fresh basil, chopped
¾ cup (6 fl oz) olive oil
4 anchovy fillets, chopped
juice of 1 lemon
salt
freshly ground black pepper
½ tablespoon capers
125 g (4 oz) tuna, diced and drained of its oil
185 g (6 oz) crab meat, cooked

1. In a salad bowl, gently combine the potatoes,
beans, olives, garlic, parsley and basil. **2.** Heat the
olive oil and add the anchovy fillets, mashing them
with the back of a fork until they are well blended.
Add the lemon juice and season, then add the
capers. **3.** Pour three-quarters of this dressing over
the salad and toss it thoroughly. **4.** In the centre of
the salad make a well and into it place the tuna.
Around it arrange the crab meat, sprinkle the rest of
the dressing over the tuna and crab meat and serve.

Roasted Celery

Sedano al Forno

Serves 4

2 heads of celery, broken into stalks and cut
into 7.5 cm (3 in) lengths
juice of ½ lemon
salt
6 tablespoons olive oil
1 onion, sliced
4 slices bacon, chopped
pepper
625 g (1¼ lb) tomatoes, peeled, seeded and
roughly chopped
3 sprigs parsley, chopped

1. Preheat oven to 180°C (350°F/Gas 4). **2.** Simmer
the celery in water, lemon juice and salt for 15 minutes, drain. **3.** In half the oil, sauté the onion and
the bacon in a frying pan for approximately 5 minutes. **4.** Arrange the celery in an ovenproof dish and
pour the onion and bacon over it. Add the tomatoes
and the rest of the olive oil. Sprinkle with salt and
pepper. **5.** Cover the dish and cook it in the
preheated oven for approximately 1 hour. **6.** Serve
it hot, sprinkled with chopped parsley.

Cauliflower Salad

Insalata di Cavolfiore

Serves 4-6

1 medium-sized cauliflower
salted water
juice of ½ lemon
salt
freshly ground black pepper
⅓ cup (2½ fl oz) olive oil
8 anchovy fillets, finely chopped
2 tablespoons capers
3 sprigs parsley, chopped
12–16 black olives

1. Boil the cauliflower in the salted water until it is
tender but firm, depending on the size, approximately 5 to 8 minutes. **2.** Drain and rinse with cold
water. **3.** Combine the lemon juice, salt and pepper
with olive oil and stir together to make a dressing.
4. Break the cauliflower into flowerets and arrange
them on a serving dish. Pour the dressing over them
and sprinkle with the anchovy fillets, capers and
parsley. **5.** Arrange the olives around the cauliflower
and serve.

Fried Cauliflower in Batter

Cavolfiore Fritto

Serves 4

1 kg (2 lb) cauliflower in one piece
¾ cup (3 oz) flour
1 egg
dry white wine
1 teaspoon aniseed liqueur (optional)
salt
freshly ground black pepper
oil for frying

1. Boil the cauliflower, covered, in salted water for 10 to 15 minutes until it is tender but still firm. **2.** To make the batter, mix the flour, egg and sufficient wine to make a batter which will be thick enough to cling to the cauliflower. Add the aniseed liqueur and season to taste. **3.** Drain the cauliflower and when cool divide it into flowerets. **4.** Heat the oil. **5.** Dip the flowerets in the batter and fry them in the oil until light brown. Sprinkle with salt and freshly ground black pepper and serve the cauliflower hot.

Asparagus Milanese Style

Asparagi alla Milanese

Serves 4

750 g (1½ lb) asparagus
water
4 eggs
125 g (4 oz) butter
salt
freshly ground black pepper
½ cup (2 oz) Parmesan cheese

1. Tie the asparagus into 4 equal bundles. If you don't have an asparagus steamer, use your tallest saucepan. Stand the bundles vertically and if they protrude above the rim, cover the saucepan with another of the same diameter, turned upside-down. **2.** Pour in about 5 cm (2 in) of water and boil for 15 minutes. **3.** In the meantime, fry the eggs in the butter. **4.** Lift the eggs out onto the dinner plates and place the asparagus next to them. Pour the butter over the asparagus and sprinkle it all with Parmesan.

Sicilian Ratatouille

Caponata alla Siciliana

A speciality of 'A Cuccagna in Palermo.

Serves 6

1 kg (2 lb) eggplants (aubergines), cut into cubes
salt
500 g (1 lb) onions, sliced
½ cup (4 fl oz) olive oil
500 g (1 lb) tomatoes, peeled, seeded and chopped
2 tablespoons capers, washed
90 g (3 oz) celery stalks, roughly chopped
½ cup (2½ oz) pickled olives, stoned
½ cup (4 fl oz) white wine vinegar
1 tablespoon sugar

1. Arrange the cubed eggplants on a rack or in a sieve. Sprinkle with salt and allow to stand for 1 to 2 hours until the liquid has completely drained off. **2.** Sauté the onions in half the oil and when golden brown add the tomatoes, capers, celery and olives. **3.** Brown all these ingredients and remove the pan from the heat. **4.** Lightly squeeze any remaining liquid from the eggplant and dry the pieces in a cloth. **5.** In the remaining oil in a separate pan, fry the eggplant and when brown, drain off the oil and add the eggplant to the above mixture. **6.** Add the vinegar and sprinkle with sugar. Mix well and continue cooking over a low heat until most of the liquid has evaporated. **7.** Caponata may be served cold as an hors d'oeuvre or hot as a vegetable with the main course.

Pickled Peppers

Peperoni Sott'aceto

From Ai Portici in Martina Franca.

large firm peppers (capsicums)
white wine vinegar

1. Cut the peppers into quarters, wash them and remove their stems and seeds. **2.** Dry and spread them out on a tray in the sun for a few hours. **3.** Place them in a glass jar, cover with the vinegar and stand in a cool place for 2 to 3 days before using them.

Stuffed Tomatoes

Pomodori Ripieni

From La Rosetta in Perugia.

Serves 4

4 large tomatoes
3 tablespoons olive oil
1 onion, chopped
1 tablespoon parsley, chopped
3 tablespoons fresh breadcrumbs
2 teaspoons capers
salt
freshly ground black pepper
¼ teaspoon nutmeg
**2 tablespoons fine dry breadcrumbs for
topping**
2 tablespoons olive oil

1. Preheat the oven to 190°C (375°F/Gas 5). **2.** Cut a slice from the base, not the stem end, of the tomatoes and reserve. Hollow out the centres. Reserve the flesh, discarding the juice and seeds. **3.** Heat the oil in a frying pan and sauté the onion. **4.** Remove the pan from the heat and add the parsley, fresh breadcrumbs, capers, salt, pepper, nutmeg and two tablespoons of the reserved tomato flesh. **5.** Mix all the ingredients thoroughly and fill the tomatoes with the stuffing. **6.** Replace the reserved tomato tops, coat the tomatoes with dry breadcrumbs and sprinkle them with oil. **7.** Arrange them on an oiled shallow baking tray and bake them in the preheated oven for 30 minutes.

Broccoli or Cauliflower, Milanese Style

Broccoli o Cavolfiori alla Milanese

Serves 4

**1 cauliflower or broccoli weighing 1–1.25 kg
(2–2½ lb)**
water
salt
¼ cup (1 oz) flour
2 eggs, whisked with a little water
1 cup (4 oz) grated Parmesan cheese
1 cup (4 oz) fine dry breadcrumbs
salt
freshly ground black pepper
250 g (8 oz) butter

1. Break up the cauliflower or the broccoli into bite-size flowerets and boil them in salted water for 5 minutes. **2.** Drain them, dust them with flour, dip them in the egg mixture, then in the cheese, again in the egg and finally in the breadcrumbs. Season. **3.** Fry them in the butter until the breadcrumbs are golden-brown.

Onion Pie

Torta di Cipolle

*This recipe comes from the Chalet Della Certosa
in Pavia.*

Makes one 23 cm (9 in) pie

600 g (1 lb 3 oz) onions, finely chopped
90 g (3 oz) smoked fat bacon, chopped
3 tablespoons oil
4 eggs
2 egg whites, beaten stiff
salt
freshly ground pepper
**puff pastry, sufficient to make 2 crusts for a
23 cm (9 in) pie dish**
egg wash to glaze

1. Preheat the oven to 190°C (375°F/Gas 5). **2.** Place the onions, bacon and oil in a frying pan and sauté them until the onions are soft. **3.** Remove from the heat and incorporate 4 eggs, lightly beaten, and the egg whites, together with some salt and pepper. **4.** Grease the pie dish and line it with the puff pastry. Pour the mixture into the pie and cover with a pastry lid. Brush the lid with egg wash. **5.** Bake the pie in the preheated oven for 45 minutes. It may be served either hot or cold.

Parmesan Spinach

Spinaci alla Parmigiana

Serves 6

1 kg (2 lb) spinach, washed and chopped
100 g (3½ oz) butter
salt
freshly ground black pepper
½ teaspoon nutmeg
½ cup (2 oz) grated Parmesan cheese

1. In a saucepan, combine the spinach and the butter. Cook for 8 to 10 minutes, add the salt, pepper and nutmeg. Mix in the Parmesan and serve very hot.

Right: Onion Pie (above) from the Chalet della Certosa in Pavia, Lombardy. The restaurant is located just outside the gates of the famous Carthusian Monastery the Certosa di Pavia. Its owner, Piero Bolfo, has always been interested in furthering the cause of regional foods and at the Chalet he serves a very impressive array of regional and local dishes.

Spinach with Pine Nuts and Raisins

Spinaci alla Liguria

Serves 4

1 kg (2 lb) spinach
2 tablespoons olive oil
1 clove garlic, crushed
4 slices bacon or 4 slices prosciutto crudo, chopped
2 tablespoons pine nuts
2 tablespoons raisins
2 tablespoons butter
salt
freshly ground black pepper

1. In a large saucepan, boil some salted water and cook the spinach in it for 5 minutes. Drain and rinse it under cold running water. **2.** Roughly chop the spinach and sauté it in olive oil with the garlic and the bacon or prosciutto. **3.** When cooked, add the pine nuts and raisins, stir in the butter and season it to taste.

Piedmontese Stuffed Mushrooms

Funghi Ripieni alla Piemontese

This recipe comes from La Maison de Filippo in Entrèves.

Serves 4 (as a first course)

4 very large or 8 medium-sized mushrooms
½ cup chopped parsley
4 anchovy fillets, finely chopped
2 onions, chopped
1 egg
½ cup (2 oz) fine dry breadcrumbs
2 tablespoons olive oil
salt
freshly ground black pepper

1. Preheat the oven to 180°C (350°F/Gas 4). **2.** If possible, select large cup-shaped mushrooms, remove the stalks and chop them for the stuffing. **3.** If you have a food processor, place all the ingredients except the whole mushrooms and the oil in the bowl and process to a fine texture. Otherwise mix the ingredients thoroughly in a bowl. **4.** Fill the mushrooms with the mixture and sprinkle the tops with some of the oil. **5.** Place the mushrooms on a baking tray and put them in the preheated oven for about 30 minutes. Check from time to time and if necessary sprinkle more oil on the mushrooms to prevent them drying out.

Trieste Potato Cake

Patate alla Triestina

From the Park Hotel Obelisco in Trieste. The Obelisco serves regional food which means that it often seems more Austrian or Yugoslav than Italian. Their jota triestina, which is a bean, potato and cabbage soup, is very similar to a Yugoslavian dish, while their excellent tarts — especially those made from almonds — taste similar to those found in Austria.

Serves 4–6

1.75 kg (3½ lb) potatoes
salt
90 g (3 oz) bacon, finely chopped
30 g (1 oz) butter
2 tablespoons olive oil
1 onion, thinly sliced
½ cup (4 fl oz) beef stock (see p. 328)

1. Boil the potatoes in salted water until they are tender. **2.** Drain, peel and cut them into slices. **3.** Lightly sauté the bacon in the butter and oil, add the onion and sauté until golden-brown. **4.** Add the potatoes, season and add the beef stock. **5.** With the back of a fork, crush the potatoes roughly. **6.** Over a low heat, cook the potatoes until the underside is brown. **7.** Slide the potato cake onto a plate and reverse the sides. Fry again, adding more butter if necessary, until the second side is brown and crisp.

Green Pea Omelette

Frittata con Piselli

Serves 4

75 g (2½ oz) butter
1 onion, finely chopped
60 g (2 oz) prosciutto, finely chopped
1 bulb fennel, finely sliced
250 g (8 oz) shelled green peas
salt
freshly ground black pepper
7 eggs, lightly beaten
3 sprigs parsley, finely chopped

1. Melt 60 g of the butter in a large frying pan, add the onion, prosciutto, fennel and peas and sauté lightly. **2.** Season and add 1 cup of water. **3.** Simmer for approximately 5 minutes, until the fennel is tender. **4.** Drain the water, add the remaining butter, pour in the beaten eggs and add the parsley. Fry until it is brown. **5.** Slip the omelette on to a large dinner plate, then turn it over and cook the other side until it is brown. **6.** Cut the omelette into four and serve the quarters hot with a mixed green salad.

FISH

Sicilian Steamed Clams
Vongole alla Siciliana

Serves 4

3 tablespoons olive oil
2 cloves garlic, crushed
2 tablespoons finely chopped parsley
freshly ground black pepper
48 clams or pippies, scrubbed

1. In a saucepan, heat the olive oil and add the garlic and parsley. Sauté for a few minutes without browning the garlic. Add some pepper. 2. Add the clams or pippies, cover the saucepan and, over a moderate heat, simmer until the clams have opened. 3. Serve the clams in their shells in soup plates with the cooking juice poured over them.

Sicilian Fish Steaks
Trance di Pesce alla Siciliana

Serves 4

½ cup (4 fl oz) olive oil
4 fish steaks (kingfish, snapper etc.)
1 tablespoon finely chopped parsley
2 cloves garlic, crushed
½ cup (4 fl oz) white wine vinegar
1 kg (2 lb) tomatoes, peeled, seeded and coarsely chopped
salt
freshly ground black pepper
1 kg (2 lb) fresh peas, shelled
4 croûtons, browned in oil

1. In a large frying pan, heat the oil and lightly brown the fish. Add the parsley, garlic and vinegar. 2. Simmer until the vinegar has almost evaporated, add the tomatoes and peas and season to taste. Simmer for a further 10 minutes or until the peas and the fish are tender. 3. To serve, arrange the pieces of fish on a serving platter and pour the tomato and pea sauce over them. Serve with croûtons.

Tuna with Olives and Capers
Tonno alla Marinara

Serves 4

4 slices tuna, about 4 cm (1½ in) thick
4 tablespoons oil
¼ cup (1 oz) dry breadcrumbs
6-8 basil leaves, chopped
12 green or black olives, stoned
3 tablespoons capers
400 g (12½ oz) ripe tomatoes, peeled and chopped
salt
freshly ground black pepper

1. Preheat the oven to 160°C (325°F/Gas 3). 2. In a heavy baking dish, lightly fry the tuna pieces in half of the oil. 3. Sprinkle the tuna with the breadcrumbs and basil leaves. 4. Mix the olives, capers and tomatoes. Season and pour the mixture over the fish. 5. Pour the remaining oil on top and cook in the preheated oven for about 40 minutes. 6. Serve straight from the baking dish.

Stuffed Cuttlefish
Seppie Ripiene

From Al Gambero in Taranto, a stark, rather uninviting looking restaurant which serves excellent seafood. One could make a meal just by eating the antipasti: seafood salads of all kinds; stuffed, crumbed and fried mussels; calamari; prawns; lobster. Their pasta with various seafood sauces are also delicious.

Serves 4

750 g (1½ lb) small cuttlefish
345 g (11 oz) mussels
345 g (11 oz) small squid, cleaned and finely chopped
¾-1 cup (1½-2 oz) fine soft breadcrumbs
¼ cup (1 oz) grated pecorino cheese
1 tablespoon capers, finely chopped
2 eggs
2 tablesoons olive oil
salt
freshly ground pepper

1. Preheat the oven to 160°C (325°F/Gas 3). 2. Clean and empty the cuttlefish and wash them well. 3. With a sharp knife open the mussels and detach the mollusc. Chop them finely. 4. Place the mussels and squid in a bowl, add the breadcrumbs, pecorino, capers and eggs. Mix together well. 5. Fill the cuttlefish with this mixture. Be careful not to overfill or they will burst. 6. Place on a baking dish, sprinkle with oil and season with salt and pepper. 7. Place in the preheated oven for ½ to ¾ hour. Serve hot.

Stuffed Mussels in Tomato Sauce

Cozze Ripiene al Sugo

From Al Gambero in Taranto.

Serves 4

1 kg (2 lb) mussels
3 tablespoons olive oil
2 cloves garlic
4 fresh tomatoes, peeled and puréed
¼ cup finely chopped basil
2 eggs, lightly beaten
2 tablespoons finely chopped parsley
sufficient soft breadcrumbs to make a firm but moist stuffing
salt
freshly ground black pepper

1. Scrub the mussels. **2.** With the sharp edge of a knife, open the raw mussels without damaging the shells. **3.** In the oil, fry one clove of garlic and when brown remove it. Add the tomato purée and sufficient water to cover the mussels. **4.** Add the basil and cook the mixture for a few minutes. **5.** Prepare the filling by mixing together the beaten eggs, parsley, the remaining garlic clove, finely chopped, and the breadcrumbs. **6.** Place a little of the mixture on each mussel in its shell. Press the shells together to close and tie white thread around them to keep the two shells together. **7.** Place the mussels in the sauce, which by now should be cooked. **8.** Simmer the mussels for 15 to 20 minutes. **9.** Remove the thread from the mussels and serve with boiled rice and the sauce.

Mussels Venetian Style

Peòci al Pangrattato

Serves 4

1 cup finely chopped parsley
3 cloves garlic, finely chopped
1 cup (4 oz) fine dry breadcrumbs
salt
freshly ground black pepper
¼ cup (2 fl oz) olive oil
2 kg (4 lb) mussels, scrubbed

1. Combine the parsley, garlic, breadcrumbs, salt and pepper. **2.** In a saucepan large enough to contain the mussels, heat most of the oil. Add the mussels, cover the pan, and heat until all the shells have opened. Remove one half-shell from each mussel and reserve the mussel liquid. **3.** Place some of the breadcrumb mixture on top of each mussel in its shell, sprinkle with the remaining oil and place them under the grill to brown the breadcrumbs. **4.** Serve with some of the mussel liquid poured over.

Pippies (Clams) Maremma Style

Arselle alla Maremmana

Pippies (clams) tend to be sandy and it is necessary to clean them. Place them in a large bowl filled with salted water and leave them to stand overnight. (1 tablespoon of salt per 4 cups (1 litre) of water.)

Serves 4

6 tablespoons olive oil
2 cloves garlic, crushed
3 sprigs fresh sage, chopped
2 kg (4 lb) pippies (clams)
1 cup (8 oz) dry white wine
salt
freshly ground black pepper
2 eggs
juice of 1 lemon
½ cup chopped parsley
12–16 1.5 cm (½ in) slices of fresh French bread

1. Put the olive oil, one of the garlic cloves and the sage in a large saucepan. Sauté for 3 to 4 minutes, then remove the garlic and sage. **2.** Put the pippies in the saucepan, add the wine and season with salt and pepper. Cook over high heat for 5 minutes or until the pippies are open. **3.** Drain the pippies and remove them from their shells. **4.** Return the pippies to the pan. **5.** In a bowl, beat the eggs with the lemon juice and season. **6.** Pour the mixture over the pippies, stir and remove from the heat. **7.** Add the parsley and the remaining garlic. **8.** Arrange the bread on heated plates and pour the pippi and egg mixture over them. (The bread may also be toasted.)

Right: Mixed Seafood Salad photographed against a background of a hand-painted horse-drawn cart. It is a speciality of the restaurant Callà in Policoro, Basilicata.

Seafood Risotto
Risotto di Mare

Serves 4

2 blue swimmer crabs or 1 small crayfish,
cooked
500 g (1 lb) shelled school prawns (shrimps),
cooked
2 carrots, chopped
2 stalks celery, chopped
1 onion, chopped
2 tablespoons butter
3 tablespoons olive oil
3 tablespoons chopped parsley
2 cups (12 oz) rice
salt
freshly ground black pepper
½ cup (4 fl oz) dry white wine
approximately 2 cups (16 fl oz) fish stock

1. Chop the crab and prawns. **2.** Sauté the carrots,
celery and onion in the butter and oil, add the
parsley and the rice and season. **3.** Gradually add
sufficient wine and fish stock to cook the rice. Simmer until the rice is cooked and the liquid has been
absorbed. **4.** Stir in the seafood and cook for another
5 minutes. Season.

Vincenza Salt Cod
Baccalà alla Vicentina

Serves 4

1 kg (2 lb) salt cod
¼ cup (2 fl oz) olive oil
2 tablespoons butter
2 onions, sliced
1 clove garlic, crushed
4 anchovy fillets, chopped
¼ teaspoon cinnamon
½ cup (4 fl oz) dry white wine
1–2 cups (8–16 fl oz) hot milk
½ cup (2 oz) grated Parmesan cheese

1. Soak the cod in cold water for several hours,
changing the water often. This will remove its salty
taste. **2.** Drain the fish, skin and bone it. **3.** Heat the
oil and butter and add the onions, garlic and anchovies and sauté for a few minutes. **4.** Cut the fish into
pieces and put them into the saucepan. Add the cinnamon, wine and sufficient hot milk to cover.
5. Stew for 2 to 3 hours: by then the sauce should
be reduced and thick. Before serving, mix in the
cheese. Serve with toasted squares of polenta.

Oysters Venetian Style
Ostriche alla Veneziana

Serves 4

¼ cup parsley, finely chopped
½ stalk celery, finely chopped
1 tablespoon finely chopped fresh oregano,
thyme or marjoram
½ cup (2 oz) fine dry breadcrumbs
olive oil
juice of 2 lemons
2 dozen oysters in their shells

1. Make a mixture of all the ingredients except the
oil, lemon juice and oysters. **2.** Put a little of it on
each oyster in its shell. **3.** Sprinkle with a few drops
of oil and place them for a few minutes under a grill.
4. Sprinkle with lemon juice before serving.

Pickled Octopus
Polpi Sott'aceto

*From Ai Portici in Martina Franca. Octopus
prepared in this way can be served as an
hors d'oeuvre or as part of a fish salad.*

1 kg (2 lb) fresh octopus, cleaned and
tenderised
12 fresh mint leaves
3 cloves garlic, sliced into thin slivers
2 cups (16 fl oz) white wine vinegar

1. Place the octopus in boiling unsalted water and
cook for approximately 1 hour, or until it feels tender when pierced with a fork. **2.** Drain and slice it
into 5 to 10 cm (2 to 4 in) pieces. **3.** Dry the octopus
and place in a glass jar, interleaving it with mint
leaves and thin slivers of garlic. Cover with vinegar,
seal the jar and preserve until ready to use.

POULTRY & GAME

Spit-roasted Chicken with Piquant Rice

Pollo allo Spiedo con Riso in Peverada

Guinea fowl is sometimes used instead of chicken in this dish.

Serves 4

1 chicken, about 1.5 kg (3 lb)
salt
freshly ground black pepper
2 tablespoons olive oil
2 cups (12 oz) rice

Peverada Sauce:
125 g (4 oz) chicken livers, chopped
4 anchovy fillets, chopped
1 clove garlic, crushed
125 g (4 oz) pickled green peppers, chopped
¼ cup (2 fl oz) olive oil
salt
freshly ground black pepper
2 tablespoons chopped parsley
¼ cup (2 fl oz) chicken stock (see p. 328)
juice of 1 lemon
1 tablespoon white wine vinegar

1. Preheat the oven to 190°C (375°F/Gas 5). **2.** Rub the chicken inside and out with salt and pepper and smear the outside with the oil. Place it in the preheated oven and spit-roast for 1¼ to 1½ hours. Baste frequently with the pan juices. **3.** To make the sauce, place the chicken livers, anchovies, garlic and green peppers in a saucepan and sauté them in the oil, add the seasoning and the parsley. **4.** Gradually add the stock, and simmer for 20 minutes. Add the lemon juice and vinegar. **5.** Boil the rice in salted water until tender. **6.** To serve, mix the peverada sauce into the rice. Serve the chicken carved into pieces surrounded by the rice.

Chicken with Peppers

Pollo con Peperoni

Serves 4

5 large green and red peppers (capsicums)
1 large onion, sliced
2 tablespoons butter
3 tablespoons olive oil
1.5 kg (3 lb) chicken, cut into pieces
salt and freshly ground black pepper
½ cup (4 fl oz) dry white wine
750 g (1½ lb) tomatoes, skinned and chopped
1 cup (8 fl oz) chicken stock (see p. 328)
3 tablespoons fresh basil, chopped

1. Place the peppers into boiling water for 1 minute. Drain, peel the skin, remove the seeds and cut the peppers into 2.5 cm (1 in) strips. **2.** Sauté the onion in the butter and oil until light brown, add the chicken and brown it on all sides. Season with salt and pepper. **3.** Add the wine and cook until it has almost evaporated, then add the tomatoes and stock. **4.** Cover and simmer over low heat, stirring occasionally for 45 minutes or until the chicken is tender. **5.** Remove the chicken to a preheated serving plate and reduce the pan juices by fast boiling. Pour them over the chicken and serve sprinkled with the basil. If basil is not available, sprinkle with chopped parsley.

Poached Chicken with Egg and Lemon Sauce

Pollo alla Maceratese

Serves 4

1.5 kg (3 lb) chicken
125 g (4 oz) chicken giblets, chopped
salt
½ cup (4 fl oz) olive oil
2 cups (16 fl oz) chicken stock (see p. 328)
2 egg yolks
juice of 1 lemon
freshly ground black pepper

1. In a deep heavy-bottomed casserole, brown the chicken and the giblets, which have been sprinkled with salt, in the olive oil. **2.** Add the stock, cover the casserole and simmer it over a low heat for approximately 1 hour. **3.** When the chicken has cooked, remove it from the casserole and keep it warm. Boil the stock until it reduces slightly. **4.** Mix the egg yolks with the lemon juice, salt and pepper, and add to the cooking juices in the casserole. **5.** Cook over a low heat for 1 to 2 minutes, stirring constantly, making sure that it does not boil and curdle. **6.** To serve, carve the chicken into pieces, arrange them on a serving platter and pour the sauce over them.

Breasts of Turkey
Filetti di Tacchino

This dish can also be prepared with chicken fillets.

Serves 4

410–500 g (13–16 oz) breast of turkey, cut into
thin slices
salt
freshly ground black pepper
¼ cup (1 oz) flour
125 g (4 oz) butter
4 slices prosciutto or cooked ham
6–8 button mushrooms, finely chopped
½ cup (2 oz) grated Parmesan cheese
½ cup (4 fl oz) chicken or turkey stock
(see p. 328)

1. Season the turkey fillets, dust them with flour and
lightly brown them in the butter. **2.** Place a slice of
ham on each slice of turkey and cover them with the
mushrooms which have been previously sautéed in
butter. Sprinkle them with the cheese and moisten
them with the stock. **3.** Place them in a pan, cover
and gently simmer for 5 to 8 minutes. If the cooking
juice has evaporated too much add more stock.
4. Serve the fillets masked with the cooking juice
which should have thickened to a cream-like
consistency.

Casserole of Turkey with Olives
Spezzato di Tacchino

Serves 6

2 cloves garlic
½ cup (4 fl oz) olive oil
1.5 kg (3 lb) turkey pieces
flour
salt
1 small piece hot chilli, finely chopped (or a
pinch of cayenne pepper)
½ cup (4 fl oz) dry white wine
24 black olives, pitted
¾ cup (6 fl oz) beef stock (see p. 328)

1. In a large heavy-bottomed frying pan, fry the garlic in olive oil until it is brown. Discard the garlic.
2. Sprinkle the turkey pieces with flour and brown
them in the garlic-flavoured oil. **3.** Add salt and the
chilli, being careful not to use too much otherwise
the dish will be too hot. **4.** Transfer everything to
a large casserole with a lid. **5.** Add the wine, olives
and the stock. **6.** Cover and simmer on a low heat
for 2 hours. **7.** Serve the turkey pieces directly out
of the casserole and mask them with the cooking
juices.

Lombardian Stuffed Turkey
Tacchina Ripiena alla Lombarda

Serves 8–10

1 turkey, about 4 kg (8 lb)
salt
freshly ground black pepper
3 tablespoons butter mixed with a little finely
chopped sage and rosemary
4 slices prosciutto
4 cups (1 litre) dry white wine

Stuffing:
250 g (8 oz) veal, minced
125 g (4 oz) lean pork, minced
125 g (4 oz) beef, minced
220 g (7 oz) chipolata sausage, chopped
3 eggs
4 tablespoons grated Parmesan cheese
¼ teaspoon nutmeg
125 g (4 oz) prunes, stoned and chopped
2–3 cooking apples, peeled and diced
15 chestnuts, boiled, peeled and mashed
2 slices bacon, coarsely chopped
salt
freshly ground black pepper

1. Preheat the oven to 180°C (350°F/Gas 4).
2. Combine all the stuffing ingredients and place
them in the cavity of the turkey. Sew up the opening. **3.** Place the turkey in a large roasting pan, dot
with the herb butter and cover the bird with
prosciutto. Add 2 cups of the wine to the pan and
place the turkey in the preheated oven. **4.** Roast it
for 2½ hours, remove the prosciutto and return the
turkey to the oven for a further 20 to 30 minutes to
brown the skin. **5.** Remove the turkey from the
roasting pan. Skim off the excess fat. Add the remaining wine, bring to the boil, season and serve
separately in a sauce-boat.

*Right: A selection of the delicious food prepared at La
Maison de Filippo in Entreves, Courmayeur. Bottom step, left
to right: Polenta; Peperoni with garlic. Second step: boiled
ham.*

Duck in Piquant Sauce
Anatra in Salsa Piccante

Serves 4

60 g (2 oz) butter
60 g (2 oz) bacon, finely chopped
1 sprig rosemary, finely chopped
3 sprigs sage, finely chopped
2 kg (4 lb) duck
1 lemon, cut into quarters
salt
freshly ground black pepper
1 tablespoon olive oil
185 g (6 oz) pork and veal mixture, finely minced
1 clove garlic, crushed
2 anchovy fillets, finely chopped
½ cup (4 fl oz) white wine vinegar
½–1 cup (4–8 fl oz) beef stock (see p. 328)

1. Preheat oven to 220°C (425°F/Gas 7). **2.** In a deep heavy casserole dish, melt the butter, add the bacon, rosemary and sage and fry for a few minutes. **3.** Add the duckling and the lemon quarters and season with pepper and salt. **4.** Place the casserole in the preheated oven and roast for approximately 30 minutes. **5.** Take the casserole out of the oven and pour off the excess fat. **6.** Return the casserole and roast it for a further 30 minutes, basting it with the cooking liquid. **7.** In a heavy-bottomed frying pan, heat the oil and fry the minced meat, garlic and anchovy fillets until brown. Add the vinegar and the beef stock and cook until the liquid has reduced a little. **8.** Remove the casserole from the oven, skim off the excess fat and cut the duckling into serving pieces. **9.** Return them to the casserole and pour the minced meat sauce over it. **10.** Reduce the heat to 150°C (300°F/Gas 2). Cover the casserole and return it to the oven to braise for 30 minutes. **11.** Before serving, season and add more beef stock if necessary.

Pigeon and Rice
Bomba di Riso

A classic dish of Piancenza, in which the pigeon is served in a mound of rice with a mushroom sauce and it is finished in the oven. A young spatchcock may be used instead.

Serves 4

2 onions, sliced
4 tablespoons butter
2 pigeons or spatchcocks
2 chicken livers, chopped
125 g (4 oz) chicken giblets, chopped
125 g (4 oz) chopped mushrooms
2 tablespoons concentrated tomato purée
1 cup (8 fl oz) white wine
salt
freshly ground black pepper
4 cups (1 litre) beef or chicken stock (see p. 328)
1¼ cups (8 oz) rice
½ cup (2 oz) grated Parmesan cheese
½ cup (2 oz) fine dry breadcrumbs

1. Brown 1 of the onions in half the butter, add the pigeons or spatchcocks, the livers, giblets, and mushrooms. **2.** When they are all browned, add the tomato purée. Cook it for 2 to 3 minutes then add the wine and seasoning. Add half the stock and simmer for 1½ hours. If necessary, from time to time add more of the stock. **3.** Cook the rice with the remaining onion, butter and remaining stock. **4.** When it is almost cooked, add the cooking juice from the pigeons. Remove the pan from the heat and mix in the Parmesan. **5.** Preheat the oven to 150°C (300°F/Gas 2). **6.** Butter the bottom and sides of a round mould or cake tin 20 cm (8 in) in diameter and sprinkle with half the breadcrumbs. **7.** Put half the rice into the tin. Cut each bird into 4 pieces and put them on top of the rice. Cover with the remaining rice, sprinkle it with the rest of the breadcrumbs and dot with butter. **8.** Place the tin in the preheated oven and cook for 1 to 1½ hours. **9.** To serve, ease it carefully onto a serving platter.

MEAT

Veal with Ham and Sage

Saltimbocca alla Romana

Serves 4

8 thin slices veal scaloppine
8 thin slices prosciutto ham
8 fresh sage leaves
1 tablespoon butter
3 tablespoons olive oil
salt
freshly ground black pepper
1 cup (8 fl oz) dry white wine

1. With a toothpick secure a slice of ham and a sage leaf to each slice of veal. **2.** In a frying pan melt the butter and add the oil. **3.** Briefly brown the ham side of the veal and then turn it to the meat side, season and add the wine. Simmer for 6 to 10 minutes. **4.** When cooked place the meat on a serving platter. Continue to boil the cooking juice to reduce it to half its volume. Season if necessary and serve with the pan juices poured over the meat.

Milanese Veal Cutlets

Costolette alla Milanese

It is said that wiener schnitzel developed from the costoletta. The main difference is that the schnitzel is cut from the fillet or leg and the costoletta is a loin chop with the bone left on.

Serves 6

6 veal loin chops
salt
freshly ground black pepper
¼ cup (1 oz) flour
1 egg, whisked with a little water
½ cup (2 oz) fine dry breadcrumbs
125 g (4 oz) butter, clarified
6 lemon wedges
6 sprigs parsley

1. Cut off any fat or gristle from the chops and flatten them with a meat hammer or rolling pin. Season. **2.** Dust the chops with flour, dip them in the egg-water mixture and generously coat them with the breadcrumbs. **3.** Fry the chops in hot clarified butter over a medium heat for 8 to 10 minutes. **4.** Serve them garnished with the lemon wedges and sprigs of parsley.

Escalopes of Veal, Milanese Style

Scaloppine alla Milanese

Scaloppine are small squares of veal, sliced very thinly and lightly cooked in butter. There are many ways of garnishing them and they form an important part of Lombardy cooking, especially that of Milan.

Serves 4

500 g (1 lb) thin veal escalopes cut from the fillet or the inside of the leg
salt
freshly ground black pepper
juice of 1½–2 lemons
¼ cup (1 oz) flour
60–125 g (2–4 oz) butter

1. Cut the escalopes thinly into 7.5 cm (3 in) squares, each weighing approximately 30 g (1 oz). Allow 3 to 4 slices per person. **2.** Beat them flat, season them and sprinkle with lemon juice. Dust them with flour. **3.** Melt the butter in a frying pan and brown the pieces on both sides.

Variations:

Scaloppine with Capers: Fry 1 chopped onion in the butter, add 2 tablespoons of capers and then cook the meat as above.

Scaloppine with Olive Oil and Lemon: Before cooking, marinate the veal in a mixture of ¼ cup (2 fl oz) olive oil and the juice of 2 lemons. Pour the marinade into the pan and cook the veal in it.

Scaloppine with Tomatoes: Fry 1 chopped onion in the butter with 2 chopped peeled tomatoes and add, then cook the veal as above.

Scaloppine in Piquant Sauce: Heat ½ cup (4 fl oz) veal stock and 2 tablespoons each of chopped mixed pickles, pickled peppers and mushrooms in the pan before the meat is cooked.

Scaloppine in Marsala: Add 2 tablespoons of Marsala to the meat in the pan and simmer for 2 minutes.

Scaloppine with Cheese: Add ½ cup (4 fl oz) white wine to the pan, cover each slice of meat with a slice of cheese, cover and simmer for 2 to 3 minutes until the cheese melts.

Veal Shanks Milan Style
Ossobuco alla Milanese

This recipe comes from Villa d'Este on Lake Como.

Serves 6

4 tablespoons butter
2 large onions, chopped
1 carrot, chopped
1 stalk celery, chopped
1 clove garlic, crushed
6–8 pieces meaty veal shanks, cut into 5 cm (2 in) slices
salt
freshly ground black pepper
½ cup (2 oz) flour
½ cup (4 fl oz) olive oil
1¼ cups (10 fl oz) dry white wine
¾ cup (6 fl oz) beef or chicken stock (see p. 328)
1 teaspoon mixed dried herbs
750 g (1½ lb) canned whole tomatoes, chopped
½ cup chopped parsley
3 bay leaves

Gremolata:
1 clove garlic, crushed
3 teaspoons grated lemon peel
3 tablespoons finely chopped parsley

1. Preheat the oven to 180°C (350°F/Gas 4). **2.** In a large frying pan, melt the butter and sauté the onions, carrots, celery and garlic. Continue cooking for 10 minutes until the vegetables have lightly browned. **3.** Season the meat and dust the pieces with flour. In another large fryng pan, heat the oil and fry the meat until it is brown all over. **4.** Place the pieces of meat side by side in a casserole and cover with the vegetables. **5.** Pour the wine into the frying pan in which the meat was cooked, add the stock, herbs, tomatoes, parsley and bay leaves. Bring to the boil, reduce slightly and then pour it over the meat. The liquid should come half-way up the side of the meat. If necessary, add more stock. **6.** Bring the casserole to the boil on top of the oven, cover and place it into the preheated oven. Cook for 1½ hours. **7.** Serve the pieces of meat on individual plates and pour the sauce over the meat, sprinkled with some gremolata.

Gremolata: Mix the garlic, lemon peel and chopped parsley together.

Bolognese Meat Sauce
Ragù alla Bolognese

This famous sauce may be used with any type of pasta.

Serves 6

90 g (3 oz) bacon, chopped
1 tablespoon butter
1 onion, chopped
1 carrot, chopped
1 stalk celery, chopped
250 g (8 oz) beef, minced
125 g (4 oz) chicken livers, chopped
2 tablespoons concentrated tomato purée
1 cup (8 fl oz) dry white wine
salt
freshly ground black pepper
¼ teaspoon nutmeg
1 cup (8 fl oz) beef stock (see p. 328)
½–1 cup (4–8 fl oz) cream (optional)

1. Brown the bacon in the butter, add the onion, carrot, and celery and sauté until brown. **2.** Add the meat and stir well to make sure that it is evenly browned. **3.** Add the chicken livers, cook for 3 to 4 minutes, then add the tomato purée and the wine. Season and add the nutmeg and stock. **4.** Cover and simmer for 30 to 40 minutes. **5.** Just before serving, add the cream, if used. **6.** To serve, pour the sauce over previously cooked pasta.

Lamb with Olives
Agnello con Olive

Serves 4

6 tablespoons olive oil
4 lamb leg steaks, about 1.5 cm (½ in) thick
salt
freshly ground black pepper
1 cup (5 oz) black olives, pitted and chopped
½ teaspoon dried oregano
3 tablespoons green peppers (capsicums), chopped
juice of ½ lemon

1. In a frying pan heat the oil and brown the steaks on both sides. Drain off some of the fat and season. **2.** Add the olives, sprinkle with the oregano, add the green peppers and lemon juice and simmer for 4 to 5 minutes before serving.

Right: A selection of cold meats forms the basis of the anti-pasto served at the Hotel Grief in Bolzano, Venezia.

Mixed Fried Meat and Vegetables

Fritto Misto

Serves 4

Batter (Pastella):
3 tablespoons olive oil
salt
½–¾ cup (4–6 fl oz) lukewarm water
1 cup (4 oz) flour
1 egg white
125 g (4 oz) calves' liver
250 g (8 oz) calves' brains
250 g (8 oz) veal fillet
12 cauliflower flowerets
2 potatoes, peeled and cut into 1.5 cm (½ in) slices
flour
salt
freshly ground black pepper
½ cup (4 fl oz) melted butter mixed with ¼ cup (2 fl oz) olive oil

1. First make the batter: stir the oil, salt and water into the flour and let it stand in the refrigerator for 2 hours. **2.** Just before using, whisk the egg white stiffly and fold it into the batter. **3.** Trim and rinse the liver, brains and veal. Cut them into bite-sized pieces. **4.** Dip them and the cauliflower and potatoes in flour, then dip them in the batter and fry them over medium heat in the butter-oil mixture for 3 to 5 minutes or until golden-brown. **5.** Drain the pieces on absorbent paper, sprinkle with salt and serve immediately.
Note: If you substitute fresh seafood for the meat in this recipe, the dish is called Fritto di Pesce.

Steak Florentine Style

Bistecca alla Fiorentina

From Buca Lapi in Florence. This dish is a very simple one and its main character depends on the use of the best quality beef and cooking it over charcoal.

Serves 4

1 large T-bone steak (approx. 1 kg (2 lb))
salt
pepper

1. If a charcoal fire is not available, grill the meat on both sides, turning it from time to time until it is well browned but rare inside. **2.** Sprinkle with salt and pepper before serving.

Italian Meat Loaf

Polpettone

As with the polpette there are many ways of varying the preparation of the polpettone.

Serves 8

1 kg (2 lb) raw meat, minced (beef, pork, veal or a mixture)
4 eggs
2 cloves garlic, crushed
½ cup chopped parsley
salt
freshly ground black pepper

Stuffing:
2 eggs, hard-boiled and chopped
60 g (2 oz) cooked ham, chopped
60 g (2 oz) provolone or Gruyère cheese, chopped
salt
freshly ground black pepper

1. Preheat the oven to 150°C (300°F/Gas 2). **2.** In a bowl mix the meat, eggs, garlic, parsley, salt and pepper. **3.** Spread the mixture on a board. **4.** In another bowl, mix together the stuffing ingredients. **5.** Spread the stuffing in the centre of the meat, leaving a border all around of 2.5 cm (1 in). **6.** Roll the meat into a loaf and place it on a buttered baking tray, or pack half the meat into a terrine, spread out the stuffing and cover with the rest of the meat. **7.** Place the meat in the preheated oven and cook for 1½ hours. **8.** Polpettone may be eaten either hot or cold.

The following are some of the variations prepared in Lombardy. Prepare as above, using the same proportions.

Polpettone di cotecchino: with veal or pork and cotecchino sausage.
Polpettone di fegato: with beef, beef liver and ham.
Polpettone di rognone: with veal, veal kidney, raw ham, sage and rosemary.
Polpettone con gli spinacci: with spinach, raw ham, egg, sage and rosemary.
Polpettone tritato arrosto: with beef, pork, veal, egg, sage and rosemary.
Polpettone tritato a lesso: with beef and mortadella sausage.

Italian Meatballs or Rissoles

Polpette

Polpette can be made with raw beef, veal, pork, liver or cooked meat. The variations are endless.

Serves 6

500 g (1 lb) raw or cooked minced meat
1 egg
2 cloves garlic, crushed
1 thick slice of bread
1 cup (8 fl oz) milk
¼ cup chopped parsley
salt
freshly ground black pepper
¼ teaspoon nutmeg
¼ teaspoon grated lemon peel
¼ cup (1 oz) flour
oil for frying

1. In a bowl, mix the meat, egg, garlic and the bread which has been previously soaked in a little of the milk. Pour in the remainder of the milk, add the parsley, season and stir in the nutmeg and lemon peel. **2.** Form the meat into small cakes 5 cm (2 in) in diameter. **3.** Dust them with flour and fry them in the oil. **4.** Serve with a tomato or potato salad.

The following are some of the variations. Use the same proportions as above.
Polpette de la serva: use a mixture of minced veal and pork with parsley and garlic.
Polpette di maiale: use pork and pork liver with breadcrumbs, grated cheese, parsley, sage, garlic, tomato and egg.
Polpette della nonna: use pickled pork and ham.
Polpette Campari: use minced pork and/or veal, bacon, bread, grated cheese, egg, onion, garlic, parsley, spices.

Mixed Boiled Meats with Green Sauce

Lesso Misto con Salsa Verde

This dish is known as bollito misto in other parts of Italy and is related to the French pot-au-feu. It can be an extravagant dish and is best suited for a large number of people since it requires many different types of meat.

Serves 12

1 kg (2 lb) shin beef
4 veal shanks
4 pig's trotters
2 pig's shanks
500 g (1 lb) cotecchino sausage, or similar
½ a calf's head
1 medium-sized chicken
water
2 onions, studded with cloves
2 carrots, chopped
3 stalks celery, chopped
salt
12 whole black peppercorns

Salsa Verde (Green Sauce):
½ cup chopped parsley
2 pickled cucumbers, chopped
4 anchovy fillets, chopped
1 clove garlic, crushed
¼ cup (2 fl oz) olive oil
1–2 tablespoons red wine vinegar

1. The total cooking time of the dish is 2 to 2½ hours and the various meats should be added to the pot at different times as their cooking times vary. Start with the calf's head and beef. Half an hour later add the veal shanks, pig's shanks and trotters, and allow approximately 1 hour for the chicken and sausage. **2.** Place the meat in a large pot and add all the non-meat ingredients. Bring to the boil and simmer for 2 to 2½ hours. If necessary during the course of cooking, add more water. **3.** Serve with boiled potatoes, or boiled white haricot beans. It is sometimes also served with stewed cabbage. **4.** To make the green sauce, combine all the ingredients and serve separately.

DESSERTS & CAKES

Caramelised Oranges

Aranci Caramellizzati

This recipe comes from Dodici Apostoli in Verona.

Serves 6

6 seedless oranges
1 cup (8 oz) sugar
1¼ cups (10 fl oz) water
1 tablespoon orange liqueur

1. With a very sharp knife, peel off the top layer of the orange skin and cut it into very fine strips. **2.** Place the strips in a saucepan and add just enough water to cover. Simmer them for 5 to 6 minutes. **3.** Peel the oranges carefully, removing all traces of white pith. **4.** In a large saucepan combine the sugar and the water and simmer, stirring constantly, until the sugar has dissolved. **5.** Boil the syrup for approximately 5 minutes, add the oranges and simmer for 2 to 3 minutes. **6.** Remove the oranges and arrange them on a serving platter. **7.** Place the strips of orange rind in the syrup and boil it gently until the syrup reaches the soft ball stage. **8.** Cool the syrup slightly and add the orange liqueur. **9.** Cool the syrup and pour it, together with the strips of rind, over the oranges. **10.** Place them in the refrigerator and serve them chilled.

Modena Macaroons

Amarelli o Amaretti di Modena

Makes 14–16 macaroons

¾ cup (4 oz) blanched almonds
1¼ cups (8 oz) caster (powdered) sugar
2–3 egg whites
2 tablespoons Kirsch

1. Preheat the oven to 180°C (350°F/Gas 4). **2.** In a mortar, a mincer or food processor grind the almonds finely. **3.** Place in a bowl, add 1 egg white, mix well and then add the sugar. Continue mixing and then add the second egg white and the Kirsch. **4.** Form the dough into small biscuits and arrange them on a buttered baking tray, keeping some distance between them as they expand while baking. **5.** Place them in a preheated oven and bake for 30 to 40 minutes.

Siena Christmas Cake

Panforte

Makes 1 cake approximately 45 × 38 cm (18 × 15 in)

200 g (6½ oz) blanched almonds
100 g (3½ oz) hazelnuts, roasted
100 g (3½ oz) glacé citron
100 g (3½ oz) glacé pumpkin
100 g (3½ oz) glacé melon rind
100 g (3½ oz) dried figs
155 g (5 oz) walnut kernels
30 g (1 oz) sweet cocoa (or drinking chocolate)
10 g (⅓ oz) powdered cinnamon
10 g (⅓ oz) mixed spices
⅓ cup (4 oz) honey
155 g (5 oz) caster (powdered) sugar
2 sheets rice paper

1. Preheat the oven to 180°C (350°F/Gas 4). **2.** Finely chop all ingredients up to and including the walnut kernels. **3.** Put them in a bowl, add the cocoa, half of the cinnamon and the mixed spices. Mix well together. **4.** Put the honey and all but a tablespoon of the caster sugar in a saucepan. Heat and stir constantly until a drop of the mixture solidifies in contact with cold water. **5.** Remove from the heat and add the nut-fruit mixture; mix well together. **6.** Line the bottom of a shallow baking dish with one of the sheets of rice paper and pour the mixture on top of it. Cover with the other sheet. **7.** Place in the preheated oven and bake for 30 minutes. **8.** Remove from the oven, cool, unmould and sprinkle with the remaining caster sugar and cinnamon. **9.** Do not serve until the next day. With a sharp knife cut it into bite-sized pieces.
Note: If glacé pumpkin and melon rind are not available, use other glacé fruits such as peaches or pineapple.

Right: Siena Christmas Cake (above) from Buca Lapi in Florence. Buca Lapi is situated in the basement of the Antinori Palace where the Antinori family (of Chianti wine fame), after more than five centuries, still resides. It is a pity that the vaulted ceilings of the ancient cellars have been spoiled by tourist posters; nevertheless, the food is good and many of the dishes served there are traditionally Florentine.

Chocolate Cream with Lady Fingers

Semifreddo di Cioccolata

Serves 4

125 g (4 oz) butter
½ cup (4 oz) sugar
2 egg yolks
¼ cup (1 oz) cocoa (if sweetened drinking chocolate powder is used, reduce the amount of sugar)
1–2 tablespoons milk
12 lady fingers, more if necessary
2 tablespoons chopped pistachio nuts
¼ cup (1 oz) hazelnuts, chopped and roasted

1. In a mixing bowl, cream the butter, add the sugar, egg yolks and the cocoa. Continue mixing for a few minutes and finally add some milk until the mixture is the consistency of thick cream. 2. In a decorative glass bowl, place a layer of lady fingers, spread them with some of the mixture and sprinkle with some of the pistachio nuts. Continue the layers finishing with a layer of the chocolate cream. Sprinkle the top with the hazelnuts and place the bowl in the freezer for 2 to 3 hours.

Cream Cheese Dessert with Rum

Crema al Mascarpone

Serves 4–6

500 g (1 lb) Mascarpone cheese or ricotta-type cream cheese
125 g (4 oz) caster (powdered) sugar
4 egg yolks
½ cup (4 fl oz) rum
juice of ½ lemon
½ teaspoon cinnamon

1. In a bowl, cream the cheese, add the sugar, egg yolks, rum and lemon juice. This may be very successfully done in a food processor. Put all the ingredients together and blend until they are smooth and creamy. 2. To serve, place the cheese mixture in glass bowls. Refrigerate and then, just before serving, sprinkle with cinnamon.

Sicilian Cream Cheese Cake

Cassata alla Siciliana

Serves 6

750 g (1½ lb) ricotta cheese
1 cup (8 oz) sugar
1 teaspoon vanilla essence
2 tablespoons crème de cacao
125 g (4 oz) bitter chocolate, coarsely grated
½ cup (3 oz) candied fruit, chopped (reserve some for decoration)
1 dozen lady fingers (sponge fingers)
½ cup (4 fl oz) brandy
¼ cup (1½ oz) icing (confectioners') sugar

1. Combine the ricotta, sugar, vanilla and crème de cacao. 2. Beat the mixture until it is smooth and fluffy. Add the grated chocolate and the candied fruit and mix well. 3. Line a circular baking dish with waxed paper. 4. Dip the lady fingers in the brandy and arrange them in a fan-shape on the bottom and sides of the baking dish. Be careful not to oversoak the lady fingers or they will fall apart. 5. Put the ricotta mixture into the baking dish, filling it right to the very top. On top of the ricotta arrange another layer of the lady fingers which have been moistened with brandy. 6. Refrigerate for a few hours or overnight. 7. Turn the cassata out of the baking dish on to a plate. If it does not come out easily, immerse the pan in boiling water. 8. To serve, sprinkle the top of the cassata with icing sugar and decorate with candied fruit.

Lemon Water Ice

Granita di Limone

Serves 6

½ cup (4 oz) sugar
2½ cups (20 fl oz) water
6–8 lemons (enough to produce 1¼ cups (10 fl oz) lemon juice)

1. Dissolve the sugar in the water and boil for 5 minutes. 2. Cool the syrup and add the lemon juice. 3. To make the granita, place it in a metal tray and freeze. 4. If you have an electric ice cream machine, churn until the granita sets.

Carnival Twists

Sfrappole

A delicious sweetmeat traditionally eaten during the Carnival period, these are also known as crespelli, chiacchiere or cenci.

Serves 6–8

500 g (1 lb) flour
¼ cup (2 oz) sugar
3 egg yolks
2 tablespoons brandy or rum
½ teaspoon grated lemon peel
60 g (2 oz) butter, melted
⅛ teaspoon salt
milk
oil for frying
icing (confectioners') sugar

1. In a bowl mix the flour, sugar, egg yolks, liquor, lemon peel, butter and salt. **2.** Gradually, while stirring constantly, add enough milk to obtain a thick mixture. **3.** Place it on a floured board and roll it out very thinly. **4.** Cut the dough into rectangles 3 by 10 cm (1¼ by 4 in). In the centre of each, make an incision 2.5 cm (1 in) long and thread one end of the rectangle through it. **5.** Preheat the oil in a saucepan and fry them to a light gold colour. **6.** When they have cooled, dust them with plenty of icing sugar. Store them in an airtight jar to preserve freshness.

Neapolitan Strawberry Ice Cream

Gelato di Fragole alla Napoletana

Serves 6

1½ cups (12 fl oz) cream
½ cup (4 oz) caster (powdered) sugar
1½ cups (12 fl oz) thick strawberry purée

1. Turn the refrigerator control to the coldest setting at least 1 hour in advance. **2.** Whip the cream with the sugar until it is thick. **3.** Gently fold in the puréed strawberries. **4.** Transfer to empty ice cube trays and freeze for 1 to 2 hours. **5.** Tip the frozen mixture into a bowl and break it up with a hand beater. **6.** Return the mixture to the trays and freeze for a further 1 to 2 hours. **7.** Repeat the beating-up and finally refreeze for 2 to 3 hours before serving.

Zabaione

Serves 4

6 egg yolks
2 whole eggs
8 tablespoons caster (powdered) sugar
1 cup (8 fl oz) Marsala

1. In a bowl, beat the yolks and the whole eggs together with the sugar until they are white and frothy. **2.** Stir in the Marsala and pour the mixture into a double boiler. **3.** While the water is boiling, whisk the mixture with a hand beater, making sure that it does not get too hot and curdle. As soon as it thickens pour the zabaione into glass dishes and serve immediately.

Stuffed Figs

Fichi Ripieni

Serves 4

12 ripe fresh figs
¼ cup (1 oz) chopped mixed nuts
1 tablespoon drinking chocolate
1 tablespoon mixed candied fruit, chopped
1 tablespoon honey
2 tablespoons icing (confectioners') sugar

1. Cut the figs in half vertically and from each piece scoop out one teaspoonful of the flesh. **2.** In a bowl mix it with the rest of the ingredients, except the icing sugar. **3.** Place this mixture back into the figs. Put the two halves together and serve them dusted with the icing sugar.

GERMANY

Germany regional food is no longer clearly defined as it was some hundred years ago, before Bismarck unified the German-speaking kingdoms, dukedoms and other states under the Imperial crown. In those days, the regional differences between the various sovereign areas were easy to identify. Today, after several wars and a great deal of social upheaval and population movement, the formal regional divisions no longer exist.

So, what has happened to the traditional cooking of Germany? Fortunately it is still a part of German life, although not as dominant as it was.

It is difficult to imagine a German table without its Kartoffeln (potatoes) in one form or another. In the Rhineland they will appear as Himmel and Erde (Heaven and Earth) cooked with apples and Blutwurst (a type of black pudding), thus combining the two most characteristic of German ingredients, potatoes and sausage. Bavaria's potato salad, and its Kartoffel Knodel (potato dumplings) are common in most parts of the country.

Hearty soups are the staple diet of cold climates, so it is not surprising that in the north of Germany one finds more soups than in the south. Fish soups are among their specialities. However, Germans love soups in general, and Mittagessen (the main midday meal) almost always includes a plate of warming soup.

Volumes could be written about German sausages, and the Wurst has a special place in every German's heart.

Germans are very fond of pork, and pigs are bred extensively in all parts of the country. Speck, the smoked bacon, is another by-product which is closely associated with German cooking. Among the best in the land is Westphalian Speck which, with Westphalian ham, finds its way to most German tables. Speck is used extensively and gives many of the country's dishes their characteristic smoky scent and flavour.

Sauerkraut, known since prehistoric times, has found its modern home in Germany. Whether cooked, raw, in salads or as part of a made-up dish, it is eaten throughout the country.

The German Konditorei, or cake shop, is an institution shared only with Austria. The Germans like their Kuchen mit Kaffee, and the pastry repertoire is extensive.

The herring is another German institution. Despite its northern origin, it is popular in all parts of the land, although it probably tastes best along the shores of the North or Baltic Seas.

There are many other characteristic German dishes which form part of a foreigner's concept of German cooking, and a great number of these are associated with specific parts of the country. I have tried to present some of the traditional German dishes, most of them collected during my trip through the country, and hope that they will inspire the traveller through Germany to seek out and enjoy the local dishes.

Right: The historic Hotel Kaiserworth, Goslar.

FIRST COURSES

Herrings in Sour Cream

Hering in Saurer Sahne

A very popular first course in north Germany.

Serves 4

6 Matjes herring fillets
1 cup (8 fl oz) sour cream
juice of 1 lemon or 2 tablespoons white wine vinegar
½ tablespoon sugar (optional)
freshly ground black pepper
1 apple, peeled, cored and cut into thin slivers
1 onion, cut into thin slices
1 tablespoon finely chopped dill

1. Cut the herring fillets into 2.5 cm (1 in) pieces and arrange them on a serving dish. **2.** Mix the sour cream, lemon juice or vinegar and (if desired) the sugar. Add the pepper and let the mixture stand for 10 minutes. **3.** Arrange the apple slivers and onion slices in a layer on the herrings. **4.** Cover with the cream and sprinkle with dill.

Rhineland Herring, Apple and Vegetable Salad

Heringssalat Rheinischer Art

Serves 6

6 pickled herring fillets, chopped
155 g (5 oz) beetroot, cooked and diced
1 large apple, cored and diced
2 medium potatoes, cooked and diced
1 small onion, finely chopped
½ cup (2 oz) chopped walnuts
½ cup (4 fl oz) sour cream
½ cup (4 fl oz) mayonnaise (see p. 330)
1 teaspoon sugar

Garnish:
1 egg, hard-boiled and sliced
6–8 slices beetroot
1 tablespoon finely chopped parsley or dill

1. Combine all the ingredients except the garnish ingredients. Mix gently together and arrange them in a salad bowl or on a serving platter. **2.** Decorate the top with the egg slices and the beetroot. Before serving, sprinkle with the parsley or dill.

Eggs in Green Sauce

Eier in Grüner Sosse

A speciality of Frankfurt.

Serves 4

½ cup (4 fl oz) sour cream
½ cup (4 fl oz) yogurt
½ cup (4 fl oz) mayonnaise (see p. 330)
3 sprigs each of the following fresh herbs (or any combination): dill, parsley, tarragon, oregano
1 small bunch chives
juice of 1 lemon
1 egg, hard-boiled and finely chopped
salt
freshly ground black pepper
½ teaspoon sugar (optional)
8 eggs, hard-boiled and cut in half
finely chopped dill for garnish

1. Combine sour cream, yogurt and mayonnaise. **2.** Finely chop the herbs by hand or in a food processor. **3.** Mix the sauce, chopped herbs, lemon juice, chopped egg, salt, pepper and (if desired) sugar. **4.** Arrange the egg halves on a serving platter, pour the sauce over them and serve chilled, garnished with chopped dill.

Cucumber Salad

Gurkensalat

Serves 4

1 large cucumber
½ teaspoon salt
1 tablespoon sugar
1 tablespoon white wine vinegar
¼ cup (2 fl oz) sour cream
1 tablespoon chopped parsley

1. Peel the cucumber leaving some of the green rind. Slice it very thinly. The cucumber may be served either fresh or marinated. When serving it fresh, sprinkle the cucumber with salt, sugar and vinegar, mix in the sour cream and sprinkle with the parsley. **2.** Alternatively, mix the salt and sugar into the vinegar, and marinate the cucumber in this mixture for 30 minutes. Drain off the liquid, mix the sour cream with the cucumber, and serve sprinkled with parsley.

Beetroot and Endive Salad

Roterüben Salat

This dish has a tasty combination of flavours. If endive is not available, firm hearts of lettuce, broken up into small pieces, may be used.

Serves 4

2 medium-sized beetroot, cooked and diced
3 endives, sliced
1 cooking apple, peeled, cored and finely diced
1 small onion, finely chopped
2 tablespoons prepared horse-radish
2 egg yolks
juice of 1 lemon
3 tablespoons sour cream
½ teaspoon mustard
1 teaspoon sugar (optional)
salt
freshly ground black pepper
3 tablespoons oil
chopped parsley for garnish

1. In a bowl mix beetroot, endives, apple, onion and horse-radish. **2.** In a mixing bowl, combine egg yolks, lemon juice, sour cream, mustard, sugar, salt and pepper. **3.** Mix for 5 minutes and then, still mixing, gradually add the oil. **4.** Pour the dressing over the salad and serve garnished with parsley.

Baked Spinach and Cheese

Überbackener Spinat mit Käse

Serves 4

750 g (1½ lb) fresh spinach leaves
100 g (3½ oz) butter
1 onion, finely chopped
1 clove garlic, crushed
salt
freshly ground black pepper
¼ teaspoon nutmeg
1 teaspoon paprika
125 g (4 oz) grated Gruyère-type cheese

1. Preheat the oven to 180°C (350°F/Gas 4). **2.** In a large saucepan boil some water. Plunge the spinach into it and boil for 5 minutes. **3.** Drain, dry and coarsely chop the spinach. **4.** In a saucepan melt the butter. Fry the onion and garlic until the onion is soft and transparent. **5.** Add the spinach and sauté lightly until most of the moisture has evaporated. **6.** Season and add nutmeg and paprika. **7.** Grease an ovenproof dish. Sprinkle the bottom and sides with half of the cheese. Place the spinach in the dish, level the top and sprinkle with the rest of the cheese. **8.** Bake for 20 to 30 minutes until the cheese melts. Serve hot.

Onion Pie

Zwiebelkuchen

Serves 8

Pastry:
2 cups (8 oz) self-raising flour
½ teaspoon salt
185 g (6 oz) butter
1 egg, beaten
1 tablespoon cream (optional)
1 egg white, lightly beaten

Filling:
250 g (8 oz) onions, chopped
2 slices bacon, diced
2 tablespoons butter
¼ teaspoon salt
1 teaspoon caraway seeds
½ tablespoon flour
½ cup (4 fl oz) cream
2 eggs, beaten

Pastry: 1. Preheat the oven to 190°C (375°F/Gas 5). **2.** Combine the flour and salt. Dice the butter and rub into the flour until the mixture is the consistency of breadcrumbs. Add the egg and blend until the dough is pliable. Add the cream if the dough is not sufficiently moist. **3.** Roll out the dough and press it into the bottom and sides of a round pie dish 23 cm (9 in) in diameter. Brush the egg white over the bottom of the dough.

Filling: 1. Sauté the onions and bacon in the butter until soft, then add the salt and caraway seeds. Stir in the flour and slowly add the cream. **2.** Remove from the heat, add the beaten eggs and mix well together. Pour into the pastry-lined pie dish. **3.** Bake until the pastry is golden and the filling is firm. Serve as a snack with white wine.

Bremen Meat Salad with Frankfurters and Mayonnaise

Fleischsalat auf Bremer Art

Serves 6

125 g (4 oz) boiled ham, cut into thin strips
2 frankfurters, diced
60 g (2 oz) salami, diced
3 gherkins, diced
¼ cup (2 fl oz) mayonnaise (see p. 330)
1 tablespoon white wine vinegar
salt
freshly ground black pepper

1. Combine all ingredients and mix them gently together. Serve on lettuce leaves.

Crayfish Salad with Cucumber

Hummersalat mit Gurken

Serves 4

flesh of 1 crayfish, diced, or 8 medium-sized king prawns (shrimps), shelled, deveined and sliced
2 large cucumbers, peeled, seeded and diced
½ cup (4 fl oz) mayonnaise (see p. 330)
1 tablespoon tomato paste
1 teaspoon dry mustard
2 tablespoons prepared mustard
2 tablespoons dry sherry
1 tablespoon brandy
juice of ½ lemon
½ small onion, finely chopped
3 sprigs dill, finely chopped
2 sprigs tarragon, finely chopped or 1 teaspoon dried tarragon
salt
freshly ground black pepper

1. Place the crayfish or prawns in a serving dish. **2.** In a bowl combine all the remaining ingredients. Mix well and pour them over the crayfish or prawns. Toss gently. **3.** Refrigerate for 2 to 3 hours and serve cold or at room temperature.

Salmon with Horse-radish Cream

Lachstüten mit Meerrettich Rahm

In Germany, horse-radish cream is a popular garnish for smoked salmon. This is one of the many ways it can be served.

Serves 4

1 cup (8 fl oz) cream, whipped
1 tablespoon horse-radish relish
1 tablespoon vinegar or juice of 1 lemon
½ teaspoon sugar
salt
freshly ground black pepper
1 teaspoon gelatine, dissolved in ¼ cup (2 fl oz) hot water, cooled
12 slices smoked salmon
2 sprigs parsley, finely chopped

1. Combine all ingredients except the smoked salmon and parsley. **2.** Form the salmon slices into cones and with a teaspoon or piping bag fill the cones with the cream. **3.** Arrange the cones on a serving platter and refrigerate for 2 hours or until the cream hardens. **4.** Serve chilled, the cream sprinkled with parsley.

Brains au Gratin

Hirn Überbacken

Serves 4

4 veal brains (or 6 lambs' brains)
2 tablespoons vinegar
1 teaspoon salt
45 g (1½ oz) butter
45 g (1½ oz) flour
⅔ cup (5½ fl oz) hot beef stock (see p. 328)
⅔ cup (5½ fl oz) hot milk
45 g (1½ oz) grated Parmesan cheese
½ teaspoon Worcestershire sauce
1 egg yolk
3 tablespoons cream
freshly ground black pepper
dry breadcrumbs

Topping:
¼ cup (1 oz) grated Parmesan cheese
30 g (1 oz) butter, cut into small pieces

1. Preheat the oven to 200°C (400°F/Gas 6). **2.** Remove the membranes from the brains. **3.** Half fill a saucepan with water, add the vinegar and salt, plunge the brains into it and simmer for 5 minutes. Remove them with a slotted spoon and rinse them under running cold water. **4.** Chop the brains into cubes. **5.** To make the sauce, melt the butter, add the flour and cook for 5 minutes. **6.** Add the hot stock and milk or, if you have no stock, use all milk. **7.** Cook, stirring constantly until the sauce is thick and smooth. **8.** Remove from the heat, stir in the cheese, Worcestershire sauce, egg yolk, cream, pepper and salt. **9.** Add the brains and pour the mixture into a buttered soufflé dish sprinkled with breadcrumbs. **10.** Sprinkle the top with the cheese and dot with pieces of butter. **11.** Place it in the preheated oven and cook for 10–15 minutes or until the top browns. **12.** Serve it with toast as a first course.

Right: Smoked Eel, which is the speciality of the restaurant Spieker in Bad Zwischenahn. The eels there are small, tender and freshly smoked, and their aroma fills the room. A pile of these eels, each with a price tag, is placed before the diners who then embark on the ritual of eating them. The skin is pulled off with an unzipping action; the eel is held at each end, and the juicy, tender flesh is chewed off the backbone. Then the waiter brings special round tin spoons which he fills with a local Schnaps. This is downed in one gulp, accompanied by an appropriate drinking rhyme and often, a beer chaser. The ritual is repeated until all the eels are eaten.

SOUPS

Liver Dumpling Soup

Leberknödelsuppe

From the Posthotel Koblerbräu in Bad Tölz.

Serves 4-6

8 stale bread rolls, cut into slices
salt
1 cup (8 fl oz) lukewarm milk
250 g (8 oz) pork or beef liver, cut into cubes
1 small onion
½ clove garlic
1 sprig parsley
2 eggs, beaten
1 tablespoon finely chopped fresh marjoram
4 cups (1 litre) strong beef stock (see p. 328)

1. Place the bread roll slices and salt in the milk and soak for 5 minutes. **2.** Squeeze out all the liquid and mix together the bread rolls, liver, onion, garlic and parsley. Put this mixture through a meat grinder or food processor. **3.** Add the eggs and marjoram and, using floured hands, make small dumplings. **4.** Heat the beef stock, place the dumplings into it and cook for approximately 20 minutes. Season to taste and serve hot.

Cold Apple Soup

Apfelsuppe

Serves 6

750 g (1½ lb) apples, peeled and cut into small pieces
3 cups (24 fl oz) water
small piece lemon rind
juice of 1 lemon
¼ cup (2 oz) sugar
1 cup (8 fl oz) dry white wine
1 tablespoon cornflour (cornstarch)
⅓ cup (2 oz) raisins or sultanas

1. In a saucepan, combine the apples, water, lemon rind, lemon juice, sugar and white wine, and cook until the apples are soft. **2.** Purée the apples with the liquid in a blender or food processor. **3.** Return the soup to the saucepan and bring to the boil. Add the cornflour (which has been mixed with a little water), and simmer gently until the soup thickens. (The flavour may be adjusted by the addition of further sugar and/or lemon juice.) **4.** Add the raisins, cool the soup, refrigerate and serve icy cold.

Cucumber Soup

Gurkensuppe

This recipe comes from the Parkhotel Fürstenhof in Celle.

Serves 4

1 large cucumber
4 cups (1 litre) water or chicken stock (see p. 328)
¼ cup (1 oz) chopped spring onions (scallions)
½ clove garlic, finely chopped
30 g (1 oz) butter
¼ cup (1 oz) flour
1 teaspoon chopped fresh marjoram
1 teaspoon chopped fresh thyme
1 teaspoon chopped fresh basil
salt
freshly ground black pepper
pinch of nutmeg
½ cup (4 fl oz) fresh cream
4 tablespoons sour cream
fresh dill, finely chopped

1. Peel the cucumber and save the skins. Cut the cucumber lengthwise and, with a tablespoon, remove and reserve the seeds. **2.** In a saucepan, cook the peelings and the seeds in the water or chicken stock for approximately 45 minutes. **3.** Cut the cucumber into slices. Sauté the cucumber with the spring onions and garlic in the butter, and sprinkle with flour. **4.** Strain the stock over the sautéed cucumber and spring onions. **5.** Add the marjoram, thyme, basil, salt and pepper and simmer for approximately 10 minutes. **6.** Add the fresh cream and heat it but do not boil. **7.** Cool the soup and refrigerate for 3 hours. **8.** Serve in individual soup bowls with a tablespoon of sour cream and a sprinkling of dill.

Cuxhaven Fish Soup

Fischsuppe 'Cuxhaven'

Serves 6-8

60 g (2 oz) butter
315 g (10 oz) potatoes, peeled and cut into cubes
1 carrot, cut into cubes
2 onions, chopped
2 stalks celery, chopped
1 leek, white part only, chopped
6 sprigs parsley, chopped
salt
freshly ground black pepper
6 cups (1.5 litres) fish stock (see p. 328)
500 g (1 lb) any white-fleshed fish, cut into chunks

1. In a large saucepan, heat the butter and lightly sauté all the vegetables and parsley. Season with salt and pepper. **2.** Add the fish stock and cook for 15 minutes. **3.** Add the fish and simmer lightly for 5 minutes. Serve immediately.

Potato Soup

Kartoffelsuppe

No set of German soup recipes would be complete without potato soup, which is a national favourite.

Serves 6

4 cups (1 litre) chicken stock (see p. 328)
2 cups (12 oz) finely diced potatoes
2 spring onions (scallions), chopped
2 cups (16 fl oz) milk
1 teaspoon Worcestershire sauce
½ cup (4 fl oz) sour cream

1. Cook the potatoes and spring onions in the chicken stock until the potatoes are soft (15 to 20 minutes). **2.** In a food processor or blender, purée the potatoes, onions and chicken stock and return them to the saucepan. **3.** Add the milk and Worcestershire sauce and heat through. Before serving, season and add the sour cream. The soup may be served hot or chilled.

Baden Leek Soup

Badische Lauchsuppe

Serves 4

3 leeks, white part only
90 g (3 oz) butter
1 large onion, chopped
4 cups (1 litre) chicken stock (see p. 328)
salt
freshly ground black pepper
1 cup (8 fl oz) milk
¾ cup (4 oz) ham, cut into julienne strips

1. Wash the leeks thoroughly and slice them into 2.5 cm (1 in) pieces. **2.** In a heavy-bottomed saucepan, melt the butter and sauté the leeks and onions until they are soft. **3.** Add the chicken stock, salt and pepper and simmer for 10 minutes, stirring occasionally. **4.** Add the milk and bring gently to the boil. **5.** Serve sprinkled with the ham.

Cheese Soup from Siegerland

Siegerländer Käsesuppe

This recipe comes from the Hotel Kaisergarten in Siegen.

Today Siegen is a modern town, but its origins are medieval and many of the old houses and churches are still preserved. Siegen's main claim to fame is that it is the birthplace of Rubens, and its art gallery contains several of his paintings. The Hotel Kaisergarten is part of modern Siegen, and while the town is not known as a great gourmet centre, very good food is served in some of its restaurants. Except for the Siegerlander Käsesuppe, a very tasty local cheese soup, most of the food served at the Hotel Kaisergarten is 'international'.

Serves 4

2 onions, cut into julienne strips
60 g (2 oz) butter
1 tablespoon flour
4 cups (1 litre) beef stock (see p. 328)
4 tablespoons grated Gruyère cheese
2 egg yolks
salt
freshly ground black pepper
⅛ teaspoon nutmeg
4 tablespoons sour cream

1. Lightly sauté the onions in the butter, and when light brown, sprinkle with flour. **2.** Heat the beef stock and slowly pour it over the onions, stirring constantly. **3.** In a separate saucepan, melt the grated cheese over low heat. Remove from the flame and mix in the egg yolks. **4.** Combine the cheese with the onions and beef stock, season lightly with salt and pepper and add the nutmeg. **5.** Serve in soup bowls and garnish each one with a tablespoon of sour cream.

VEGETABLES

Sour Horse-radish Potatoes

Saure Meerrettichkartoffeln

A very tasty way of giving potatoes a new and interesting flavour. Dill, marjoram or parsley may be used instead of horse-radish.

Serves 4–6

6 medium-sized potatoes, peeled and cut into 6 mm (¼ in) slices
2 cups (16 fl oz) milk or beef stock (see p. 328)
salt
freshly ground black pepper
75 g (2½ oz) Speck or smoked bacon, finely diced
¼ cup (1 oz) flour
1½ tablespoons wine or cider vinegar
3 tablespoons prepared horse-radish
½ teaspoon sugar
3 tablespoons sour cream (optional)
2 sprigs parsley, finely chopped

1. Boil the potatoes in milk with salt and pepper until they are soft. **2.** Drain and reserve the milk. **3.** Place the potatoes in a glass or china serving dish and keep them warm while preparing the sauce. **4.** In a heavy frying pan fry the Speck or bacon until it is crisp and golden. **5.** Stir in the flour and cook on a low heat until the flour is a light golden colour. **6.** Slowly add the hot milk and stir to a thick, smooth consistency. **7.** Add the vinegar and simmer for 5 minutes. **8.** Add horse-radish and sugar and, for a richer sauce, the sour cream. Heat but do not boil. Season. **9.** Pour the sauce over the potatoes, mix in gently and sprinkle with parsley. Serve as a vegetable accompanying sausages and smoked meat cuts.

Red Cabbage and Apples

Rotkohl

Serves 4–6

45 g (1½ oz) butter
500–750 g (1–1½ lb) red cabbage, shredded
juice of 1 lemon
2 apples, peeled and diced
2 tablespoons redcurrant jelly
2 cloves
2 tablespoons beef stock (see p. 328)

1. In a heavy-bottomed casserole melt the butter. Add the cabbage and pour over the lemon juice (this will help to preserve the colour). Add the apples, redcurrant jelly, cloves and beef stock. **2.** Mix all the ingredients together and simmer for 10 to 20 minutes. The cabbage should not be overcooked.

Puréed Potatoes and Apples with Black Pudding

Himmel und Erde ('Heaven and Earth')

One of the most famous traditional Rhineland dishes.

Serves 4

4 large potatoes, peeled and diced
3 cooking apples, peeled, cored and quartered
salt
freshly ground black pepper
1 tablespoon sugar
75 g (2½ oz) butter
500 g (1 lb) Blutwurst (black pudding)

1. In a saucepan, cook the potatoes in salted water for 15 minutes. **2.** Drain off most of the water and add the apples. Cook until tender. **3.** Mash the potato and apple mixture, and season with the salt and pepper. Add the sugar and 60 g of the butter. **4.** Slice the Blutwurst and fry in the remaining butter until brown on each side. **5.** To serve, arrange the fried slices of sausage over the mashed potato and apple mixture.

Westphalian Broad Beans

Westfälische Dicke Bohnen

Serves 4

1 kg (2 lb) broad beans
salt
100 g (3½ oz) Speck or smoked bacon, diced
freshly ground black pepper
3 sprigs parsley, finely chopped
2 sprigs marjoram, finely chopped

1. Shell the beans and cook them in salted water for 20 minutes, drain. **2.** Fry the Speck or bacon until the fat is rendered and the meat is crisp but not burnt. **3.** In a serving dish mix the beans with the Speck or bacon. Add salt and pepper and toss them with parsley and marjoram. **4.** Serve hot with mashed potatoes.

Right: *Crayfish Soup and Red Fruit Dessert (see page 105) from the Schabbelhaus restaurant in Lübeck.*

Lentils with Bacon

Berliner Linsentopf

Serves 6

375 g (12 oz) green lentils, soaked overnight
5 cups (1.25 litres) beef stock (see p. 328)
2 potatoes, diced
3 tablespoons vinegar
3 tablespoons sugar
salt
freshly ground black pepper
250 g (8 oz) smoked Speck or bacon, chopped
2 onions, finely chopped
3 tablespoons finely chopped parsley

1. In a heavy-bottomed saucepan, cook the lentils in the beef stock for 45 minutes. **2.** Add the potatoes and cook for a further 15 minutes. **3.** Add the vinegar, sugar, salt and pepper. **4.** In a frying pan, melt and brown the Speck or bacon. Add the onions and fry lightly. **5.** Add the Speck, onions and parsley to the lentils and mix well. Serve hot as a vegetable with meat.

Pears, Beans and Bacon

Birnen, Bohnen und Speck

A speciality of Westphalia.

Serves 6

6 ripe pears, peeled and sliced
½ teaspoon grated lemon rind
½ cup water
1 teaspoon salt
6 slices bacon or heavy smoked Speck
¼ cup (2 oz) sugar
2 tablespoons vinegar
1 teaspoon lemon juice
500 g (1 lb) green beans, cut into 2.5 cm (1 in) lengths

1. In a saucepan cook the pear slices and lemon rind in the water for 10 minutes. **2.** Meanwhile chop the bacon and fry it in a pan until it is crisp. Remove and drain on absorbent paper. **3.** Add the sugar, vinegar and lemon juice to the bacon fat. Cook for 3 minutes. **4.** Add the beans and salt to the pears and pour this sauce over them. Continue cooking until tender. **5.** Just before serving, add the crisp pieces of bacon to the beans and pears. Serve as a vegetable dish.

Carrots and Green Beans with Bacon and Apples

Blindes Huhn ('Blind Hen')

Serves 6

4 large carrots, diced
250 g (8 oz) green beans, cut into 2.5 cm (1 in) pieces
3 slices bacon, diced
1 tablespoon butter
2 onions, sliced
3 cooking apples, peeled and sliced
1 tablespoon sugar
2 tablespoons white wine vinegar
salt
freshly ground black pepper

1. In a saucepan, cook the carrots and beans in salted water until they are almost tender. Drain and set the vegetables aside. **2.** Sauté the bacon in the butter until crisp then remove and set aside. **3.** Cook the onions in the bacon fat and butter until they are soft but not brown. Add the apples, sugar and vinegar and the partially cooked carrots and beans. Add the crisp bacon and season. **4.** Cover and cook until the vegetables are heated through.

Swabian Sauerkraut

Schwäbisches Sauerkraut

Serves 6

1 kg (2 lb) fresh Sauerkraut
3 apples, peeled and diced
1 onion, sliced
2 tablespoons lard
½ teaspoon crushed juniper berries
1 teaspooon sugar
2 tablespoons flour
2 cups (16 fl oz) dry white wine
½ teaspoon salt
freshly ground black pepper

1. Sauerkraut may be bought in tins or in bulk. For best results, rinse the Sauerkraut in warm water and drain well. **2.** Sauté the apples and onions in the lard until light brown. Add the juniper berries, sugar and Sauerkraut. Cover and simmer for 30 minutes. **3.** Add the flour and stir in well, then add the wine, salt and pepper. Continue simmering for approximately 1 hour until the Sauerkraut is tender.
Note: Sauerkraut may be served with Spätzle (see p. 331).

Stewed Cucumbers with Sour Cream and Dill

Schmorgurken

Serves 6

1.5 kg (3 lb) fresh cucumbers
1 teaspoon salt
30 g (1 oz) butter
60 g (2 oz) onions, finely chopped
1½ tablespoons flour
1¾ cups (14 fl oz) milk
1½ tablespoons sour cream
1 tablespoon chopped parsley
1 tablespoon chopped dill
salt
freshly ground pepper

1. Peel the cucumbers, cut them in half lengthways, and with a small spoon remove the seeds. Cut the halves crosswise into 2.5 cm (1 in) pieces. **2.** Place them in a bowl and sprinkle with salt. Let the cucumbers stand for 30 minutes then drain off the liquid. **3.** In a frying pan, melt the butter and sauté the onions until light brown. Add the flour and cook until the flour turns light brown. **4.** Add the milk, stirring constantly and boil for 3 to 4 minutes. **5.** Add the cucumbers and simmer for 10 to 15 minutes. The cucumber must be tender but still quite firm. **6.** Add the sour cream, parsley and dill. Season to taste.

Leipzig Mixed Vegetable Platter

Leipziger Allerlei

Serves 6

250 g (8 oz) cauliflower, cut into flowerets
2 large carrots, diced
500 g (1 lb) shelled green peas (buy 1 kg (2 lb)
fresh peas)
250 g (8 oz) green beans, sliced
125 g (4 oz) button mushrooms
45 g (1½ oz) butter
¼ cup chopped parsley

1. The traditional recipe calls for the vegetables to be cooked in separate saucepans. However, if the vegetables are added at intervals, they can all be cooked in one saucepan. **2.** Start with the cauliflower and carrots. Cook them in boiling salted water for 5 minutes, then add the peas and beans. Cook for a further 10 minutes or until the vegetables are cooked but still crisp. Drain, and save ½ cup of the liquid in which the vegetables have cooked. **3.** Arrange the vegetables on a platter and keep them warm. **4.** Sauté the mushrooms in the butter until they are light brown. Add them to the serving platter and sprinkle them with a little of the butter in which they are cooked. Pour the reserved liquid over them and sprinkle with the chopped parsley.

Berlin Pea Purée

Berliner Erbsenpüree

This is served as a vegetable accompanying meat dishes

Serves 4-6

500 g (1 lb) dried yellow peas, soaked
overnight
2 onions, chopped
60 g (2 oz) bacon, chopped
salt
freshly ground black pepper

1. Drain the peas and place them in a heavy-bottomed saucepan. Cover with fresh water and cook slowly until the peas are soft. Drain them, reserving ½ cup of the liquid. **2.** In a frying pan, fry the onions with the bacon. **3.** Add the onions and bacon to the peas and season with salt and pepper. **4.** One cup at a time, place the peas in a food processor and purée. Add some of the reserved liquid if the purée is too thick.

Sweet-Sour Beans

Süss-Saure Grüne Bohnen

Serves 4

500 g (1 lb) stringless beans cut into 5 cm (2 in)
lengths
2 cups (16 fl oz) beef stock (see p. 328)
salt
freshly ground black pepper
60 g (2 oz) butter
1 tablespoon flour
juice of 1 lemon
1 teaspoon white wine vinegar
1 tablespoon sugar
1 onion, chopped

1. In a saucepan, cook the beans in the beef stock together with the salt and pepper for approximately 15 minutes. **2.** Soften 45 g of the butter and mix it with the flour, then add to the beans and beef stock. **3.** Add lemon juice, vinegar and sugar and mix well. **4.** In the remaining butter, lightly fry the onions and add them to the beans. Cook this mixture for a further 15 minutes. **5.** Traditionally these beans are served with pork dishes.

FISH

King Prawns in Dill Sauce
Kaiser Krabben mit Dillsosse

Serves 4

2 celery sprigs, chopped
1 onion, chopped
750 g (1½ lb) fresh prawns (shrimps) in their shells
45 g (1½ oz) butter
1 tablespoon flour
1 tablespoon finely chopped fresh dill
½ cup (4 fl oz) sour cream
salt
freshly ground black pepper

1. Cook the celery and onions in a little salted water for 10 minutes. **2.** Add the prawns and cook until they turn pink (approximately 2 to 3 minutes). **3.** Cool the prawns in the stock. Remove and shell them, strain and reserve the stock. **4.** To make the sauce, melt the butter in a saucepan, stir in the flour and cook for a few minutes without browning. **5.** Add the dill and 1 cup of the prawn stock. **6.** Cook for a few minutes until the sauce thickens. Finally add the sour cream and the prawns. Season before serving.

Fried Eel with Herbs
Aal mit frischen Kräutern gebraten

From the Waldschlösschen Bösehof in Bederkase.

Serves 4

1 kg (2 lb) eel, cut into 10 cm (4 in) pieces
salt
freshly ground black pepper
½ cup (2 oz) flour
90 g (3 oz) butter
½ cup chopped fresh herbs (oregano, thyme, tarragon, etc.)
1 clove garlic, finely chopped
2 tomatoes, peeled and diced
6 champignon-type mushrooms, diced

1. Season the eel and dust with flour. **2.** In a frying pan, melt the butter and fry the eel. Add the herbs, garlic, tomatoes and mushrooms and cook for a further 5 minutes. **3.** Traditionally, fried eel is served with parsley potatoes and a lettuce salad.

Jellied Trout
Gesülzte Forellen

Serves 4

6 cups (1.5 litres) water
½ cup (4 fl oz) wine vinegar
salt
12 peppercorns
1 onion, chopped
3 bay leaves
3 stalks celery, chopped
1 cup (8 fl oz) dry white wine
4 small trout
6 teaspoons gelatine
2 egg whites, whipped
8 slices lemon
small sprigs parsley
1 egg, hard-boiled and sliced
1 tablespoon capers

1. In a fish kettle or large saucepan combine the water, vinegar, salt, peppercorns, onions, bay leaves, celery and white wine. **2.** Bring to the boil and simmer for 30 minutes. **3.** Reduce the heat, add the trout and cook slowly for 5 minutes. Cool the trout in the liquid. **4.** Remove the trout and save the cooking liquid. **5.** Cool the trout and carefully remove the flesh from the bones, in whole fillets on each side. **6.** Arrange the fillets on a serving dish and refrigerate. **7.** Strain the liquid and return it to the saucepan. **8.** Heat it, and with a wire whisk mix the egg whites into it. Cook for 5 minutes. This will clarify the stock. **9.** Filter the stock through a cloth and if necessary adjust the seasoning. **10.** Remove 1 cup of the stock and dissolve the gelatine in it, then return it to the remaining stock, stirring well. **11.** Decorate the top of the fillets and the serving dish with the lemon slices, parsley, hard-boiled egg and capers. **12.** Carefully pour the liquid into the serving dish so that it covers the fish by 1 cm (½ in). **13.** Refrigerate until the jelly sets and serve with mayonnaise (see p. 330) and salad.

Right: Jellied Trout (above). Instead of carrots, the dish can be decorated with hard-boiled egg and capers.

Poached Rhine Salmon

Rheinsalm

Unfortunately there are hardly any fish left in the River Rhine and there are certainly no more salmon. Trout may be used as a substitute in this recipe (either a very large trout cut into 4 pieces, or 4 whole small trout).

Serves 4

2 cups (16 fl oz) dry white wine
1 cup (8 fl oz) water
1 onion, cut into small pieces
2 bay leaves
12 peppercorns
½ teaspoon salt
4 salmon steaks, 4 pieces of trout, or 4 whole trout
1 cup (8 fl oz) cream
3 egg yolks, beaten
salt
freshly ground black pepper

1. Combine the wine, water, onion, bay leaves, peppercorns and salt and cook for approximately 10 minutes. **2.** Reduce the heat and place the fish in the saucepan. Cover and simmer for approximately 10 minutes. **3.** Remove the fish and keep warm. **4.** Continue boiling the mixture until it is reduced to 1½ cups. Strain and return it to the rinsed-out pan. **5.** Mix the cream and the egg yolks. **6.** Using a whisk, beat a quarter of the reduced liquid into the egg mixture. **7.** Place the saucepan on a low flame and mix in the rest of the liquid. Cook gently until the mixture thickens, making sure that it does not curdle. Season. **8.** Serve the fish with the sauce poured over.

Fish with Mushrooms, Tomatoes and Artichokes

Heilbutt Filet, Gebraten mit Steinpilzen, Tomaten und Artischoken

A recipe from Waldschlösschen Bösehof in Bederkase.

Serves 4

4 fillets of halibut, flounder or John Dory
juice of 1 lemon
salt
3 tablespoons flour
90 g (3 oz) butter
250 g (8 oz) mushrooms, sliced
4 artichoke hearts, cut into quarters
½ cup (4 fl oz) demi-glace sauce (see p. 329)
⅓ cup chopped parsley
4 tomatoes, peeled and cut into small dice
4 potatoes, peeled and cut into small dice
⅓ cup (2½ fl oz) vegetable oil
freshly ground black pepper

1. Sprinkle the fillets with the lemon juice and salt and dust them with the flour. **2.** In a frying pan, melt half the butter and fry the fillets lightly. **3.** In a separate pan, fry the mushrooms and artichoke hearts in the remaining butter. **4.** Add the demi-glace, parsley and tomatoes to the mushrooms and artichokes. Cook for about 5 minutes. **5.** Fry the potatoes in a separate pan in the vegetable oil until they are crisp. Season. **6.** To serve, arrange the fillets on plates and garnish with the mushroom and artichoke sauce. Serve the potatoes separately.

Baked Pike, Moselle Style

Gebratener Moselhecht

Serves 4

125 g (4 oz) butter
2 spring onions (scallions), chopped
1 carrot, finely diced
1 tablespoon chopped parsley
1 kg (2 lb) pike, or any available fish, cleaned
salt
1 cup (8 fl oz) fish stock (see p. 328)
½ cup (4 fl oz) sour cream
1 egg
½ cup (2 oz) grated Gruyère cheese

1. Preheat the oven to 180°C (350°F/Gas 4). 2. Using half the butter, grease a shallow baking dish. Scatter the vegetables and parsley on the bottom and place the fish on top of them. Sprinkle with salt, dot with the remaining butter and add the fish stock. 3. Cover the dish with foil and place it in the oven for 10 minutes. 4. Combine the sour cream and the egg. Remove the foil and spread the cream and egg mixture on top of the fish. Sprinkle with the cheese and increase the oven temperature to 200°C (400°F/Gas 6). 5. Return the dish to the oven and bake for a further 10 to 15 minutes.

Matjes Herrings in Cream Sauce

Matjesheringe in Rahmsosse

Serves 6

8 herring fillets
1 cup (8 fl oz) buttermilk or milk
½ cup (4 fl oz) sour cream
¼ cup (2 fl oz) yogurt
salt
freshly ground black pepper
1 teaspoon sugar
juice of 1 lemon
1 onion, grated
1 tablespoon tomato purée
2 tablespoons prepared horse-radish
2 apples, peeled, cored and finely diced
1 sour cucumber, finely diced
2 tablespoons finely chopped dill

1. Place the fillets in the buttermilk for 2 to 3 hours. This will reduce the salty flavour of the herrings. 2. To prepare the cream sauce, combine the sour cream, yogurt, salt and pepper, and whisk lightly. 3. Add the sugar, lemon juice, onion, tomato purée, horse-radish, apples and cucumber, and mix them thoroughly together. 4. The drained fillets can be arranged whole or cut into pieces on a serving platter with the sauce poured over. Refrigerate for several hours before serving, and garnish with finely chopped dill.

Hamburg Seafood Pie

Hamburger Fischpastete

The traditional recipe calls for halibut and sole or flounder. If these fish are not available, other similar fish may be used.

Serves 6–8

Filling:
1 kg (2 lb) halibut
500 g (1 lb) sole or flounder
1 carrot, chopped
1 stalk celery, chopped
1 onion, chopped
¼ cup chopped parsley
750 g (1½ lb) raw shelled prawns (shrimps)
1 can (approximately 400 g) (12½ oz) asparagus tips, drained
60 g (2 oz) butter
3 tablespoons flour
¼ cup (2 fl oz) sour cream
1 egg yolk
salt
freshly ground black pepper

Pastry:
1 cup (4 oz) self-raising flour
¼ teaspoon salt
125 g (4 oz) butter
1 egg, beaten (reserve 1 teaspoon and mix with a few drops of water for glazing)
1 teaspoon grated lemon peel

Filling: 1. Gently poach the fish in enough water to cover it, together with the carrot, celery, onion and parsley for 15 minutes. Cool the fish in the stock. When it is cold, remove the flesh from the bones. Discard the skin. **2.** Strain the stock. **3.** Add the prawns to the stock and simmer until they turn pink (approximately 2 to 3 minutes). Remove the prawns and save the stock. **4.** Place the fish in a shallow ovenproof dish. Arrange the prawns and the asparagus tips on top. **5.** Make a roux by melting the butter and adding the flour to it. Cook it for 4 to 5 minutes. Heat 2 cups of the fish stock and gradually add it to the roux. Cook for 5 to 10 minutes until the sauce is smooth and thick. **6.** Beat the sour cream and the egg yolk together, add some of the hot sauce to it and then pour the cream and egg mixture back into the sauce. Season. **7.** Pour the sauce over the fish in the ovenproof dish.

Pastry: 1. Preheat the oven to 190°C (375°F/Gas 5). **2.** Combine the flour and the salt. Chop the butter into small pieces and mix it with the flour until it resembles fine breadcrumbs. Add the egg and lemon peel and, with the minimum of kneading, prepare the dough. **3.** Roll it out to the size of the ovenproof dish and lay it over the seafood mixture. **4.** Brush the egg and water mixture over the pastry and bake the pie in the oven until the pastry is golden-brown and crisp.

POULTRY & GAME

Pheasant with Sauerkraut

Fasan mit Sauerkraut

Serves 4

1 pheasant
salt
freshly ground black pepper
3 slices bacon
3 onions, chopped
90 g (3 oz) butter
1 kg (2 lb) fresh Sauerkraut
2 cups (16 fl oz) chicken stock (see p. 328)
1 cup (8 fl oz) dry white wine
2 tablespoons brandy

1. Preheat the oven to 200°C (400°F/Gas 6).
2. Rub the pheasant inside and out with salt and
pepper. **3.** Wrap the bacon around the bird, place it
in a shallow ovenproof dish and bake it for 20 minutes. **4.** Sauté the onions in the butter. **5.** Add the
Sauerkraut to the onions. Cover and simmer for 15
minutes. **6.** Remove the bird from the baking dish.
Add the chicken stock and white wine to the pan
juices. Cook until the liquid has reduced by half.
7. Add the Sauerkraut to the reduced cooking juices
and mix well. **8.** Place the pheasant on top of the
Sauerkraut, using some of it to cover the bird
lightly. **9.** Return the pheasant to the oven, reduce
the heat to 180°C (350°F/Gas 4) and cook for 1
more hour. **10.** Arrange the Sauerkraut on a serving
plate and place the bird on top of it. Pour the cooking juices over the pheasant. Warm the brandy, pour
it over the bird, ignite it and serve it flaming.

Roast Goose Stuffed with Prunes and Apples

Gänsebraten

Serves 6–8

4–5 kg (8–10 lb) goose
salt
freshly ground black pepper
2 onions, chopped
3–4 cups (24 fl oz–1 litre) water
2 cups (12 oz) pitted and chopped prunes
4 apples, peeled, cored and diced
1–1½ cups (2–3 oz) fresh, coarse, rye
breadcrumbs
2 tablespoons sugar
75 g (2½ oz) flour

1. Twenty-four hours before roasting, rub the goose
with salt and pepper and refrigerate. **2.** Place the
goose in a large saucepan with the onions and water,
and simmer, covered, for 1 hour. **3.** Strain the stock,
skim off the fat and reserve. **4.** Rub the goose again
with salt and pepper. **5.** Preheat the oven to 220°C
(425°F/Gas 7). **6.** Combine the prunes, apples,
breadcrumbs, sugar, salt and pepper and stuff the
cavity of the bird. Use skewers to hold the opening
together. **7.** Place the goose breast side down on a
rack in a roasting pan and bake for 45 minutes.
8. Drain the fat from the roasting pan, reduce the
temperature to 190°C (375°F/Gas 5) and roast the
goose for a further 1 to 1¼ hours. **9.** Again, drain
the fat from the pan. Turn the goose breast side up
and increase the temperature to 240°C (475°F/Gas
9). Roast for 15 minutes or until the breast is golden-
brown. **10.** Remove the goose and keep it warm.
11. Skim off the fat from the roasting pan but leave
the cooking juices in it. Combine the flour with the
reserved goose stock and add the mixture to the pan.
12. Slowly simmer until the sauce thickens. Season
and serve it with the goose.

*Right: Foreground — Roast Goose stuffed with Prunes and
Apples (above); background left: Blackforest Cherry Cake (see
page 109); right: rollmops*

Duck with Sauerkraut, Apples and Grapes

Ente mit Sauerkraut auf Nürnberger Art

Serves 4

**2–2.5 kg (4–5 lb) duckling
juice of 1 lemon
salt
freshly ground black pepper
1 onion, peeled
1 kg (2 lb) Sauerkraut
2 cooking apples, peeled and diced
2 cups (16 fl oz) dry white wine
60 g (2 oz) seedless grapes
2 tablespoons flour**

1. Preheat the oven to 180°C (350°F/Gas 4). **2.** Rub the skin of the duckling with lemon juice and sprinkle with salt and pepper. **3.** Put the onion in the cavity and place the duck on a rack in a baking dish. **4.** Cook in the oven for 1 hour. Drain off the excess fat from the pan while the duck is roasting. **5.** Mix the Sauerkraut, apples and half a cup of the wine together and simmer for 30 minutes. **6.** Arrange the Sauerkraut in a casserole and half an hour before the duck is ready, remove it from the oven and place it on top of the Sauerkraut mixture. Sprinkle with the grapes, cover, and return to the oven to bake for a further 30 minutes. **7.** In the meantime, remove as much of the fat as possible from the cooking juices. Mix a little of the juice with the flour to make a smooth paste and then stir this into the remainder. Add the remaining wine, season to taste and simmer for 15 minutes. **8.** When the duck is cooked, carve it and arrange on a platter. **9.** Add half the gravy to the Sauerkraut and serve the rest in a sauce-boat. Traditionally, the dish is served with mashed potatoes.

Venison Pepper Stew

Schwarzwälder Rehpfeffer

This recipe comes from the Burghotel in Sababurg.

Serves 4–6

**1 kg (2 lb) venison (neck, shoulder or breast meat), cut into cubes
2 cups (16 fl oz) dry red wine
3 bay leaves
8 juniper berries, crushed
½ teaspoon dried thyme
1 onion studded with 6 cloves
6 peppercorns
2 slivers of lemon peel
125 g (4 oz) Speck or bacon, diced
salt
freshly ground black pepper
2 cups (16 fl oz) beef stock (see p. 328)
½ cup (4 fl oz) sour cream
3 tablespoons redcurrant jelly, heated, to liquefy
white pepper
½ teaspoon grated lemon rind**

1. Place the meat in a marinade of wine, bay leaves, juniper berries, thyme, onion and cloves, peppercorns and lemon peel. Refrigerate for 24 hours. **2.** Drain the meat and reserve the marinade. **3.** Lightly sauté the Speck or bacon to render the fat. **4.** Add the venison to the pan and fry until brown. Season and add 1 cup of the stock. Cover and simmer over low heat for 50 minutes or until the meat is tender. **5.** During that time gradually add the rest of the stock and all the strained marinade. **6.** Add the sour cream, redcurrant jelly, sufficient white pepper to make the stew quite peppery, and the lemon rind. **7.** Continue cooking gently for a further 5 minutes. Season to taste. **8.** Serve with Spätzle (see p. 331), stewed apples and cranberries.

MEAT

Sauerbraten Rhineland Style

Rheinischer Sauerbraten

Sauerbraten is marinated for 2 to 3 days in red wine before it is cooked.

Serves 8

2 kg (4 lb) rump steak in one piece
¼ cup (1 oz) flour
90 g (3 oz) butter
2 carrots, sliced
2 onions, quartered
1 tablespoon concentrated tomato purée
75 g (2½ oz) ginger biscuits or gingerbread, crushed
2 tablespoons sugar
½ cup (4 fl oz) red wine
1 cup (5 oz) raisins
½ cup (2 oz) slivered almonds
salt
freshly ground black pepper
cranberry preserve for garnish

Marinade:
4 cups (1 litre) dry red wine
1 cup (8 fl oz) water
juice of 1 lemon
125 g (4 oz) onions, thinly sliced
6 peppercorns
2 bay leaves
1 teaspoon finely chopped thyme
2 cloves
¼ teaspoon nutmeg
5 sprigs parsley, chopped

1. Place the meat in a bowl. In a saucepan, combine all the ingredients for the marinade, except the parsley, and bring to the boil. Pour over the meat and cool. Add the chopped parsley. **2.** Refrigerate the marinated meat for 2 to 3 days, turning from time to time. **3.** Remove the meat and strain the marinade. Wipe the meat dry, sprinkle it with flour, and in a saucepan sauté it in the butter until it is brown on all sides. **4.** Add the carrots, onions, tomato purée and 1 cup of the strained marinade. **5.** Cover the saucepan and simmer for 2½ to 3 hours or until the meat is tender. **6.** Remove the meat. **7.** Purée the sauce in a blender and strain it, then add the rest of the marinade, the ginger biscuits, sugar, wine and raisins. **8.** Boil the mixture until it thickens. Add the almonds and cook for another 5 minutes. Taste, and if necessary, adjust the seasoning. **9.** Carve the meat into slices, pour the sauce over it and serve it with the cranberry preserve. The dish should be accompanied by potato dumplings, Spätzle (see p. 331) or egg noodles.

Beef Cooked in Milk

Siebenbürgerfleish

Serves 4

60 g (2 oz) speck or smoked bacon, roughly chopped
1 kg (2 lb) beef rump or silverside
1 onion, roughly chopped
3 celery stalks, sliced
1 turnip, sliced
1 tablespoon dried basil
salt
freshly ground black pepper
3 cups (24 fl oz) milk
15 g (½ oz) butter
½ teaspoon sugar
2 tablespoons flour
1½ cups (12 fl oz) beef stock (see p. 328) or water
4 tablespoons sour cream
2 tablespoons tomato paste

1. Place the speck or bacon in a heavy-bottomed, lidded casserole. **2.** Add the meat, onion, celery, turnip, basil, salt, pepper and milk. **3.** Cover, bring to the boil and gently simmer for 2 hours. **4.** In the meantime, melt the butter, add the sugar and cook until it is light yellow. Add the flour and cook until it becomes golden-yellow. Be very careful not to burn it, or it will taste bitter. **5.** Add the stock or water and simmer for 10 minutes. **6.** Pour this sauce over the meat for the last 10 minutes of cooking. **7.** Mix the sour cream and tomato paste together and add it to the meat. Cook for 2 minutes more. If necessary adjust seasoning. **8.** Remove the meat from the sauce, let it stand for 10 minutes and carve it into slices. Serve with the sauce and boiled potatoes or dumplings.

Pork Fillet with Beer Sauce

Schweinefilet mit Biersosse

Serves 4

750 g (1½ lb) pork fillets
150 g (5 oz) Speck or smoked bacon slices
2 spring onions (scallions), chopped
salt
freshly ground black pepper
1 cup (8 fl oz) cream
½ cup (4 fl oz) beer
600 g (1 lb 3½ oz) leeks, sliced
60 g (2 oz) butter

1. Preheat the oven to 200°C (400°F/Gas 6).
2. Trim the fat and sinews from the fillets and wrap
the Speck or bacon around them, securing with
toothpicks. **3.** Heat a frying pan and brown the
Speck-wrapped fillets on all sides. **4.** Place the fillets
in a baking dish and cook in the preheated oven for
15 minutes. **5.** Remove the fillets and keep them
warm. **6.** Sauté the spring onions in the fat remaining in the baking dish. Add the cream and reduce by
half. Add the beer and simmer. Season. **7.** Remove
the Speck from the fillets, finely chop it and set
aside. **8.** Lightly sauté the leeks in the butter and
season them. **9.** To serve, slice the fillet and arrange
the slices on a bed of leeks, sprinkled with chopped
Speck and masked with the sauce.

Calves' Liver with Apples and Onion

Gebratene Kalbsleber auf Berliner Art

Serves 4

125 g (4 oz) butter
2 onions, cut into thin slices and pushed into
rings
750 g (1½ lb) cooking apples, peeled, cored
and sliced
salt
freshly ground black pepper
500 g (1 lb) calves' liver, cut into 6 mm (¼ in)
slices
flour

1. Melt half the butter in a frying pan. Fry the onion
rings and apple slices until they are light brown.
Season with salt and pepper. Set aside and keep hot.
2. Dust the liver slices with flour. Fry them in the
remaining butter, allowing approximately 2 minutes
each side. Do not overcook. **3.** Serve the liver slices
garnished with the apples and onions.

Beef Tongue with Raisin Sauce

Weimarer Ochsenzunge

Serves 6–8

1 fresh uncooked beef tongue (1.5–2 kg/3–4 lb)
1 onion, chopped
1 carrot, chopped
3 stalks celery, chopped
6 peppercorns
3 bay leaves
1 clove garlic, crushed

Sauce:
2 tablespoons butter
2 tablespoons flour
salt
2 tablespoons wine vinegar
3 tablespoons sour cream
1 teaspoon sugar
¾ cup (4 oz) raisins
freshly ground black pepper

1. Place the tongue in a large saucepan with the
onion, carrot, celery, peppercorns, bay leaves and
garlic. Cover with salted water and simmer for 2
hours. **2.** Strain and reserve the stock and keep the
tongue hot. **3.** To make the sauce, melt the butter,
add the flour and cook for 5 minutes. **4.** Add 1½
cups (12 fl oz) of the reserved stock, the vinegar,
sour cream, sugar and raisins. Cook together on a
low heat for 3 minutes. Season. **5.** Serve the tongue
sliced with the raisin sauce.

*Right: Breakfast at the Gasthof Schütte. Clockwise from
bottom left: German breads; Ham on the bone; Liver sausage;
Black pudding.*

Homemade Brawn

Hausmacher Sülze

From the Brauereiausschank Schlenkerla in Bamberg. It is customary to have a beer 'bar' attached to a brewery, and while they originally served only beer, such places have often developed into restaurants. The Schlenkerla brewery has been making a special type of smoked-flavoured beer since 1678. Today the adjoining restaurant specialises in local peasant-type dishes: pig's trotters, veal knuckles, local sausages, brawns and pickled meats, all served with sauerkraut and potato salad in the Bavarian tradition. Everything they serve has a rich flavour and the aroma fills the ancient beamed and panelled rooms. The place is always packed with people who come from far and wide to enjoy the friendly atmosphere. Plenty of beer flows to wash down the highly flavoured fare.

Serves 6

½ **pig's head**
4 **pig's trotters**
6 **tablespoons vinegar**
8 **juniper berries**
4 **bay leaves**
8 **peppercorns**
2 **onions, cut into quarters**
3 **cloves**
1 **tablespoon salt**
3 **tablespoons sugar**
16 **cups (4 litres) water**

1. Place all the ingredients in a large saucepan and slowly bring them to the boil. Continue boiling for 1½ hours or until the meat is soft. **2.** Remove the meat from the liquid and continue cooking until the liquid has reduced to approximately 6 cups. **3.** Strain the solids out of the liquid and allow it to cool. Remove any fat. **4.** Taste the liquid, and if necessary season or add more vinegar. **5.** Remove the meat from the pig's head and the trotters and cut it into small cubes. **6.** Place the meat into a decorative form or pâté mould and carefully pour the cold liquid over it. **7.** Place it in a refrigerator and serve when it has set. Traditionally, fried potatoes and Schlenkerla smoked beer are served with the brawn.

Pickled Pork with Sauerkraut

Eisbein gekocht mit Sauerkraut

Serves 4

30 g (1 oz) **lard**
2 **onions, chopped**
750 g (1½ lb) **Sauerkraut**
2 **cooking apples, peeled, cored and roughly chopped**
6 **juniper berries, crushed**
freshly ground black pepper
2 **cloves**
1 **clove garlic, crushed**
2 **cups (16 fl oz) beef stock (see p. 328) or water**
2 **hands or knuckles of pickled pork**

1. In a large, lidded saucepan melt the lard and lightly fry the onions. **2.** Add the Sauerkraut, apples, juniper berries, pepper, cloves, garlic and stock and cook for 10 minutes. **3.** Make a well in the Sauerkraut, add the meat and cover with Sauerkraut. **4.** Cover the saucepan and simmer over very low heat for 2 hours. **5.** Remove the pork from the pan, take the meat off the bones and cut it into serving pieces. **6.** If necessary, season the Sauerkraut, place it on a serving platter and arrange the meat on top of it. Serve with boiled potatoes or dumplings.

DESSERTS

Red Fruit Dessert

'Rode Grütt' (Rote Grütze)

Traditionally, redcurrant juice is used in this recipe. However, if this is not available, the juice or purée of strawberries, raspberries, apricots or cherries may be used.

Serves 4–6

6 cups (1.5 litres) red fruit juice
4–6 tablespoons honey (depending on the acidity of the fruit juice)
1 cup (8 fl oz) dry red wine
⅔ cup (3 oz) cornflour (cornstarch)

1. Bring the fruit juice to the boil, then add the honey and wine. **2.** Mix the cornflour with a little water. Reduce the heat, and while stirring vigorously, add the cornflour to the juice. Continue stirring and boil slowly for 1 to 2 minutes. **3.** To serve, pour the mixture into dessert glasses and refrigerate. Garnish with the same type of fruit used for the juice.

Beer Fruit Cup

Altbier Bowle

This recipe comes from the Waldhotel Krautkrämer in Münster-Hiltrup. If the fruit listed below is not available, use any fruit in season.

Serves 6

1 cup strawberries, hulled
2 peaches, peeled and stoned
2 slices pineapple
2 oranges, peeled and cut into segments
4 cups (1 litre) beer
1 tablespoon sugar (optional)

1. Cut the fruit into small pieces and marinate them in the beer for 12 to 14 hours. **2.** Before serving, taste and, if necessary, add the sugar. Place the fruit and the beer in which it was marinated into 6 glasses and top with fresh beer.

Steamed Chocolate Pudding

Schokoladenpudding

Serves 6–8

1½ cups (12 oz) caster (powdered) sugar
250 g (8 oz) dark chocolate, cut into chunks
1 teaspoon instant coffee
250 g (8 oz) softened unsalted butter
10 egg yolks
300 g (10 oz) blanched almonds, coarsely chopped and roasted
10 egg whites, stiffly beaten
2 cups (16 fl oz) fresh cream
3 tablespoons icing (confectioners') sugar
⅛ teaspoon vanilla essence

1. Preheat oven to 180°C (350°F/Gas 4). **2.** Sprinkle 2 to 3 tablespoons of the sugar into a greased 8 cup (2 litre) pudding basin to coat the bottom and sides. **3.** Melt the chocolate in a double boiler and mix in the coffee. **4.** In a large mixing bowl cream the butter and the remaining caster sugar. Add the egg yolks, one at a time, beating constantly, and then add the chocolate. Beat until the mixture is smooth. **5.** Add the almonds. **6.** Fold one quarter of the egg whites into the egg-chocolate mixture and in turn mix it into the rest of the egg whites. **7.** Pour the mixture into the pudding basin. Smooth the top and cover the basin. **8.** Place the basin in a large saucepan and pour in enough water to come two-thirds up the side of the basin. **9.** Bring the water to a boil and simmer over low heat for 1 hour. **10.** Remove the basin and turn the pudding out onto a serving dish. **11.** Whip the cream with the icing sugar and vanilla essence until it is stiff. **12.** Serve the pudding hot together with the whipped cream presented separately in a bowl.

Lemon Cream
Zitronencreme

Serves 6–8

1½ tablespoons gelatine
½ cup (4 fl oz) cold water
4 egg yolks
½ cup (4 oz) sugar
juice of 2 lemons
½ tablespoon grated lemon rind
4 egg whites, stiffly beaten
1 cup (8 fl oz) cream, whipped
4 macaroons, broken into small pieces
3 tablespoons Kirsch (optional)
lemon rind slivers for garnish

1. In a small bowl or cup combine the gelatine with water and soak for 10 to 15 minutes. Place the bowl in a saucepan of boiling water and simmer until the gelatine dissolves. **2.** Cream the egg yolks and sugar in a bowl until the mixture is pale yellow and thick. Add the lemon juice and rind. **3.** Place the mixture in a saucepan and heat gently (do not boil). Beat constantly until the volume increases. **4.** Remove from the heat and, still constantly beating, add the dissolved gelatine. (Make sure that the mixture and the gelatine are at approximately the same temperature.) **5.** Allow to cool. Gradually fold in one-third of the beaten egg whites. **6.** Mix the rest of the egg whites with the whipped cream and incorporate it into the basic mixture. **7.** Fold in the macaroons and for greater flavour mix in the Kirsch. **8.** Pour the mixture into glass dessert bowls and refrigerate until stiff. Before serving, garnish with thin slivers of lemon rind.

Rye Bread and Apple Pudding
Bettelmann ('Beggar's Dessert')

Serves 6

345 g (11 oz) dark rye bread, 2–3 days old
1 cup (8 fl oz) apple juice
1½ cups (12 fl oz) dry white wine
750 g (1½ lb) green cooking apples, peeled, cored and thickly sliced
5 tablespoons sugar
½ teaspoon cinnamon
½ cup (3 oz) raisins
60 g (2 oz) butter

1. Preheat the oven to 200°C (400°F/Gas 6). **2.** Cut the bread into small cubes, place in a bowl and pour the apple juice and wine over it. **3.** Butter an ovenproof earthenware or glass dish. Place one thick layer of the bread on the bottom, and on top of that place a layer of apples. Sprinkle with cinnamon and sugar. Continue layering until the bread and apples are used up. Cover the final layer of apples with raisins, and finish with a layer of bread. **4.** Dot the top layer with knobs of butter and cook in the oven for approximately 45 minutes. Serve hot.

Souffléed Pancake
Kaiserschmarren

Serves 6

2¼ cups (10 oz) flour
salt
2 cups (16 fl oz) milk
6 egg yolks
60 g (2 oz) butter, melted
½ cup (3 oz) raisins or sultanas, soaked in lukewarm water for 1 hour and drained
2 tablespoons rum
6 egg whites, beaten until stiff
butter, for frying
icing (confectioners') sugar

1. Prepare a batter from the flour, salt, milk and egg yolks. Add the melted butter, the raisins or sultanas and the rum and mix well together. **2.** Gradually fold the beaten egg whites into the batter. **3.** In a frying pan melt some butter and pour in a layer approximately 1 cm (½ in) of batter. **4.** Fry until brown then turn to brown the other side. **5.** When both sides have been browned, using two forks, tear the pancake into approximately 2.5 cm (1 in) square pieces. Add a little more butter and continue frying until all the pieces are brown all round. **6.** As each batch is cooked place the pieces on a serving dish, and serve hot sprinkled with icing sugar. **7.** Traditionally, Kaiserschmarren is served with a dried fruit compote.

Right: A selection of German cakes including the famous Blackforest Cherry Cake and Apple Strudel.

CAKES

Bee Sting Cake
Bienenstich

Traditionally this cake is made with yeast, but the self-raising flour version is simpler to prepare and equally tasty.

Makes one 23 cm (9 in) cake

Cake:
1½ cups (6 oz) self-raising flour
pinch salt
155 g (5 oz) butter
⅓ cup (3 oz) sugar
2 eggs
¼ tablespoon vanilla essence
½ cup (4 fl oz) milk

Topping:
½ cup (2 oz) slivered almonds, toasted
¼ cup (2 oz) sugar
60 g (2 oz) butter
1 tablespoon milk

Filling:
¼ cup (2 oz) sugar
2 tablespoons cornflour (cornstarch)
3 egg yolks, beaten lightly
1 cup (8 fl oz) milk
few drops almond or vanilla essence

1. Preheat the oven to 190°C (375°F/Gas 5). **2.** To make the cake, combine the flour and salt. **3.** Cream the butter and gradually add the sugar. Add the eggs, one at a time, beating vigorously, then add the vanilla essence. **4.** Alternately and gradually, add the milk and flour. **5.** Pour the mixture into a springform pan. **6.** Make the topping by combining the almonds, sugar, butter and milk, and heating them until the sugar is dissolved. **7.** Sprinkle the cake mixture in the pan with flour and pour the topping over it. **8.** Bake in the oven for 25 to 30 minutes, then allow it to cool. **9.** To prepare the filling, mix the sugar, cornflour and egg yolks in the top of a double boiler. **10.** Heat the milk, and while stirring with a whisk, pour it over the egg yolk mixture. **11.** Cook over boiling water until smooth and thick. Do not boil. Stir in the almond or vanilla essence and cool. **12.** Cut the cake horizontally in half and spread the bottom piece with the filling. Replace the top with the topping side up. **13.** Refrigerate before serving.

Almond Torte
Mandeltorte

Hazelnuts or walnuts may be used instead of almonds.

Makes one 20 cm (8 in) torte

½ cup (2 oz) fine dry breadcrumbs
½ cup (4 fl oz) milk
1 tablespoon rum
90 g (3 oz) butter
⅓ cup (3 oz) sugar
6 egg yolks
6 egg whites, beaten stiff
1 cup (3½ oz) ground roasted almonds

Cream Filling:
2 cups (16 fl oz) cream
2 tablespoons caster (powdered) sugar
1 tablespoon rum
¼ cup (1 oz) chopped roasted almonds

1. Preheat the oven to 180°C (350°F/Gas 4). **2.** Soak the breadcrumbs in the milk and rum. **3.** Cream the butter and sugar. Add the egg yolks and the creamed butter to the soaked crumbs. Fold in the egg whites and stir in the almonds. **4.** Divide the mixture into 3 parts and bake each one in a greased 20 cm (8 in) cake tin for 30 to 40 minutes. Cool and turn out on a rack. **5.** Prepare the cream filling by whipping the cream and sugar until stiff. Add the rum. **6.** Divide the cream into 3 parts and spread it between each layer and on top of the torte. Sprinkle the nuts on top. To serve, cut into wedge-shaped portions.

Apple, Pear or Plum Cake
Apfel, Birnen oder Zwetschgen Kuchen

Makes one 25 cm (10 in) flan

unbaked sweet pastry dough (see p. 331)
750 g–1 kg (1½–2 lb) apples, pears or plums, sliced
2–3 tablespoons dry breadcrumbs (optional)
3–4 tablespoons (2–3 oz) caster (powdered) sugar (optional, to be used if fruit is not very sweet)
2–3 tablespoons icing (confectioners') sugar

1. Preheat the oven to 220°C (425°F/Gas 7). **2.** Make the flan as described in the recipe for Mürbeteig. **3.** Arrange the fruit in the flan. If the fruit is particularly juicy, sprinkle the bottom of the flan with breadcrumbs. Sprinkle the top of the fruit with sugar if the fruit is not very sweet. **4.** Bake in the oven for 30 to 45 minutes. **5.** Allow to cool, and before serving sprinkle with the icing sugar.

Blackforest Cherry Cake
Schwarzwälder Kirschtorte

Makes one 23–25 cm (9–10 in) cake

125 g (4 oz) butter
½ cup (4 oz) sugar
6 egg yolks
few drops vanilla essence
125 g (4 oz) dark chocolate, grated
1¼ cups (4 oz) ground almonds
1 cup (4 oz) self-raising flour
6 egg whites, beaten stiffly
butter and flour, for greasing pan
¼ cup (2 fl oz) Kirsch
¼ cup (2 fl oz) cherry syrup from preserved cherries

Filling and Topping:
3 cups (24 fl oz) cream
¼–⅓ cup (2–3 oz) caster (powdered) sugar
3 tablespoons Kirsch
750 g (1½ lb) stoned preserved sour cherries, chopped

Garnish:
250 g (8 oz) dark chocolate curls
fresh or maraschino cherries with stems, drained and rinsed

1. Preheat the oven to 180°C (350°F/Gas 4). **2.** Cream the butter and gradually add the sugar (reserve 1–2 tablespoons for the egg whites) and egg yolks. The mixture should be light and frothy. **3.** Gradually add the vanilla essence, chocolate, almonds and flour. Finally, fold in the egg whites, beaten with the reserved sugar. **4.** Pour the mixture into a buttered and floured springform pan. Bake for 45 minutes to 1 hour. **5.** Cool for a few minutes and then remove the cake from the pan. When cold, cut the cake horizontally into 3 slices. **6.** Mix the Kirsch and cherry syrup and sprinkle the slices with the mixture. **7.** For the filling and topping, whip the cream with the sugar and Kirsch. Fold in the cherries. **8.** Spread each layer with the whipped cream mixture and put them together. Spread the top and sides with the remaining cream. **9.** Sprinkle the side with the chocolate curls and decorate the top with the cherries.

Piped Biscuits (Cookies)
Spritzgebäck

Makes 60 biscuits

250 g (8 oz) butter, softened
1¼ cups (8 oz) caster (powdered) sugar
5 egg yolks or 3 whole eggs
¼ tablespoon vanilla essence or grated rind from ½ lemon
1¼ cups (4 oz) ground almonds or hazelnuts
3 cups (12 oz) flour

1. Preheat the oven to 190°C (375°F/Gas 5). **2.** Cream the butter and gradually add the sugar. Beat in, one at a time, the egg yolks or whole eggs. Add the vanilla essence or lemon rind. While beating well, gradually add the nuts and flour. Knead the dough briefly. **3.** To form the biscuits, use either a piping bag or a biscuit press fitted with a forming tube of the desired shape. **4.** Press the dough onto a baking sheet in rounds, rings, sticks or 's' shapes, making sure they are spaced at least 2.5 cm (1 in) apart. **5.** Bake them for approximately 10 minutes or until they are light brown. Remove the biscuits from the baking sheet and allow to cool. **6.** As a variation, 90 g (3 oz) grated dark chocolate or 2 to 3 tablespoons of cocoa powder may be used in the dough to produce a chocolate biscuit.

Honey and Spice Biscuits (Cookies)
Nürnberger Busserl

Makes 100–120 biscuits

2 cups (1 lb) sugar
4 eggs
3 tablespoons honey
½ teaspoon ground cloves
1 tablespoon cinnamon
90 g (3 oz) glazed lemon peel, chopped
½ cup (3 oz) almonds or hazelnuts, blanched and chopped
4¾ cups (1 lb 3 oz) self-raising flour
½ cup (4 fl oz) half and half mixture of honey and water for glazing

1. Preheat oven to 180°C (350°F/Gas 4). **2.** Cream the sugar and eggs and gradually add the honey, cloves, cinnamon, lemon peel, nuts, and flour. **3.** The dough should be soft but firm enough to form into balls. **4.** With floured hands roll regular-sized small balls. Place them on a floured baking tray and with the palm of your hand flatten them a little. Space them at least 2.5 cm (1 in) apart. **5.** With a pastry brush, brush them with the honey-water mixture. **6.** Bake them in the preheated oven until they are crisp on the outside but still soft inside. Cool them on a wire cake rack.

BRITAIN

The collection of British recipes in this book is in no way complete. I am not even sure if it is typical. But it is the result of a genuine attempt to record the sort of food to be found in Britain today.

In my search I was greatly assisted by Catherine Althouse of the British Tourist Authority who mapped out my journey through England, Wales and Scotland which took me to many restaurants where local dishes are prepared. Yet during my travels I found that regional food was not commercially available to the same degree as in the rest of Europe. There are many reasons for this.

In Britain the most drastic change in the eating habits of the people came with the Industrial Revolution in the first half of the 19th century. When huge segments of the rural population shifted to the towns, regional traditions, developed over the centuries, were suddenly, and in many cases, brutally destroyed. Until then the majority of the population was in one way or another connected with the land.

Suddenly being cut off from the roots of their rural existence and losing the sources of their traditional food supplies, the traditional ways of preparing the ingredients were also lost. What replaced their simple but healthy food was a diet unrelated to anything previously experienced, and barely sufficient for survival.

Of course, this is not the complete picture. The Industrial Revolution did result in the emergence of a prosperous middle class which tried to imitate the customs of established upper classes, which in turn, had adopted many foreign, especially French, traditions.

Eating habits in Britain were further complicated by the availability of foods from the colonies, by wars and the austerity measures they brought, and finally, by the results of the progress in food technology such as preserving and freezing which made food from all over the world available all year. In general terms, the food of Britain today bears little resemblance to the traditions of eating of one or two hundred years ago.

This of course does not mean that regional, traditional cooking has been completely forgotten. It is alive and well and in recent years many cookbooks have been written about it. There is a definite awakening of interest in traditional regional cooking. However, the interest is not yet universal and the prejudice of many years has to be overcome until it again dominates the cooking scene.

Food resources vary from county to county and this difference has been responsible for the development of regional dishes. In Britain the differences are not as strongly pronounced as in other countries. However, nobody would mistake the cooking of England for that of Scotland or Wales.

Today a culinary journey through the counties of England, Scotland and Wales is still a rewarding challenge which yields to a gourmet unexpected pleasures at the table.

Right: A cobblestone lane in Ledbury in the county of Hereford and Worcester.

SOUPS

Watercress Soup

This recipe comes from the Bush Hotel at Farnham in Surrey.

Serves 4

30 g (1 oz) butter
1 small onion, finely chopped
1 small leek, finely chopped
1 bunch watercress, washed
2½ cups (20 fl oz) chicken or veal stock
250 g (8 oz) potatoes, peeled and sliced
pepper
salt
¼ cup (2 fl oz) cream

1. Melt the butter in a saucepan and sauté the onion and leek in it, without allowing them to brown. **2.** Chop the watercress, reserving a few leaves for garnish. **3.** Add the chopped watercress to the onion and leek in the pan and cook for a few minutes. **4.** Pour in the stock and add the potatoes, salt and pepper. **5.** Simmer for 30 minutes. **6.** Pass the soup through a coarse strainer, return it to the pan and add the cream. **7.** Reheat gently, being careful that it doesn't boil. **8.** Pour into warm soup bowls, float the reserved watercress leaves on top and serve.

Cream of Leek Soup

Cawl Cennin a Hufen

From the King's Head Hotel at Monmouth in Wales. The leek is the national emblem of Wales so it is not surprising that it appears in many fine dishes. Cream of Leek Soup, a refined version of leek and potato soup, does justice to this great vegetable.

Serves 8

625 g (1¼ lb) leeks, washed
60 g (2 oz) butter
375 g (12 oz) celery, chopped
7½ cups (1.75 litres) lamb or chicken stock (see p. 328)
30 g (1 oz) parsley, finely chopped
salt and pepper
60 g (2 oz) diced cooked chicken or lamb (optional)
⅔ cup (5 fl oz) cream
sippets

1. Slice the leeks thinly and reserve some of the green slices for garnish. **2.** Melt the butter in a large pan and cook the leeks and celery over gentle heat with the lid on the pan until the leeks are soft but not brown. **3.** Add the stock, bring to the boil and simmer for 1 hour, skimming if necessary. **4.** Purée the soup in a blender, return it to the pan and add the parsley, reserved leek slices and diced meat. Season with salt and pepper. **5.** Add the cream and reheat the soup without allowing it to boil. Serve with sippets.

Meat Broth

Potes Cig

This recipe comes from the Chequers Restaurant in Clwyd, Wales.

Serves 6–8

500 g (1 lb) corned (salt) beef
500 g (1 lb) bacon in one piece
250 g (8 oz) carrots, finely chopped
500 g (1 lb) cabbage, finely chopped
250 g (8 oz) swede, finely chopped
1.5 kg (3 lb) potatoes, peeled and cut in half
pepper and salt

1. Put the beef, bacon, carrots, cabbage and swede into a saucepan with the pepper and salt. Cover it with water and bring to the boil. Cook for 2 hours or until the meat is almost tender. **2.** Add the potatoes and boil for a further 20 minutes. **3.** Remove the meat and vegetables from the pan and serve. **4.** In Wales, the broth is kept until the next day when it is reheated, poured over small pieces of bread and served for breakfast. This dish is called Brwes.

Carrot Soup

Serves 4

375 g (12 oz) carrots, chopped
100 g (3⅓ oz) turnips, chopped
100 g (3⅓ oz) onions, chopped
2 stalks celery, chopped
125 g (4 oz) potatoes, peeled and diced
50 g (1¾ oz) chopped ham
30 g (1 oz) butter
1 teaspoon tomato purée
5 cups (1.25 litres) chicken stock (see p. 328)
3 sprigs fresh herbs, chopped
salt and freshly ground pepper
⅔ cup (5 fl oz) cream
chopped watercress for garnish
fried sippets

1. Sauté the vegetables and ham in the butter.
2. Add the tomato purée, stock, herbs, salt and pepper. **3.** Simmer for 1½ hours. **4.** Cool and rub it through a sieve or purée in a food processor or blender. **5.** Heat the purée, add the cream and serve garnished with watercress and sippets.

Friar's Chicken Soup

Serves 6-8

1 kg (2 lb) veal knuckle, cut into pieces
8 cups (2 litres) water
1.3 kg (2 lb 10 oz) chicken, cut into bite-sized pieces
salt and pepper
5 sprigs parsley, chopped
3 eggs, well beaten

1. Simmer the veal, covered, in the water for 2 hours. Strain and save the stock. The veal may be minced and made into meat croquettes. **2.** Add the chicken pieces to the boiling stock, season and simmer for 20 minutes. **3.** Add two-thirds of the parsley and continue simmering for a further 30 minutes. **4.** When the chicken is tender, stir in the eggs, remove from the heat and serve hot, sprinkled with the remaining parsley.

Pea and Bacon Rib Soup

From the Waterside Restaurant at Romiley, Manchester.

Serves 8

500 g (1 lb) bacon ribs, soaked overnight in water
30 g (1 oz) butter
125 g (4 oz) onions, chopped
125 g (4 oz) carrots, diced
60 g (2 oz) celery, diced
500 g (1 lb) dried split peas
salt and pepper

1. Put the bacon in a large pan and cover with 10 cups (2.5 litres) water. Bring to the boil and simmer for 1 hour. **2.** Melt the butter in a pan and cook the onion, carrots and celery for 8 minutes, making sure you don't allow them to brown. **3.** Add the peas and cook for a further 2–3 minutes, stirring well. **4.** Add this to the stock and ribs, season, bring to the boil and simmer for 2–3 hours. Skim when necessary. **5.** Remove the ribs and put the soup through a blender. Return the soup to the rinsed-out pan, add the ribs and reheat. **6.** Serve with sippets.

FIRST COURSES

Asparagus and Game Mousse

From The George Hotel in Chollerford, Northumberland. The George Hotel, which is situated on the banks of the river North Tyne, serves a wide range of dishes, including some local or regional fare. Spiced beef, pease pudding and crown of lamb are amongst them. Asparagus and Game Mousse is a speciality and in the Apple and Bramble Fool (p. 137), apples and blackberries combine in a tasty mixture.

Serves 4-6

2½ cups (20 fl oz) water
1 tablespoon gelatine, softened in a little cold water
125 g (4 oz) fresh cooked asparagus, chopped, plus extra cooked asparagus tips for garnish
250 g (8 oz) cooked pheasant or guinea fowl, minced
1 cup (8 fl oz) cream
salt
freshly ground black pepper

1. Bring the water to the boil and add the gelatine. Stir until it has dissolved. Add the asparagus and game, stirring well. Set the mixture aside to cool to lukewarm. **2.** Add the cream, salt and pepper and pour the mixture into a mould. Refrigerate until set. **3.** Remove the mousse from the mould and decorate with asparagus tips.

Smoked Mackerel with Gooseberry Sauce

This recipe comes from The Open Arms in Dirleton in East Lothian, Scotland.

Serves 4

4 smoked mackerel fillets
4 lettuce leaves
4 lemon wedges
2 tomatoes, cut into wedges
60 g (2 oz) gooseberries, poached
1¼ cups (10 fl oz) cream, lightly whipped

1. Place the mackerel fillets on the lettuce and garnish with lemon and tomato wedges. **2.** Finely chop the poached gooseberries (or purée them) and mix with the cream to make a gooseberry sauce. Serve with the mackerel.

Potted Duck

From Chequers Inn, Fowlermere, Near Royston.

meat and liver from one duckling
250 g (8 oz) finely minced veal
½ cup (2 oz) dry breadcrumbs
2 tablespoons finely chopped onion
1 tablespoon finely chopped chervil
3 sprigs parsley, finely chopped
salt and freshly ground black pepper
grated rind from half an orange
2 tablespoons brandy or dry sherry
2 eggs, lightly beaten
2–3 slices bacon

1. Preheat oven to 160°C (325°F/Gas 3). **2.** Finely mince the duck meat and liver. **3.** Mix it with the veal, breadcrumbs, onion, chervil, parsley, salt and pepper. **4.** Stir in the orange rind, brandy or sherry and eggs. **5.** Spoon into a greased terrine dish and cover with bacon. **6.** Bake in a baking tin half filled with hot water for 1¾ hours. **7.** Remove from the oven, allow to cool and refrigerate overnight. Serve at room temperature with hot buttered toast.

Right: *A selection of traditional English dishes prepared at the Chequers Inn at Fowlmere. Clockwise from bottom left: Potted Duck (above); Fillet of Pork in Pastry; Prawn Mousse; Chicken in a Lavender Sauce; Chocolate Raisin and Rum Cheesecake.*

Kipper Cheese Puffs

Serves 8

300 g (10 oz) kipper fillets
30 g (1 oz) butter
¼ cup (1 oz) flour
1¼ cups (10 fl oz) hot milk
½ cup (2 oz) grated Lancashire cheese
salt and freshly ground pepper
375 g (12 oz) defrosted puff pastry
1 egg, lightly beaten
lemon wedges for garnish

1. Preheat oven to 220°C (425°F/Gas 7). **2.** Poach the fillets in water for 2–3 minutes, drain, save the water. Skin the fillets, remove all bones and chop the flesh into small pieces. **3.** In a saucepan, melt the butter, add the flour and cook for a few minutes without colouring. **4.** Stir in the milk and if it looks too thick add a little of the poaching liquid. Cook for a few minutes, stirring continuously. **5.** Remove from the heat, stir in the cheese and the kippers, season and let it cool. **6.** Roll out the pastry 25 × 50 cm (10 × 20 inches) and cut it into eight pieces 12.5 cm (5 inches) square. **7.** Place the pastry on a greased baking tray and put a portion of the kipper mixture on each. **8.** Brush the edges with the egg, fold the square into a triangle and seal the edges firmly. **9.** Brush them with egg and bake for approximately 20 minutes or until golden-brown.

Smoked Trout

From The Open Arms in Dirleton, in East Lothian, Scotland.

Serves 4

4 whole smoked trout
4 large lettuce leaves
4 lemon wedges
2 tomatoes, cut into wedges
1¼ cups (10 fl oz) cream, whipped
30 g (1 oz) grated horse-radish
mustard and cress for garnish

1. Skin the trout and place on the lettuce leaves. **2.** Garnish with lemon and tomato wedges. **3.** Mix the cream and horse-radish and serve separately. **4.** Decorate with mustard and cress.

Potted Silloth Shrimps

From The Pheasant Inn on Bassenthwaite Lake in Cumberland. Potting shrimps is an old way of preserving a surplus catch. Those from Morecombe have been well known for their delicate flavour since the 18th century.

Serves 2

125 g (4 oz) brown 'Silloth' shrimps (or small raw prawns)
60 g (2 oz) butter
salt and black pepper
1 tablespoon dry white wine

1. Bring a large pan of salted water to the boil. Drop in the shrimps and boil for 3 minutes. **2.** Plunge the shrimps immediately into cold water, then shell and devein them. **3.** Put the shrimps into a bowl and sprinkle them with the wine. Leave to marinate for 1 hour. **4.** Force the shrimps into small pots and top each one with a layer of butter. Chill until needed. **5.** Serve on a bed of lettuce with tomato, cucumber, watercress, lemon wedges and thin slices of brown bread and butter.

Anglesey Eggs

Wyau Mon

From the King's Head Hotel in Monmouth, Wales.

Serves 4

8 eggs
750 g (1½ lb) potatoes, peeled and cut into quarters
6 leeks, washed
knob of butter

Cheese Sauce:
30 g (1 oz) butter
¼ cup (1 oz) flour
1¼ cups (10 fl oz) milk
90 g (3 oz) Caerphilly cheese, grated

1. Hard-boil the eggs, shell them and leave them in a bowl of cold water. **2.** Boil the potatoes, strain and mash them. **3.** Slice the leeks into thin rings and boil them in salted water for 10 minutes. Drain. **4.** Add the leeks to the mashed potato with the knob of butter and beat well. **5.** To make the sauce, melt the butter in a saucepan, add the flour and stir to make a roux. Add the milk and cook the sauce, whisking constantly with a wire whisk, until it is smooth. Add 75 g of the cheese and cook for a few minutes longer. **6.** Preheat the oven to 200°C (400°F/Gas 6). **7.** Place the potato mixture on the bottom and around the sides of a warmed ovenproof dish. Cut the eggs in half lengthwise and put them, cut side down, in the centre of the dish. **8.** Coat the eggs with the sauce and sprinkle with the remaining grated cheese. **9.** Cook in the oven for 20 minutes or until the top is golden.

VEGETABLES

Bacon Floddies

From the Bush Hotel at Farnham in Surrey. Bacon floddies are a variation of potato floddies which are known in many parts of the country. Grated cheese, chopped herbs, minced or sausage meat, can be added to the batter and it can be served as a light supper dish.

Serves 2–3

1 large potato, peeled and grated
1 small onion, finely chopped
60 g (2 oz) bacon, rinds removed and finely chopped
30 g (1 oz) mushrooms, finely chopped
pinch thyme
salt
pepper
1 egg, beaten
dripping or oil for frying

1. Place the potato, onion, bacon, mushrooms, thyme, salt and pepper in a bowl and mix in the egg. **2.** Heat 1 cm (½ inch) dripping or oil in a frying pan and drop large spoonfuls of the mixture into it. **3.** Fry over low heat, turning once. **4.** Serve hot with mustard pickle.

Northumbrian Leek Pudding

Serves 6

1.75 kg (3½ lb) suet pastry (see p. 331)
1.25 kg (2½ lb) leeks, cleaned and chopped
125 g (4 oz) butter
salt and freshly ground pepper

1. Line a 5 cup (1.25 litre) pudding basin with three-quarters of the suet pastry. **2.** Fill the basin with leeks, dot with butter and season with salt and pepper. **3.** Cover with the rest of the pastry, tie down with foil and place the basin in a saucepan half-filled with water. Cover and steam it for 2 hours. Traditionally, this is served with stews.

Welsh Onion Cake

Serves 6

1 kg (2 lb) potatoes, peeled and sliced
250 g (8 oz) onions, finely chopped
90 g (3 oz) butter, melted
salt and freshly ground pepper

1. Preheat the oven to 190°C (375°F/Gas 5). **2.** Grease an 18 cm (7 inch) soufflé dish and place a layer of potatoes on the bottom and then a layer of onions, dot with butter and sprinkle with salt and pepper. **3.** Repeat the layers, finishing off with potatoes. Brush with butter and bake for 1–1¼ hours. **4.** Turn out and serve hot.

Parsnips, Potatoes and Bacon

Serves 6

500 g (1 lb) parsnips, peeled and diced
500 g (1 lb) potatoes, peeled and thickly sliced
250 g (8 oz) bacon slices, chopped
1¼ cups (10 fl oz) chicken stock (see p. 328)
salt and freshly ground pepper

1. Preheat oven to 180°C (350°F/Gas 4). **2.** Mix parsnips, potatoes and bacon together and place them in a greased ovenproof dish. **3.** Add the stock, salt and pepper. **4.** Cover the dish and bake for 1 hour or until vegetables are tender. Serve with grilled or roast meat.

Potato Cakes

From the Waterside Restaurant in Romiley, Manchester.

Serves 4

250 g (8 oz) cooked, cold potatoes
15 g (½ oz) butter, melted
½ teaspoon salt
½ cup (2 oz) flour or fine oatmeal
½ teaspoon baking powder

1. Mash the potatoes and add butter and salt. **2.** Work in as much flour mixed with baking powder as you need to make a pliable dough. **3.** Roll it out thinly, cut in rounds with a bread and butter plate and then mark into quarters. **4.** Prick with a fork and cook on a hot griddle for 5 minutes each side. **5.** Serve with plenty of butter.

Anglesey Mushrooms

Wyau Yns Mon

From The Chequers in Northophall Village in Clwyd, Wales.

Serves 2

125 g (4 oz) button mushrooms, stems chopped
1¼ cups (10 fl oz) Béchamel sauce (see p. 329)
1 small clove garlic, crushed
1 large potato, peeled, boiled and mashed with butter
2 thick slices bread, toasted

1. Add the mushrooms to the Béchamel sauce and simmer for 5 minutes. **2.** Add the garlic and cook for a further 2 minutes. **3.** Preheat the grill (broiler) to high. **4.** Place each slice of toast on a large heatproof plate and pipe mashed potato around the toast. **5.** Pour the mushroom Béchamel over the toast and put the plates under the hot grill. It is ready to serve when the potato browns.

Devonshire Stew

Serves 8

1 kg (2 lb) mashed potatoes
500 g (1 lb) boiled shredded cabbage
500 g (1 lb) boiled chopped onions
salt and freshly ground black pepper
100 g (3½ oz) butter

1. Combine the potatoes with the cabbage and onions and season with salt and pepper. **2.** In a large frying pan or casserole, melt the butter and fry the mixture until brown. Serve hot.

Pease Pudding

This recipe comes from The George Hotel in Chollerford, Northumberland.
A dish which dates back to the Middle Ages and was originally known as pease porridge. It is really a pea purée which is served with pickled pork or boiled beef.

Serves 4-6

250 g (8 oz) yellow split peas
4 cups (1 litre) stock made from ham or bacon bones
salt
freshly ground black pepper

1. Place the peas in a muslin bag allowing plenty of room for them to swell up. Put the bag into the pan of hot stock and leave them to soak for 3 hours. **2.** Bring the stock (with the bag of peas) to the boil, then simmer for about 45 minutes or until the peas are soft. **3.** Remove the peas from the bag and place them into a bowl. Beat them with a wooden spoon until they are creamy. **4.** Reheat them for a few minutes over low heat and serve immediately with salted meat.

Right: Some of the traditional Welsh dishes served at the Chequers Hotel, Northophall Village, Mold, Clwyd. Clockwise from bottom left: Trout with Bacon (see page 121); Tournados Glantreath (see page 128); Anglesey Mushrooms (see page 118); St Tudno's Pork; Supremes of Chicken Llandrillo; Potes Cig (see page 112). The Chequers is a 19th century Welsh manor house converted into a comfortable country hotel.

FISH

Salmon en Croûte

From The Open Arms in Dirleton in East Lothian, Scotland.

Serves 4-6

1 salmon or a large trout
6 asparagus tips, steamed for 5 minutes
6 slices streaky (fat) bacon
puff pastry
egg wash (1 egg yolk, mixed with a little cold water)
lettuce, tomato, cucumber and lemon to garnish

1. Preheat the oven to 180°C (350°F/Gas 4). **2.** Remove the head and tail of the fish and cut along the backbone until you have two sides of boneless salmon. Skin both sides. **3.** Fill the centre of the salmon with asparagus, put the two sides together and wrap in bacon. **4.** Roll out the puff pastry and wrap the fish in it. Brush with egg wash. **5.** Bake for 30 to 40 minutes or until the pastry is golden-brown and the fish is cooked. Leave it to cool. **6.** Serve it cut into slices with lettuce, tomato, cucumber and wedges of lemon.

Fried Scallops

Serves 4

1 tablespoon olive oil
juice of ½ lemon
salt and freshly ground pepper
3 sprigs parsley, chopped
12–16 scallops
75 g (2½ oz) ham, finely chopped
½ cup (2 oz) dry breadcrumbs
2 tablespoons grated Parmesan cheese
1 small onion, finely chopped
flour
1–2 eggs, lightly beaten
oil for deep frying
lettuce leaves and lemon wedges

1. Combine the oil, lemon juice, salt, pepper and parsley and marinate the scallops in the mixture for 30–45 minutes. **2.** Combine the ham, breadcrumbs, cheese, onions, salt and pepper. **3.** Drain the scallops, dust them with flour, dip them in the egg and coat them with the ham-breadcrumb mixture. **4.** Deep-fry them in the heated oil until golden brown. **5.** Serve on lettuce leaves garnished with lemon wedges.

Sewin (Sea Trout) Baked in butter with Sorrel Sauce

Sewin is a delicious pink firm-fleshed fish, believed by many connoisseurs to be as good as or better than salmon. If it is not available, freshwater trout may be used. This recipe comes from Ty Mawr in Brechfa, Wales. Run by Cliff and Jill Ross, the Ty Mawr is a 16th century house which has been converted into a small comfortable hotel. Its setting in a picturesque, Welsh-speaking village on the banks of the Marlais is very pretty.

Serves 4-6

1 large or 2 smaller trout
1 tablespoon butter, melted
1 large onion, chopped
2 bay leaves, crumbled
salt and pepper
pinch of dried dill
sea salt
1 cup (8 fl oz) dry white wine

Sorrel Sauce:
60 g (2 oz) butter
3 spring onions (scallions), finely chopped
250 g (8 oz) fresh sorrel, chopped
½ cup (2 oz) flour
1¼ cups (10 fl oz) chicken stock (see p. 328)
½ teaspoon sugar
salt and pepper

1. Preheat the oven to 190°C (375°F/Gas 5). **2.** Brush a large sheet of foil with melted butter and place the cleaned trout in the centre. **3.** Stuff the cavity with the onion, bay leaves, salt and pepper. **4.** Rub the skin with sea salt. **5.** Add the wine and loosely wrap the fish in the foil. Place it in a baking dish and bake for 10 minutes per 500 g. **6.** When it is cooked, remove it from the oven but leave it wrapped in foil for a further 20 minutes. **7.** To make the sauce, melt the butter and cook the spring onions and sorrel in it over low heat for 10 minutes. **8.** Stir in the flour and add the stock, sugar and seasoning. Cook for a further 20 minutes. **9.** Put the sauce through a blender or food processor until it is smooth and creamy. **10.** Return it to the pan and reheat it gently. **11.** When the fish has finished cooking, carefully remove the skin and remove the light-brown bits near the head with a knife. **12.** Serve the fish and the sauce separately.

Note: The fish may also be served cold. In this case, cool the sauce and mix it with 1 cup (8 fl oz) of mayonnaise.

Cornish Roast Lobsters

This recipe dates back to 1727. It comes from The Coachmakers Arms in Callington, Cornwall. Cornwall is famous for its harvest of the sea. Some of the best fish in the country comes from the many fishing villages dotted along the rugged coast.

Serves 4

1 small onion, chopped
1 cup (8 fl oz) water
1 cup (8 fl oz) white wine vinegar
bouquet garni, consisting of 1 sprig fresh thyme, 3 sprigs fresh parsley and 1 bay leaf, tied up with string
pepper
salt
2 live lobsters

Sauce:
30 g (1 oz) butter
1 small tin anchovy fillets, drained and chopped
1 cup (8 fl oz) white wine
1 tablespoon lemon juice or white wine vinegar
pinch of grated nutmeg
pinch of ground mace
pepper
¼ cup (½ oz) fresh breadcrumbs

1. Preheat the oven to 180°C (350°F/Gas 4). **2.** Put the onion, water, vinegar, bouquet garni, pepper and salt in a pan and bring it to the boil. Simmer for 5 minutes. **3.** Wash the lobsters and roast them on a spit in the oven or in a baking dish for 45 minutes, basting them frequently with the above mixture. **4.** Meanwhile, make the sauce. Melt the butter in a pan and add the anchovies, mashing them well with a wooden spoon. **5.** Add the wine, lemon juice, nutmeg, mace and pepper and simmer, stirring occasionally, for 5 minutes. **6.** Stir in the breadcrumbs and simmer for a few minutes longer. **7.** Remove the lobsters from the oven, split them, remove their intestines, crack the claws and serve with the hot sauce.

Trout Agincourt

From the King's Head in Monmouth, Wales.

Serves 4

4 trout, cleaned and heads removed
1 tablespoon seasoned flour
1 egg, beaten
2 tablespoons dry breadcrumbs
oil for deep frying

Forcemeat:
30 g (1 oz) butter
1 onion, finely chopped
60 g (2 oz) mushrooms, finely chopped
1 teaspoon dried dill
125 g (4 oz) prawns, peeled, deveined and finely chopped
1 cup (2 oz) fresh white breadcrumbs
salt and pepper
1 egg yolk

1. Coat the trout in the flour, then the egg and breadcrumbs and deep fry in the hot oil for a few minutes only — just until they are golden-brown. Remove them and drain them on kitchen paper. **2.** To make the forcemeat, melt the butter in a frying pan and add the onion, mushrooms and dill. Fry for about 5 minutes, until the onion is soft, but not brown. Add the prawns and cook for a few minutes longer. **3.** Add the breadcrumbs and season with salt and pepper. **4.** Remove the pan from the heat and bind the forcemeat together with the egg yolk. **5.** Spoon some of this mixture into the cavity of each trout. **6.** Preheat the oven to 180°C (350°F/Gas 4). **7.** Lay the trout in an oiled baking dish and bake for 10–15 minutes or until cooked through. **8.** Serve garnished with lemon wedges, parsley and cooked king prawns.

Trout with Bacon

Brithyll yr Afon gyda Chig Moch

This recipe comes from The Chequers in Clwyd, Wales.

Serves 4

4 small trout, split and cleaned
500 g (1 lb) spinach, well washed
½ cup (3 oz) raisins
4 slices bacon
2 tablespoons melted butter

1. Cook the spinach in very little water for 6 to 8 minutes. Drain it well and chop it finely. **2.** Mix the raisins into the spinach and add a knob of butter. **3.** Stuff each trout with a little of this mixture and brush their skins with melted butter. **4.** Grill the trout for 5 minutes each side. **5.** A few minutes before the trout are ready, grill the bacon slices. **6.** Serve the trout and bacon together.

Trout with Lemon Cucumber Butter

From the Cavendish Hotel, Baslow, Bakewell, Derbyshire

Serves 4

4 trout
½ cup (2 oz) seasoned flour
juice of 1 lemon
2 sprigs thyme, finely chopped
125 g (4 oz) butter, melted

Lemon Cucumber Butter:
125 g (4 oz) softened butter
100 g (3⅓ oz) cucumber, finely chopped, peeled and seeded
juice of 1 lemon
grated rind of 1 lemon
salt and freshly ground pepper

1. Preheat oven to 200°C (400°F/Gas 6). **2.** Roll the trout in seasoned flour and sprinkle the inside with some of the lemon juice and the thyme. **3.** Place the trout in a baking dish and pour the rest of the lemon juice and the melted butter over it. **4.** Place it in the preheated oven and bake for 8–10 minutes, turning it once. **5.** To serve, place it on a serving dish with the lemon cucumber butter. **6.** To make the lemon cucumber butter, mix the ingredients together, roll it in aluminium foil, refrigerate until firm and cut into slices to serve.

Mussel and Onion Stew

From The Open Arms in Dirleton in East Lothian, Scotland. This is an ancient Scottish dish dating back to the Middle Ages.

Serves 4

90 g (3 oz) butter
1 large onion, sliced
½ cup (2 oz) flour
2½ cups (20 fl oz) fish stock (see p. 328)
salt and black pepper
750 g (1½ lb) mussels, shelled
1 cup (8 fl oz) white wine
3 tablespoons fresh parsley, finely chopped
pinch of dried mixed herbs

1. Melt the butter in a pan and add the onion. Cook over gentle heat until the onion is soft. **2.** Add the flour, stir well, then add the fish stock. Stir until smooth and then simmer for a few minutes. **3.** Add the mussels and white wine, bring to the boil then simmer for about 10 minutes. **4.** Add the cream, parsley and herbs and serve in an earthenware or porcelain terrine.

Dover Sole in Cider

From the Bush Hotel in Farnham, Surrey. Dover sole has the reputation of being the finest of all flat-type fish. It is delicate and has a flavour which distinguishes it from other similar looking fish such as lemon sole or flounder.

Serves 4

4 spring onions (scallions), finely chopped
8 fillets of Dover sole (or John Dory) weighing about 90 g (3 oz) each
pinch of dried rosemary
salt
pepper
2 cups (16 fl oz) cider
¼ cup (1 oz) grated Cheddar cheese
¼ cup (2 fl oz) cream
1 egg
1 tablespoon finely chopped parsley
mashed potatoes for serving

1. Preheat the oven to 180°C (350°F/Gas 4). **2.** Sprinkle half the chopped spring onions on the bottom of an ovenproof casserole. **3.** Tuck under the two ends of the fish fillets and lay them on the onions. **4.** Sprinkle with the remaining onions, the rosemary, salt and pepper and pour over the cider. **5.** Bake for 15 minutes. **6.** Remove the fish with a slotted spoon, place them on a serving dish and sprinkle them with cheese. **7.** Reduce the cooking liquid to about half its original volume by fast boiling. **8.** Beat the cream and egg together, add a little of the hot cooking liquid to it, then return it to the pan, stirring constantly and making sure it doesn't boil. **9.** When it has thickened slightly, pour it over the fish. **10.** Glaze under a hot grill, sprinkle with parsley and serve surrounded by piped mashed potato.

Essex Whitebait in Batter

Serves 4

1 cup (4 oz) flour
pinch of salt
1 egg, lightly beaten
⅔ cup (5 fl oz) milk
500 g (1 lb) whitebait
flour
salt, freshly ground pepper
oil for deep frying
lemon wedges and parsley sprigs for garnish

1. Make a batter by combining the flour, salt, egg and milk, and leave it to rest for 30 minutes before using it. **2.** Dust the whitebait with seasoned flour. **3.** Dip the fish in the batter and deep fry in hot oil until golden-brown. **4.** Serve hot garnished with lemon wedges and parsley.

Right: *Fresh trout.*

POULTRY & GAME BIRDS

Hindle Wakes Chicken

From the Waterside Restaurant in Romiley, Manchester. This dish was brought to England by Flemish spinners in the 12th century. It was served during the annual Wakes Week near Bolton where the spinners settled.

Serves 4-6

1 large onion, finely chopped
1 cup (2 oz) soft breadcrumbs
2 cups (12 oz) stoned prunes, chopped
1 tablespoon grated suet
1 tablespoon mixed herbs
pinch mace and cinnamon
juice of 1 lemon
1 large boiling fowl
½ cup (4 fl oz) white wine vinegar
2 tablespoons brown sugar

Sauce:
30 g (1 oz) butter
¼ cup (1 oz) flour
¼ cup (2 fl oz) milk
juice and rind of 1 lemon
⅔ cup (5 fl oz) cream
⅔ cup (5 fl oz) stock from chicken

Garnish:
12 prunes, stoned, halved and soaked in water
1 lemon, thinly sliced
grated lemon rind
parsley

1. Mix together the onion, breadcrumbs, prunes, suet, herbs, spices, and lemon juice and stuff the bird with it. **2.** Put it into a large pot and cover with water into which you have mixed the vinegar and brown sugar. **3.** Cover the pan and simmer for 2½–3 hours or until the fowl is tender. **4.** Leave the bird to cool in the stock. **5.** Drain it, skin it and place it on a serving dish. **6.** To make the sauce, melt the butter, stir in the flour and cook, stirring constantly, for 2 minutes then add the milk. **7.** Stir well, add the degreased chicken stock and simmer for 5 minutes. Season, add the lemon juice and rind and the cream. **8.** Simmer for 5 minutes, then leave to cool. **9.** Coat the chicken with the sauce, sprinkle with grated lemon rind and decorate with prunes, lemon slices and parsley. Serve cold.

Devonshire Chicken Dumplings

Serves 4-6

250 g (8 oz) cooked chicken livers
2 chicken livers, fried
2 slices of bacon, fried
2 cups (8 oz) dried breadcrumbs
2 eggs, lightly beaten
salt and pepper
2 sprigs parsley, finely chopped
flour
3-4 cups (24 fl oz–1 litre) chicken stock
(see p. 328)
2 egg yolks, lightly beaten
⅔ cup (5 fl oz) cream
½ cup (2 oz) grated cheese
finely chopped parsley for garnish

1. Mince the chicken meat, livers and bacon together and mix it with breadcrumbs, eggs, salt, pepper and parsley. **2.** Roll the mixture into balls the size of walnuts and sprinkle them with flour. **3.** Over low heat simmer them in chicken stock for 12–15 minutes. **4.** Remove them to an ovenproof dish and keep them warm. **5.** To make the sauce, combine the egg yolks, cream and 1¼ cups (10 fl oz) of the cooking liquid. Season to taste and simmer over low heat without boiling. **6.** Pour the sauce over the dumplings, sprinkle with cheese and brown under a hot grill. Serve hot, sprinkled with parsley.

Chicken Casserole with Potatoes and Onions

Serves 4

1.3 kg (2 lb 10 oz) chicken, cut into 4 portions
flour
30 g (1 oz) butter
2 onions, sliced
500 g (1 lb) peeled, sliced potatoes
salt and freshly ground pepper
2 cups (16 fl oz) hot chicken stock (see p. 328)
or water
¼ cup (1 oz) grated cheese
chopped parsley

1. Preheat oven to 180°C (350°F/Gas 4). **2.** Dust the chicken pieces with flour and fry in butter until light brown. **3.** Place a layer of onions and potatoes in a casserole and sprinkle them lightly with salt and pepper. **4.** Put the chicken pieces on top and cover them with the remaining potatoes and onions, season. **5.** Add the hot stock, or water, cover with a lid and cook in the oven for 1 hour. **6.** Turn the heat up to 200°C (400°F/Gas 6), sprinkle the top with cheese and return to the oven, uncovered, for 30 minutes or until the top is brown. Serve hot sprinkled with parsley.

Roast Borrowdale Duckling with Bilberry and Apple Sauce

This recipe comes from The Pheasant Inn on Bassenthwaite Lake in Cumberland. The building which houses The Pheasant Inn dates back to the 16th century and it is what a country pub ought to look like: whitewashed walls with black trim. Inside there are low cosy rooms with beamed ceilings and a particularly pleasant old worldly, tobacco smoke-stained bar.

Serves 4

2–2.5 kg (4–5 lb) oven-ready duckling
¼ cup (3 oz) honey
salt and black pepper

Sauce:
3 cooking apples, peeled, cored and diced
30 g (1 oz) butter
¾ cup (6 oz) sugar
250 g (8 oz) bilberries (or substitute cranberries)
juice of 1 lemon
salt and black pepper
1 tablespoon soy sauce
1 teaspoon Worcestershire sauce
⅓ cup (2½ fl oz) water
3 tablespoons cornflour (cornstarch)

1. Preheat the oven to 190°C (375°F/Gas 5). **2.** Truss the duckling and place it on a rack in a roasting dish. **3.** Season it with salt and pepper and spread the breast liberally with honey. **4.** Bake for 1 hour or until cooked.

Sauce: 1. Place the apples, butter and sugar in a pan and cook until very soft. **2.** Add the bilberries and lemon juice and continue cooking for 5 minutes. **3.** Add pepper and salt, soy sauce, Worcestershire sauce and water and bring to the boil. **4.** Mix the cornflour to a paste with a little water and add it to the sauce mixture. Stir until sauce is thick, then serve with the duck.

Welsh Salted Duck

Mwyaden Hallt Gymreig

From the King's Head Hotel in Monmouth, Wales. This dish is a typical Welsh speciality. The process of salting the duck for several days gives the bird a particular flavour much appreciated in Wales.

Serves 3–4

1 duck, weighing 1.5–2 kg (3–4 lb)
1 onion
1 teaspoon finely chopped fresh sage
1 teaspoon sea salt

Sauce:
2½ cups (20 fl oz) Béchamel sauce (see p. 329)
1 onion, finely chopped
salt and pepper

1. Preheat the oven to 190°C (375°F/Gas 5). **2.** Stuff the duck with the whole onion. Sprinkle sage and salt all over the skin, pressing down well. **3.** Roast the duck for about 1½ hours, depending upon its size (allow 20 minutes per 500 g plus an extra 20 minutes). **4.** Remove the onion from the duck and purée it in a blender. Add it to the hot Béchamel sauce along with the chopped raw onion, salt and pepper. Cook for 5 minutes. **5.** Cut the duck into portions and serve decorated with watercress. Serve the sauce separately.

Duckling in Honey Sauce

Serves 4

100 g (3½ oz) butter
2 small ducklings (about 1.2 kg/2 lb 6 oz) each
½ cup (4 fl oz) dry white wine
salt, freshly ground black pepper
2 onions, finely chopped
¼ cup (2 fl oz) honey
2 sprigs thyme, finely chopped
juice of ½ lemon
1¼ cups (10 fl oz) cream
3 sprigs parsley, finely chopped

1. Preheat oven to 180°C (350°F/Gas 4). **2.** Melt half of the butter in an ovenproof dish and sauté the duckling until light brown all round. **3.** Add the wine, salt and pepper, tightly cover with foil and place it in the preheated oven for 1½ hours or until cooked. **4.** In a large frying pan, melt the rest of the butter and slowly sauté the onions until light golden-brown. **5.** Skim the surplus fat from the duck cooking liquid and add the liquid to the onions. **6.** Mix in the honey, thyme, lemon juice and cream, season to taste and cook for 5 minutes. **7.** Split each duckling lengthwise into two. **8.** Place the duckling halves on a preheated serving platter and strain the hot sauce over them. Serve sprinkled with parsley.

Pheasant in Cider

Serves 4

60 g (2 oz) butter
2 small pheasants
juice of 1 lemon
2 sprigs rosemary, finely chopped
2 sprigs thyme, finely chopped
salt and freshly ground pepper
3 cooking apples, peeled, cored and sliced
½ teaspoon cinnamon
1 cup (8 fl oz) cider
¼ cup (2 fl oz) cream
finely chopped parsley for garnish

1. Preheat oven to 180°C (350°F/Gas 4). **2.** In a casserole melt half of the butter and brown the pheasants all round. **3.** Remove the pheasants from the casserole and sprinkle the insides with lemon juice, rosemary, thyme, salt and pepper. **4.** Melt the rest of the butter and lightly sauté the apples. **5.** Return the pheasants to the casserole and pour a mixture of cinnamon, cider and cream over them. **6.** Cover the casserole and put it in the preheated oven for 50–60 minutes or until the pheasants are cooked. **7.** Season to taste, split the pheasants into two, lengthwise, and place them on a heated serving platter. Arrange the apples round them, pour the sauce over the birds and serve sprinkled with parsley.

Guinea Fowl with Tudor Sauce

From The Bell Inn, Long Hanborough, Oxfordshire.

Serves 6

3 guinea fowl
45 g (1½ oz) butter
2 large onions, finely chopped
125 g (4 oz) mushrooms, finely chopped
2 tablespoons flour
1¼ cups (10 fl oz) dry red wine
salt and freshly ground pepper

1. Preheat oven to 200°C (400°F/Gas 6). **2.** Place the guinea fowl and one-third of the butter in the preheated oven and cook for 30 minutes, basting occasionally with the butter. Reduce the heat to 150°C (300°F/Gas 2) and cook until tender. **3.** Melt the remaining butter and sauté the onions until soft, add the mushrooms and cook for 5 minutes. **4.** Add the flour, cook for 3–4 minutes, add the wine and stir well. Season and cook the sauce for 5–8 minutes. **5.** Rub the sauce through a sieve. **6.** Split the birds into two, lengthwise, and serve with the sauce poured over.

Stuffed Boiled Turkey with Celery Sauce

Serves 6

1 small turkey (about 3 kg/6 lb)
250 g (8 oz) minced veal and pork
100 g (3⅓ oz) dried apricots, soaked overnight and finely chopped
125 g (4 oz) ham, finely chopped
2 cups (4 oz) fresh breadcrumbs
4 sprigs parsley, chopped
juice of 1 lemon
salt and freshly ground pepper
1 egg, lightly beaten
4 sprigs of fresh herbs, bound together
1 onion, studded with 6 cloves
4 stalks celery, cut into 2 cm (1 inch) lengths
2 carrots, chopped
6 peppercorns
2 bay leaves
30 g (1 oz) butter
¼ cup (1 oz) flour

1. To make the stuffing, mix together well the minced meat, apricots, ham, breadcrumbs, parsley, lemon juice, salt, pepper and egg. **2.** Stuff the turkey and secure the opening. **3.** Place the turkey in a large saucepan, add the herbs, onion, celery, carrots, peppercorns, bay leaves and salt. **4.** Cover with water, bring slowly to the boil and skim if necessary. **5.** Cover and simmer over low heat for approximately 1½ hours or until the turkey is tender. **6.** Remove the turkey from the liquid and keep it warm. **7.** To make the sauce, strain and save the cooking liquid. Take out the celery and rub it through a sieve, reserve the purée. **8.** Melt the butter, add the flour and without browning, cook for 2 minutes, add 2½ cups (20 fl oz) of the hot cooking liquid and mix to a smooth sauce. **9.** Add the celery purée, season to taste and cook for 3–4 minutes. **10.** Carve the turkey and arrange the meat and stuffing on a preheated serving plate. Garnish with sprigs of parsley. **11.** Rub the sauce through a sieve and serve it separately in a sauce-boat.

Right: *From the kitchen at the Bell Inn, Long Hanborough, Oxfordshire. Clockwise from bottom left: Love Apple Cocktail; Huntsman's Game Pies; Guinea Fowl with Tudor Sauce (see page 126); Venison, Beefsteak and Mushroom Casserole (see page 129); Brandy Pralines; Vegetables for Guinea Pie.*

MEAT

Roast Beef

As prepared by the chef at the Black Bull Inn, Moulton, Richmond, Yorkshire. The timing and the temperatures are rather unusual but since I have partaken of the dinner at which it was served, I can vouch for its excellence. As much higher temperatures are required for the Yorkshire Pudding, it has to be cooked separately.

9 kg (18 lb) rib roast at room temperature

1. Preheat the oven to 150°C (300°F/Gas 2). **2.** Place the roast on top of a rack, fat side up. **3.** Roast it for 4 hours, then reduce the heat to 70°C (160°F) and cook it for 1 hour more. **4.** Remove the roast from the oven and let it stand for 15 minutes before carving. **5.** Serve with its cooking juices, Yorkshire Pudding and horse-radish.

Note: If cooking smaller quantities, allow approximately 375 g (12 oz) gross weight of meat and bones per person. Cook in a 240°C (475°F/Gas 9) oven for the first 30 minutes, then reduce temperature to 180°C (350°F/Gas 4) and roast for a further hour. Use a meat thermometer 60°C (140°F) for rare, 60°-70°C (149°-150°F) for medium and 75°C (167°F) for well done.

Yorkshire Pudding

500 g (1 lb) flour
pinch of salt and pepper
4 eggs
2½ cups (20 fl oz) milk
1¼ cups (10 fl oz) water
dripping

1. Preheat oven to 230°C (450°F/Gas 8). **2.** Mix the flour, salt and pepper together. **3.** Make a well in the middle, add the eggs and gradually the milk and water to make a batter. **4.** Allow the batter to stand for an hour before use. **5.** Heat the dripping in a mould until very hot, pour in the batter. **6.** Cook in the preheated oven until it has risen then lower the temperature to 180°C (350°F/Gas 4) and cook for 40-45 minutes.

Glantraeth Tournedos

From The Chequers in Mold, Clwyd, Wales.

Serves 4

4–250 g (8 oz) fillet steaks
250 g (8 oz) country-style pâté
seasoned flour
1 egg, beaten
1 cup (5 oz) rolled oats
½ cup (4 fl oz) vegetable oil
¼ cup (2 fl oz) dry sherry
½ cup (4 fl oz) cream
salt and pepper

1. Preheat the oven to 180°C (350°F/Gas 4). **2.** Make an incision along one side of each steak right through to the centre. **3.** Fill this cavity with the pâté. **4.** Roll the steaks in flour, then egg then rolled oats. **5.** Heat the oil in a frying pan and fry the steaks on both sides until well browned. **6.** Transfer the steaks to a baking dish and bake for 8-10 minutes. **7.** Add the sherry to the frying pan and with a wooden spoon scrape up all the brown bits clinging to the pan. Add the cream and heat gently. **8.** Pour the sauce over the steaks and serve.

Spiced Beef

From the George Hotel, Chollerford, Northumberland.

Serves 6-8

1 teaspoon salt
1 teaspoon sugar
1 teaspoon allspice
10 peppercorns
10 cloves
2 kg (4 lb) brisket or leg of beef
250 g (8 oz) fat or lard
2½ cups (20 fl oz) water

1. Mix together the salt, sugar, allspice, peppercorns and cloves and place them on a large dish. **2.** Roll the meat in them, cover with foil and refrigerate for three days, turning it in the spices every day. **3.** On the fourth day, wash the meat, dry it well and tie it into a roll. **4.** Heat the fat in a pan until it is smoking and add the meat. Seal it on all sides then add the water and simmer for 3-4 hours, or until it is tender. **5.** Remove the meat from the pan and place it in a mould. Cover with a heavily weighted plate and leave to cool. **6.** Serve with salad.

English Oxtail with Dumplings

From the Cavendish Hotel, Baslow, Bakewell, Derbyshire. The Cavendish Hotel has a very tasteful interior and could certainly be a home away from home for many of its guests. From the outside it looks like an opulent manor house and commands a view over the gentle, undulating Derbyshire landscape.

Serves 8

4 oxtails cut into pieces
seasoned flour
30 g (1 oz) dry English mustard
125 g (4 oz) onions, chopped
125 g (4 oz) mushrooms, chopped
2 bay leaves
125 g (4 oz) carrots
salt, freshly ground pepper
1¼ cups (10 fl oz) dry red wine

Brown Sauce:
4 onions, chopped
90 g (3 oz) dripping
5 tablespoons flour
5 cups (1.25 litres) beef stock (see p. 328) or water
3 tablespoons Worcestershire sauce
3 tablespoons vinegar

Dumplings:
125 g (4 oz) suet
500 g (1 lb) flour
1 tablespoon baking powder
salt and pepper
water
chopped parsley for garnish

1. Soak the oxtail in cold water for 24 hours. **2.** Dry and roll in a mixture of seasoned flour and mustard. **3.** Place it in a dry stewpan and fry. The oxtail will render its own fat. **4.** Add the onions, mushrooms, bay leaves, carrots, salt and pepper and sauté lightly. **5.** Add the wine and brown sauce. **6.** Cover the pan, cook the oxtail for 2½ hours or until the meat is tender and falls off the bones. **7.** Garnish with parsley and serve with dumplings, broad beans and boiled new potatoes.

Brown Sauce: Sauté the onions in the dripping until they are browned. Drain off fat. Add the flour and cook until it browns. Add the stock or water and stir until it boils. Add the Worcestershire sauce and vinegar and simmer for 10 minutes. Strain.

Dumplings: Mix together the suet, flour, baking powder, salt and pepper, add enough water to make a firm soft dough. Roll into 16 small balls and simmer in a pan of salted water for about 30 minutes.

Venison, Beefsteak and Mushroom Casserole

From the Bell Inn, Long Hanborough, Oxfordshire.

Serves 6

750 g (1½ lb) venison, cut into 1.25 cm (½ inch) dice
750 g (1½ lb) beef, cut into 1.25 cm (½ inch) dice
60 g (2 oz) lard
2 large onions, chopped
2 tablespoons flour
1¼ cups (10 fl oz) redcurrant wine or any sweet red wine
250 g (8 oz) mushrooms, sliced
salt and freshly ground pepper

1. Preheat the oven to 150°C (300°F/Gas 2). **2.** Sauté the venison and beef in the lard until brown. Remove from the pan. **3.** Add the onions to the remaining fat and sauté until soft. **4.** Add the flour and cook for 2–3 minutes. **5.** Add the wine and stir until smooth. Cook for 2–3 minutes. **6.** Transfer the meat, onions and sauce to a casserole, add the mushrooms and season to taste. **7.** Cover the casserole and cook in the oven for 2½–3 hours or until the meat is tender.

Cider Baked Pork Chops

From The Anglers' Rest, Fingle Bridge, Exeter.

Serves 5

250 g (8 oz) cooking apples, peeled, cored and sliced
1 large onion, sliced
125 g (4 oz) mushrooms, sliced
salt
pepper
5 pork chops
1¼ cups (10 fl oz) cider
1 cup (4 oz) grated Cheddar cheese
½ cup (2 oz) browned breadcrumbs
watercress for garnishing

1. Preheat the oven to 200°C (400°F/Gas 6). **2.** Grease a shallow baking dish. **3.** Place the apples, onion and mushrooms on the bottom of the dish and sprinkle with salt and pepper. **4.** Lay the pork chops on top and pour over the cider. **5.** Mix together the cheese and breadcrumbs and sprinkle it over the chops. **6.** Bake, uncovered, for 1¼–1½ hours or until the chops are cooked through. **7.** Serve, garnished with watercress.

St Tudno's Pork

From The Chequers in Mold, Clwyd, Wales.

Serves 4

1½ cups (12 fl oz) Béchamel sauce (see p. 329)
2 large tomatoes, peeled and cut into quarters
1 cup (8 fl oz) fish stock (see p. 328)
125 g (4 oz) small cooked prawns
4 pork chops
pepper and salt

1. Heat the Béchamel sauce and add the quartered tomatoes. Cook for 10 minutes, mashing the tomatoes well. **2.** Add the fish stock and cook for a further 10 minutes. Strain. **3.** Put the sauce back into the washed-out pan and add the prawns. Reheat just until the prawns are hot. **4.** Grill the pork chops and when they are cooked pour the prawn sauce over them and serve.

Toad-in-the-Hole

A homely dish, using meat leftovers. Today the Yorkshire Pudding batter is poured over slices of sausage but originally any leftover meat was used. This recipe, from the Cavendish Hotel, in Baslow, Derbyshire, is a rather more sophisticated version.

Makes four 12.5 cm (5 inch) puddings

500 g (1 lb) rump steak, cubed
125 g (4 oz) kidney, chopped
1 onion, chopped
60 g (2 oz) mushrooms, chopped
60 g (2 oz) butter
3 tablespoons plain flour
⅔ cup (5 fl oz) dry red wine
salt and freshly ground pepper

Yorkshire Pudding Batter:
1½ cups (6 oz) flour
3 eggs
1¼ cups (10 fl oz) milk
dripping

1. To make the filling, fry the meat, kidney, onion and mushrooms in the butter until golden-brown. **2.** Sprinkle with flour, add the wine and, if necessary, some water to make a sauce. Season to taste. **3.** Simmer over low heat for 30–40 minutes or until the liquid has reduced by half. **4.** To make Yorkshire puddings, beat the flour, eggs and some of the milk to make a paste, season and add the rest of the milk. **5.** Rest the batter for 2 hours. **6.** Preheat the oven to 200°C (400°F/Gas 6). **7.** Preheat the pudding dishes, add some dripping, divide the batter into four and pour it into the dishes. **8.** Place them into the preheated oven and bake for approximately 35–45 minutes. The puddings will rise at the sides leaving a well in the centre. **9.** To serve, take the puddings out of the dishes and fill them with the meat mixture.

Crown of Lamb

From the George Hotel, Chollerford, Northumberland.

Serves 6

1 crown of lamb of 12 ribs
1 cup (8 fl oz) port
60 g (2 oz) tomato purée
1 cup (4 fl oz) flour
2½ cups (20 fl oz) chicken stock (see p. 328)
pepper and salt

1. Preheat the oven to 180°C (350°F/Gas 4). **2.** Trim the lamb if the butcher hasn't already done so and cover the bones with foil. **3.** Roast for 45 minutes, then remove it from the oven and keep it warm while you make the gravy. **4.** Skim the fat from the pan juices and stir in the flour. **5.** Put the roasting tin over a high heat and stir well until the flour has browned. Add the tomato purée, port, stock, pepper and salt, bring to the boil, stirring constantly, and simmer for 3–4 minutes until the gravy is smooth. **6.** Place cutlet frills on the lamb bones and serve it with vegetables, redcurrant jelly and the gravy.

Devon Lamb Stew

Serves 4

8 lamb chops trimmed of all fat
30 g (1 oz) butter
400 g (12½ oz) small potatoes, peeled
10 small pickling-type onions
16 button mushrooms
½ cup (4 fl oz) hard cider (alcoholic)
1 cup (8 fl oz) beef stock (see p. 328)
½ cup (4 fl oz) cream
salt and freshly ground pepper
2 bay leaves
2 sprigs thyme, chopped
4 sprigs parsley, finely chopped

1. In a casserole, brown the chops in the butter. **2.** Remove the meat and lightly brown the potatoes, onions and mushrooms. **3.** Drain off excess fat. **4.** Add the cider, stock, cream, salt, pepper, bay leaves, thyme and half the parsley and mix thoroughly. **5.** Return the meat to the dish, cover and simmer over low heat for 1 hour or until the meat is tender. Serve garnished with the rest of the parsley.

Right: *Charles Somerville, the chef at the Black Bull in Moulton, Richmond, Yorkshire, proudly displaying his renowned Roast Beef with Yorkshire Pudding (see page 128).*

Thirlmere Forest Casserole of Venison

This recipe comes from Yan Tyan Tethera in Keswick, Cumbria. These are the words still used by genuine Cumbrian shepherds to count sheep. It is an ancient local language which is similar to Welsh, Cornish and the language of Brittany.

Serves 4–6

Marinade:
1 onion, chopped
1 carrot, chopped
½ stick celery, chopped
6 peppercorns
4 juniper berries, crushed
2 tablespoons olive oil
red wine

Casserole:
1.25 kg (2½ lb) venison
155 g (5 oz) streaky (fat) bacon, cut into strips
1 tablespoon olive oil
250 g (8 oz) onions, chopped
250 g (8 oz) carrots, chopped
250 g (8 oz) celery, chopped
1 cup (4 oz) flour
salt
1–2 tablespoons redcurrant jelly

1. Place all the marinade ingredients except the wine in a large bowl, place the piece of venison on top and pour over enough red wine to cover the meat. Leave to marinate 24 hours, turning occasionally. **2.** Remove the venison from the marinade, dry it well with paper towels and cut it into 2.5 cm (1 inch) cubes. **3.** Heat the oil in a frying pan and add the bacon and venison. Fry on all sides to seal the meat. **4.** Add the vegetables, then the flour, stirring well. **5.** Add sufficient strained marinade to almost cover the meat and vegetables. **6.** Simmer the liquid, stirring constantly, until it has thickened. Cover the pan and cook very slowly for 2–4 hours depending upon the age of the meat. Test after 2 hours — the meat should not be chewy, but it must not fall apart either. **7.** Add the redcurrant jelly to taste. **8.** Traditionally, this is served with jacket potatoes and red cabbage.

Baked Gammon with Cumberland Sauce

From the Parkend Restaurant in Wigton, Cumbria. Cumberland Sauce derives its name from Ernest, Duke of Cumberland. It is most often served with game, ham and poultry.

Serves 8

piece of corner or middle gammon weighing 2.5 kg (5 lb), soaked overnight in cold water
1¼ cups (10 fl oz) cider
cloves

Glaze:
4 tablespoons dark brown sugar
1 teaspoon dry mustard
pinch of mace
grated rind and juice of 1 orange

Cumberland Sauce:
juice and rind of 2 oranges or 1 orange and 1 lemon
4 tablespoons redcurrant jelly
1 teaspoon dry mustard
½ cup (4 fl oz) port or red wine
salt and black pepper
pinch ground ginger

1. Drain the gammon and put it into a large pot. Cover with fresh cold water, bring to the boil and simmer for 1 hour. Preheat the oven to 180°C (350°F/Gas 4). **2.** Remove the gammon from the pan, wipe it dry, wrap it loosely in foil, put it in a baking tin and bake for 45 minutes. **3.** Remove the gammon from the oven and carefully lift off the skin. (To do this, lift the corner of the skin with a knife and pull the skin off with your fingers. If the joint is cooked, it should come away easily.) **4.** Score the fat in a diamond pattern with a sharp knife. **5.** Mix together all the glaze ingredients. **6.** Spread this mixture over the fat, stud with cloves, pour the cider around it and return it to the oven for a further 20 minutes, basting occasionally with the cider, until the glaze is crisp and golden. **7.** Serve hot or cold, garnish with watercress and fruit in season, e.g. slices of orange or pineapple or poached apricots and Cumberland Sauce.

Cumberland Sauce: 1. Cut the fruit rind into fine matchsticks. Blanch for 5 minutes in boiling water then drain. **2.** Heat the jelly and mustard together over low heat, stirring until smooth. **3.** Add the fruit juice, wine, pepper, salt and ginger. **4.** Stir in the peel and simmer for about 5 minutes, then pour into a sauce-boat or glass bowl and serve cold.

PIES

Lancashire Steak Pie

This recipe comes from the Waterside Restaurant in Romiley, Manchester.

Serves 4

1 tablespoon vegetable oil
1 large onion, finely chopped
1 small stick celery, finely chopped
250 g (8 oz) minced beef
salt and pepper
1 tablespoon Worcestershire sauce
500 g (1 lb) short crust pastry (see p. 331)
6 slices black pudding

1. Heat the oil in a pan and sauté the onion and celery for about 5 minutes or until the onion is transparent. **2.** Add the minced beef, salt, pepper and Worcestershire sauce and cook until the meat is well browned. **3.** Preheat the oven to 180°C (350°F/Gas 4). **4.** Roll out the pastry and, using two-thirds of it, line a shallow round pie dish. **5.** Spoon in the meat mixture and arrange the black pudding slices on top. **6.** Roll out the remaining pastry and cover the pie with it, crimping the edges together. **7.** Bake for 30–35 minutes or until the pastry is golden.

Our Game Pie

This is a speciality of Invereshie House, Kincraig, Inverness-shire, Scotland.

Serves 6–8

1 kg (2 lb) stewing venison, diced
125 g (4 oz) bacon, finely chopped
2 onions, chopped
2 carrots, chopped
4 pigeons or 6 quail
1–2 cups (8–16 fl oz) dry red wine
3 sprigs parsley, chopped
2–3 sprigs of several fresh herbs, chopped
1 clove garlic, crushed
salt and freshly ground pepper
puff pastry
egg wash (1 egg yolk mixed with a little cold water)

1. Preheat oven to 180°C (350°F/Gas 4). **2.** Place all ingredients except puff pastry and egg wash in a casserole, cover and cook in the preheated oven for about 1½ hours. **3.** When cool take the meat off the bones and chop it. **4.** Increase the temperature of the oven to 220°C (425°F/Gas 7). **5.** Place all the ingredients in a pie dish, cover with the rolled out puff pastry, decorate the top with pastry leaves and roses, brush it with egg wash and bake in the oven until golden-brown.

Cornish Pasties

From The Coachmakers Arms in Callington, Cornwall.

Makes 2 large pasties

Pastry:
2 cups (8 oz) flour
pinch of salt
90 g (3 oz) dripping or lard
cold water

Filling:
250 g (8 oz) stewing steak, chopped into small dice
2 large potatoes, peeled and diced
1 large onion, finely chopped
1 medium turnip, peeled and diced
salt and pepper

1. To make the pastry, sift the flour and salt into a bowl, rub in the dripping with your fingers and add enough cold water to make a stiff dough. **2.** Preheat the oven to 220°C (425°F/Gas 7). **3.** Mix the chopped vegetables together and sprinkle with salt and pepper. **4.** Roll the pastry out into 2 large circles. **5.** Place half the vegetables on one half of each circle and put the meat on top. **6.** Dampen the edges of the pastry and fold them over, pressing the edges together well. **7.** Put the pasties on a baking sheet and bake for 20 minutes, then reduce the oven temperature to 180°C (350°F/Gas 4) and bake for a further hour.

Squab Pie

In Cornwall and Devon in the 18th century, squab took on the meaning of mutton or lamb and squab pie is made in these counties in this way, without squab or pigeon. This recipe comes from The Coachmakers Arms in Callington, Cornwall.

Serves 4–6

500 g (1 lb) stewing lamb or mutton, cut into cubes
500 g (1 lb) apples, peeled, cored and sliced
¾ cup (4 oz) currants or sultanas
500 g (1 lb) onions, finely chopped
1 tablespoon brown sugar
salt
pepper
water
125 g (4 oz) short crust pastry (see p. 331)
egg wash (1 egg yolk, mixed with a little cold water)

1. Preheat oven to 220° (425°F/Gas 7). **2.** Put layers of the lamb, apples, currants, and onions into a pie dish, sprinkle with the sugar, salt and pepper and pour in just enough cold water to moisten it. **3.** Roll out the dough and cover the pie dish with it. Brush with egg wash. **4.** Bake for 15 minutes then lower the oven temperature to 180°C (350°F/Gas 4) and bake for a further 1¾ hours. **5.** Serve hot.

Stargazy Pie

From The Coachmakers Arms in Callington, Cornwall. It is said that the best pilchards have always come off the Cornish fishing boats and for centuries the pilchard industry has flourished. In the Stargazy Pie, whole fish are used and while the head is inedible it does contain oils which add to the flavour of the dish.

Serves 4

8–10 small fresh pilchards, herrings or mackerel
salt
pepper
3 tablespoons finely chopped parsley
1 cup (4 oz) dry breadcrumbs
3 slices bacon, rinds removed
6 eggs
½ cup (4 fl oz) cream
125 g (4 oz) short crust pastry (see p. 331)
egg wash (1 egg yolk mixed with a little cold water)

1. Scale the fish, leaving their heads on. Open them out flat, remove their backbones and season the inside with salt and pepper. **2.** Put a generous amount of parsley into each cavity and press the fish into shape again. **3.** Butter a pie dish and sprinkle with a thick layer of breadcrumbs. Put half the fish on top of this then another layer of breadcrumbs. **4.** Arrange the remaining fish so that their heads face the centre of the pie dish and cover with the bacon. **5.** Beat the eggs well and mix them with the cream. **6.** Pour this over the fish. **7.** Preheat the oven to 220°C (425°F/Gas 7). **8.** Roll out the pastry and cover the pie with it. Make slits in the pastry and pull out the heads of the fish so that they are looking upwards. **9.** Brush the pie with egg wash and bake for 15 minutes then reduce the oven temperature to 180°C (350°F/Gas 4) and cook for a further 45 minutes. **10.** Serve hot.

Melton Mowbray Pork Pie

Serves 8

1 kg (2 lb) pork shoulder meat, diced into 0.5 cm (¼ inch) pieces
1 teaspoon salt and freshly ground pepper
½ teaspoon ground sage or 2–3 fresh leaves, chopped
a pinch each of dry mustard and allspice
pork and veal bones
2 onions, chopped
1 bay leaf
2–3 sprigs of marjoram and thyme
250 g (8 oz) lard
500 g (1 lb) flour
⅔ cup (5 fl oz) milk mixed half and half with water
1 egg, lightly beaten

1. Mix the meat, salt, pepper, herbs and spices and set aside. **2.** To make the stock, boil bones, onions, bay leaf, herbs, salt and pepper in 4 cups (1 litre) of water for 2 hours or until the liquid is reduced to 2⅓ cups (18 fl oz). Cool, degrease and refrigerate until it starts to jell. **3.** To make the pastry, rub 60 g (2 oz) of the lard into the flour mixed with a teaspoon of salt until it is the consistency of breadcrumbs. **4.** Boil the rest of the fat with the milk and water. **5.** Make a well in the mound of flour and while stirring with a wooden spoon, mix in the boiling liquid. **6.** Knead and leave to rest for 10 minutes. **7.** To make the casing or 'coffyn', roll out three-quarters of the dough into a circle 2 cm (¾ inch) thick. Flour the outside of a cake tin and stand it in the centre of the dough. Work the dough up the sides of the tin and then gently remove the tin, leaving you with a pie casing. **8.** Fill it immediately with the meat mixture as it is likely to collapse. **9.** Roll out the remaining dough into a circle slightly larger than the diameter of the casing, to form the lid. **10.** Preheat the oven to 200°C (400°F/Gas 6). **11.** Dampen the top edge of the pie and gently press on the lid. Crimp the edge. Make a hole in the centre of the lid and decorate it with pastry leaves. **12.** Place on a baking dish and bake in the preheated oven for 20 minutes and then reduce the heat to 150°C (300°F/Gas 2) and bake for 1¾ hours. If necessary place some aluminium foil on the top to prevent burning. **13.** Remove from the oven and allow to cool completely. Pour the chilled stock through the hole in the lid and refrigerate. Serve cold.

Right: A fine display of Cornish dishes from the Coachmaker's Arms in Callington, Cornwall. Clockwise from bottom left: Cornish Pasties (see page 133); Cornish Roast Lobster (see page 121); Stargazy Pie (above); Squab Pie (see page 133); Smoked Mackerel.

DESSERTS

Strawberry Muffins

From the Hunters' Lodge Restaurant, Broadway, Worcestershire.

Serves 4–6

½ cup (4 oz) caster (powdered) sugar
500 g (1 lb) strawberries, sliced
1¼ cups (10 fl oz) cream, stiffly whipped

Muffins:
500 g (1 lb) flour
pinch of salt
2 teaspoons sugar
1¼ cups (10 fl oz) warm milk
2 teaspoons dry yeast
1 egg, well beaten
30 g (1 oz) butter, melted
icing (confectioners') sugar for garnish

1. Sprinkle sugar over strawberries and refrigerate for 30 minutes. **2.** Fold in cream and return to refrigerator until ready to use. **3.** To make the muffins combine the flour and salt. **4.** Dissolve the sugar in the milk and add the yeast. Stand it in a warm place for 10 minutes. **5.** Add the yeast mixture and the egg to the flour, stir in the melted butter and knead for 10 minutes to a soft dough. **6.** Place the dough in an oiled bowl, cover and leave to rest in a warm place until it has doubled in size. **7.** Turn out onto a floured board, punch it down and roll it out 1.5 cm (½ inch) thick. **8.** Cut it into 7.5 cm (3 inch) rounds, place them on a floured board, dust them with flour, cover with a tea towel and leave until double in size. **9.** Lightly grease a hot griddle and cook the muffins for about 8 minutes on each side. **10.** To serve, split the muffins in half, toast on both sides, spread one side with butter, heap the strawberries and cream on the bottom half, place the other half on top and sprinkle with icing sugar.

Rose Cream

Hufen Rhosyn

From Ty Mawr in Brechfa, Wales.

Serves 4–6

4 egg yolks
1½ tablespoons caster (powdered) sugar
1¾ cups (15 fl oz) milk, scalded
500 g (1 lb) raspberries
1 tablespoon rosewater
15 g (½ oz) gelatine, dissolved in 2 tablespoons cold water
whipped cream for decoration

1. Cream the egg yolks and sugar together until they are thick and pale coloured. **2.** Pour the milk over them and put the mixture into a saucepan. Heat it, stirring constantly, until it thickens. Do not allow it to boil. **3.** Cool it over a bed of ice. **4.** Stir in the gelatine. **5.** Reserve a few of the raspberries for decoration and put the rest in a blender or food processor and purée. Pour it through a sieve into the custard mixture. **6.** Add the rosewater and mix well. **7.** Pour the mixture into a lightly oiled jelly mould and leave it to set in the refrigerator. **8.** When it has set, unmould it and decorate it with reserved raspberries and whipped cream.

Monmouth Pudding

Pwdin Mynwy

From the King's Head Hotel in Monmouth, Wales.

Serves 4–6

6 cups (12 oz) fresh white breadcrumbs
3 tablespoons sugar
4 drops vanilla essence
⅔ cup (5 fl oz) boiling milk
2 tablespoons melted butter
3 egg whites, stiffly beaten
500 g (1 lb) strawberry or raspberry jam

1. Place the breadcrumbs into a warmed bowl and pour the boiling milk over them. Cover the bowl and leave it to stand for 15 minutes. **2.** Preheat the oven to 120°C (250°F/Gas ½). **3.** Stir the breadcrumb and milk mixture with a fork and add the sugar and melted butter. **4.** Fold the beaten egg whites gently into the mixture. **5.** Grease an ovenproof dish with butter and spread half the jam on the bottom of it. **6.** Spoon half the breadcrumb mixture on top of the jam, then spread over the remaining jam and finally the remaining breadcrumb mixture. **7.** Bake for 30 minutes and serve either hot or warm.

Baked Devonshire Apple Dumplings

From The Anglers' Rest, Fingle Bridge, Exeter. In this Devon speciality, the name 'dumpling' is a misnomer because the pastry is wrapped around the apple and then it is baked, whereas normally one would expect to boil dumplings.

Serves 4

250 g (8 oz) sweet short crust pastry (see p. 331)
4 apples, each weighing about 125 g (4 oz)
¼ cup (2 oz) sugar
4 cloves
1 egg yolk, mixed with a little cold water

1. Preheat the oven to 180°C (350°F/Gas 4). **2.** Roll out the pastry fairly thinly and cut it into 4 squares big enough to completely enclose an apple. **3.** Peel and core the apples, fill their centres with sugar and pierce each one with a clove. **4.** Place an apple on each pastry square, brush the edges of the pastry with water and fold it over to completely seal the apple. **5.** Decorate the tops with offcuts of pastry cut into shapes. **6.** Brush the pastry with the egg yolk and water mixture. **7.** Place the apples on a lightly greased baking sheet and bake for 30 minutes or until the pastry is golden-brown. **8.** Serve with whipped cream.

Bakewell Pudding

From the Cavendish Hotel, Baslow, Bakewell, Derbyshire. The Cavendish Hotel is only a few kilometres from Bakewell where this famous dish originated.

Serves 8

250 g (8 oz) sweet short pastry (see p. 331)
30 g (1 oz) raspberry jam
4 eggs
½ cup (4 oz) sugar
125 g (4 oz) butter, melted
1¼ cups (4 oz) ground almonds

1. Preheat oven to 200°C (400°F/Gas 6). **2.** This dish is usually made in a traditional oval Bakewell pudding tin with sloping sides but a 20 cm (8 inch) flan may be used instead. **3.** Line the greased dish or flan with the pastry. **4.** Cover the pastry with the jam. **5.** Beat the eggs and sugar until the mixture is pale and creamy. **6.** While stirring constantly, pour the butter into it. **7.** Mix in the almonds and pour it over the jam. **8.** Bake in a preheated oven for 30–35 minutes or until the filling has set.

Apple and Bramble Fool

This recipe comes from the George Hotel in Chollerford, Northumberland. The combination of a fruit purée and cream was once considered foolish, hence the name. Different types of fruit are used and the dessert is very popular in many parts of England.

Serves 4–6

250 g (8 oz) Granny Smith apples, peeled, cored and sliced
155 g (5 oz) blackberries
¼ cup (2 fl oz) water
½ cup (4 oz) sugar
2½ tablespoons cornflour (cornstarch)
1 cup (8 fl oz) milk

1. Put the apples and blackberries in a pan with the water and ⅓ cup of the sugar. Bring slowly to the boil, stirring until the sugar has dissolved, then simmer until the mixture has reduced to a purée. **2.** Mix the cornflour with a little of the milk to make a smooth paste. **3.** Put the remaining milk and sugar into a pan, heat and stir until the sugar has dissolved then bring to the boil. **4.** Add the cornflour mixture and boil for 3 minutes. **5.** Cool the milk mixture slowly and add the fruit. **6.** Pour into tall glasses and refrigerate until set. Serve decorated with whipped cream and cherries.

Chester Pudding

From the Waterside Restaurant in Romiley, Manchester.

Serves 6–8

1 cup (4 oz) self-raising flour
125 g (4 oz) shredded suet
2 cups (4 oz) soft breadcrumbs
¼ cup (2 oz) caster (powdered) sugar
⅓ cup (4 oz) blackcurrant jam
1 egg, lightly beaten
milk

1. Mix all the dry ingredients together with the jam. **2.** Add the egg and enough milk to make a smooth dough. **3.** Spoon the mixture into a greased 5 cup (1.25 litre) pudding basin and steam over hot water for 3 hours. Serve with blackcurrant jam.

Cumberland Rum Nicky

This recipe comes from the Parkend Restaurant in Wigton, Cumbria. This is what is known as a plate pie, i.e. a two-crust pie with a fruit filling. It appears in many parts of England with various fillings.

Serves 6–8

375 g (12 oz) short crust pastry (see p. 331)
1⅔ cups (8 oz) stoned dates, chopped
1½ cups (8 oz) sultanas or seedless raisins
60 g (2 oz) butter
⅓ cup (2 oz) soft brown sugar
30 g (1 oz) stem ginger, finely chopped
2 cooking apples, peeled and diced
3 tablespoons rum

1. Preheat the oven to 190°C (375°F/Gas 5). **2.** Roll out the pastry thinly, and, using two-thirds of it, line a 23 cm (9 inch) flan ring. **3.** Mix all the remaining ingredients together, spoon them into the pastry shell, smoothing the mixture out well. **4.** Cover the pie with the remaining pastry, seal the edges, prick the top with a fork, brush with milk and sprinkle brown sugar lightly over the top. **5.** Bake for 20 minutes or until the pastry is crisp and golden. **6.** Serve warm or cold with lightly whipped cream.

Cumberland Rum Butter

From Yan Tyan Tethera in Keswick, Cumbria. The tale goes that a ship from the Cumbrian coast had collected its cargo of spices, rum and sugar from the West Indies, called on Ireland for butter, and then encountered a storm which loosened the various barrels. The resultant mixture tasted so good it became a Cumbrian speciality. Traditionally, rum butter is served at christenings or, with whipped cream added, with Christmas Pudding.

Serves 6

500 g (1 lb) dark brown sugar
220 g (7 oz) butter, softened
1 teaspoon mixed spices
1 teaspoon cinnamon
¼ cup (2 fl oz) Jamaican rum

1. Cream the sugar and butter together until it is light. **2.** Add the spices, cinnamon and rum. **3.** Form into a block, wrap in foil and keep in the refrigerator.

Devonshire Junket

From The Anglers' Rest, Fingle Bridge, Exeter.

Serves 6–8

1 litre (4 cups) milk
¾ cup (5 fl oz) brandy
60 g (2 oz) sugar
2 tablespoons rennet
1 cup (8 fl oz) Devonshire clotted cream (thickened cream)
¼ tablespoon cinnamon
2 tablespoons sugar

1. Warm the milk and brandy to blood temperature. **2.** Stir in the sugar and rennet. **3.** Leave to set. **4.** Just before serving, garnish with the clotted cream and sprinkle with cinnamon and sugar. The junket may also be decorated with apricot or strawberry jam.

Peil Wyke Raspberry Syllabub

This recipe comes from the Pheasant Inn in Cumberland. Syllabubs are a traditional English dessert in which wine, sherry or brandy is mixed with whipped cream. They are usually made several hours before they are served to permit the liquid to separate from the cream.

Serves 6–8

2½ cups (20 fl oz) cream
½ cup (4 oz) caster (powdered) sugar
315 g (10 oz) fresh raspberries
4 egg whites
150 ml (5 fl oz) dry white wine

1. Whip the cream until it is thick, then fold in the caster sugar. **2.** Put the raspberries in a pan with a tablespoon of water and stew over gentle heat for a few minutes. Leave to cool. **3.** Whip the egg whites until they form stiff peaks and fold them into the cream mixture. **4.** Gently fold the raspberries and wine into the cream mixture and spoon the mixture into champagne glasses. Serve decorated with a raspberry and a raspberry leaf.

***Right:** Guinness Christmas Pudding (see page 157); Peil Wyke Raspberry Syllabub (above).*

Westmorland Dream Cake

From Yan Tyan Tethera in Keswick, Cumbria.

Serves 6

Base:
1 cup (4 oz) flour
125 g (4 oz) butter
2 tablespoons soft brown sugar

Topping:
1½ cups (8 oz) soft brown sugar
¼ cup (1 oz) flour
pinch salt
1 cup (4 oz) walnuts, chopped
1 cup (3 oz) desiccated coconut
½ teaspoon baking powder
2 eggs, beaten

1. Preheat the oven to 180°C (350°F/Gas 4). **2.** Rub the butter into the flour and then add the sugar, mixing in well. **3.** Press this mixture into a Swiss (jelly) roll tin and bake for 20 minutes. Allow to cool. **4.** To make the topping, mix together all the dry ingredients then mix in the eggs. **5.** Spread the mixture on top of the cooled base and bake a further 20 minutes or until it browns. **6.** Leave to cool in the tray before cutting into slices.

Saffron Cake

From the Coachmakers Arms, Callington, Cornwall.

Serves 6-8

4½ cups (1 lb 2 oz) flour
pinch of salt
125 g (4 oz) butter
125 g (4 oz) lard
⅓ cup (3 oz) sugar
pinch of freshly grated nutmeg
pinch of saffron
1⅔ cups (8 oz) currants
⅓ cup (2 oz) mixed peel
15 g (½ oz) fresh yeast
warm milk

1. Sift the flour and salt into a bowl and rub the butter and lard into it with your fingertips. **2.** Add the sugar, nutmeg, saffron, currants and peel and mix well. **3.** Put the yeast into a cup with a pinch of sugar and a little warm milk. **4.** When the yeast mixture becomes foamy, make a well in the centre of the flour mixture and pour the yeast into it. **5.** Beat the mixture well, adding enough warm milk to make a soft dough. **6.** Leave the mixture to rise in a warm place until it has doubled in bulk. **7.** Preheat the oven to 180°C (350°F/Gas 4). **8.** Put the mixture into a greased loaf tin and bake for 50–60 minutes or until it is cooked through. **9.** Cool on a wire rack and serve sliced with butter.

Carmarthen Yeast Cake

From Ty Mawr in Brechfa, Wales.

Serves 6

250 g (8 oz) flour
1 teaspoon mixed spice
pinch of salt
1½ cups (8 oz) mixed dried fruit
45 g (1½ oz) butter
45 g (1½ oz) lard
⅓ cup (3 oz) caster (powdered) sugar
2 teaspoons golden syrup (light corn syrup)
1 egg
⅔ cup (5 fl oz) milk, warmed
15 g (½ oz) fresh yeast
½ teaspoon bicarbonate of soda (baking soda)

1. Sift the flour, mixed spice and salt into a large bowl. Add the dried fruit. **2.** In another bowl, beat the butter, lard, sugar and syrup together until it is creamy. Add the egg and mix well. **3.** Dissolve the yeast in half the warmed milk and the bicarbonate of soda in the other half. **4.** Add both mixtures to the creamed butter mixture and beat thoroughly. **5.** Fold this butter-yeast mixture into the flour and mix to a soft dough. **6.** Preheat the oven to 220°C (425°F/Gas 7). **7.** Put the dough into a greased loaf tin and leave in a warm place until it has doubled in size. **8.** Bake it for 1½–2 hours or until a skewer inserted in the centre comes out clean. **9.** Cool on a wire rack and serve in slices, spread with butter.

Chorley Cakes

From the Waterside Restaurant, Romiley, Manchester.

Makes 4 cakes

500 g (1 lb) rich short crust pastry (see p. 331)
¾ cup (4 oz) currants
icing (confectioners') sugar

1. Preheat the oven to 180°C (350°F/Gas 4). **2.** Roll the pastry out 6 mm (¼ inch) thick and cut into 4 rounds the size of a dinner plate. **3.** Place the currants in the centre of the circles, moisten the edges of the pastry with water and bring the edges together in the centre, pressing to seal well. **4.** Roll out the cakes until the currants show through, keeping to the round shape. **5.** Place the rounds on baking trays and bake for 30 minutes. **6.** When cool, sprinkle with icing sugar.

Yorkshire Parkin

From The Black Bull Inn, Moulton, Richmond, Yorkshire.

Serves 6

½ cup (3 oz) brown sugar
90 g (3 oz) margarine
185 g (6 oz) golden syrup (light corn syrup)
185 g (6 oz) medium oatmeal
1½ cups (6 oz) flour
½ teaspoon mixed spices
½ teaspoon ginger
½ teaspoon bicarbonate of soda (baking soda)
1 egg

1. Preheat the oven to 180°C (350°F/Gas 4). **2.** Melt the sugar, margarine and syrup together. **3.** Add the dry ingredients, mix well and beat in the egg. **4.** Pour the mixture into a shallow cake tin and bake in the preheated oven for approximately 1 hour. When cold cut into squares. (The Chef recommends that it be kept for at least 2 days in an airtight tin before serving.)

Tipsy Hedgehog

From the Waterside Restaurant, Romiley, Manchester.

Serves 6

500 g (1 lb) Digestive (wheatmeal) biscuits
125 g (4 oz) dark (semi-sweet) chocolate, grated
2½ cups (20 fl oz) port wine
whipped cream

1. Line a bowl with foil and press in the biscuits and half the grated chocolate. **2.** Pour in the port and allow it to soak in the refrigerator overnight. **3.** Turn out onto a serving dish, shape into a 'hedgehog' shape and coat in whipped cream. Decorate with the remaining grated chocolate.

Devonshire Apple Cake

From The Anglers' Rest, Fingle Bridge, Exeter. Devon is well known for its apples and they are used in many local dishes. However, nowhere do they taste as well as in the Devonshire Apple Cake, especially as it was baked and served at the Anglers' Rest.

Serves 6

2 cups (8 oz) self-raising flour
¾ cup (4 oz) brown sugar
125 g (4 oz) butter
⅓ cup (2 oz) currants
250 g (8 oz) peeled and chopped apple
milk

1. Preheat the oven to 220°C (425°F/Gas 7). **2.** Put the flour and sugar into a bowl and rub the butter into it with your fingertips. **3.** Add the currants and apple, and if the mixture is too dry, add a little milk. **4.** Grease a 20 cm (8 inch) cake tin and press the mixture well into it. **5.** Bake for 10 minutes at 220°C (425°F/Gas 7) then reduce the temperature to 140°C (275°F/Gas 1) and cook for a further hour. **6.** Sprinkle with a little extra brown sugar before serving.

Cranachan

This recipe comes from The Open Arms Hotel in Lothian, Scotland. Cranachan is very Scottish, served traditionally at Halloween when charms with special significance were folded into the mixture. You might find a ring for marriage, a button for bachelorhood, a thimble for spinsterhood, coins for wealth and horseshoes for luck.

Serves 6–8

1¼ cups (4–6 oz) pinhead oatmeal
5 cups cream, beaten until thick
honey
whisky
strawberries or any fresh fruit in season
petticoat tails or shortbread biscuits

1. Preheat the oven to 180°C (350°F/Gas 4). **2.** Put the oatmeal in a baking dish and bake until light brown. **3.** Mix the oatmeal and cream together, flavour with honey and whisky according to your taste. **4.** Serve in individual glass dishes topped with strawberries and garnished with a petticoat tail.

IRELAND

Historically, nobody would suggest that the Irish have had a sheltered existence, so it is interesting to note that while the people of Ireland have been knocked about in one way or another, their eating habits have remained almost unchanged for hundreds of years.

The Romans, who exerted a strong influence wherever they went, did not quite make it across the Irish Sea, the Normans had their hands full in England so that they, too, left no mark on local eating habits. Ireland also missed out on the returning Crusaders bringing back the many interesting and tasty spices and unknown oriental delicacies which are absorbed into European cooking.

The Irish climate is temperate and the soil fertile, so that for centuries, while nobody but the landlords lived in luxury, nobody, thanks to good crops and plenty of dairy herds, pigs and sheep, had to starve.

The 16th century saw the introduction of the potato by Sir Walter Raleigh. Easy to cultivate, growing underground and reasonably protected from adverse external conditions, it soon became the mainstay of Irish cooking with the major part of the cuisine containing potatoes in one form or another.

Irish cooking was, in the true sense of the word, a peasant cuisine where products grown by the individual were the basis of their own cooking. The ingredients were simple: potatoes, home-grown vegetables, buttermilk and curds from their own cow, fruit and their own honey, which was the main sweetening agent. Those along the shores supplemented their diet with the catch from the sea. Recipes were handed down by word of mouth and there were only slight regional variations.

Today, very few traditional dishes are offered in public eating places. There is the occasional and delicious Irish Stew, and Boxty Bread and Pancakes make an appearance, but there is nothing on the scale of many Continental countries where regional food is the pride of the table.

What has happened to traditional Irish cooking? During the last two hundred years, traditional Irish cooking, the simple but wholesome fare of the Irish farmhouse, has been associated with poverty and misfortune. When people started to become more prosperous, they discarded Irish food in favour of new, foreign flavours. The result is that today a great effort will have to be made to search out what little can be found of the old and forgotten traditions. The older generation may still hold the memories of the food of their childhood, but unless a concerted effort is made soon, a valuable cultural asset will be lost forever.

Some of the best seafood can be found in the coastal waters around Ireland. The Dublin Bay Prawn, not a prawn at all but a small type of Norwegian lobster, bred all year round, is probably the most famous and certainly the most delicious local product of the sea. Cockles, scallops and oysters, especially those from County Galway, have a quality of their own, while sole and mackerel deserve the reputation they enjoy. Famous also are the Irish salmon and local trout.

Local hams are good and that from Limerick, smoked with juniper branches and berries, has a taste of its own.

Right: Kylemore Abbey in Co. Galway.

SOUPS

Irish Potato Soup

Serves 6

1 kg (2 lb) potatoes, peeled and diced
2 large onions, sliced
90 g (3 oz) butter
5 cups (1.25 litres) water
3 tablespoons mixture of finely chopped
parsley, thyme and sage
salt
freshly ground pepper
1¼ cups (10 fl oz) milk
2 tablespoons cream
2 tablespoons chopped chives or mint

1. Sauté the potatoes and onions in the butter for approximately 15 minutes but do not brown. 2. Place them in a large saucepan, add water, herbs, salt and pepper and simmer for approximately 30 minutes until the vegetables are tender. Remove from the heat and allow to cool. 3. In a blender or food processor purée the mixture. 4. Transfer to the saucepan, add the milk and bring to the boil. 5. Serve hot garnished with cream and the chopped chives or mint.

Irish Turnip Soup

Serves 6

3 large turnips, chopped
1 large onion, chopped
60 g (2 oz) butter
4 cups (1 litre) chicken stock (see p. 328)
2 cloves
¼ cup (1 oz) flour
2 cups (16 fl oz) milk
2 teaspoons sugar
salt
freshly ground pepper

1. Place the turnips, onions and butter in a heavy-bottomed saucepan. Cover and cook gently for 30 minutes. 2. Add the chicken stock and cloves, cover and simmer for a further 30 minutes. Discard the cloves. 3. Purée the mixture in a blender or food processor and return to the saucepan. 4. Mix the flour to a smooth paste with some of the milk. 5. Add the flour, the milk and sugar and season. Cook for a further 10 minutes.

Mussel Soup

Serves 6

4 dozen mussels
60 g (2 oz) butter
2 tablespoons flour
4 cups (1 litre) of the water from the mussels
2 cups (16 fl oz) milk
2 tablespoons chopped parsley
2 stalks celery, chopped
salt
freshly ground pepper
½ cup (4 fl oz) cream

1. Clean the mussel shells thoroughly and place them in a large saucepan. Cover and simmer for approximately 5 minutes until the shells open. Do not continue cooking once the shells are open. 2. When the mussels have cooled remove them from their shells and reserve them. 3. In a saucepan melt the butter, add the flour and gradually add the cooking water from the mussels and the milk, stir constantly making sure the mixture is smooth. If there is not enough water from the mussels add milk or water. 4. Add the parsley, celery, pepper and salt and cook for 10–15 minutes. 5. Just before serving add the mussels, heat gently and serve with the fresh cream.

Crubins Pea Soup

Also called Crubeens, the Irish name for pig's trotters.

Serves 6

3 pig's trotters
500 g (1 lb) dried peas, soaked overnight
8 cups (2 litres) water
1 bunch celery, chopped
3 onions, chopped
1 bay leaf
6 peppercorns
salt
chopped fresh herbs or parsley for garnish

1. Simmer the pig's trotters for 3 hours. 2. Add the rest of the ingredients and simmer for a further hour. 3. Take out the trotters, cool them, pick off all the meat, chop it roughly and set it aside. 4. Rub the vegetables and liquid through a fine sieve. 5. Return the meat to the soup, reheat, adjust seasoning if necessary and serve it hot, sprinkled with herbs or parsley.

FIRST COURSES

Galway Oyster Soufflé

Serves 4

24 oysters
juice of ½ lemon
½ cup (2 oz) fresh breadcrumbs
½ cup (4 fl oz) cream
2 egg yolks, lightly beaten
salt and pepper
pinch of mace
2 egg whites, stiffly beaten

1. Oysters in shells or bottled oysters may be used. Chop 20 of the oysters and save 4 for garnish. **2.** Mix the oyster liquid and lemon juice, heat it and pour it over the breadcrumbs, stir in the chopped oysters, cream and egg yolks. Season and add mace. **3.** Fold in the egg whites. **4.** Pour the mixture into one large or several individual buttered soufflé dishes. Do not fill them right to the top. Cover with aluminium foil, place them in a baking dish filled with hot water, cover the dish with foil and steam them over medium heat for 1 hour for the large basin and 40–45 minutes if using small dishes. To serve, turn them out onto plates and serve hot.

Closheens (Scallops) in White Wine

Serves 4

15 g (½ oz) butter
1 onion, finely chopped
1 clove garlic, crushed
1 tablespoon flour
1¼ cups (10 fl oz) dry white wine
4 sprigs parsley, finely chopped
2 sprigs thyme, finely chopped
salt and freshly ground pepper
24 scallops

1. In a saucepan melt the butter, add the onion and garlic and sauté until it is soft and transparent. **2.** Add the flour and cook it for 2–3 minutes without browning it. **3.** Gradually stir in the wine and add half the parsley, the thyme, salt and pepper. Cook for 5 minutes. **4.** Add the scallops and cook over low heat for a further 3 minutes. Serve hot sprinkled with the remaining parsley.

Sweetbreads and Bacon

Serves 6

6 sweetbreads
salt
3 slices bacon, cut in two
1 onion, finely chopped
3 tomatoes, peeled and sliced
1 cup (8 fl oz) chicken stock (see p. 328)
4 sprigs parsley, chopped

1. Preheat oven to 180°C (350°F/Gas 4). **2.** Soak the sweetbreads in water for 30 minutes. **3.** Salt the water, bring it to the boil and simmer the sweetbreads for 8 minutes. Strain and cool them and remove the membrane. **4.** Wrap a piece of bacon around each sweetbread and secure it with a toothpick. **5.** Place them in a buttered ovenproof dish on a bed of onion and tomato slices. **6.** Add the stock, sprinkle with half of the parsley and pepper and bake in the preheated oven for 35–45 minutes.

7. Serve hot sprinkled with fresh parsley.

Irish Rarebit

Serves 4

2 cups (8 oz) grated (Irish) Cheddar cheese
15 g (½ oz) butter
⅓ cup (2 fl oz) milk
½ tablespoon vinegar
1 teaspoon mustard
salt and freshly ground pepper
30 g (1 oz) chopped gherkins
slices of buttered toast

1. In a saucepan combine cheese, butter and milk. Heat and stir until it is creamy. **2.** Add the vinegar, mustard, salt, pepper and gherkins. **3.** Spoon the mixture on the toast and brown it under a preheated grill, serve hot.

Kippers on Toast

Serves 4

250 g (8 oz) kipper fillets, flaked
2 tablespoons cream
2 hard-boiled eggs, chopped
salt and freshly ground pepper
juice of ½ lemon
2 sprigs parsley, finely chopped
4 slices of buttered toast

1. Combine kippers, cream, eggs, salt, pepper, lemon juice and parsley. **2.** Spoon it on to the pieces of toast and heat it under a hot grill. Serve it garnished with lemon twists and olives.

VEGETABLES

Leeks in Cream Sauce

Serves 4

8 leeks, white parts only, split in half and washed
50 g (1⅔ oz) butter
½ cup (2 oz) flour
½ cup (4 fl oz) cream
salt
pepper

1. Preheat oven to 200°C (400°F/Gas 6). **2.** Boil the leeks in salted water for 10 minutes or until they are tender, save the water. **3.** To make the sauce, melt the butter and stir in the flour. Cook for 2–3 minutes without browning. **4.** Add enough of the hot leek cooking water to make a thick smooth sauce. Simmer for 5 minutes. **5.** Add cream and season to taste. **6.** Arrange the leeks in an ovenproof dish and pour the sauce over. **7.** Bake in the preheated oven until the top turns light brown.

Potato Oat Cakes

Pratie Oaten

Serves 6

1⅔ cups (8 oz) oatmeal
500 g (1 lb) mashed potatoes
salt and freshly ground pepper
milk
melted butter

1. Combine the oatmeal, potatoes, salt, pepper, and enough milk to make a firm dough. **2.** Sprinkle some oatmeal on a board and roll out the mixture approximately 2 cm (¾ inch) thick. **3.** Cut it into small rounds, triangles or squares and cook on a hot griddle or fry them in butter. Serve hot with melted butter.

Colcannon

Serves 4

1 kg (2 lb) potatoes, peeled, boiled and mashed
250 g (8 oz) mashed cooked cabbage
2 small leeks cooked and mashed
30 g (1 oz) butter
1 tablespoon finely chopped onion
2 tablespoons cream
salt
freshly ground pepper

1. Place the potatoes in a large bowl and, while beating with a wooden spoon, add the cabbage and the leeks. Mix in the butter and onion and finally add the cream. If the mixture is too thick, more cream or milk may be added. Season to taste. **2.** Place this mixture in a saucepan and heat gently for approximately 5 minutes.

Irish Mashed Potatoes

Champ

Serves 4

8 potatoes
1 onion, thinly sliced
1½ cups (12 fl oz) milk or buttermilk
4 spring onions, finely chopped
90 g (3 oz) butter
salt and freshly ground pepper

1. Boil the potatoes in salted water until soft. Drain. **2.** Cook the onion in the milk for 5 minutes. **3.** Pour the milk and onion on to the potatoes and mash them until creamy. **4.** Beat the spring onions, butter, salt and pepper into the potatoes. Serve hot.

Right: Potatoes and leeks, the 'Irish' vegetables.

FISH

King Prawns in Whiskey Sauce

From Marlfield House in Gorey, Co. Wexford. Marlfield House is a beautifully restored Regency period house which was originally the Dower House on the estate of the Earls of Courtown.

Serves 4

30 g (1 oz) butter
30 g (1 oz) onions, chopped
1 small capsicum (pepper), chopped
15 g (½ oz) flour
30 g (1 oz) tomatoes, peeled and chopped
1 clove garlic, chopped
1 tablespoon fennel leaves, chopped
salt
freshly ground pepper
⅔ cup (5½ fl oz) dry white wine
250 g (8 oz) fresh king prawns
¼ cup (2 fl oz) Irish whiskey

1. In a frying pan melt the butter and sauté the onions and capsicum until they are soft but not brown. **2.** Stir in the flour, add the tomatoes, garlic, fennel and seasoning. **3.** Add the wine and the shelled prawns and cook for 3–5 minutes. **4.** Finally, add the whiskey and cook for a further 2 minutes. **5.** The prawns and sauce are usually served with boiled rice.

Clarinbridge Oyster Stew

Serves 4

3 dozen oysters
60 g (2 oz) butter
salt
freshly ground pepper
1 bay leaf
2 cups (16 fl oz) milk
2 cups (4 oz) white breadcrumbs
½ tablespoon paprika
juice of ½ lemon
2 tablespoons chopped parsley

1. Open the oysters, clean them and save the juice. **2.** In a saucepan lightly sauté the oysters in the butter for not more than 2–3 minutes. Season with salt and pepper and add the bay leaf, milk and juice of the oysters. **3.** Cook for a further 2–3 minutes. **4.** To thicken, add the breadcrumbs. **5.** Finally, add the paprika and lemon juice and serve garnished with the chopped parsley.

Jellied Eel

Serves 4-6

1 kg (2 lb) eels
3-4 cups (24-32 fl oz) water
3 bay leaves
juice of 1 lemon
2 onions, chopped
salt and freshly ground pepper
¼ teaspoon nutmeg
pinch of mixed spices
30 g (1 oz) gelatine
3 sprigs dill, chopped

1. Skin the eels and cut into small lengths. **2.** Put them in a saucepan and add enough cold water to cover. Slowly bring to the boil and skim off the scum and fat. **3.** Add the bay leaves, lemon juice, onions, salt, pepper, nutmeg and spices. **4.** Simmer over low heat for 10–15 minutes until the eels are cooked. **5.** Take out the fish, remove the flesh from the bones and cut it into small pieces. **6.** Place them into a bowl or a mould and sprinkle with dill and parsley. **7.** Strain the cooking liquid and skim off all fat. **8.** Dissolve the gelatine in some of the warm liquid and add it to the rest. Season to taste. **9.** Pour it over the fish, cool and refrigerate. Serve with a tossed salad.

Baked Galway Cod with Mussels

Serves 4

3 dozen mussels
1 kg (2 lb) cod, cut into steaks
salt
freshly ground pepper
2 tablespoons chopped thyme
12 small potatoes, cooked
8 small onions, cooked
60 g (2 oz) melted butter
1 tablespoon chopped parsley
1 tablespoon chopped fennel
4 slices of lemon

1. Preheat the oven to 200°C (400°F/Gas 6).
2. Clean the mussels and place them in a saucepan with a little water, cover and cook for approximately 5 minutes until the mussels are open. Cool the mussels. **3.** Remove the mussels from the shells and set aside. Reserve the liquid. **4.** Place the cod steaks in a greased baking dish, season and sprinkle with the thyme. **5.** Place the cooked potatoes and onions around the fish. Add the melted butter to the mussel liquid and pour it over the fish. **6.** Bake in the preheated oven for approximately 20 minutes. **7.** Serve the fish topped with the mussels and sprinkled with the chopped parsley and fennel. Decorate it with the lemon slices.

Prawns with Mushrooms

Serves 4

250 g (8 oz) button mushrooms, sliced
60 g (2 oz) butter
¼ cup (1 oz) flour
1 cup (8 fl oz) cream
salt
freshly ground pepper
500 g (1 lb) uncooked, shelled prawns
1 tablespoon Irish whiskey

1. In a saucepan fry the mushrooms in the butter.
2. Sprinkle the mushrooms with the flour and mix well. **3.** Lightly heat the cream and while continuously stirring pour it over the mushrooms and cook until creamy. **4.** Add the prawns and continue simmering for 3–5 minutes. **5.** Before serving, check the seasoning, sprinkle with the Irish whiskey and serve with boiled rice.

Dressed Crab

This recipe is featured at Ballymaloe House in Shangarry, Co. Cork. Myrtle Allan, who with her husband Ivan, runs the Hotel and Restaurant, is the author of the 'Ballymaloe Cookbook' which is a collection of recipes from her repertoire at Shangarry. Mrs Allan notes in her book that 500 g (1 lb) cooked crab in a shell will yield about 120–180 g (4–6 oz) of crab meat.

Serves 4-6

3 cups crab meat (2 or 3 crabs should yield this)
1¾ cups (3½ oz) soft breadcrumbs
½ tablespoon white vinegar
2 tablespoons fruit chutney
30 g (1 oz) butter
1 generous pinch dry mustard
salt
freshly ground pepper
½ cup Béchamel sauce (see p. 329)
1 cup (4 oz) fine dry breadcrumbs
60 g (2 oz) butter

1. Preheat the oven to 200°C (400°F/Gas 6). **2.** Mix together all ingredients except the breadcrumbs and butter, and taste for seasoning. **3.** Pack the mixture into the crab shells, top it with the breadcrumbs and cover it with dobs of butter. **4.** Place the crab shells in the preheated oven and cook until thoroughly heated through and browned on top — approximately 20–30 minutes.

Baked Trout with Cream and Cucumber

Serves 4

4 plate-sized trout
60 g (2 oz) softened butter
3 sprigs parsley, chopped
salt
freshly ground pepper
1 cup (8 fl oz) cream
1 large cucumber, peeled, seeded and cut into small cubes
juice of 1 lemon

1. Preheat the oven to 185°C (350°F/Gas 4). **2.** Rub the trout with the softened butter and sprinkle them with parsley, salt and pepper. Pour the cream around the trout, cover the baking dish with a lid or foil and bake it in the preheated oven for 15 minutes. **3.** Remove from oven and add the cucumber and lemon juice. **4.** Return it to the oven for a further 15 minutes. **5.** To serve, arrange the trout on a serving dish and pour the cream and cucumber over the fish.

MEAT

Irish Beef Stew

Serves 4–6

45 g (1½ oz) dripping
500 g (1 lb) shin beef cut into 2.5 cm (1 inch) cubes
3 carrots, sliced
2 onions, sliced
3 stalks celery, chopped
¼ cup (1 oz) flour
2 cups (16 fl oz) beef stock (see p. 328)
1 tablespoon tomato paste
salt and freshly ground pepper
8–12 small potatoes
4–6 slices of bacon, cut into large pieces

1. Preheat oven to 160°C (325°F/Gas 3). 2. In a casserole melt the fat and brown the meat all round. 3. Take out the meat and in the remaining fat sauté the vegetables until slightly browned. 4. Mix in the flour, gradually add the stock, mix in the tomato paste and season to taste. 5. Return the meat to the casserole, cover and cook in the preheated oven for 45 minutes. 6. Place the potatoes on top, cover again and continue cooking for a further 45 minutes or until potatoes and meat are done. 7. Grill the bacon and serve the stew out of the casserole topped with the bacon.

Irish Hunter's Pie

Serves 6

60 g (2 oz) butter
1 onion, finely chopped
1 carrot, finely chopped
2 stalks celery, finely chopped
1¾ cups (14 fl oz) beef stock (see p. 328)
6 mutton or lamb chops
1.5 kg (3 lb) mashed potatoes
salt and freshly ground pepper

1. Melt half of the butter and lightly sauté the onion, carrot and celery. 2. Add the stock, place the chops on top, cover and braise the meat over low heat for 30 minutes. 3. Preheat the oven to 200°C (400°F/Gas 6). 4. Lift out the chops and rub the vegetables and liquid through a fine sieve. Reserve the purée. 5. Place two-thirds of the potatoes in a buttered pie dish, place the chops on top, season and cover with the rest of the potatoes. Dot the top with the rest of the butter and bake in the preheated oven until brown. 6. Make a hole in the top layer of potatoes and pour in some of the vegetable purée. Serve the rest with the pie.

Braised Beef with Guinness and Prunes

Serves 6

30 g (1 oz) dripping
1 kg (2 lb) shin beef cut into large cubes
2 onions, sliced
3 carrots, sliced
2 tablespoons flour
⅔ cup (5 fl oz) Guinness
⅔ cup (5 fl oz) water
3 sprigs parsley, chopped
3 bay leaves
salt and freshly ground pepper
1 cup (6 oz) soaked prunes

1. Preheat oven to 140°C (275°F/Gas 1). 2. In a casserole heat the fat and brown the meat. 3. Add the onions and carrots and brown them lightly. 4. Add the flour, cook for a few minutes, add the Guinness, water, parsley, bay leaves and seasoning. 5. Cover and cook in preheated oven for 1½ hours. Mix in the prunes and cook for a further hour or until the meat is tender.

Spiced Beef

A traditional Christmas dish.

Serves 8

1.5 kg (3 lb) silverside or brisket
1 cup (8 oz) coarse salt
⅓ cup (2 oz) brown sugar
½ teaspoon allspice
½ teaspoon nutmeg
½ teaspoon ground cloves
¼ teaspoon dry thyme
freshly ground pepper
½ teaspoon ground bay leaves
1 tablespoon saltpetre
60 g (2 oz) black treacle
250 g (8 oz) carrots, sliced
1 onion, finely chopped

1. Rub the meat with salt and leave it overnight. 2. Combine the sugar, allspice, nutmeg, cloves, thyme, pepper, bay leaves and saltpetre. 3. Rub the salt off the meat and wipe dry. 4. Rub the meat with the spice mixture, cover it and refrigerate it for 2 days. 5. Heat the treacle and pour it over the meat. 6. Refrigerate for a week and during that time, every day, rub the treacle and spices firmly into the meat. 7. Roll the meat lightly and tie it firmly with some string. 8. Place it in a saucepan with enough water to cover it. Add carrots and onions and simmer over low heat for 3 hours. 9. Cool it in the liquid. Place it between two plates and press it down with heavy weights overnight. Serve cold and sliced.

Right: Traditional Irish fare: Soda Bread (see page 154) and Irish Stew (see page 152).

Corned Meat and Cabbage

Corned silverside or pickled pork may be used.

Serves 6–8

1.5 kg (3 lb) corned meat, soaked in water to remove excess salt
2 onions, chopped
2 carrots, sliced
3 stalks celery, chopped
2 sprigs thyme, chopped
2 sprigs parsley, chopped
4 bay leaves
6 peppercorns
1 large cabbage cut into 6–8 pieces

1. In a large saucepan combine all the ingredients except the cabbage and cover with water. **2.** Slowly bring to the boil, cover and simmer over low heat for 1 hour. If necessary take off any scum which may float to the top. **3.** Add the cabbage and under cover simmer for a further 2 hours. **4.** When cooked take out the meat, rest it for 10 minutes, slice it and serve on a serving platter surrounded with the cabbage and vegetables. If it's not too salty, the stock can be used to make a lentil or pea soup.

Irish Stew

From Gregans Castle in Ballyvaugham, Co. Clare.

Serves 4–6

1 kg (2 lb) lamb neck chops
salt
freshly ground pepper
6 medium sized onions, chopped
1 kg (2 lb) potatoes, peeled and sliced
2½ cups (20 fl oz) water
2 tablespoons parsley, chopped

1. Preheat the oven to 175°C (350°F/Gas 4). **2.** Place the meat in the bottom of a heavy, cast iron casserole and cover it with a layer of chopped onions and a layer of the sliced potatoes. Add a little water and boil on the top of the stove for 15 minutes. **3.** Add the rest of the water, cover the casserole and place it in the oven for 1 hour. **4.** Add the remaining onions and potatoes. **5.** Cover again and return to the oven for a further hour, or until the vegetables are cooked and the meat is tender. **6.** Serve directly from the casserole, garnished with parsley.

Dublin Coddle

Serves 6

6 thick bacon slices
6 pork sausages
1 litre (4 cups) boiling water
3 large onions, sliced
750 g (1½ lb) potatoes, peeled and sliced
3 tablespoons chopped parsley
salt
freshly ground pepper

1. Preheat the oven to 150°C (300°F/Gas 2). **2.** In a saucepan, boil the bacon and sausages in the water for 5 minutes. **3.** Drain the water and reserve it. **4.** On top of the sausages and bacon place layers of onions and potatoes and the chopped parsley. Season lightly, keeping in mind the saltiness of the bacon. Cover with the liquid. **5.** Cover the saucepan with a lid and place it in the preheated oven for approximately 1 hour. The ingredients must be cooked but not be too soft. **6.** Traditionally this dish is served with soda bread and Guinness.

Irish Pig's Trotters

Crubeens

Serves 6

12 pig's trotters
3 stalks celery
3 onions, chopped
3 carrots, sliced
6 peppercorns
3 bay leaves
½ teaspoon dry thyme
3 sprigs parsley, chopped
salt
flour
2 eggs, lightly beaten
¼ teaspoon English mustard
breadcrumbs seasoned with salt and pepper
dripping

1. In a large saucepan combine trotters, celery, onions, carrots, peppercorns, bay leaves, thyme, parsley and salt. Add enough water to cover. **2.** Bring to the boil, reduce heat to low and simmer for 2½ hours or until the meat is tender. **3.** Take the trotters out of the liquid and remove the meat from the bones. Strain and keep the liquid for later use as stock. **4.** Dust the meat with flour, dip it in a mixture of egg and mustard and coat it in breadcrumbs. **5.** Heat the dripping and fry the meat until brown and crisp. It can be served in a piquant sauce made with stock.

POULTRY

Stuffed Goose with Apple Sauce

What makes this recipe typically Irish is the use of potatoes in the stuffing.

Serves 8

1 × 3–4 kg (6–8 lb) goose
1 cup (8 fl oz) chicken stock in which the goose giblets have been cooked

Stuffing:
750 g (1½ lb) cooked, diced potatoes
2 onions, chopped
3 slices bacon, chopped
salt
freshly ground pepper
liver of the goose, chopped
2 tablespoons parsley, chopped
1 tablespoon fresh sage, or 2 teaspoons dried

Apple Sauce:
250 g (8 oz) peeled, cored apples, cut into pieces
½ cup (4 fl oz) chicken stock (see p. 328)
30 g (1 oz) butter
1 tablespoon sugar
pinch of nutmeg
salt

1. Preheat oven to 200°C (400°F/Gas 6). **2.** Mix all the stuffing ingredients together and put them into the main cavity of the bird. Secure the opening with a skewer. **3.** Place the bird, breast side down, on a rack in a roasting pan. **4.** Place the roasting pan in the preheated oven and roast for 45 minutes. **5.** Reduce the oven temperature to 160°C (325°F/Gas 3) and continue roasting for 1 hour. **6.** At the end of the hour, turn the bird breast side up, and roast at the same temperature for 30–45 minutes, until the breast is golden-brown. During this time, baste with the cooking juices and the stock. If necessary, add a further cup of stock. **7.** To prepare the apple sauce, cook the apples in the stock until they are tender. Purée the apples in a blender or food processor. Add the butter, sugar and pinch of nutmeg and serve hot with the goose. **8.** The goose should be carved and arranged on a serving platter with the stuffing surrounding the pieces of meat.

Roast Chicken with Bread Sauce

Serves 4

1 × 1.75 kg (3½ lb) chicken
30 g (1 oz) softened butter
freshly ground pepper

Stuffing:
breadcrumbs made from 4 large slices of white bread
½ cup (4 fl oz) milk
2 tablespoons chopped parsley
1 tablespoon chopped thyme
1 clove garlic, crushed
pinch of nutmeg
salt
freshly ground pepper

Bread Sauce:
6 cloves
1 large onion
2 cups (16 fl oz) milk
2 bay leaves
pinch of powdered mace
10 peppercorns
1 cup brown breadcrumbs
15 g (½ oz) butter
2–3 tablespoons cream
salt
freshly ground pepper

1. Preheat oven to 180°C (350°F/Gas 4). **2.** To make the stuffing, soak the bread in the milk for 10–15 minutes then squeeze out all the liquid. **3.** Combine all the ingredients together. **4.** Fill the cavity of the chicken with the stuffing and with a skewer, close up the opening. **5.** Place the chicken on the roasting pan. Rub it with softened butter and roast in the preheated oven for 1¼ hours. **6.** Remove the chicken from the baking dish and keep hot. **7.** Strain off the fat, add 2 cups of the chicken stock to the cooking juices and continue cooking until it reduces and thickens. **8.** To prepare the bread sauce, stick the cloves into the onion and place it in a saucepan with the milk, bay leaves, mace and peppercorns. **9.** Boil it gently for approximately 15 minutes and leave it aside for a further 30 minutes so that the liquid can absorb the flavours of the ingredients. **10.** Strain the milk into another pan and add the breadcrumbs. **11.** Return it to the heat and stir it until the breadcrumbs have absorbed the milk. Continue boiling it gently for 2–3 minutes. Season. **12.** Before serving add the butter and the cream. **13.** The chicken is served with the bread sauce and the gravy in two separate sauce-boats.

BREAD, CAKES & DESSERTS

Irish Soda Bread

This recipe comes from Gregans Castle in Ballyvaugham, Co. Clare. The traditional recipe requires the use of buttermilk or sour milk; however, if fresh milk is used one teaspoon of cream of tartar should be added to the dry ingredients.

Serves 6

6 cups (1½ lb) flour
¼ tablespoon bicarbonate of soda
¼ teaspoon salt
1 cup (8 fl oz) buttermilk or sour milk

1. Preheat the oven to 200°C (400°F/Gas 6). **2.** Mix all the dry ingredients in a basin and make a well in the centre. **3.** Stir in the milk vigorously. If necessary add more milk, but the mixture should not be too thin. **4.** On a floured board flatten the dough into a circle approximately 4 cm (1½ inches) thick. **5.** With a floured knife make a cross in the dough. **6.** Place the baking sheet into the preheated oven for approximately 40 minutes.

Note: Brown Irish Soda Bread may be made as above but using 500 g (1 lb) wholewheat flour and 250 g (8 oz) plain white flour — a little more milk may be required to mix the dough.

Chocolate Whiskey Cake

From Marlfield House in Gorey, Co. Wexford.

Serves 6

250 g (8 oz) Digestive biscuits (Graham Crackers, Granita)
250 g (8 oz) dark cooking chocolate
250 g (8 oz) butter
2 eggs
⅓ cup (3 oz) caster (powdered) sugar
60 g (2 oz) glacé cherries
60 g (2 oz) walnuts, chopped
½ cup (4 fl oz) Irish whiskey
¼ cup (2 fl oz) whipped cream

1. Crush the biscuits coarsely and set them aside. **2.** In a double boiler, melt the chocolate together with the butter. **3.** Cream the eggs and sugar until they are light in colour. **4.** Add the chocolate and butter to the eggs while stirring constantly. **5.** Add three-quarters of the glacé cherries and the walnuts, save the rest for garnish. Add the crushed biscuits and all except one tablespoon of the whiskey. **6.** Butter a 23 cm (9 inch) baking dish and pour the mixture into the mould. **7.** Decorate the top with the remaining cherries and walnuts and place in the refrigerator for several hours. Remove it approximately 30 minutes before serving. **8.** Decorate the top of the cake with the whipped cream to which the remaining tablespoon of whiskey has been added.

Guinness Cake

Makes one 20 cm (8 inch) cake

125 g (4 oz) butter
1½ cups (8 oz) brown sugar
3 eggs, lightly beaten
3 cups (12 oz) self-raising flour
pinch of salt
pinch of mixed spice
125 g (4 oz) raisins, soaked
60 g (2 oz) mixed peel, chopped and soaked
250 g (8 oz) sultanas, soaked
60 g (2 oz) glacé cherries
½ cup (4 fl oz) Guinness

1. Preheat the oven to 180°C (350°F/Gas 4). **2.** Cream the butter and sugar until the sugar is dissolved. Beat in the eggs, add the flour, salt, mixed spice and the soaked dried fruit. Finally, mix in the Guinness. **3.** Pour the mixture into a greased cake tin. **4.** Place the cake tin into the preheated oven and bake for 2 hours. To prevent burning, cover the top with foil for the last 30–45 minutes of the baking. **5.** When baked, allow it to cool, remove from cake tin and cut into portions.

Right: An Irish Afternoon Tea — Scones (see page 156) and Guinness Cake (above).

Irish Boiled Cake

90 g (3 oz) golden syrup (light corn syrup)
⅔ cup (5 fl oz) water
½ cup (4 oz) caster (powdered) sugar
¾ cup (4 oz) currants
¾ cup (4 oz) sultanas
125 g (4 oz) butter
2 cups (8 oz) flour
¾ teaspoon baking powder
1 teaspoon mixed spice
1 teaspoon ground ginger
1 egg, lightly beaten

1. Preheat the oven to 180°C (350°F/Gas 4). **2.** In a saucepan, combine the syrup, water, sugar, currants, sultanas and butter and boil for 8–10 minutes, stirring occasionally. Set aside and cool. **3.** Mix together the flour, baking powder, spice and ginger and stir it into the liquid. Mix in the egg. **4.** Pour the dough into a baking tin and bake for 1½–2 hours or until cooked. Cool the cake on a rack and serve it sliced.

Scones

Makes 15 scones

4 cups (1 lb) self-raising flour
pinch of salt
125 g (4 oz) margarine
⅓ cup (3 oz) sugar
milk
1 egg yolk mixed with a little cold water

1. Preheat the oven to 190°C (375°F/Gas 5). **2.** Sift the flour and salt into a bowl. **3.** Rub in the margarine with your fingertips. **4.** Add the sugar and then the milk, a little at a time, until it is a soft consistency. **5.** Roll out on a floured board to about 2 cm (¾ inch) thick. **6.** Cut into rounds about 6 cm (2½ inches) in diameter and place on a lightly greased baking sheet. **7.** Paint with the egg yolk and water mixture and bake for 20 minutes or until they are golden-brown. **8.** Remove from the oven and cool on a wire rack.

Irish Almond Cheese Cake

250 g (8 oz) short crust pastry
(see p. 331)
60 g (2 oz) butter
⅓ cup (3 oz) caster (powdered) sugar
3 eggs, lightly beaten
1 cup (4 oz) chopped blanched almonds
grated rind of ½ lemon
juice of ½ lemon

1. Preheat oven to 180°C (350°F/Gas 4). **2.** Roll out the pastry and line a greased flan dish. **3.** Cream the butter and sugar until light and fluffy and gradually add the eggs. **4.** Add the almonds, lemon rind and juice. **5.** Spoon it into the flan and bake it in the preheated oven for 30–40 minutes or until set.

Honey Mousse

1⅓ cup (1 lb) liquid honey
4 egg yolks
4 egg whites, stiffly beaten

1. Mix the honey and egg yolks. **2.** Cook in a double boiler until the mixture thickens like a custard. **3.** Cool it and fold in the egg whites. **4.** Pour into a glass serving bowl or individual dessert dishes and refrigerate it for 4–6 hours before serving.

Potato Scones

15 g (½ oz) butter, melted
½ teaspoon salt
250 g (8 oz) cold mashed potatoes
½ cup (2 oz) oatmeal
½ teaspoon baking powder

1. Add the butter and salt to the potatoes. **2.** Add enough oatmeal and the baking powder to make a pliable dough. **3.** Roll it out thick and using a saucer approximately 14 cm (7½ inches) in diameter, cut it into rounds, prick the top with a fork and score it into quarters without cutting them right through. **4.** Cook them on a hot griddle for 3–4 minutes each side. Serve hot with butter.

Guinness Christmas Pudding

375 g (12 oz) sultanas
125 g (4 oz) glacé cherries
250 g (8 oz) raisins
125 g (4 oz) mixed peel
1½ cups (8 oz) brown sugar
250 g (8 oz) chopped suet
1 cup (4 oz) flour
2 cups (4 oz) soft breadcrumbs
pinch of salt
pinch of cinnamon
pinch of mixed spice
¾ cup (6 fl oz) Guinness

1. Soak the sultanas, cherries, raisins and mixed peel in water until they are soft. **2.** In a mixing bowl, combine the sugar, suet, flour, breadcrumbs, salt, cinnamon and mixed spice and mix until it is the consistency of breadcrumbs. **3.** Add the soaked fruit and stir in the beaten eggs. Finally, add the Guinness. **4.** Mix well and pour the mixture into one large, or two small, greased pudding bowls. **5.** Cover with foil and tie down with some string. **6.** Steam the pudding for 4–5 hours. **7.** When completed, remove from the water. Serve immediately or store and reheat for 1–2 hours before serving. **8.** Traditionally, this Irish Christmas pudding is served with Irish Whiskey Butter.

Irish Whiskey Butter

½ cup (4 oz) caster (powdered) sugar
60 g (2 oz) butter
2 tablespoons Irish whiskey

1. Cream the sugar and the butter until the sugar is dissolved, gradually add the whiskey. Refrigerate and serve with the pudding which has been flamed with Irish whiskey.

Boxty Bread

Makes 4 cakes

500 g (1 lb) raw potatoes, grated
500 g (1 lb) cooked mashed potatoes
500 g (1 lb) flour
salt
freshly ground pepper
¼ cup (2 fl oz) melted bacon fat

1. Preheat the oven to 160°C (325°F/Gas 3). **2.** Place the grated potatoes in a cloth over a basin and wring out as much liquid as possible. Let it stand until the starch has sunk to the bottom. **3.** In a bowl, mix the grated potatoes with the mashed potatoes, add the flour, pepper and salt. **4.** When the starch has sunk to the bottom, pour off the liquid from the top and scrape the starch into the other ingredients. **5.** Add the melted bacon fat and combine all the ingredients thoroughly. **6.** Divide the dough into four parts and on a floured board form them into round flat cakes. **7.** Make a cross in the top of the cakes and place them on a greased baking dish. **8.** Bake them in the preheated oven for approximately 40–50 minutes. **9.** Serve hot split into four and covered with butter.

Irish Mist Cream

2½ cups (20 fl oz) milk
4 egg yolks
2 tablespoons honey
7 teaspoons gelatine
¼ cup (2 fl oz) Irish Mist liqueur
1¼ cups (10 fl oz) cream, whipped
4 egg whites, stiffly beaten

1. Bring the milk to boiling point. **2.** In a bowl stir yolks and honey together and while continuing to stir, incorporate the milk into the yolk mixture. **3.** Pour back into the saucepan and over low heat, stirring constantly, cook the mixture until it thickens, do not boil. **4.** Dissolve the gelatine in warm water and mix it in. Continue to stir until the mixture cools. **5.** Incorporate the Irish Mist and three-quarters of the cream and fold in the egg whites. **6.** Spoon it into one large or several small moulds. Refrigerate and when set serve it in the moulds or unmould it and decorate it with the remaining cream.

HUNGARY

Although one-fifth of the nation lives in their beloved capital city of Budapest, most Hungarians have close links with the country and it is through this bond with the land that the best of Hungarian cooking has filtered through to the cities, for the Hungarian gastronomy is basically a peasant cuisine.

In 1526 the Hungarians were defeated by the Turks at Mohacs and, from the culinary point of view, the consequences were significant. It was during that time that paprika, or capsicum, was first planted by the victors, who used it extensively in their own cooking. Today, rightly or wrongly, it is paprika that is considered to be the best-known ingredient of Hungarian cooking. Together with the use of lard as a cooking medium, onions and sour cream, it gives the national dishes what could be termed the 'Hungarian flavour'. The four well-known groups of dishes in which paprika is used are the various gulyás, pörkölt, tokány and paprikás.

In 1683 the Turks were defeated near Vienna and when three years later the Habsburgs chased the Turks out of Buda, the nation exchanged the Turkish presence for Austrian domination. At the time, Austrian cooking was influenced by the French and so traditional Hungarian dishes of the time became lighter under the French influence, but without losing their local characteristics and originality.

The Hungarians share with Austrians a very sweet tooth and they satisfy this appetite with a huge range of cakes and desserts. The Hungarians, to the great distress of the Austrians, maintain that they taught the Austrians how to make strudel. Rétes, as it is known in Hungarian, is of course an adaptation of the Middle Eastern baklava. Both countries inherited it from the Turks and both versions are equally good.

Among other vegetables, fresh cabbage enjoys great popularity. Kohlrabi and marrow are also eaten frequently, while dill and marjoram appear in countless dishes.

Hungarian fruit is particularly good, especially from the district of Kecskemét where the best apricots are grown. Consequently, apricot brandy distilled in that area enjoys great popularity. Fruit is used extensively in traditional cooking and Hungarian fruit soups are very tasty.

Hungary has no direct access to the sea but many lakes, rivers and mountain streams yield excellent fish and freshwater crayfish. Lake Balaton is a popular summer holiday area and produces the famous fogas, a pike-perch type of fish with a delicate flavour.

It is on festive and religious occasions that some of the best of the traditional dishes make their appearance. Poppy-seed noodles and a thin brown soup are eaten on Good Friday. Easter Sunday is celebrated with broth, boiled chicken and bread, while Christmas Day seems to be the most inviting day with roasted ducks and chickens, dishes from the festive pig-killing, and lots of fancy cakes. Goose is eaten on festive occasions and many experts consider Hungarian foie gras equal to that of France.

Right: St Andrews at Szentendre.

SOUPS

Fish Soup

Halászlé

From the Apostolok Restaurant, Budapest. This fish soup is as traditional as Hungarian Goulash and in different regions different types of fish are used. Traditionally carp is the main ingredient but perch, sturgeon, and other freshwater fish can be used. The soup is not thickened and is a thin, fiery red coloured soup with the fish served in chunks. The degree of hotness can be adjusted by using more or less chilli.

Serves 4

4 onions, sliced
5 cups (1.25 litres) water
2 tablespoons paprika
2 whole chillies, or less, to taste
1 kg (2 lb) any white-fleshed fish, cut into chunks
salt
2 green peppers (capsicums), cut into chunks
2 tomatoes, peeled and chopped

1. Combine the onions, water, paprika and chillies and simmer for 20 minutes. **2.** Add the fish to the broth. **3.** Season with salt and add the peppers, and tomatoes. **4.** Simmer on very low heat for 45 minutes, do not stir. **5.** Serve as soon as it is cooked.

Goulash Soup

Serves 6–8

3 onions, finely chopped
60 g (2 oz) speck, diced
1 teaspoon paprika
1 pinch chilli powder (cayenne pepper)
750 g (1½ lb) shin beef, cut into cubes
salt
1 clove garlic, crushed
½ teaspoon caraway seeds
2 green peppers (capsicums), seeded and sliced
2 tomatoes, peeled and roughly chopped
1 kg (2 lb) potatoes, peeled and cut into cubes

1. Sauté the onions in the melted speck for 3–4 minutes, sprinkle with paprika and chilli powder. **2.** Add the beef, garlic and caraway seeds, add half a cup of water, simmer gently and as the water evaporates add more; keep simmering until the meat softens. **3.** Add the peppers, tomatoes and potatoes and enough water to cover all the ingredients. **4.** Simmer until the potatoes are cooked. Taste and season before serving.

Cold Morello Cherry Soup

Hideg Meggyleves

From the Arany Sarkany Restaurant, Szantendre.

Serves 4–6

750 g (1½ lb) sour cherries, pitted (fresh or canned)
⅓ cup (3 oz) sugar
½ teaspoon cinnamon
2 cloves
juice of ½ lemon
½ cup (4 fl oz) dry red wine
1 cup water or juice from stewed cherries
2 cups (16 fl oz) milk
½ cup (4 fl oz) cream
½ cup (2 oz) flour
extra cream and cherries for garnish

1. If using fresh sour cherries, cook them with the sugar, cinnamon, cloves, lemon juice, red wine and water until they are soft, approximately 15–20 minutes. **2.** If using canned cherries, drain and mix with the same ingredients as for fresh cherries. **3.** Add the milk and then the cream mixed with the flour. **4.** Mix all ingredients well together and bring to the boil. Simmer for 5 minutes. **5.** Refrigerate and serve cold with some cherries and a spoonful of cream on each serving.

SAUCES

Dill Sauce

Makes 3 cups

1 onion, finely chopped
45 g (1½ oz) butter
½ cup (2 oz) flour
1 small bunch dill, chopped
1-1½ cups chicken stock (see p.328)
1 teaspoon sugar
juice of ½ lemon
1 cup (8 fl oz) sour cream
salt
freshly ground black pepper

1. Lightly fry the onions in butter, add the flour and cook the roux for 5 minutes without browning it. **2.** Add three-quarters of the chopped dill and the chicken stock. Simmer for 20 minutes. **3.** Purée this mixture in a blender or food processor and pass it through a fine sieve. Return it to the saucepan. **4.** Add the sugar, lemon juice and sour cream and season to taste. Gently simmer for another 2–3 minutes. **5.** Just before serving, mix in the remainder of the chopped dill.

Mushroom Sauce

Gombamártás

From the Sziget Czarda Restaurant, Harkany.

Makes 3 cups

150 g (5 oz) mushrooms, sliced
1 onion, chopped
4 sprigs parsley, chopped
45 g (1½ oz) lard
1 tablespoon flour
1 cup (8 fl oz) beef stock (see p. 328)
salt
freshly ground black pepper
½ teaspoon paprika
½ cup (4 fl oz) sour cream

1. Fry the mushrooms, onion and parsley in the lard for 5–10 minutes. **2.** Sprinkle with flour and mix in well. **3.** Pour over the beef stock, add salt, pepper and paprika and cook for 10 minutes. **4.** Finally, add the sour cream and if necessary adjust the seasoning.

Paprika Sauce

Makes 2 cups

1 onion, finely chopped
4 large green peppers (capsicums), seeded and cut into pieces
2 tomatoes, peeled and roughly chopped
45 g (1½ oz) lard
30 g (1 oz) paprika
½ cup (4 fl oz) red wine
¼ cup (2 fl oz) sour cream
salt

1. Fry the onion, peppers and tomatoes in the lard for about 10 minutes, add the paprika and the red wine, continue simmering for 20 minutes. **2.** Purée the mixture in a blender or food processor and rub it through a fine sieve. **3.** Return to the saucepan and cook for 5 minutes. To finish, add the sour cream, salt and freshly ground black pepper.

VEGETABLES & SALADS

Cucumber and Sauerkraut Salad

Paprika Sauerkraut
From the Ködmön Czarda Restaurant, Eger.

Serves 4-6

500 g (1 lb) sauerkraut, drained and rinsed
2 cucumbers, peeled, seeded and sliced
2 red peppers (capsicums), cut into strips
1 teaspoon paprika
½ clove garlic, crushed
½ teaspoon caraway seeds
1-2 teaspoons sugar (according to taste)
¼ cup vegetable oil

1. In a salad bowl, mix all the ingredients together except for half the strips of pepper. **2.** To serve, garnish with the remaining strips of red pepper and serve as a salad.

Lecsó

In Hungary, preserved Lecsó is used during winter in many of the goulashes and stews. Prepared in the following way it may be used as a vegetable to accompany meat.

Serves 6

90 g (3 oz) lard
90 g (3 oz) smoked speck or bacon, diced
4 onions, finely chopped
1 teaspoon paprika
1 kg (2 lb) tomatoes, peeled and roughly chopped
1.25 kg (2½ lb) green peppers (capsicums), seeded and cut into strips
salt

1. In a large heavy-bottomed saucepan melt the lard and fry the smoked speck or bacon. **2.** Add the onions and sauté them until light brown; add the paprika. **3.** Add the tomatoes and peppers and season with salt. **4.** Simmer gently for 30-45 minutes.

Mushrooms in Sour Cream

Serves 4-6

3 onions, finely chopped
60 g (2 oz) butter
500 g (1 lb) mushrooms
salt
1 teaspoon paprika
3 sprigs parsley, finely chopped
½ tablespoon flour
1½ cups (12 fl oz) sour cream

1. In a heavy-bottomed saucepan, sauté the onions in the butter until light brown. **2.** Add the mushrooms and sauté for 3-5 minutes, season with salt, add the paprika and parsley and cook for a further 2-3 minutes. **3.** Sprinkle with flour, mix it in well and then add the sour cream. Simmer gently for a further 2-3 minutes. **4.** Season if necessary. In Hungary, Mushrooms in Sour Cream are served with fried eggs.

Hungarian Dried Beans

Serves 6

500 g (1 lb) dried beans (any type)
salt
2 bay leaves
3-4 smoked bacon ribs *or* 1-2 smoked pig's trotters
30 g (1 oz) lard
½ onion, chopped
¼ cup (1 oz) flour
1 teaspoon paprika
½ cup (4 fl oz) sour cream
½ teaspoon sugar
1 tablespoon white wine vinegar
freshly ground black pepper

1. Soak the beans overnight. **2.** Place the beans in a large saucepan, add some water, salt, bay leaves, the bacon ribs or pig's trotters and cook until the beans are almost tender. (At this stage the beans should not be overcooked otherwise they will become mushy.) **3.** In a large frying pan, melt the lard and sauté the onions lightly, add the flour and cook for 2-3 minutes; add enough water from the beans to make a fairly thin sauce. **4.** Add the paprika, sour cream, sugar and vinegar, mix together and cook for 2-3 minutes. **5.** Remove the pork ribs or trotters from the beans and with a sharp knife scrape off the meaty parts from the bones. Return the meat to the beans. **6.** Add the sauce to the beans, mix them together and heat for a few minutes before serving.

Right: Three of the dishes served at the Arany Sarkany Restaurant in Szentendre. Clockwise from bottom left: Tomato Salad; Cold Morello Cherry Soup (see page 160); Smoked Goose Breast with Baked Beans.

Cabbage and Tomato

Serves 4-6

1 medium-sized fresh cabbage, shredded
1 kg (2 lb) tomatoes, peeled, seeded and
chopped
30 g (1 oz) lard
1 onion, chopped
½ cup (2 oz) flour
½ cup (4 fl oz) hot beef stock (see p. 328)
1 tablespoon sugar
salt
freshly ground black pepper

1. Place the cabbage and tomatoes in a large sauce-pan and cook until the liquid from the tomatoes has reduced. **2.** Melt the lard and lightly fry the onion. Add the flour and cook the roux for 5 minutes to brown it then mix in the hot beef stock to make a sauce. **3.** Add the sauce to the cabbage and tomato mixture, add the sugar and season with salt and pepper. **4.** Cook for a further 10 minutes, season if necessary and serve hot.

Paprika Sauerkraut

Serves 4-6

60 g (2 oz) speck, diced
1 kg (2 lb) sauerkraut
¼ teaspoon caraway seeds
1½ cups (12 fl oz) beef stock (see p. 328)
60 g (2 oz) lard
1 onion, finely chopped
½ cup (2 oz) flour
1 clove garlic, crushed
1 teaspoon paprika
3 tablespoons sour cream
3 sprigs dill, finely chopped

1. In a heavy-bottomed casserole, fry the speck until it melts. Rinse the sauerkraut under cold running water, squeeze it out and add it to the speck. Add the caraway seeds and 1 cup of stock. **2.** Cook on a low heat for approximately 45 minutes. **3.** In a frying pan, melt the lard and fry the onions until light golden-brown. **4.** Add the flour and cook for a further 4–5 minutes to brown it. **5.** Heat the remaining stock and add it to the roux to make a fairly thick sauce. If necessary add more stock. **6.** Add the garlic, paprika and sour cream and cook it for 4–5 minutes. **7.** Add the sauce to the sauerkraut. Before serving, sprinkle with dill.

Potatoes with Dill Cucumbers

Serves 6-8

1½ kg (3 lb) medium-sized potatoes
30 g (1 oz) lard
½ onion, finely chopped
¼ cup (1 oz) flour
3 sprigs parsley, chopped
3 sprigs dill, finely chopped
beef stock (see p. 328)
salt
freshly ground black pepper
100 g (3⅓ oz) dill cucumbers, peeled and
sliced
½ cup (4 fl oz) sour cream

1. Cook the potatoes in their jackets until soft, let them cool and then peel them. **2.** In a frying pan, melt the lard and lightly sauté the onions, add the flour, parsley and dill and cook for 3–5 minutes. **3.** Add enough stock to make a sauce of medium density; season with salt and pepper. **4.** Place the sliced potatoes in a large saucepan and add the cucumbers. Pour the sauce over them and then add the sour cream. Heat but do not boil. Serve hot.

Potato Paprikash

Serves 8

100 g (3⅓ oz) lard
2 onions, finely chopped
1 clove garlic, crushed
¼ teaspoon caraway seeds
1 teaspoon paprika
2 kg (4 lb) potatoes, peeled and cut into chips
2 green peppers (capsicums), seeded and cut
into strips
4 tomatoes, peeled, seeded and roughly
chopped
salt

1. In a heavy-bottomed casserole, melt the lard and lightly fry the onions and garlic, add the caraway seeds and paprika and pour in 1–2 cups of water. **2.** Add the potatoes, peppers and tomatoes and season with salt. Simmer for approximately 30 minutes **3.** Potato Paprikash can be improved by adding, halfway through the cooking, some sliced Vienna sausage.

FISH

Fish with Paprika Cream Sauce

Serves 6

125 g (4 oz) onions, finely chopped
60 g (2 oz) butter
1 tablespoon paprika
¾ cup (6 fl oz) sour cream
1 kg (2 lb) fish fillets, cut into cubes
1 green pepper (capsicum), seeded and cut into strips
2 tomatoes, peeled, seeded and roughly chopped
salt

1. Sauté the onions in butter until transparent, sprinkle with paprika and add the sour cream, fish pieces, green pepper, tomatoes and salt. **2.** Simmer for 30 minutes. **3.** Traditionally, this fish dish is served with galuskas (see p. 173), small spätzlé type noodles.

Crayfish Pörkölt

This dish may also be prepared with prawns or lobster. The flavour of caraway seeds and paprika enhances the flavour of the crustacea.

Serves 6

30 live freshwater crayfish (yabbies) (or green prawns)
4 sprigs parsley, roughly chopped
¼ teaspoon caraway seeds
salt
125 g (4 oz) butter
1 teaspoon paprika
extra caraway seeds (optional)

1. Simmer the crayfish or prawns in boiling water for 10 minutes, together with the parsley, caraway seeds and salt. **2.** Remove them from the water and peel them. If necessary, remove the vein. **3.** In a frying pan, heat the butter with the paprika and a few caraway seeds. Add the crayfish or prawn meat and lightly sauté for 2–3 minutes. Season to taste. **4.** Serve hot, poured over rice or buttered noodles.

POULTRY

Braised Szekely Goose

Serves 6

1 × 4–5 kg (8–10 lb) goose, cut into pieces
salt
freshly ground black pepper
60 g (2 oz) lard
3 onions, finely chopped
1 clove garlic, crushed
1 teaspoon paprika
2 cups beef stock (see p. 328)
60 g (2 oz) smoked speck, diced
4 green peppers (capsicums), seeded and cut into pieces
500 g (1 lb) tomatoes, peeled and roughly chopped
4 sprigs parsley, finely chopped

1. Season the goose pieces with salt and pepper. Melt the lard in a heavy cast iron casserole and fry the pieces of goose until they are brown. **2.** Add the onions and garlic and also fry them lightly, add the paprika and beef stock, cover and simmer for 1 hour. **3.** In the meantime, melt the speck in some lard, add the peppers and tomatoes and sauté them lightly for about 10 minutes. **4.** When the goose has been braised for 1 hour, add the peppers and tomatoes, cover and continue braising for a further 30 minutes or until the meat is tender. **5.** Spoon off any excess fat from the sauce. **6.** Arrange the meat on a large platter, mask with the cooking juices and sprinkle with parsley.

Chicken in Lecsó

Serves 6

3 onions, finely chopped
30 g (2 oz) lard
½ teaspoon paprika
1 × 1½ kg (3 lb) chicken, cut into pieces
salt
1 clove garlic, crushed
60 g (2 oz) speck, diced
30 g (1 oz) lard
1 kg (2 lb) green peppers (capsicums), seeded
and cut into strips
750 g (1½ lb) tomatoes, peeled and roughly
chopped

1. In a large saucepan, fry the onions in the lard, add the paprika, chicken pieces, salt and garlic. Add 2 cups of water, cover the saucepan with a lid and simmer for 30 minutes. **2.** In a large frying pan or saucepan, fry the speck in the lard, add the green peppers and tomatoes, cover and simmer for 10 minutes, stirring occasionally. **3.** Add the pepper-tomato mixture to the chicken, cover with a lid and simmer gently for a further 30 minutes. **4.** To serve, arrange the chicken on a serving platter and pour the pepper-tomato sauce over it. **5.** Traditionally, this dish is served with boiled parsley potatoes.

Stuffed Chicken

From the Hotel Danube International, Budapest.

Serves 4

1 × 1.5 kg (3 lb) chicken
90 g (3 oz) butter
2 eggs
1 egg yolk
salt
freshly ground black pepper
3 slices white bread soaked in 1 cup warm milk
2 sprigs marjoram, finely chopped
3 sprigs parsley, finely chopped
1 teaspoon paprika
½ cup melted butter

1. Preheat the oven to 190°C (375°F/Gas 5). **2.** Cream the butter with the eggs and egg yolk, add the salt and pepper. **3.** Squeeze the milk out of the bread and mash the bread finely. **4.** Add it to the butter-egg mixture and at the same time add the marjoram, parsley and paprika. **5.** Mix all the ingredients well together. **6.** With a sharp knife, separate the skin along the breast of the chicken and into the cavity distribute the stuffing evenly. **7.** Use skewers to secure any loose ends so that the stuffing does not ooze out. **8.** Place the chicken into a baking dish, pour the melted butter over it and sprinkle it with pepper and salt. **9.** Roast the chicken for approximately 1 hour or until golden-brown, basting with the melted butter every 10 minutes. **10.** Traditionally, the chicken is served with sautéed potatoes.

Szeged Chicken Goulash with Csipetke Noodles

Serves 6–8

125 g (4 oz) lard
2 onions, chopped
1–2 cloves garlic, crushed
2 stalks celery, chopped
1 carrot, chopped
1 parsnip, chopped
1 × 1½ kg (3 lb) chicken, cut into pieces
125 g (4 oz) chicken giblets, chopped
½ teaspoon caraway seeds
1 teaspoon paprika
125 g (4 oz) tomato purée
1 kg (2 lb) potatoes, peeled and cut into cubes
salt
3 sprigs parsley, chopped

Csipetke:
¾ cup (6 oz) flour
1 egg, lightly beaten
salt

1. In a large saucepan, melt the lard and sauté the onions, garlic, celery, carrots, and parsnip. Add the chicken pieces, giblets, caraway seeds, paprika and tomato purée. **2.** Add sufficient water to cover and simmer for 30–40 minutes. **3.** Add the potatoes and salt to taste. **4.** Continue simmering for a further 30 minutes. **5.** Traditionally, Szeged Chicken Goulash is served with Csipetke noodles.

Csipetke noodles: 1. Mix the flour with the lightly beaten egg and add salt. **2.** Place the dough on a wooden board and with a knife cut off small portions and drop them into simmering salted water. Continue cooking until they rise to the surface. **3.** Drain the noodles and place them into the chicken goulash. **4.** Sprinkle each serving with parsley.

Right: *From the Csarda restaurant in the Danube International Hotel, Budapest. Clockwise from bottom right: Grilled Rumpsteak; Saddle of Veal; Stuffed Chicken (above).*

MEAT & GAME

Veal Paprika Stew
Veal Pörkölt

Serves 6

2 onions, finely chopped
60 g (2 oz) lard
1 teaspoon paprika
1 cup (8 fl oz) water
1 kg (2 lb) shoulder of veal, cut into large cubes
2 tomatoes, peeled and roughly chopped
2 green peppers (capsicums), seeded and cut into small pieces
1 cup (8 fl oz) sour cream
salt

1. Lightly sauté the onions in the lard, add the paprika, water and meat. **2.** Cover the saucepan with a lid and braise the meat for approximately 45 minutes or until tender. **3.** Add the tomatoes and peppers, cover and continue cooking for a further 15 minutes. **4.** Add the sour cream, season with salt and heat gently but do not boil it once the cream has been added. **5.** Serve with noodles, dumplings or steamed rice.

Veal Cutlets with Paprika

Serves 6

6 veal cutlets (about 2.5 cm (1 inch) thick)
90 g (3 oz) lard
2 onions, sliced
1 teaspoon paprika
1 cup (8 fl oz) beef stock (see p. 328)
salt
1 tablespoon flour
1 cup (8 fl oz) sour cream
3 green peppers (capsicums), seeded and sliced
3 tomatoes, peeled and roughly chopped

1. Fry the veal cutlets in the lard until they are light brown. **2.** Remove them and in the same pan lightly sauté the onions. Add the paprika, beef stock and salt and simmer for 5 minutes. **3.** Add the cutlets to this mixture, cover with a lid and gently simmer until the meat is tender. **4.** Mix the flour into the sour cream and while stirring add it to the veal cutlets. **5.** Add the peppers and tomatoes, cover and simmer for 15 minutes. **6.** Traditionally, this dish is served with either noodles or fried potatoes and onions.

Székely Goulash

Serves 6

1 kg (2 lb) shoulder of pork, cut into large cubes
375 g (12 oz) onions, chopped
90 g (3 oz) lard
½ teaspoon caraway seeds, crushed
1 clove garlic, crushed
2 sprigs dill, chopped
1–2 cups beef stock (see p. 328)
1 kg (2 lb) sauerkraut, rinsed in cold water and drained
1 teaspoon paprika
1 cup (8 fl oz) sour cream
salt

1. In a large saucepan, lightly sauté the meat and the onions in the lard. **2.** Add the caraway seeds, garlic, dill and the stock. **3.** Simmer for 45 minutes. **4.** Add the sauerkraut and the paprika and simmer for a further 30 minutes. Before serving add the sour cream, heat gently and if necessary season, but be careful because the sauerkraut is sometimes very salty.

Braised Beef Esterhazy

Serves 6

1½ kg (3 lb) rump, in one piece
salt
freshly ground black pepper
60 g (2 oz) lard
1 carrot, sliced
1 parsnip, sliced
1 stalk celery, chopped
2 onions, sliced
2 tablespoons flour
1 teaspoon paprika
2 cups beef stock (see p. 328)
1 tablespoon capers
1 cup (8 fl oz) sour cream
6 slices lemon

1. Preheat the oven to 175°C (350°F/Gas 4). **2.** Season the meat and in a large, heavy-bottomed cast iron casserole, brown it in the lard. Add the carrots, parsnips, celery and onions and fry them until the onions are a light golden colour. **3.** Sprinkle the vegetables with flour, add the paprika and the beef stock. **4.** Cover the casserole and place it in the preheated oven. **5.** Braise the beef for approximately 1½ hours or until the meat is tender. **6.** Remove the meat and keep it warm for 10 minutes before carving it. **7.** In the meantime, add the capers and sour cream to the vegetables and mix them well in. Heat gently but do not allow it to boil once the sour cream has been added. **8.** To serve, cut the meat into slices and arrange them on a platter. Mask the meat with the sauce and vegetables and decorate with the lemon slices. **9.** Serve with noodles or rice.

Stuffed Green Peppers

Serves 6

Tomato Sauce:
2 onions, chopped
30 g (1 oz) lard
1 kg (2 lb) tomatoes, peeled and roughly chopped
3 green peppers (capsicums), seeded and roughly chopped
½ teaspoon paprika
salt
pepper

Stuffed Peppers:
12 green peppers (capsicums), seeded
100 g (3⅓ oz) rice, parboiled
500 g (1 lb) minced lean pork
2 onions, chopped and fried
3 sprigs parsley, chopped
1 egg
1 egg yolk
1 sprig marjoram, chopped
½ clove garlic, crushed
salt
pepper

1. Preheat oven to 190°C (375°F/Gas 5). **2.** To prepare the tomato sauce, sauté the onions in the lard for 10 minutes, add the tomatoes, green peppers, paprika, salt and pepper. **3.** Simmer for 30 minutes until the sauce thickens. **4.** Prepare the stuffing by mixing the parboiled rice together with the pork, sautéed onions, parsley, egg, egg yolk, marjoram, garlic, salt and pepper. Mix all ingredients well together. **5.** Divide the stuffing into 12 equal portions and stuff the green peppers. **6.** Pour the tomato sauce into a baking dish large enough to hold the stuffed peppers and arrange them next to each other in the dish. Place the baking dish into the preheated oven and cook for approximately 30 minutes or until the peppers are tender. **7.** Serve 2 peppers per person with some tomato sauce poured over the peppers.

Hungarian Cabbage Rolls

Serves 6

1 large cabbage (1.5 kg (3 lb))
30 g (1 oz) speck, finely chopped
3 onions, finely chopped
1 clove garlic, crushed
500 g (1 lb) minced pork-veal mixture
1 cup cooked rice
2 eggs, lightly beaten
2 tablespoons paprika
1 sprig marjoram, finely chopped
salt
freshly ground black pepper
1 kg (2 lb) sauerkraut, rinsed in cold water and drained
1 cup (8 fl oz) water
1 cup (8 fl oz) tomato purée
45 g (1½ oz) butter
2 tablespoons flour
1 cup (8 fl oz) sour cream

1. In a large saucepan, boil up enough salted water to cover the cabbage and simmer the cabbage for 10 minutes. **2.** Remove the cabbage, drain it and break off enough large leaves to make 12 cabbage rolls. Drain them and leave to cool. **3.** In a frying pan, melt and fry the speck, add the onions and garlic and sauté until the onions are transparent. **4.** Place the onions in a mixing bowl, add the minced meat, rice, eggs, paprika and marjoram and season with salt and pepper, mix together with a wooden spoon. Place approximately 2 tablespoons of the mixture in the centre of each cabbage leaf. **5.** Roll the cabbage leaf, starting at the thick end of the leaf. **6.** Fold the sides over and roll the cabbage leaf tightly. **7.** In a large, heavy-bottomed casserole, spread out the sauerkraut and place the cabbage rolls on top of it. **8.** Mix the water and the tomato purée and pour it over the cabbage rolls. **9.** Cover the casserole and simmer for approximately 1 hour. **10.** Place the cabbage rolls into a dish and keep them warm. **11.** In a small frying pan, melt the butter and stir in the flour until the roux browns slightly, add the cream and continue cooking until the sauce thickens. **12.** Mix the sauce into the sauerkraut and simmer for 10 minutes, taste and if necessary adjust the seasoning. **13.** To serve, arrange the sauerkraut on a serving dish and place the cabbage rolls on top of it with the liquid poured over the cabbage rolls. **14.** If there is any sauce left, serve it in a sauce-boat.

Tokay Pork Chops with Red Cabbage

Serves 6

12 small pork chops
2 tablespoons flour
salt
freshly ground black pepper
90 g (3 oz) lard
1 tablespoon tomato purée
¾ cup water
1 cup Tokay wine (or any sweet white wine)
1 small red cabbage, shredded
60 g (2 oz) smoked speck, diced
1 tablespoon vinegar
1 onion, chopped
½ tablespoon sugar
2 firm tart apples, peeled and diced

1. Dust the pork chops in flour and season them with salt and pepper. **2.** In a large, heavy-bottomed frying pan, heat the lard and lightly fry the chops to seal them. **3.** Place the chops in a casserole. **4.** In the frying pan, boil together the tomato purée, water and one-third of the wine. Pour the mixture over the chops. **5.** Cover the casserole and braise the chops gently until they are tender. **6.** In a frying pan, melt and fry the speck. **7.** Add the cabbage, vinegar, onion, sugar and apples. **8.** Braise the cabbage until it is soft, season with salt and pepper. **9.** To serve, arrange the chops on a large platter and place the braised cabbage around the chops.

Braised Pork Loin

*From the Happy Miller Inn (Vigmolnar Czarda),
Lake Balaton.*

Serves 6

1.5 kg (3 lb) loin of pork
salt
freshly ground black pepper
3 onions, sliced
90 g (3 oz) smoked speck, diced
1 clove garlic, crushed
125 g (4 oz) mushrooms, sliced
½ teaspoon caraway seeds
1 cup beef stock (see p. 328)

1. Preheat the oven to 190°C (375°F/Gas 5). **2.** Rub the pork with salt and pepper and place it into a casserole. **3.** Lightly fry the onions in the speck and add it to the casserole together with the rest of the ingredients. **4.** Cover the casserole and place it in the preheated oven. **5.** Braise for approximately 2 hours. **6.** Remove the meat from the casserole and let it stand for 10 minutes before carving it into slices. **7.** Remove any excess fat from the cooking liquid and taste it for flavour, if necessary adjust the seasoning. **8.** The cooking juice together with the solid ingredients can be served as a sauce with the sliced meat. **9.** Sautéed potatoes and onions are usually served with this dish.

Saddle of Venison Szekszárd Style

Özgerinc Szekszárdi Módra

*From the 'Vadvendéglö' (Venison Restaurant),
Pecs.*

Serves 6–8

1 × 2–3 kg (4–6 lb) saddle of venison
2 tablespoons tomato purée
2–4 tablespoons redcurrant jelly
1 tablespoon paprika
salt
pepper

Marinade:
1 cup white wine vinegar
2 cups dry red wine
1 clove of garlic, crushed
6 peppercorns
2 bay leaves
6 juniper berries, crushed
3 sprigs parsley, chopped
2 sprigs marjoram, chopped
1 carrot, chopped
2 stalks celery, chopped
1 onion, chopped
4 cups (1 litre) water

1. Combine the marinade ingredients and boil them for 30 minutes. Allow to cool. **2.** Place the saddle of venison in the cooled marinade and refrigerate for 2 days. The original recipe requires the venison to be marinated for 4 days but this may be excessive. **3.** Preheat the oven to 190°C (375°F/Gas 5). **4.** Remove the meat from the marinade and wipe off excess moisture. **5.** The sauce should be prepared first and the meat should be roasted at the last moment. It is essential to keep the meat rare or underdone. **6.** To prepare the sauce, boil the marinade for approximately 1 hour. **7.** Cool, then sieve it, forcing through as much of the solids as possible. **8.** Return the sieved liquid to a saucepan and add the tomato purée. Cook this liquid until it has reduced to approximately 4 cups. **9.** Add the redcurrant jelly and paprika, season and cook for a further 15 minutes. **10.** Place the meat in the preheated oven and roast for approximately 20–30 minutes, making sure that it is still pink inside. **11.** Remove the meat from the oven, let it stand for 10 minutes, cut it off the bone and then cut each fillet into slices. Arrange them on a serving platter and mask them with the sauce. **12.** In the Vadvendéglö restaurant, venison is served with crumbed potato croquettes.

Right: A colourful centrepiece of sausages at the Baricska Czarda Restaurant in Balatonfured.

DESSERTS & PASTRY

Fruit Cream

Strawberries, raspberries or any fruit purée may be used in this dessert.

Serves 4-6

¾ cup (6 fl oz) milk
½ cup (4 oz) sugar
2 egg yolks
10 g (⅓ oz) gelatine, dissolved in 2 tablespoons hot water
125 g (4 oz) any fruit purée
1½ cups (10 fl oz) cream
2½ tablespoons caster (powdered) sugar

1. Boil the milk with half of the sugar. **2.** In the top of a double boiler, over simmering water, cream the eggs with the rest of the sugar. **3.** Gradually, while whipping constantly, add the milk to the egg yolks and continue stirring until the mixture thickens into a custard. **4.** Remove it from the heat and continue stirring until the mixture is lukewarm. **5.** Add the gelatine and mix it in well. **6.** Add the fruit purée. **7.** Whip the cream with the caster sugar and fold it into the fruit custard mixture. **8.** Pour the mixture into dessert glasses, refrigerate and serve chilled, decorated with some whipped cream.

Layered Pancakes

Serves 4-6
(Makes 12 pancakes)

Pancake Batter:
1¼ cups (5 oz) flour
2 eggs, lightly beaten
1 egg yolk
1 cup (8 fl oz) milk
1 teaspoon sugar
pinch of salt
butter for frying

Filling:
150 g (5 oz) walnuts, ground
½ cup (4 oz) caster (powdered) sugar
220 g (7 oz) cream cheese
3 egg yolks, lightly beaten
30 g (1 oz) raisins
60 g (2 oz) cocoa
185 g (6 oz) apricot jam
5 egg whites, beaten stiff with some sugar and a few drops of vanilla essence
1 tablespoon vanilla sugar

1. Preheat oven to 175°C (350°F/Gas 4). **2.** To make the pancake batter, mix the flour, eggs, egg yolk, milk, sugar and a pinch of salt. **3.** Make 12 pancakes and set aside. **4.** The filling ingredients will make four different types of filling. **5. Filling No. 1**: combine the walnuts with one-third of the sugar; set aside. **6. Filling No. 2**: cream the cheese with a further one-third of the sugar, the egg yolks and raisins; set aside. **7. Filling No. 3**: combine the cocoa with the rest of the sugar; set aside. **8. Filling No 4**: plain apricot jam. **9.** Butter a soufflé dish, preferably the same diameter as the pancakes. **10.** Place a pancake on the bottom of the dish and on top of that place one-third of the walnut-sugar mixture. **11.** Place another pancake on top of that and spread it with one-third of the cream cheese mixture. **12.** Place a further pancake on top of that and sprinkle it with the cocoa and sugar mixture. **13.** Place a pancake on top of that and spread it with one-third of the apricot jam. **14.** Repeat the layers, finishing with a layer of apricot jam. **15.** Place the dish in the preheated oven and bake for 30 minutes. **16.** Remove it from the oven, turn down the heat and spread the top layer of jam with the beaten egg whites. **17.** Return the dish to the oven and leave it long enough for the meringue to set and brown slightly on top. **18.** Serve hot, sprinkled with the vanilla sugar.

Fried Crisp Puffs

Lángos

From the Malomczárda (Mill Inn), Lake Balaton. Lángos are very popular in Hungary and can be bought at street-side stalls.

1 packet dry active yeast (7 g–¼ oz)
lukewarm water
pinch of sugar
3¼ cups (13½ oz) flour
1½ teaspoons salt
lard for deep frying

1. Mix the dry active yeast with ¾ cup of lukewarm water to which a pinch of sugar has been added. Let it stand for approximately 10 minutes until it becomes frothy. **2.** In a large mixing bowl, combine the flour and salt. When the yeast is ready, pour it into the flour and add additional lukewarm water to make a medium soft dough. **3.** Knead the dough for 5–8 minutes. **4.** Return the dough to the bowl, cover it with a tea towel and place it in a warm, draught-free spot to rise for approximately 1 hour, until double its volume. **5.** Heat the lard in a frying pan. **6.** With a tablespoon, take out some of the dough and with wet hands pull it out into a thin round pancake approximately the size of the frying pan. **7.** Place the pancake into the hot fat and fry it until one side is brown, turn it over and fry the other side until it is brown and the pancake is crisp. **8.** Lángos can also be made with cooked or raw potatoes. For potato Lángos, add to the dough approximately 200 g (7 oz) cooked mashed potatoes or grated raw potatoes and make the dough slightly firmer by using less water. Fry the potato Lángos in the same way as in the standard recipe. **9.** At the Mill Inn at Lake Balaton the Lángos are served with leg of pork roasted with pepper, salt and garlic.

Cherry Pie

6 egg yolks
60 g (2 oz) butter, softened
⅔ cup (6 oz) sugar
grated rind of ½ lemon
6 egg whites
1 cup (4 oz) fine dry breadcrumbs
500 g (1 lb) pitted fresh or preserved cherries, well drained
icing (confectioners') sugar

1. Preheat the oven to 180°C (350°F/Gas 4). **2.** Cream the egg yolks, the butter and half of the sugar until fluffy and thick, then add the grated lemon rind. **3.** Beat the egg whites until very stiff, gradually adding the remainder of the sugar. **4.** Add the breadcrumbs alternately with the beaten egg whites to the yolk mixture. **5.** Pour the mixture into a round, buttered pie dish. **6.** Place the cherries on top of the mixture, pressing them in lightly. **7.** Bake in the preheated oven for 25–30 minutes. **8.** Serve hot, cut into wedges and sprinkled with icing sugar.

Pork Crackling Scones

Pogásca

From the Apostolok Restaurant, Budapest.

1 sachet dry active yeast
2 cups (16 fl oz) lukewarm milk
8 cups (2 lb) flour
500 g (1 lb) pork crackling, chopped
salt
freshly ground black pepper
1½ cups dry white wine (lukewarm)
250 g (8 oz) butter, softened
1–2 egg whites, lightly whisked with 2–4 tablespoons water

1. Preheat the oven to 200°C (400°F/Gas 6). **2.** Dissolve the yeast in ¾ cup of lukewarm water and let it stand for approximately 10 minutes until it becomes frothy. **3.** Place the flour, pork crackling, salt and pepper in a large mixing bowl and mix the ingredients together. **4.** Add the softened butter and, using your hands, make sure that it is well incorporated into the flour. **5.** Add the yeast, the rest of the milk and wine and mix well together. The dough should be of a firm consistency. If it is too dry, add more liquid, if it is too soft, add a little more flour. **6.** Knead the dough for 5–8 minutes. **7.** Cover the bowl and place it in a warm draught-free spot to rise until it has doubled in volume. **8.** Punch the dough down and knead it lightly. Roll it out and fold it two or three times, as for puff pastry (see p. 331). **9.** Return it to the bowl and refrigerate, preferably overnight. **10.** Before baking, roll it out and fold it, then roll it out again. **11.** With a biscuit cutter, cut out round shapes. **12.** Place the scones on a buttered baking sheet and make a network of incisions on top of each scone. **13.** Brush the top with the egg and water mixture. **14.** Leave the scones to rise for 15–20 minutes. **15.** Bake in the preheated oven for approximately 20–30 minutes.

Noodles

Galuskas

1 egg
1 cup (8 fl oz) water
1 teaspoon salt
4 cups (1 lb) flour

1. Combine the egg with the water and salt and mix this into the flour to make a medium firm dough. **2.** In a saucepan, boil 4 cups of salted water and, with your thumb and index finger, break off small pieces of the dough and drop them into the boiling water. **3.** Boil the Galuskas until they rise to the surface, drain, then rinse them under cold water. **4.** Galuskas are extensively used in various meat, fish and poultry dishes.

SWITZERLAND

When does the cooking of a country become a cuisine? It's hard to tell. The Swiss are not really worried, they do not claim this distinction for their indigenous cooking.

The plain, hearty and nutritious dishes of that country are a true product of the climate and the proverbial Swiss thrift. Heavy but tasty cheese dishes, plain flavoursome cured meats and aromatic smoked sausages, heavy, filling soups and stews, plain fresh vegetables, ripe, juicy fruit, wholesome and delicious breads, rich cakes and sweet desserts are their claim to culinary fame.

During the past 100 years or more, the Swiss have successfully supplemented their basic earnings with tourism; the by-product of this is the development of an interesting hybrid style of cooking in which local ingredients and styles are influenced by and mix with the cuisines of its neighbour. The result: the Swiss international cuisine. Dishes such as Eminence de Veau, the succulent strips of veal cooked with white wine and cream, Veal Cordon Bleu, crumbed slices of veal with ham and cheese have become favourites on the menus of many countries.

I appreciate the refinement of that style of cooking, but I do love the simple and unpretentious farm-house cooking of the Swiss.

One of its attractions is the way the cooking follows the seasons, feast days and the many other annual events in local life.

In summer, when the fruit is ripe, the Wähen, the large fruit tarts, can be found in most houses, while garden fresh vegetables and salads are eaten with every meal. In autumn and winter when the gardens are empty and the trees are bare, preserved fruit and vegetables are part of the seasonal fare. The famous cured and dried meats of the Canton of Grisons, the so-called Bündenerfleisch, originally the preserved meat for winter, is now an all-year-round favourite of the Swiss table.

Swiss cheese is also eaten all year round, but prepared in the many hearty and warming cheese dishes it is at its best when eaten in winter. I have pleasant memories of evenings spent in the old village of Verbier where after an exhilarating day's skiing we enjoyed plates of raclette prepared for us by the patron, melting the cheese in front of the crackling log fire.

After Swiss watches, cheese is undoubtedly the most famous product of the land. We, as outsiders tend to think in terms of the famous Gruyère and Emmantaler as being the 'Swiss Cheeses'. But countless local traditional cheeses are made in all the mountain cantons while new varieties of soft cheeses, cheeses with white and blue veins, dessert and fresh cheeses are constantly being developed by the cheese industry. During my all too brief gastronomic tour of Switzerland I had the opportunity of trying some of the many tasty dishes of the Swiss kitchen.

My visit was arranged with Swiss efficiency and attention to detail by Peter Kuehler the head of Ambassador Service Hotels, an organisation linking some 80 hotels in all parts of the country. Each is serving local indigenous Swiss fare as part of its menu.

Right: The village of Gruyère, where the famous cheese is made.

SOUPS

Barley Soup

Bündner Gerstensuppe

From the Hotel Duc de Rohan, Chur.

Serves 6–8

2 parsnips, peeled and finely diced
100 g (3½ oz) finely chopped celery
2 large potatoes, peeled and finely diced
2 leeks, white part only, finely sliced
2 celery leaves, chopped
4–5 cabbage leaves, chopped
1 veal knuckle
1 tablespoon melted butter
90 g (3 oz) barley
8 cups (2 litres) meat stock (see p. 328)
salt, freshly ground pepper
1 onion spiked with 6 cloves
100 g (3½ oz) smoked speck or bacon
300 g (10 oz) smoked pork neck
200 g (7 oz) smoked beef
1 egg yolk
⅓ cup (3 fl oz) cream

1. In a saucepan, combine the vegetables, the veal knuckle and butter. 2. While stirring lightly, sauté the mixture. 3. Add the barley and sauté for a few minutes longer. 4. Add the stock, season and add the onion, speck or bacon, pork and beef. 5. Bring to the boil over low heat, simmer for 2½ hours. 6. Remove the onion and all the meat. 7. First remove the veal from the bone and, together with the other meat, cut into small dice. 8. Return the diced meat to the broth. 9. Beat the yolk with the cream and mix it into the soup. 10. Heat it but do not boil. Check the seasoning and serve the soup as a one-pot meal.

Cheese Soup

Käsesuppe

Serves 6

500 g (1 lb) stale bread, cut into small cubes
6 cups (1.5 litres) hot meat stock (see p. 328)
2 onions, chopped
100 g (3½ oz) butter
2½ cups (9 oz) grated Swiss cheese
salt
freshly ground pepper
2 onions, sliced

1. Soak the bread in the hot stock for 1 hour. Strain it through a sieve and reserve the stock. Squeeze out as much liquid from the bread as possible. 2. Sauté the onions in half of the butter, add the bread and fry it for a few minutes. 3. With a potato masher, mash the bread and onions, adding a little of the remaining stock. 4. Mix in the cheese. The mixture should not be too thick, so if necessary add more stock or water. Season to taste. 5. Cook over low heat until the cheese melts. 6. Sauté the sliced onions in the remaining butter and serve the soup hot, sprinkled with the onions and butter.

Pea Soup

Berner Erbsensuppe

Serves 6

2½ cups (1 lb) yellow or green split peas
8 cups (2 litres) water
125 g (4 oz) speck or bacon cut into small dice
2 onions, chopped
1 leek, white part only, sliced
3 sticks celery, sliced
1 parsnip, sliced
salt and pepper
6 slices of bread
60 g (2 oz) butter

1. Soak the peas in the water overnight. 2. Fry the speck or bacon and when it has rendered the fat, sauté the onions, leek, celery and parsnip. 3. Add it to the peas and water, season, bring to the boil and simmer over low heat for 1½–2 hours. 4. Cut the bread into cubes and fry it golden-brown in the butter. 5. Serve the soup hot with the sippets served separately.

FIRST COURSES

Lenten Ravioli

Ravioli di Magro Olivella

From the Hotel Olivella au Lac, Lugano-Moncota.

Pasta:
4 cups (16 oz) flour
5 eggs
1 tablespoon olive oil
pinch of salt

Stuffing:
250 g cooked chopped spinach or silver beet
30 g (1 oz) butter
salt
freshly ground pepper
200 g (6½ oz) fresh ricotta cheese
3 egg yolks
pinch of nutmeg

Pasta: 1. Place the flour in a mound on the working surface and form a well in the top. **2.** Place the eggs in it, add the oil and salt and with a fork stir it together. **3.** Knead the dough with your fingers and the heel of your palms for 10–15 minutes. If you have a pasta machine make the dough a little firmer, do not knead by hand but pass the dough through the machine several times until the dough is fine and smooth. **4.** Wrap the dough in a floured cloth and rest it for 15–20 minutes. **5.** Divide the dough into two, leave one part wrapped and roll out the other into a thin sheet. **6.** Leave it to dry a little (but not too dry) before using it to make the ravioli.

Stuffing: 1. Over medium heat, toss the spinach in the butter for 5 minutes. Season. **2.** Remove from the heat, stir in the ricotta, egg yolks and nutmeg. **3.** With a serrated pastry wheel cut the thinly rolled out pasta into 5 × 5 cm (2 × 2 inch) squares and place a small mound of the stuffing on half of the squares. Moisten the edges, cover with the remaining squares and, with your fingers, press firmly together. **4.** Cook in plenty of lightly salted water for 3–4 minutes until they are still firm and chewy. **5.** Drain the water, sprinkle the ravioli with grated Parmesan cheese and serve with thinly sliced mushrooms sautéed in butter.

Fondue

This famous Swiss cheese dip is considered to be the country's national dish. Traditionally, it is prepared in a glazed pottery dish called a caquelon. There are many variations of fondue, the main difference being the type of cheese used.

Serves 4

Basic Recipe:
1 clove garlic
5¼ cups (19 oz) grated cheese
1¼ cups (10 fl oz) dry white wine
2 teaspoons cornflour (cornstarch)
½ cup (4 fl oz) Kirsch
freshly ground pepper
pinch of nutmeg

1. Rub the dish with the garlic clove. **2.** Mix the cheese and wine together over a low heat and, stirring constantly, bring to the boil. **3.** Mix the cornflour and Kirsch together and stir it into the cheese mixture. Boil it briefly and season with pepper and nutmeg. **4.** To serve, place the fondue dish on top of a burner with an adjustable flame. **5.** To eat the fondue, spike a cube of bread on a fork and dip it in the cheese mixture. From time to time, stir it with a fork and bread. Tradition requires that anyone who loses the piece of bread off their fork stands a round of drinks!

Note: The flavour of fondue depends on the type of cheese used. Try the following regional variations. In the Canton of Vaud, where the romantic township of Gruyère is located, Gruyère cheese is used exclusively; also the garlic is finely chopped and sautéed and added to the mixture. In Fribourg, a 50–50 mixture of Fribourg Vacherin and Gruyère is used while in Neuenburg they use half Gruyère and half Emmentaler.

Ham Pastie

Schinken Pastete

Serves 4

300 g (9½ oz) leg ham, fincly chopped
3 sprigs parsley, finely chopped
⅓ cup (2½ fl oz) sour cream
¼ teaspoon powdered rosemary
salt
freshly ground black pepper
1 packet defrosted frozen puff pastry
1 egg, lightly beaten

1. Preheat the oven to 200°C (400°F/Gas 6). **2.** Combine the ham, parsley, cream, rosemary, salt and pepper. **3.** Roll out the pastry and cut it into a rectangle. **4.** Place the stuffing in a rectangular heap on top, fold at the short end and roll it lengthwise. Prick it with a fork, brush with the egg and bake it on a buttered baking sheet in the preheated oven for approximately 20 minutes or until golden-brown. Cut into slices and serve hot.

VEGETABLES

Maluns

A potato dish from Graubünden
From the Hotel Duc de Rohan, Chur.

Serves 4

1.2 kg (2 lb 7 oz) potatoes
3¼ cups (13 oz) flour
salt
a pinch of nutmeg
100 g (3⅓ oz) butter

1. The day before they are required, cook the potatoes in their jackets; be careful not to overcook them. **2.** When cold, peel them and grate them on the largest holes of the grater. **3.** Add the flour, salt and nutmeg and, with your fingers, gently mix until all the flour is absorbed. Refrigerate until the next day. **4.** Heat one-third of the butter in a heavy, preferably cast iron, frying pan. **5.** Fry over low heat, stirring and turning the mixture constantly and gradually adding the rest of the butter. If preparing it in the traditional manner, this should take up to 40 minutes until the mixture becomes light brown and is broken up into small, flake-like, soft pieces. It is important not to add too much butter at once or the Maluns will be too hard. Keep a little of the butter to add just before serving. Traditionally, this delicious potato dish is served with apple mousse, Swiss cheese and milk coffee and is eaten as a supper dish.

Grated Potato Cake

Berner Rösti

From the Hotel Bären, Berne.

Serves 4

800 g (1 lb 10 oz) potatoes
30 g (1 oz) lard
60 g (2 oz) butter
80 g (1⅔ oz) speck or bacon, diced
salt
freshly ground pepper

1. Cook the potatoes in their jackets and refrigerate until the next day. **2.** Peel the cold potatoes and grate them on the largest holes of the grater. **3.** Heat the lard and butter and sauté the speck. **4.** Mix in the potatoes and with an egg-slice flatten them down into a cake. **5.** Cover with a lid or plate and fry over low heat until both sides are crisp.

EGG & CHEESE

Cheese Fritters

Beignets Soufflés au Gruyère

From the Hotel Carlton, Lausanne.

Serves 4

¾ cup (6 fl oz) milk
50 g (1⅔ oz) butter
1 cup (4 oz) flour
4 eggs
salt, pepper
1 pinch of nutmeg
1 cup (4 oz) grated Gruyère cheese
oil for frying

1. In a saucepan, bring the milk and butter to the boil. **2.** Add the flour all at once, stir vigorously with a wooden spoon over the heat until the pastry comes away from the sides of the pan. **3.** Remove from the heat, beat in the eggs one at a time making sure that the mixture is not too thin. Add salt, pepper and nutmeg. **4.** Cool it and stir in the cheese. Refrigerate for 1 hour. **5.** Preheat the oil to approximately 180°C (350°F) and with a tablespoon form small balls. Fry the fritters until golden-brown and serve them hot with a piquant tomato sauce.

Berne Fried Cheese Sandwich

Berner Käseschmitte

From the Hotel Bären, Berne.

Serves 4

1½ cups (6 oz) grated Emmentaler cheese
2 egg yolks
⅓ cup (2½ fl oz) milk
1 teaspoon Kirsch
salt, pepper
2 egg whites, stiffly beaten
8 slices rye or brown bread
butter

1. Mix the cheese, egg yolks, milk, Kirsch, salt and pepper, and finally fold in the egg whites. **2.** Thickly coat each slice with the mixture. **3.** Heat the butter in a frying pan and fry the slices until crisp and light brown.

Right: A selection of traditional Swiss dishes from the Hotel International in Basle. Clockwise from bottom centre: Grated Potato Cake (above); Ice Cream Mousse with Kirsch (see page 185); Roast Fillet of Beef with Mushrooms; Sour Calf's Liver (see page 182).

FISH

Fillets of Perch with Parsley and Chives

Fillets de Perch Persiboulette

From the Hotel Carlton, Lausanne.

Serves 4

2 tablespoons softened butter
4–8 fillets (depending on size) perch, bream or snapper
salt
freshly ground pepper
½ cup (4 fl oz) dry white wine
juice of 1 lemon
6 sprigs parsley, chopped
1 small bunch chives, finely chopped

1. Preheat the oven to 200°C (400°F/Gas 6). **2.** Butter an ovenproof dish, arrange the fillets skin side down next to each other, season and sprinkle them with wine and lemon juice. **3.** Bake them in the preheated oven for 8–10 minutes. **4.** Remove from the oven, place on a heated platter and keep them warm. **5.** Pour the cooking liquid into a saucepan and boil until reduced to half. **6.** Add the parsley and chives and pour the sauce over the fish. Serve with boiled potatoes.

Trout with Cream

Truite à la Crème des Alpes

From the Hotel Duc de Rohan, Chur.

Serves 1

30 g (1 oz) butter
2 spring onions (scallions), chopped
60 g (2 oz) button mushrooms
¼ cup (2 fl oz) dry white wine
½ cup (4 fl oz) fish stock (see p. 328)
salt
freshly ground pepper
one 300 g (9 oz) trout
¼ cup (2 fl oz) cream
1 sprig parsley, finely chopped
1 sprig dill, finely chopped
1 tablespoon beurre manié (½ tablespoon butter mixed with ½ tablespoon flour)

1. In the butter, lightly sauté the onions and mushrooms. **2.** Add the wine, stock, salt and pepper. **3.** Add the trout, cover with a lid and poach for 10 minutes or until the trout is done. **4.** Place the trout on a heated dinner plate, remove the skin and keep the fish warm. **5.** Reduce the cooking liquid to half by boiling over high heat. **6.** Add the cream, parsley and dill and thicken with the beurre manié. **7.** Adjust seasoning, pour the sauce over the fish and serve hot.

Freshwater Crayfish Tails in Dill Sauce

Queues d'Ecrevisses aux Aneth

From the Hotel Nicoletta, Zermatt.

Serves 4

24–32 freshwater crayfish (yabbies)
3 tablespoons wine vinegar
salt
juice of 1 lemon
1 teaspoon Worcestershire sauce
30 g (1 oz) butter
4 sprigs dill, finely chopped
2 cups (16 fl oz) dry white wine
1 cup (8 fl oz) cream

1. Blanch the crayfish for 1 minute in boiling water to which the vinegar has been added. **2.** Peel the tails and, if suitable, also the claws. **3.** Sprinkle the flesh with a mixture of salt, lemon juice and Worcestershire sauce. **4.** In a saucepan, heat the butter and briefly sauté the tails and claws. **5.** Add the dill and wine. **6.** Remove the crayfish, add the cream and gently simmer for 30–45 minutes or until reduced to a sauce-like consistency. **7.** To heat, briefly place the tails and claws back into the sauce. **8.** Place on a heated platter, sprinkle with fresh dill and serve with rice and a julienne of vegetables.

POULTRY & GAME

Spatchcock in Cream Sauce

Mistchratzerli

From the Hotel Bären, Berne.

Serves 1

1 × 350–400 g (11–14 oz) spatchcock
salt and ground pepper
30 g (1 oz) butter
50 g (1⅔ oz) speck or bacon, diced
4 button mushrooms
2 pickling onions
3 tablespoons cream
3 tablespoons meat stock (see p. 328)
1 teaspoon finely chopped rosemary

1. Preheat the oven to 180°C (350°F/Gas 4). **2.** Split the spatchcock along its backbone and flatten it out. **3.** Season it and lightly sauté in the butter until it is almost cooked. **4.** Take out the spatchcock and put it into a casserole. **5.** Sauté the speck or bacon, mushrooms and onion in the remaining butter. **6.** Add the cream, meat stock and rosemary and bring it to the boil. Season to taste. **7.** Pour the sauce over the spatchcock, cover the casserole and cook it in the preheated oven for about 15 minutes.

MEAT

Berner Mixed Grill with Rösti

Berner Ratsherrentopf mit Speckrösti

From the Hotel Hirschen at Gunten on the Lake of Thun.

Serves 1

1 slice each beef fillet, veal fillet, pork fillet, smoked speck, veal liver
1 lamb chop
½ lamb's kidney
1 chipolata sausage
1 marrow bone
salt
freshly ground pepper
250 g (8 oz) potatoes in their jackets
1 slice smoked speck, diced
½ onion, finely chopped
30 g (1 oz) butter or lard

1. Grill the meats and marrow bone to your liking and serve them with the rösti, scraping the marrow out of the bone with a spoon. **2.** To cook the rösti, parboil the potatoes and peel them while they are still warm. **3.** Refrigerate the potatoes for a few hours and then grate them on the largest holes of the grater. **4.** In a small omelette pan, sauté the speck and onions in the butter. **5.** Mix in the potatoes, season, and with a pallet knife or egg slice, press the potatoes down firmly. **6.** Cover tightly with a lid or plate and turn the heat down to low. Cook for 25 minutes, then, with the help of a plate or lid, turn the potatoes over without breaking the 'cake'. Fry on the second side until brown. Serve hot.

Veal Schnitzels Valais Style

Escalope de Veau 'Valaisanne'

From the Hotel Nicoletta, Zermatt.

Serves 4

4 veal schnitzels
60 g (2 oz) butter
salt
freshly ground pepper
6 tomatoes, peeled, seeded and finely chopped
12 basil leaves, chopped
2 sprigs oregano, finely chopped
1½ cups (12 fl oz) dry white wine
4 slices prosciutto
4 slices Raclette cheese

1. Quickly sauté the veal in the butter. **2.** Season and add the tomatoes, basil, oregano and wine. **3.** Bring to the boil, take out the veal and keep it warm. **4.** Cook the sauce for 5 minutes. **5.** To serve, place the meat on individual plates, cover it with the prosciutto and cheese. **6.** Place each plate under the griller until the cheese has melted and is light brown. Serve with the sauce.

Emmentaler Schnitzel

From the Hotel Bären, Berne.

Serves 4

4 veal schnitzels
seasoned flour
1 egg, lightly whipped with 2 tablespoons water
½ cup (2 oz) fine, dry breadcrumbs
3 tablespoons grated Emmentaler cheese
oil
4 slices Emmentaler cheese

1. Dust the schnitzels in the seasoned flour, dip them in the egg wash and coat them with a mixture of breadcrumbs and cheese. **2.** Fry them in the oil until light brown and cooked through. **3.** Place them on a heatproof serving dish, put a slice of cheese on each piece of meat and grill them under the preheated griller until the cheese melts. **4.** Traditionally, this dish is served with rösti potatoes (see p. 178) and a fresh salad.

Lamb Ragout

Emmentaler Lammvoressen

From the Hotel Bären, Berne.

Serves 4

600 g (1¼ lb) boneless lamb shoulder cut into 5 cm (2 inch) cubes
50 g (1⅔ oz) butter
2 onions, chopped
2 stalks celery, chopped
1 parsnip, sliced
1 leek, white part only, sliced
salt
freshly ground pepper
1½ cups (12 fl oz) meat stock (see p. 328)
4 bay leaves
1 clove
1 tablespoon flour
½ teaspoon saffron
½ cup (4 fl oz) dry white wine
⅓ cup (2½ fl oz) cream

1. In a saucepan, sauté the meat in the butter. **2.** Add the onions, celery, parsnip and leek. Season and sauté for a few more minutes. **3.** Add the stock, bay leaves and clove. Cook over low heat for 45 minutes. **4.** Remove the bay leaves. Mix together the flour, saffron and wine, add it to the meat and cook for a few minutes to thicken the sauce. **5.** Add the cream, cook it gently without allowing it to boil, season to taste and serve with boiled potatoes.

Sour Calf's Liver

Suuri Laeberli Spalenberg

From the Hotel International, Basle

Serves 4

600 g (1¼ lb) calf's liver, sliced
salt and ground pepper
4 onions, chopped
50 g (1⅔ oz) butter
2 tablespoons wine vinegar
3 tablespoons dry white wine
⅓ cup (2½ fl oz) reduced meat stock (see p. 328)
4 sprigs parsley, finely chopped

1. Season the liver, and, with the onions, fry it in the butter. Do not overcook, it should be pink inside. **2.** Place the liver on a preheated plate and keep it warm. **3.** To the remaining butter and onions add the vinegar, wine and stock. Cook briskly for a few minutes. **4.** To serve, arrange the liver on a platter, pour the sauce over it and sprinkle with parsley. Serve with rösti potatoes (see p. 178).

Right: From the Hotel Hirschen, on the shores of the Lake of Thun. Centre: Berner Mixed Grill with Rösti (see page 181); above: Fish Fillets with White Wine Sauce; right: Meringues Chantilly (see page 184).

DESSERTS & CAKES

Engadin Nutcake

Engadiner Nusstorte

From the Hotel Duc de Rohan, Chur.

Makes one 26 cm (10½ inch) cake

2½ cups (10 oz) flour
200 g (6½ oz) butter, cut into small pieces
a pinch of salt
1⅔ cups (13 oz) sugar
2 eggs, lightly beaten
2½ cups (8 oz) walnut kernels
1 cup (4 fl oz) cream
1 tablespoon honey

1. Preheat the oven to 180°C (350°F/Gas 4).
2. Working quickly, combine the flour, butter, salt and ⅔ cup of the sugar until they are the texture of coarse breadcrumbs. **3.** Mix in the eggs. **4.** Refrigerate for 20 minutes. **5.** Place the rest of the sugar in a dry frying pan and stir over medium heat until it is light brown. **6.** Add the nuts and continue roasting for 2–3 minutes. **7.** Add the cream and dissolve the sugar. **8.** Add the honey. **9.** Roll out two-thirds of the pastry 3 mm (⅛ inch) thick. **10.** Butter a springform tin and line it with the pastry, making the sides approximately 5 cm (2 inches) high. **11.** Place the walnut mixture into the pastry case, making sure that the filling is slightly below the top of the pastry case. **12.** Roll out the remaining pastry to make a lid. **13.** Place it on top of the filling. Wet the edges of the pastry case and fold them over the lid. **14.** Pierce the lid uniformly with a sharp fork. **15.** Bake in the preheated oven for 1 hour until the top of the cake is light brown. If necessary, cover the cake with aluminium foil towards the end of the baking time. **16.** Cool the cake and serve cut into wedges.

Meringues Chantilly

From the Hotel Hirschen at Gunten on the Lake of Thun.

Makes 8 shells

5 egg whites
a pinch of salt
½ cup (4 oz) sugar
3½ tablespoons cornflour (cornstarch)
½ cup (4 oz) caster (powdered) sugar
1 cup (8 fl oz) cream
6 drops vanilla essence
4 tablespoons brandy
chocolate shavings

1. Preheat the oven to 120°C (250°F/Gas ½).
2. Beat the egg whites with the salt until stiff and frothy. **3.** Add the sugar and cornflour and continue beating until thick. **4.** Fold in the caster sugar, saving one tablespoon. **5.** With a piping bag fitted with a star-shaped nozzle, pipe the mixture onto a sheet of dampened aluminium foil or greaseproof paper to form 8 nests. **6.** Bake in the preheated oven for 1–1½ hours, or until dry. **7.** Whip the cream with the remaining tablespoon of caster sugar, the vanilla essence and the brandy. **8.** When the shells are cool, carefully remove them from the aluminium foil or paper. **9.** To serve, fill the shells with the cream and sprinkle them with chocolate shavings.

Apple Fritters

Apfelchüechli

From the Hotel Bären, Berne.

Serves 4

4 cooking apples, peeled and cored
2 tablespoons sugar
juice of ½ lemon
1 tablespoon Kirsch
1 cup (4 oz) flour
pinch of salt
⅔ cup (5 fl oz) beer
1 egg yolk
1 egg white, stiffly beaten
oil
4 tablespoons sugar mixed with 1 teaspoon cinnamon

1. Cut the apples into 1 cm (⅜ inch) thick slices and place them in a shallow dish. **2.** Sprinkle with sugar, lemon juice and Kirsch and set aside. **3.** Mix the flour and salt with the beer and egg yolk to make a batter. Set aside to rest for 1–2 hours. **4.** Before using, fold in the egg white. **5.** Drain the liquid from the apple slices, dust them in flour and dip them in the batter. **6.** Deep fry them in the hot oil for 2–3 minutes. **7.** Serve sprinkled with cinnamon sugar.

Pear Tart

Birnenkuchen nach Winzerart

Makes one round tart 25 cm (10 in) in diameter

2 cups (8 oz) flour
¼ cup (2 oz) sugar
125 g (4 oz) butter, cut into cubes
water
3 apples, peeled and cored
8 pears, peeled and cored
90 g (3 oz) sugar
1¼ cups (10 fl oz) dry red wine
juice of ½ lemon
pinch of cinnamon
pinch of ground cloves
2 tablespoons redcurrant jelly
whipped cream

1. To make the pastry, combine the flour and sugar, add the butter and rub it with your fingertips until it is the consistency of firm breadcrumbs. **2.** Add enough water to make a firm pastry dough. Do not overwork the dough. Refrigerate for 2 hours. **3.** Preheat the oven to 220°C (425°F/Gas 7). **4.** Cut the apples and two of the pears into small slices and cook them with the sugar, wine, lemon juice, cinnamon and cloves until soft. **5.** Pour it through a strainer and reserve the juice. **6.** Halve the remaining pears and cook them in the juice until still firm. Set them aside. **7.** Roll out the dough approximately 3 mm (⅛ in) thick and larger than the tin to allow for double thickness on the sides. **8.** Line the tin, making the sides twice as thick as the bottom. Prick with a fork. **9.** Combine the juice with the cooked apple and pear slices and rub them through a sieve to make a purée. **10.** Return this to the saucepan and cook until it reduces to a thick purée; set aside to cool. **11.** Spread it over the pastry and bake in the preheated oven for 30 minutes. **12.** Arrange the pear halves in concentric circles on top and return it to the oven for a further 10 minutes. **13.** When the tart has cooled slightly but the pears are still lukewarm, spread them with the redcurrant jelly. Refrigerate it until the jelly sets. Cut the tart into slices and serve with whipped cream.

Ice Cream Mousse with Kirsch

Crème Glacée au Kirsch

From the Hotel International, Basle.

Serves 4

8 scoops vanilla ice cream, slightly softened
2 tablespoons Kirsch
4 teaspoons sugar
juice of 2 lemons
1 cup (4 fl oz) cream, whipped

1. Mix the ice cream, Kirsch, sugar and lemon juice. **2.** Fold in the cream and serve in chilled glass dessert dishes.

Plums in Red Wine

Zwetschgen in Rotwein

Serves 4–6

2½ cups (20 fl oz) dry red wine
1 clove
1 cinnamon stick
⅓ cup (3 oz) sugar
2–3 pieces lemon rind
500 g (1 lb) plums
whipped cream

1. In a saucepan, combine the wine, clove, cinnamon stick, sugar and lemon rind and boil for 5 minutes. **2.** Prick the plums several times with a needle so that they do not burst while cooking. **3.** Place them in the wine and cook them only long enough to soften; they should still be firm. Remove the clove, cinnamon and lemon rind and serve with plenty of whipped cream.

Apricot Tart

Waadtländer Aprikosenkuchen

Makes 1 medium-sized round or rectangular tart

2 cups (8 oz) flour
¼ cup (2 oz) sugar
125 g (4 oz) butter, cut into cubes
water
¼ cup (1 oz) hazelnuts, grated
1 kg (2 lb) apricots, cut in half, stones removed
sugar for sprinkling
whipped cream

1. Preheat the oven to 220°C (425°F/Gas 7). **2.** In a mixing bowl, combine the flour and sugar, add the butter and rub it in with your fingertips until the mixture is the consistency of breadcrumbs. **3.** Add enough water to make a firm dough. Work as quickly as possible and do not overwork the dough. Refrigerate for 2 hours. **4.** Roll out the pastry approximately 3 mm (⅛ inch) thick and larger than the tin to allow for a double thickness on the sides. **5.** Line a buttered tin with the pastry, making the sides twice as thick as the bottom. Prick the bottom with a fork and sprinkle it with the nuts. **6.** Arrange the apricots with the cut surface up in concentric circles if you are using a round tin or in rows in a rectangular tin. **7.** Place the tart in the preheated oven and bake for 10 minutes; generously sprinkle with sugar and return the tart to the oven for another 20–25 minutes or until done. **8.** When the tart cools, cut it into slices and serve with whipped cream.

YUGOSLAVIA

Yugoslavia as we know it today is a country of many nations, speaking their own languages and preserving their own traditions and eating habits.

In the past they have maintained their separate life styles and were exposed to different influences. Of the six republics which make up the Federal Republic of Yugoslavia, Croatia, Slovenia and Bosnia-Herzegovina were under the Austro-Hungarian rule, while Macedonia, Montenegro and Serbia were dominated by the Turks for some 500 years.

However they share one common characteristic: a sense of genuine hospitality. In Bosnia-Herzegovina they will welcome you with a cup of Turkish coffee and Ratluk, a local version of Turkish delight. In Slovenia your host will insist that you have some stewed fruit, while in Montenegro you will be offered a glass of milk or honey. In Macedonia and in Serbia it will be a glass of Rakija, a plum brandy and Turkish coffee or Slatka, a whole fruit preserve cooked in heavy sugar syrup served with a glass of water.

In the south, Macedonian cooking shows a strong Turkish and Greek influence. Here the cooking fat is oil and hot peppers and the use of spices give the food a distinctive flavour. Yogurt plays an important part in local cooking. Rivers and lakes abound in fish and there are many tasty preparations for carp, eel and trout. Desserts are typically oriental: Halva, Turkish Delight and many sweets made with heavy sugar syrup. Here lamb and mutton are the most popular meats simply prepared in stews and rice pilafs.

Turkish cooking has also left its mark on the eating habits in Bosnia and Herzegovina but the food is less spicy. Lamb and mutton are still the principal meats and vegetables, especially okra, are used in most dishes. The region shares with its southern neighbour a taste for strong cheeses and in both areas the Pita is a popular speciality. The Pita is a type of pie with savoury or sweet fillings made with Katmer puff pastry.

Dalmatia is my favourite part of Yugoslavia. Its spectacular coastline, the mild maritime climate and some of the best seafood make it one of the most popular tourist areas in Europe. There is hardly a better place where all of this can be enjoyed more than Dubrovnik. With its mediaeval walls and ancient buildings, it's one of the most attractive towns I have visited. When there enjoy the rich harvest of the blue Adriatic sea, especially when simply prepared in some of the local dishes like the Dalmatian Fish Stew.

Of all parts of Yugoslavia, Slovenia has a style of cooking most related to that of Central Europe. Pastries and many of the desserts are of Viennese origin, while some of the pasta dishes may have come across the border from Italy. It boasts the best hunting grounds in the country and its repertoire includes tasty preparations for quail, partridge, hare and venison. Vineyards and orchards yield quality grapes and the best of fruits. Local wines enjoy a high reputation among the connoisseurs.

From the Western dishes of the north to the Middle Eastern style in the south, Yugoslavia presents an interesting range of culinary delights.

Right: Dubrovnik.

SOUPS

Fisherman's Soup

Alaska Corba

From the "Venecija" Restaurant, Belgrade.

Serves 6

3 onions, chopped
¼ cup (2 fl oz) oil
3 sprigs parsley, chopped
2 stalks celery, chopped
2 green peppers (capsicums), seeded and cut into pieces
2 bay leaves
pinch of ground hot red peppers
3 tablespoons tomato purée
juice of 1 lemon
salt, freshly ground pepper
6 cups (1½ litres) water
2 kg of several types of fish fillets

1. In a casserole, fry the onions in the oil until golden-brown. **2.** Add the rest of the ingredients, except the fish, and bring to the boil. **3.** Add the fish and simmer for 10–15 minutes.

Veal Soup

Serves 6-8

300 g (9½ oz) boned veal, chopped
2 carrots, sliced
2 stalks celery, sliced
4 sprigs parsley, chopped
1 onion, chopped
salt
pepper
3 tablespoons oil
25 g (¾ oz) flour
1 teaspoon ground red pepper
60 g (2 oz) tomato purée
2 tablespoons sour cream
1 egg lightly beaten
juice of 1 lemon
chopped parsley
1 large red pepper (capsicum), seeded and thinly sliced

1. Cook the meat and vegetables in 8 cups (2 litres) water until the meat is tender. **2.** Make a roux from the oil, flour, ground pepper and tomato purée; stir it into the soup. **3.** Beat the sour cream and egg together and add it to the soup. Add the lemon juice. **4.** Serve sprinkled with parsley and garnished with the red pepper.

Chicken Soup with Liver Dumplings

Serves 4

Soup:
1.5 kg (3 lb) chicken
6 cups (1.5 litres) water
4 carrots, sliced
2 parsnips, sliced
½ celery root, chopped
3 stalks celery, sliced
3 sprigs celery, chopped
2 bay leaves
6 peppercorns
salt

Liver Dumplings:
1 calf's liver, finely minced
2 egg yolks
15 g (½ oz) softened butter
3 sprigs parsley, finely chopped
salt
2–3 tablespoons breadcrumbs
2 egg whites, stiffly beaten
finely chopped parsley for garnish

1. Put the chicken in a saucepan with the water and simmer for half an hour. **2.** Add the vegetables, bay leaves, peppercorns and salt and simmer for a further half hour or until the chicken is cooked. **3.** Take out the chicken and save for other use, such as Chicken Cocktail (p. 192). **4.** Strain the vegetables and discard them. Cool the liquid and remove excess fat. **5.** To make the dumplings, combine all the ingredients and then fold in the egg whites. If the mixture is too thin add more breadcrumbs. **6.** Bring the soup to the boil. Dip a teaspoon into the hot liquid and drop spoonfuls of the dumpling mixture into the soup. When cooked, the dumplings will rise to the surface. Check the seasoning and serve the soup hot, sprinkled with parsley.

VEGETABLES

Spinach Pies

Pita Leljanica

From the Moniča Han Restaurant, Sarajevo.

Serves 4

½ quantity of puff pastry (see p. 331)
500 g (1 lb) cooked, drained, chopped spinach
3 eggs
150 g (4¾ oz) cottage cheese
salt and pepper
½ cup (4 fl oz) hot melted butter
¼ cup (2 fl oz) sour cream

1. Preheat the oven to 200°C (400°F/Gas 6).
2. Roll out the pastry until very thin. 3. Mix the spinach, eggs and cheese and add seasoning. 4. Arrange the filling in rectangular heaps, cut the pastry to fit and shape into small rolls. 5. Brush with oil and bake in the oven for about 30–45 minutes or until golden brown. 6. Pour the butter over the pies and serve with sour cream.

Zucchini with Cream

Serves 6

1 kg (2 lb) zucchini (courgettes)
salt
1 tablespoon vinegar
45 g (1½ oz) butter
¼ cup (1 oz) flour
1 cup (8 fl oz) chicken or meat stock (see p. 328)
3 tablespoons tomato purée
½ cup (4 fl oz) sour cream

1. On the largest cutters of a grater, grate the zucchinis into long strips, lengthwise. Sprinkle with salt and vinegar and let it stand for 1 hour. 2. Heat the butter, add the zucchini, sprinkle with the flour and cook for a few minutes. Add the stock and the tomato purée mixed with the cream. If necessary, adjust the seasoning. Serve hot.

Stuffed Green Peppers with Cream Cheese

Serves 4

4 large green or red peppers (capsicums)
500 g (16 oz) sheep's cheese, grated (or cottage cheese)
2 eggs
salt
freshly ground pepper
2 tablespoons oil
¾ cup (6 fl oz) sour cream
2 teaspoons paprika

1. Preheat the oven to 240°C (475°F/Gas 9). 2. Cut a round lid from the stalk end of each pepper. Remove the seeds. 3. With a fork, mix the cheese, eggs, salt and pepper and stuff the mixture into the peppers. 4. Oil a baking dish and stand the peppers next to each other. Put some sour cream on top of each, sprinkle with paprika, salt and pepper and bake for 15–20 minutes or until the peppers are cooked. While baking, baste them from time to time with the sour cream.

Serbian Eggplant and Green Pepper Purée

Serves 6

2 large eggplant (aubergines)
8 green peppers (capsicums)
salt and pepper
1 clove garlic, crushed
3 sprigs parsley, finely chopped
juice of 1–2 lemons (to taste)
½ cup (4 fl oz) oil

1. Preheat the oven to 200°C (400°F/Gas 6). 2. Bake the eggplant and green peppers for approximately 30–40 minutes or until they are soft (green peppers will take a little less time). 3. Skin the eggplant and peppers, remove the seeds from the peppers and purée the vegetables. (A food processor is ideal for this purpose.) 4. Season, whip in the garlic, parsley, lemon juice and oil. Refrigerate and serve either as a dip, a spread, or as a vegetable.

FISH

Prawns Dalmatian Style

Serves 6-8

3 onions, finely chopped
½ cup (4 fl oz) oil
1 clove garlic, crushed
1½ cups (6 oz) breadcrumbs
2 kg (4 lb) uncooked prawns
1 cup (8 fl oz) dry white wine
5 sprigs parsley, finely chopped
salt
freshly ground pepper

1. Sauté the onions and garlic in the oil. Add the breadcrumbs and cook until brown and crisp. **2.** Add the prawns and stir fry them over low heat. **3.** When almost cooked, add the wine, parsley, salt and pepper.

Marinated Tuna

From the Jadran Restaurant, Dubrovnik.

Serves 4

1 kg (2 lb) tuna
flour
¾ cup (6 fl oz) oil
60 g (2 oz) carrots, thinly sliced
2 onions, thinly sliced
3 sprigs parsley, finely chopped
6 peppercorns
2 bay leaves
1½ cups (12 fl oz) dry white wine
¾ cup (6 fl oz) vinegar
½ lemon, sliced
1 teaspoon mustard seeds
1 teaspoon salt

1. Cut the fish into 2.5 cm (1 inch) cubes. **2.** Dust them with flour and fry them lightly in the hot oil. Set aside. **3.** In the same oil, fry the carrots and onions, add the parsley, peppercorns, bay leaves, wine, vinegar, lemon slices and mustard seeds. **4.** Bring to the boil and simmer for 2-3 minutes. Add the salt and let the marinade cool. **5.** In a glass or enamelled dish, arrange the fish in layers with some of the marinade poured over each layer. Refrigerate for at least 12 hours before serving.

Dalmatian Fish Stew

From the Jadran Restaurant, Dubrovnik.

Serves 4-6

½ cup oil
2 onions, sliced
1.25 kg (2½ lb) fish fillets, cut into bite size pieces
6 tomatoes, peeled, seeded and roughly chopped
salt and pepper
2 tablespoons vinegar
½ cup (4 fl oz) dry white wine
chopped parsley

1. In the hot oil sauté the onions, add the fish and brown lightly. **2.** Add the tomatoes, salt, pepper, vinegar and wine. **3.** Simmer in an open pan, over a low heat for 1 hour. **4.** Serve sprinkled with parsley and accompanied with polenta or cooked rice.

Squid Risotto

Serves 6

½ cup oil
1 teaspoon sugar
1 tablespoon flour
1 onion, finely chopped
3 sprigs parsley, finely chopped
4 cups (1 litre) water
1 tablespoon vinegar
salt
1 kg (2 lb) cleaned squid tubes, cut into small squares
500 g (16 oz) rice
180 g (6 oz) grated cheese made from sheep's milk

1. Heat together the oil, sugar and flour, add the onion and parsley and sauté for a few minutes. **2.** Mix in the water, vinegar and salt. Bring to the boil. **3.** Add the squid and simmer for 1 hour or until the squid is tender. Add more water to make up the original amount. **4.** Stir in the rice, cover and cook until the rice is tender. **5.** Stir in one-third of the cheese and serve sprinkled with the remaining cheese.

***Right:** In the colonnaded courtyard of the 13th Century former convent, now the Jadran restaurant in Dubrovnik, you can eat excellent seafood.*

POULTRY

Chicken Cocktail

Serves 6-8

2 cups (13 oz) mayonnaise (see p. 330)
2 tablespoons tomato ketchup
2 tablespoons Worcestershire sauce
3 tablespoons slivovic (Yugoslavian plum
brandy) or plain brandy
salt and pepper
chopped lettuce
300 g (10 oz) cooked chicken meat, cut into thin
strips
lemon slices

1. Combine the mayonnaise, ketchup, Worcestershire sauce and brandy. Season to taste and mix well together. **2.** In the bottom of shallow champagne glasses arrange some chopped lettuce and chicken. **3.** Spoon the sauce over the chicken and garnish with lemon slices.

Chicken with Mustard Sauce

Serves 6

1.5 kg (3 lb) chicken
oil for basting
salt and freshly ground pepper
150 g (5 oz) giblets
3 chicken livers
4 egg yolks
1-2 tablespoons vinegar, according to taste
1 cup (8 fl oz) stock (see p. 328)
1 cup (8 fl oz) sour cream
2 tablespoons French mustard
1 tablespoon slivovic (Yugoslavian plum
brandy) or plain brandy

1. Preheat the oven to 180°C (350°F/Gas 4). **2.** Brush the chicken with oil, season it inside and out and place it in the oven. **3.** Roast the chicken for 1¼-1½ hours or until cooked, golden-brown and crisp. Take it out of the oven, carve it, arrange the pieces on a serving platter and keep it warm. **4.** While the chicken is roasting, boil the giblets for 45 minutes. **5.** Chop them finely, also chop the livers. **6.** To make the sauce, whisk the yolks and the vinegar in a double boiler until the sauce starts to thicken. **7.** Add the stock, sour cream, mustard, brandy, giblets and livers. Bring to the boil and season if necessary. **8.** Pour the sauce over the chicken and serve with dumplings (see recipe above).

Chicken Stew with Dumplings

Serves 4-6

2 slices bacon, chopped
1 onion
1.5 kg (3 lb) chicken, cut into pieces
1 cup (8 fl oz) dry white wine
salt
2 tablespoons paprika
2 tablespoons flour
½ cup (4 fl oz) sour cream
2 tablespoons tomato purée

Dumplings:
60 g (2 oz) butter
2 egg yolks
½ teaspoon salt
1¾ cups (5 oz) flour
¼ teaspoon baking powder
¾ cup (6 fl oz) milk
2 egg whites, stiffly beaten

1. To make the stew, fry the bacon until the fat has melted, add the onions and sauté them lightly. **2.** Add the chicken pieces, wine, salt and paprika and simmer for about 45 minutes or until the chicken is tender. **3.** Mix the flour, sour cream and tomato purée together and stir it into the stew. Continue cooking for a few minutes. **4.** To make the dumplings, mix together the butter and egg yolks until creamy. **5.** Sift together ¾ cup of the flour, the salt and baking powder. **6.** Add the remaining flour and the milk to the creamed butter and let it stand for 30 minutes. **7.** Fold in the egg whites and the sifted flour. Mix well together. **8.** With a spoon, form the dumplings, drop them into boiling water and cook for 8-10 minutes. Serve hot with the chicken stew.

Turkey with Sauerkraut

Serves 6 8

1 × 2 kg (4 lb) turkey or a boned turkey
breast
oil
salt, pepper
3 slices of smoked speck or bacon, chopped
2 onions, sliced
1 clove garlic, crushed
6 juniper berries, crushed
1 tablespoon honey
1.5 kg (3 lb) sauerkraut
2–3 cups (16–24 fl oz) dry white wine

1. Preheat the oven to 180°C (350°F/Gas 4).
2. Brush the bird with oil and season it inside and
out. **3.** Melt the speck or bacon and sauté the onions
and garlic. Add the juniper berries, honey,
sauerkraut and wine. Mix well together. **4.** Put the
mixture in the bottom of a roasting dish. Place the
turkey on top and roast it in the oven for 2–2½
hours or until the turkey is cooked. During cooking,
baste the bird frequently with the liquid in the
sauerkraut. Occasionally stir the sauce and if necessary add more wine or water to keep it moist. **5.** To
serve, arrange the sauerkraut on a heated serving
platter, carve the turkey and place the meat on top.

Roast Quail with Rice

Serves 4

8 quail
salt
freshly ground pepper
8 slices of bacon
1½ cups (12 fl oz) meat stock (see p. 328)
1 onion, finely chopped
butter
¾ cup (5 oz) rice
1 sprig each of thyme, oregano and rosemary,
finely chopped
1 chicken liver, finely chopped
finely chopped parsley

1. Preheat the oven to 180°C (350°F/Gas 4).
2. Season the birds inside and out, cover them with
the bacon slices and roast them for 30 minutes until
cooked. Occasionally baste with some of the stock.
3. In a saucepan, sauté the onions in a little butter.
4. Take the quail out and keep them warm. **5.** Pour
the cooking juices and the rest of the stock into the
saucepan with the onions, add the rice and herbs,
cover and simmer until the rice is cooked. Season
and stir in the chicken liver. Heat to cook the liver.
6. Place the rice on a preheated serving platter, arrange the quail on top, sprinkle with parsley and
serve with mixed pickles.

MEAT

Bosnian Casserole

Bosanski Lonac

*From the Monica Han Restaurant, Sarajevo.
This flavoursome stew is prepared with a number
of different meats and takes hours to cook but the
result is well worth while. It is always prepared
for at least 8 to 10 people.*

Serves 10

500 g (1 lb) shin beef
500 g (1 lb) shoulder of lamb
500 g (1 lb) shoulder of pork
4 pigs' trotters or
2 calves' feet, split
125 g (4 oz) bacon or speck, diced
2 onions, sliced
2 carrots, sliced
3 stalks celery, sliced
2 parsnips, sliced
750 g (1½ lb) potatoes, peeled and diced
4 sprigs parsley, chopped
salt and pepper
enough water to cover
2 tablespoons vinegar
2½ cups (20 fl oz) dry white wine

1. Preheat the oven to 150°C (300°F/Gas 2).
2. Cut the beef, lamb and pork into 3.75 cm (1½
inch) cubes. **3.** Brown the meat in the melted bacon.
4. In an earthenware or cast iron casserole, arrange
the meat, vegetables and herbs in alternating layers.
Season. **5.** Pour in the water, vinegar and wine.
6. Cover the casserole with a lid, or waxpaper or foil
tightly tied. **7.** Place the casserole in the oven and
cook for 4–6 hours. **8.** Serve hot directly from the
lonac (pot).

Serbian Veal Cutlets

From the Vinogradi Restaurant, Grocka.

Serves 6

1.5 kg (3 lb) veal cutlets
oil
3 onions, sliced
6 green peppers (capsicums), seeded and roughly chopped
6 tomatoes, peeled and chopped
1 kg (2 lb) potatoes, peeled and thickly sliced
1¼ cups (10 fl oz) dry white wine
salt and pepper
pinch of ground hot red pepper
¾ cup (6 fl oz) sour cream

1. Preheat the oven to 220°C (425°F/Gas 7). **2.** Brown the meat in some of the oil. **3.** Separately sauté the onions and green peppers, add the tomatoes, potatoes, the wine and the seasonings. **4.** In a casserole, arrange alternate layers of meat and vegetables. **5.** Bake in the oven for 30–45 minutes or until the meat is tender. **6.** Pour the sour cream on top and serve immediately.

The original recipe calls for *kajmak* which is made from boiling cow's or sheep's milk which has been poured into shallow wooden bowls called *karlice*. As the milk cools the cream rises to the surface. This layer is removed and stored in another wooden vessel. This process is repeated and several layers accumulate. Each layer is sprinkled with salt.

Breast of Veal Stuffed with Spinach

Serves 6

2 tablespoons oil
2 tablespoons flour
2 cups (16 fl oz) milk
750 g (1½ lb) spinach
3 slices of stale bread soaked in milk
½ cup (4 fl oz) sour cream
1 egg, lightly beaten
salt
freshly ground pepper
1 boned and skinned breast of veal
¼ cup (2 fl oz) melted butter

1. Preheat the oven to 180°C (350°F/Gas 4). **2.** To make the white sauce, heat the oil, add the flour and milk and cook for 5 minutes. The sauce should have a rather heavy consistency. **3.** Blanch the spinach in boiling water, squeeze out the water and chop the spinach finely. **4.** Squeeze the bread dry. **5.** Mix together the white sauce, spinach, bread, sour cream, egg, salt and pepper. **6.** Stuff the veal and sew it up to form a roll. **7.** Place the meat in the preheated oven and bake it for 1½ hours, basting it occasionally with the butter and cooking juices. **8.** Take the meat out of the oven and let it stand for 5 minutes before carving it into slices. Pour the seasoned cooking juice over the meat and serve with boiled potatoes and a tossed green salad.

Shisk Kebabs

Šiš-ćeoap

From the Monića Han Restaurant, Sarajevo. The name Šiš is derived from the Turkish word meaning "sword".

Serves 6

500 g (1 lb) leg of lamb cut into 3.25 cm (1½ inch) cubes
salt and pepper
4 green and red peppers (capsicums), seeded and cut into large pieces
4 tomatoes, cut into quarters
12–16 small pickling-type onions, blanched
4–5 potatoes peeled, partly cooked and cut into thick slices
oil for frying

1. Season the meat. **2.** Arrange the ingredients on skewers, alternating the meat and vegetables but starting and finishing with meat. **3.** Heat the oil in a large frying pan and fry the kebabs until the meat and vegetables are cooked. **4.** Towards the end of the cooking add a little water. Season and serve hot on a bed of cooked rice.

Lamb with Okra

Bamja s Jagnjetinom

From the Monića Han Restaurant, Sarajevo.

Serves 6

500 g (1 lb) okra (ladies' fingers)
2 onions, finely chopped
¼ cup (2 fl oz) oil
750 g (1½ lb) leg of lamb, cut into 3.5 cm (1½ inch) cubes
1 tablespoon flour
pinch of ground hot peppers (to taste)
salt
4 sprigs parsley, finely chopped
¾ cup (6 fl oz) water
¾–1 cup (6–8 fl oz) tomato purée
3 cups (1½ lb) yogurt

1. Preheat the oven to 180°C (350°F/Gas 4). **2.** Bring a saucepan full of water to the boil and boil the okra for a few seconds. Take them out and drain them. **3.** Sauté the onions in the oil, add the meat and fry them together. **4.** Sprinkle with flour, add the hot pepper, salt and okra. **5.** Mix the water with the tomato purée and pour it over the meat and okra. **6.** Cover and bake in the oven for 2 hours. Serve hot with yogurt.

Right: *The Ima Dana restaurant in Skadarlija in Belgrade serves the Serbian speciality of grilled meat. Included in the Mixed Grill (see page 196) are Shisk Kebabs (see page 194) and Grilled Meat Balls (see page 196).*

Mixed Grill

From the Ima Dana Restaurant, Skadarlija, Belgrade.

Serves 6-8

**500 g (1 lb) pork fillet cut into 3.75 cm
(1½ inch) cubes
400 g (13 oz) calves' liver cut into 3.75 cm
(1½ inch) cubes
500 g (1 lb) spicy sausages
350 g (11 oz) veal medallions
300 g (9½ oz) ćevapčiči (meatballs) below
salt and pepper**

1. Grill the ingredients on a charcoal fire or electric grill to your liking, season and serve them with a garnish of sautéed, chopped onions and sprigs of parsley.

Grilled Meatballs

Ćevapčiči

From the Ima Dana Restaurant, Belgrade.

Makes 60 ćevapčiči

**1 kg (2 lb) minced beef (if possible use a
mixture from the neck, breast, shoulder and
flank)
salt
freshly ground pepper
1 onion, finely chopped
2 cloves garlic, crushed**

1. The meat should be minced and kneaded 2 or 3 times. **2.** Add the rest of the ingredients and mix well together. **3.** Shape the mixture into cylinders 2.5 cm (1 inch) in diameter and 5 cm (2 inches) long. Refrigerate them until the mixture becomes firm. **4.** Thread the meatballs onto skewers, 3 to 5 on each skewer. Ćevapčiči may be cooked either over an open grill or barbecue, fried in a pan with lard or grilled under a griller. **5.** Serve them sprinkled with chopped onions.

Bosnian Meat Pie

Pita Burek

From the Moniča Han Restaurant, Sarajevo. "Katmer" puff pastry is used for this and other types of pies.

Serves 8-10

**Pastry:
4 cups (1 lb) flour
1 tablespoon oil
2 eggs
pinch of salt
¾ cup (6 fl oz) lukewarm water**

**Filling:
300 g (9½ oz) minced meat
2 onions, finely chopped
200 g (6½ oz) mashed potatoes
salt
freshly ground pepper**

Pastry: 1. Mix the flour, oil, eggs and salt together. **2.** Add enough water to form a stiff dough. **3.** Knead until bubbles of air appear. **4.** Shape into a ball and flatten it. **5.** Brush with oil and let it stand for 20 minutes. **6.** Dust the board with flour and roll the dough into a large rectangle 0.5 cm (¼ inch) thick. **7.** Brush with oil, fold it over and roll it again. Cut the dough into rectangles 7.5 × 5 cm (3 × 2 inch).
Filling: 1. Preheat the oven to 200°C (400°F/Gas 6). **2.** Mix all the ingredients together and spread it on the rectangles leaving a 2 cm (¾ inch) border all round. Roll the rectangles, cigarette fashion, moistening the edge with water and pressing to seal. Brush with oil and bake in the oven for 30 minutes or until golden-brown. Eat the pies while they are hot.

Bosnian Cabbage Stew

Serves 4

**1 kg (2 lb) boned shoulder of lamb, cut into
5 cm (2 inch) cubes
60 g (2 oz) lard
1 onion, finely chopped
1 kg (2 lb) cabbage, trimmed, core removed
and roughly chopped
salt
freshly ground pepper
3 tomatoes, peeled and sliced
2 cloves garlic, crushed
1-2 cups (8-16 fl oz) dry white wine
1 tablespoon paprika**

1. Brown the lamb in the lard, add the onions and sauté them until they are soft. **2.** Put the lamb and onion mixture in the bottom of a casserole, arrange the cabbage over it and season with salt and pepper. Lay the tomato slices and garlic on top. **3.** Cover the casserole and cook over low heat for 2-3 hours. Add the wine gradually while the stew is cooking. **4.** Half an hour before the end of the cooking time, sprinkle the stew with paprika. Do not stir the stew. **5.** Serve hot with chunks of crusty bread and generous amounts of chilled dry white wine.

DESSERTS & PASTRY

Dalmatian Pancakes
Palacinke

Serves 6

12 thin pancakes
200 g (6½ oz) sugar
1 cup (8 fl oz) orange juice
185 g (6 oz) finely chopped almonds
juice of 1 lemon
30 g (1 oz) butter
icing (confectioners') sugar

1. In a frying pan, caramelise the sugar until it is light golden in colour, add the orange juice, half of the almonds and the lemon juice. Mix well. **2.** Remove from the heat, add the cream and butter. **3.** Sprinkle the pancakes with the remaining almonds, roll them up and warm them in the sauce. **4.** Serve the pancakes with the sauce poured over them and dusted with icing sugar.

Almond Chocolate Biscuits

Makes approximately 24

1⅓ cups (5 oz) ground toasted almonds
125 g (4 oz) grated chocolate
1 egg white
¾ cup (4 oz) icing (confectioners') sugar
1 cup (4 oz) flour
125 g (4 oz) softened butter
1 egg, lightly beaten
20–24 blanched almonds

1. Preheat the oven to 180°C (350°F/Gas 4). **2.** Combine all ingredients, except the egg and the blanched almonds, and knead them together. **3.** Butter a rectangular baking dish and pour the mixture into it. Brush the surface with the egg and then place the almonds at regular intervals over it. **4.** Bake for 35–40 minutes. Before it cools cut it into squares, with an almond in the middle of each.

Semolina Halva

Serves 6

1¼ cups (4 oz) ground blanched almonds
1 cup (5 oz) semolina
3 cups (24 fl oz) water
185 g (6 oz) butter
2 cups (16 oz) sugar
vanilla-flavoured icing (confectioners') sugar

1. Toast the almonds and semolina in a heavy-bottomed pan. **2.** Put the water, butter and sugar in a saucepan and bring it to the boil. **3.** Slowly pour it over the almonds and semolina and cook over low heat until the mixture thickens. Cover the saucepan with a lid and let the halva cool. **4.** The halva may be poured into a shallow baking tray or into wet bowls. When it sets, unmould and serve sprinkled with vanilla-flavoured icing sugar.

Honey Biscuits

Makes approximately 4 dozen

½ cup (5 oz) honey
⅔ cup (5 oz) sugar
2½ cups (10 oz) flour
185 g (6 oz) softened butter
5 egg yolks
1 teaspoon baking powder
pinch of cinnamon
pinch of ground cloves
grated rind of 1 lemon
juice of 1 lemon
1 egg yolk mixed with 2 tablespoons water

1. Preheat the oven to 190°C (375°F/Gas 5). **2.** Boil the honey and sugar together. Transfer to a mixing bowl, mix in the flour and stir until the mixture cools. **3.** Cream the butter with the egg yolks, stir in the baking powder, cinnamon, cloves, lemon rind and juice. **4.** Combine the two mixtures. **5.** Transfer to a board, knead and then roll out 1.5 cm (⅝ inch) thick. With a round 5 cm (2 inch) cookie cutter, cut out the biscuits. **6.** Place them on a buttered baking sheet and bake in the oven for 20 minutes. Let them cool and store them in an airtight jar for one or two days before eating them.

AUSTRIA

The Austrian cooking repertoire can easily be considered the melting pot of the east-west and north-south movement in European history, of which Vienna has been the focal point as early as the Roman days.

Their early contact with the East, which continued for centuries, put them in contact with the sweetmeats of the Byzantine people, the Arabs and the Turks. It is therefore not surprising that the Viennese have developed a sweet tooth unmatched by any other people and which is satisfied by a range of pastries which places them at the top of any pastry makers in the world.

Where else could the strudel pastry have originated but in Constantinople, from where it reached Vienna via Hungary. There was also friendly contact with the gastronomes of the court of the Medicis in Florence, where during the Renaissance chefs were creating pastries and sweets which had never been heard of before.

The most famous of Viennese dishes, the schnitzel, is said to be of Milanese origin, but whereas the Costoletta alla Milanese is a loin chop, in Vienna it comes from the leg or fillet and is therefore completely different from the sacred Wiener Schnitzel. Vienna shares other specialities with Milan — the fafelspitz and the lesso misto — and undoubtedly there is a family connection between the panettone and the kugelhof.

My travels through the provinces took me first south of Vienna into part of lower Austria where the cooking reflects the specialities of the capital. Throughout the Austrian provinces the cooking is good and tasty. In most parts a well-cultivated countryside produces all the ingredients for a simple, wholesome, farmhouse type of cooking.

They call Styria the green heart of Austria. Indeed, fruit and vegetables grow prolifically and their white wines are among the best in the land. The extensive forests harbour good game, chickens are bred everywhere and it is not surprising therefore to find a large number of poultry specialities. Graz, Styria's capital, is among Austria's finest cities.

My next stopover was in Klagenfurt, the capital of Carnithia, the southernmost of the country's provinces. Many lakes in the region provide the ingredients for local fish specialities and the large forests yield fine game for the table.

The highlight of my journey was without doubt my visit to Salzburg. While Salzburger Nockerln, the soufflé-like dessert, is the best-known speciality of the town and region, it is not only for its gourmet delights that I travel to this wonderful city. The visual delight of its baroque and rococo streets, the backdrop of its castle as viewed from the Mirabell Gardens, the squares, churches and alleys, all of this surrounded by picturesque hills is a sight never to be forgotten. To have all this and the heritage of Mozart, well, it's just too much!

My farewell to Austria was in Tyrol, the best-known of Austria's provinces. The grandeur of its mountains, the picturesque setting of its villages and lakes is what most travellers expect to see in Austria. The climate here is fairly severe and so the food is homely, heart-warming and satisfying.

Right: The picturesque village of Millstatt am See overlooking the beautiful Millstatt Lake.

SOUPS

Chicken Mushroom Soup

Habsburger Suppe

Serves 6–8

90 g (3 oz) butter
4 tablespoons flour
12 cups (2.5 litres) chicken stock (see p. 328)
salt
150 g (5 oz) mushrooms, sliced
½ cup green peas, puréed
1 egg yolk
¼ cup (2 fl oz) cream
meat from one roasted chicken, cut into small pieces

1. Melt 60 g (2 oz) of the butter, add the flour and cook the roux for 2–3 minutes. **2.** Add heated chicken stock and salt to taste. Simmer gently for a few minutes, stirring continuously. **3.** Sauté the mushrooms in the remaining butter and add them to the soup; add the pea purée. **4.** Combine the egg yolk and cream and add this mixture to the soup; heat but do not allow it to boil. Just before serving add the chicken meat.

Ultener Peasant Soup

Ultener Bauernsuppe

From the Goldener Adler, Innsbruck.

Serves 8

250 g (8 oz) sauerkraut
250 g (8 oz) potatoes, peeled and cut into small cubes
3 cups (24 fl oz) beef stock (see p. 328)
½ cup (4 fl oz) dry white wine
½ cup (4 fl oz) cream
1 onion, chopped
½ clove garlic, chopped
30 g (1 oz) butter

1. Cook the sauerkraut and potatoes in the stock for 30 minutes. **2.** In a blender or food processor purée the sauerkraut and potatoes. **3.** Return the purée to the saucepan, add the wine and cream, cook for a further 5 minutes. **4.** Fry the onions and garlic in the butter until golden-brown and add to the soup. Stir in and cook for another 5 minutes. **5.** If the soup is too thick it may be thinned by adding beef stock. Serve hot.

South Tyrolean Sour Soup

Bozner Sauer Suppe

Serves 6

500 g (1 lb) tripe
8 cups (2 litres) water
1 onion, chopped
3 stalks celery, chopped
1 parsnip, chopped
20 g (⅔ oz) lard
¼ cup (1 oz) flour
1 teaspoon sugar
6 cups (1.5 litres) beef stock (see p. 328)
4 tomatoes, peeled and chopped
1 onion, chopped
2 bay leaves
3 sprigs parsley, chopped
juice of ½ lemon
3–4 tablespoons vinegar
½ cup (4 fl oz) red wine
salt
freshly ground black pepper
90 g (3 oz) Parmesan cheese, grated

1. Cook the tripe in the water together with the onions, celery, parsnip and salt for 2 hours until soft. **2.** In a saucepan melt the lard, add the flour and sugar and brown lightly. Gradually add the heated beef stock and cook for 3–4 minutes. **3.** Add the tomatoes, onions, bay leaves, parsley, lemon juice, vinegar, red wine, salt and pepper. **4.** Cut the tripe into small strips and add them to the soup. **5.** Simmer for approximately 10 minutes, season with salt and pepper. **6.** Serve, sprinkled with grated Parmesan cheese, in individual bowls.

Beef Soup with Pancake Strips

Fritattensuppe

From the Gasthof Auerhahn, Salzburg.

Serves 6

5 cups (1.25 litres) beef stock (see p. 328)
1 cup (8 fl oz) milk
1 egg
salt
4½ tablespoons flour
fat for frying

1. In a bowl combine the flour, salt, egg and milk and stir until it forms a fairly thin batter. **2.** In a small frying pan make the pancakes. Stack two or three pancakes on top of each other and roll them up. With a sharp knife cut thin strips along the length. **3.** Place the strips of pancake into the preheated beef stock and serve immediately.

Goulash Soup
Gulyássuppe

Serves 6

3 onions, sliced
125 g (4 oz) speck, diced
1 teaspoon paprika
1 tablespoon vinegar
500 g (1 lb) beef shank, diced
salt
1 tablespoon fresh chopped marjoram
1 teaspoon caraway seeds
6 cups (1.5 litres) water
3 tablespoons flour
250 g (8 oz) potatoes, peeled and diced

1. Fry the onions and the speck until the onions are light brown. **2.** Add the vinegar and half the paprika. **3.** Add the meat, salt, marjoram and caraway seeds. **4.** Add 2 cups (16 fl oz) of the water, cover the saucepan and simmer gently for 1 hour. **5.** Add the potatoes. Mix the flour with the rest of the water and add it to the soup. **6.** Cook the soup gently until the potatoes are soft. Season with the remaining paprika before serving.

South Tyrolean Wine Soup
Terlaner Weinsuppe

From the Europa Hotel, Innsbruck.

Serves 4–6

2 cups (16 fl oz) beef stock (see p. 328)
1 cup (8 fl oz) dry white wine
4 egg yolks
½ cup (4 fl oz) cream
pinch of cinnamon
pinch of salt
30 g (1 oz) butter
4 slices brown bread, crusts removed and cut into cubes
pinch of cinnamon

1. Mix the stock, white wine, egg yolks, cream, cinnamon and salt in a saucepan and heat slowly, stirring constantly, until it has a creamy consistency. Do not overheat. **2.** Fry the cubes of bread in the butter, sprinkle with cinnamon and serve as an accompaniment to the soup.

Styrian Cream Soup
Steirische Rahmsuppe

From the Hotel Erzherzog Johann, Graz.

Serves 6

4 cups (1 litre) beef stock (see p. 328)
salt
pepper
pinch of caraway seeds
1 cup (8 fl oz) sour cream
¼ cup (1 oz) flour
1 tablespoon chives

1. Heat the stock with salt, pepper and caraway seeds. **2.** Mix the sour cream with the flour and add to the simmering stock, stirring continuously. **3.** Cook for 10 minutes, adjust seasoning and just before serving, sprinkle with chives.

Vienna Tomato Soup
Wiener Tomatensuppe

From the Hotel Sauerhof, Baden bei Wien.

Serves 8

1 kg (2 lb) tomatoes
1 onion, chopped
40 g (1½ oz) butter
¾ cup diced ham
1 turnip, sliced
2 tablespoons flour
6 cups (1.5 litres) beef stock (see p. 328)
1 clove garlic
¼ tablespoon chopped rosemary
1 sprig each of basil, thyme and parsley
salt
pepper
sugar to taste

1. Preheat the oven to 150°C (350°F/Gas 4) and bake the tomatoes on a baking tray for 30 minutes. **2.** In a large saucepan, sauté the onion in the butter until transparent. **3.** Add the ham and turnip. **4.** Stir in the flour and gradually add the boiling beef stock. **5.** Add the garlic, rosemary, basil, thyme and parsley. **6.** Cover the saucepan and slowly bring to the boil. **7.** Add the tomatoes and simmer the soup for approximately 30 minutes. **8.** Cool the soup and put it through a blender or food processor. **9.** Strain it through a sieve, season and add sugar to taste.

Brown Beef Soup

Braune Rindsuppe

Serves 4-6

30 g (1 oz) lard
60 g (2 oz) calf's liver
2 kg (4 lb) beef bones
2 carrots, sliced
½ parsnip, chopped
3 stalks celery, chopped
1 onion, roughly chopped
12 cups (2.5 litres) water
salt
6 peppercorns
2 bay leaves
1.25 kg (2½ lb) shin beef
2 egg whites
1 tablespoon water

1. In a large saucepan melt the lard and add the calf's liver, beef bones, carrots, parsnip, celery and onions. Fry them until they are light brown. Add the water, salt, peppercorns, bay leaves and beef. **2.** Bring slowly to the boil and simmer for 2–3 hours. **3.** Remove the beef and serve it separately as a main course. Strain off the liquid and cool it; skim off the fat. **4.** Brown beef soup is served like a consommé and should be clarified. **5.** To clarify, beat the egg whites with the cold water. **6.** Put the soup in a large saucepan and add the egg whites. While whipping constantly, bring the liquid to the boil and cook it for 5 minutes. **7.** Strain the liquid through a fine linen cloth. **8.** Traditionally this soup is served with various garnishes. The following recipes give some of them.

Small Butter Dumplings

Kleine Butterknockerln

(Garnish for Brown Beef Soup)

Serves 6-8

125 g (4 oz) butter
2 egg yolks
2 tablespoons milk
¼ teaspoon salt
1½ cups (6 oz) flour
2 egg whites, stiffly beaten
salted water

1. In a mixing bowl cream the butter, add the egg yolks, milk and salt. Stir in the flour and gently fold in the egg whites, mixing well together. **2.** With a teaspoon drop small pieces of the mixture into boiling salted water. **3.** Simmer for 10 minutes. Drain. **4.** Place the dumplings into the Brown Beef Soup before serving.

Brain Soufflé

Hirndunstkoch

(Garnish for Brown Beef Soup)

Serves 8

½ onion, finely chopped
3 sprigs parsley, finely chopped
20 g (approx. ¾ oz) butter
½ veal brain, blanched, skinned and chopped
3 white bread rolls or 6 slices of white bread
1 cup (8 fl oz) milk
45 g (1½ oz) butter
3 egg yolks
½ teaspoon salt
freshly ground black pepper
3 egg whites, stiffly beaten

1. Lightly sauté the onions and parsley in the butter, add the chopped brains and sauté for 5 minutes. **2.** Add the bread rolls or bread slices which have been previously soaked in the milk, squeezed dry and rubbed through a strainer. **3.** Cream the butter, add the egg yolks and add this to the brain mixture. Add the salt and pepper. **4.** Gently fold in the egg whites. **5.** Pour the mixture into a greased pudding mould and cook in a pan half filled with hot water for 1 hour. Do not allow the water to evaporate. **6.** Turn out the soufflé, slice it and serve as an accompaniment to Brown Beef Soup.

Ham Biscuits

Schinkenschöberln

(Garnish for Brown Beef Soup)

Serves 6-8

60 g (2 oz) butter
3 egg yolks
3 white bread rolls or 6 slices of white bread
soaked in milk or water
125 g (4 oz) ham, finely chopped
salt
3 egg whites, stiffly beaten

1. Preheat oven to 190°C (375°F/Gas 5). **2.** Cream the butter, add the egg yolks. **3.** Squeeze the bread rolls or sliced bread dry and add them to the butter and egg yolk mixture. **4.** Add the ham and salt and gently fold in the egg whites. **5.** Spread the mixture over the bottom of a baking dish and cook in the preheated oven for 15–20 minutes. **6.** To serve, cut the biscuit into small squares and serve as an accompaniment to Brown Beef Soup.

***Right:** From the Gasthof Auerhahn in Salzburg, clockwise from bottom left: Beef Soup with Pancake Strips (see page 200); Bauernschmaus; Salzburg Soufflé (see page 225).*

DUMPLINGS

Cheese Dumplings
Pinsgauer Kasnockn

From the Cafe Eichenhof, Zell am See.

Serves 4

500 g (1 lb) flour
½ teaspoon salt
1 egg
½ cup (4 fl oz) cold water
200 g (6½ oz) Emmentaler type cheese, cut into thin strips
100 g (3½ oz) butter
salt
pepper
4 tablespoons chopped chives

1. In a mixing bowl combine the flour, salt, egg and water and mix it into a smooth paste. **2.** In a large saucepan, boil some salted water. Using a teaspoon drop small amounts of the mixture into the water and boil the dumplings slowly for 3–4 minutes. **3.** When they are cooked, drain the dumplings. **4.** In a large frying pan, melt the butter and fry the dumplings lightly, add salt, pepper and the cheese, mix well but do not melt the cheese completely. **5.** Serve with the butter and cheese poured over the dumplings and garnished with the chives.

Almond Croquettes
Mandelkroketten

From the Berghotel Tulbinger Kogel, Wienerwald.

Makes approximately 20 croquettes

500 g (1 lb) mashed potatoes
2 egg yolks
75 g (2½ oz) butter
salt
nutmeg
flour for coating
1 egg, lightly beaten
breadcrumbs
½ cup finely chopped almonds
oil for deep frying

1. Mix the mashed potatoes, egg yolks, softened butter, salt and nutmeg. **2.** Form the dough into a thin sausage 2.5 cm (1 inch) in diameter and cut it into pieces approximately 4–5 cm (1½–2 inches) long. **3.** Roll these in the flour, dip them in the beaten egg and then roll them in a mixture of the breadcrumbs and chopped almonds. **4.** Fry the croquettes in deep fat until they are golden-brown. Drain and serve hot as an accompaniment to Roast Saddle of Venison (see p. 217).

Potato Pancakes
Kartoffelpuffer

Serves 4–6

1 kg (2 lb) potatoes
2 slices white bread soaked in milk and mashed
½ cup (4 fl oz) milk
2 eggs
2–3 tablespoons flour
salt
freshly ground black pepper
250 g (4 oz) lard

1. Peel and grate the potatoes into cold water so that they do not discolour. **2.** Drain them and squeeze out all the liquid. **3.** Mix the potatoes, bread, eggs, flour, salt and pepper. **4.** Using a tablespoon, place small amounts of the mixture into the hot fat and flatten them with the back of the spoon. **5.** Fry until crisp and serve hot.

Cream Cheese Dumplings

Topfengriessknödel

Serves 4-6

125 g (4 oz) butter, softened
5 egg yolks
500 g (1 lb) cream cheese or ricotta
pinch of salt
125 g (4 oz) semolina
2–3 tablespoons sugar
6 egg whites, stiffly beaten
¾ cup (3 oz) dry breadcrumbs
125 g (4 oz) butter for frying

1. Cream the butter and add the egg yolks, cream cheese, salt, semolina and sugar (the amount of sugar can vary according to taste). 2. Combine all the ingredients and set aside for 30 minutes. 3. Gently fold in the egg whites. 4. With two spoons, form small dumplings and cook them in boiling salted water for approximately 15 minutes. 5. To serve, sprinkle them with the breadcrumbs which have been fried crisp in the butter. 6. Traditionally, the dumplings are served with a side dish of stewed fruit such as plums, cherries etc.

Spätzle

From the Kärntner Stub'n Restaurant, Millstätter See.

225 g (7 oz) flour
1 egg, beaten
¾ cup (6 fl oz) water
salt
¼ cup (2 fl oz) sour cream
60 g (2 oz) butter, melted

1. Mix the flour, eggs, water and salt together. 2. The consistency of the batter should be fairly stiff. 3. Set the batter aside for 30 minutes. 4. Put the batter on a wooden board and with a knife cut off small pieces of dough and drop them into a large saucepan of boiling salted water. 5. Cook gently, the spätzle will rise to the surface when they are cooked. 6. Drain the spätzle and transfer them to a heated serving dish. 7. To serve, pour the warmed sour cream over the spätzle, mix well and then pour the melted butter over them.

Potato Dumplings

Kartoffelknödel

From the Altes Haus, Grinzing.

Serves 6-8

6 slices white bread, cut into cubes
40 g (1½ oz) butter, for frying the sippets
125 g (4 oz) butter or pork fat
3 eggs
1 kg (2 lb) potatoes, cooked and mashed
½ cup (2 oz) flour
salt
freshly ground pepper

1. Fry the cubed bread in the butter until golden-brown. 2. Cream the butter or pork fat, add the eggs, sippets, mashed potatoes, flour, salt and pepper. Stir all ingredients together and form the dumplings approximately 5 cm (2 inches) in diameter. Cook the dumplings in boiling salted water until they rise to the surface, approximately 5 minutes.

White Bread Dumplings

Semmelknödel

From the Weisser Schwan, Vienna.

2 eggs, well beaten
¾ cup (6 fl oz) milk
2½ cups (10 oz) flour
salt
100 g (3½ oz) bread, cut into cubes and fried crisp in butter
90 g (3 oz) butter

1. Mix the eggs with the milk and gradually add the mixture to the flour. Add the salt and bread cubes and mix well together. 2. Shape the mixture into dumplings approximately 6 cm (2½ inches) in diameter. 3. Boil the dumplings in salted water for approximately 15 minutes. 4. To serve, the dumplings can be sliced and covered with brown butter.

SAUCES

Mustard Sauce

Senfsauce

Makes approximately 2 cups (16 fl oz)

3 egg yolks
4 tablespoons mild mustard
3 tablespoons flour
½ cup (4 fl oz) water
¼ cup (2 fl oz) dry white wine
salt
freshly ground black pepper
pinch of sugar

1. In the top of a double boiler combine the egg yolks, mustard, the flour mixed with the water, and the wine. **2.** While stirring constantly with a whisk, cook the sauce over hot water until it thickens. **3.** Season with salt, pepper and sugar. **4.** Serve the sauce as soon as it is cooked.

Chive Sauce

Schnittlauch Sauce

From the Hotel Sauerhof, Baden bei Wien.

Makes 2½ cups (20 fl oz)

60 g (2 oz) butter
½ cup (2 oz) flour
1 cup (8 fl oz) cream
1 cup (8 fl oz) chicken stock (see p. 328)
salt
freshly ground pepper
4 tablespoons chopped chives

1. Melt the butter, add the flour, make a roux and cook approximately 5 minutes without browning it. **2.** Gradually add the hot cream. **3.** Stir until the sauce is smooth. **4.** Pour the sauce into the top of a double boiler over simmering water. **5.** Add hot chicken stock, salt and pepper. **6.** Cook the sauce for 30 minutes. **7.** Just before serving stir in the chives.

Horse-radish Sauce

Krensauce

60 g (2 oz) butter
4 tablespoons flour
1 cup (8 fl oz) beef stock (see p. 328)
½ cup cream
juice of ½ lemon
1 teaspoon sugar
4 tablespoons prepared horse-radish sauce
salt
freshly ground pepper

1. In a saucepan melt the butter and add the flour. Cook the roux for 2–3 minutes. **2.** Add the beef stock and cook for a further 5 minutes. **3.** Finally add the cream, lemon juice and sugar. **4.** Cook for a further 5 minutes. **5.** Take off the heat and add the prepared horse-radish sauce. Taste and season. **6.** Serve with boiled beef.

Apple Horse-radish Sauce

Apfelkren

From the Hotel Sauerhof, Baden bei Wien.

Makes 1 cup (8 fl oz)

⅔ cup (5 fl oz) cream
1 tablespoon lemon juice
salt
pinch of sugar
1 apple, peeled and cored
2 tablespoons prepared horse-radish sauce

1. Whip the cream, add the lemon juice, salt and sugar. **2.** Grate the apple and immediately add it to the cream otherwise it will go brown. Finally, add the prepared horse-radish sauce. **3.** Mix well together and serve it in a sauce-boat.

Cold Raisin Sauce

Kalte Rosinensauce

Makes approximately 2½ cups (20 fl oz)

150 g (5 oz) seedless raisins
1 cup (8 fl oz) port
½ cup (4 fl oz) fresh orange juice
⅓ cup (3 oz) sugar
pinch of salt
pinch each of cloves and cinnamon

1. Combine all the ingredients and heat in a saucepan without allowing it to boil. **2.** Cool the sauce and serve cold.

Right: Three dishes from the Goldener Adler restaurant in Innsbruck. Centre: Roast Pickled Pork (see page 214); Right: Pheasant Soup (see page 200); Left: Small doughnuts with poppy seed sauce (see page 225).

VEGETABLES & SALADS

Marrow in Sour Cream Sauce

Kürbiskraut

Serves 4-6

1 medium-sized marrow
salt
2 slices speck, diced
½ onion, finely chopped
2 tablespoons flour
2 sprigs parsley, chopped
2 sprigs dill, chopped
½ teaspoon paprika
1–2 cups hot beef stock (see p. 328)
½ cup (4 fl oz) sour cream
juice of 1 lemon
½ teaspoon sugar

1. Peel the marrow, cut it into sections and remove the seeds. **2.** Shred the marrow, sprinkle it with salt and let it stand for 45 minutes. **3.** In a saucepan, melt the diced speck, add the onion and fry it lightly. **4.** Add the flour, parsley, dill and paprika and cook for 2–3 minutes. **5.** While stirring, gradually add enough hot beef stock to make a light sauce. **6.** Add the sour cream, lemon juice and sugar and season to taste. **7.** Squeeze out all moisture from the marrow and add it to the sauce. Cover with a lid and simmer for 30 minutes.

Cabbage Cooked in Wine

Weinkraut

From the Goldener Adler, Innsbruck.

Serves 6

3 slices bacon or speck, cut into cubes
½ onion, chopped
1 small green cabbage, shredded
1 cup (8 fl oz) dry white wine
salt
freshly ground pepper
1 tablespoon sugar

1. In a large saucepan, melt the bacon or speck, add the onions and sauté them for 3–4 minutes. **2.** Add the cabbage, wine, salt and pepper and braise in the uncovered saucepan for approximately 30 minutes. Add the sugar during the last 5 minutes of cooking.

Beetroot Salad

Roter Rubensalat

Serves 6

6 beetroots
½ cup (4 fl oz) white wine vinegar
½ cup (4 fl oz) water
1 teaspoon caraway seeds
2 cloves
4 peppercorns
1 bay leaf
salt
1 tablespoon sugar
2 tablespoons freshly grated or prepared horse-radish

1. Simmer the beetroots in salted water to which 2 tablespoons of the vinegar has been added. Cook until tender — approximately 30 minutes. **2.** While still warm, peel the beetroots and cut them into thin slices. **3.** Arrange them in a glass serving dish and keep them warm. **4.** Prepare the marinade. Cook the remaining vinegar, water, caraway seeds, cloves, peppercorns, bay leaf, salt and sugar for 10 minutes. **5.** Pour the hot marinade over the warm beetroot slices. **6.** Mix in the horse-radish and refrigerate for 12 hours before serving.

Watercress and Mushroom Salad

Brunnenkress mit Schwämmerln

Serves 6

155 g (5 oz) mushrooms, thinly sliced
1 onion, finely sliced
½ cup (4 fl oz) oil
¼ cup (2 fl oz) white wine vinegar
1 tablespoon sour cream
salt
freshly ground black pepper
½ teaspoon sugar
1 apple, peeled, cored and sliced
1 bunch of watercress (leaves only)
½ tablespoon finely chopped chives

1. In a bowl, marinate the mushrooms and onions in a mixture of oil, vinegar, sour cream, salt, pepper and sugar for 1 hour. **2.** To serve, combine the apple and the watercress leaves and pour the marinade and mushrooms over the watercress. Serve sprinkled with chives.

Old Vienna Orange and Apple Salad

Alter Wienersalat

Serves 6

3 oranges, peeled and sliced
⅓ cup (3 oz) sugar
juice of ½ orange
juice of ½ lemon
6 small apples, peeled and cored
3 tablespoons apricot jam
2 tablespoons sugar
30 g (1 oz) butter

1. Preheat the oven to 150°C (350°F/Gas 4).
2. Arrange the orange slices on the bottom of a glass serving dish. Sprinkle each layer with sugar and pour the orange and lemon juice on top. **3.** Rub the apples with some lemon juice so they do not discolour. Place equal amounts of apricot jam into each of the cored apples. **4.** Arrange the apples on a buttered ovenproof dish. Sprinkle them with sugar and place pieces of butter on them. **5.** Bake the apples in the preheated oven for approximately 20–30 minutes until they are soft. **6.** To serve, place the apples on top of the orange slices. Refrigerate and serve cold.

Cabbage Salad

Krautsalat

From the Weisser Schwan, Vienna.

Serves 6-8

1 medium-sized white cabbage, shredded
1 cup (8 fl oz) mayonnaise
2 tablespoons tomato purée
60 g (2 oz) walnuts, chopped
grated rind 1 orange
segments from 1 orange, peeled
salt
freshly ground pepper
2-3 tablespoons grated fresh horse-radish

1. Soak the shredded cabbage in iced water in the refrigerator for approximately 2 hours. **2.** Drain the water and dry the cabbage with a tea towel. **3.** Combine the mayonnaise and tomato purée and mix it into the shredded cabbage. **4.** Add the walnuts, orange rind, orange segments and salt and pepper to taste. **5.** To serve, arrange the salad in a bowl and sprinkle the top with horse-radish.

Paprika Potato Stew

Gulyáskartoffeln

Serves 6-8

100 g (3⅓ oz) pickled pork, diced
60 g (2 oz) lard
4 onions, sliced
1–2 teaspoons paprika
1 tablespoon white wine vinegar
2 kg (4 lb) potatoes, peeled and quartered
1 tablespoon salt
freshly ground black pepper
2-3 tablespoons tomato purée
beef stock (see p. 328)

1. Fry the pork in the lard, add the onions and sauté until the onions colour. Add the paprika, vinegar, potatoes, salt, pepper and tomato purée. **2.** Cover with stock and simmer for 20–30 minutes or until the potatoes are cooked.

Red Cabbage with Apples

Rotkraut mit Äpfeln

From the Berghotel Tulbinger Kogel, Wienerwald.

Serves 6-8

1 medium-sized red cabbage
salt
pepper
1 slice of bacon or speck
½ cup (4 fl oz) tarragon vinegar
½ cup dry red wine (optional)
3 tablespoons sugar
3 tablespoons water
2 apples, peeled, cored and thinly sliced
½ cup dry red wine
2 tablespoons redcurrant jelly
pinch powdered cloves
pinch caraway seeds

1. Shred the red cabbage and sprinkle with salt and pepper. **2.** Cut the bacon or speck into small pieces and melt it in a large saucepan. **3.** Add the cabbage and sprinkle with the tarragon vinegar, mix it in well and cook over low heat. If necessary add half a cup red wine. **4.** Cook the sugar and water together until the syrup is brown. **5.** Add the caramelised sugar to the cabbage and cover the pan. **6.** Simmer the cabbage for 1½ hours. **7.** Add the apples, red wine, redcurrant jelly, cloves and caraway seeds. **8.** Cover and simmer for a further 20 minutes. **9.** Drain surplus liquid and serve the cabbage as a vegetable.

Sauerkraut with Tomatoes
Sauerkrat mit Paradeis

Serves 4–6

1 onion, chopped
60 g (2 oz) butter
3 tablespoons flour
½ cup (4 fl oz) hot beef stock (see p. 328)
1 tablespoon sugar
salt
freshly ground black pepper
4 large tomatoes, peeled, stewed and mashed
375 g (12 oz) sauerkraut, cooked and drained

1. Sauté the onions in the butter until they are lightly coloured, add the flour and cook for 2–3 minutes. **2.** Add the beef stock, sugar, salt and pepper. **3.** Add the tomatoes and cook for 5 minutes. **4.** Finally, add the sauerkraut and mix well; simmer uncovered for 30 minutes, stirring frequently. **5.** If necessary add more beef stock.

Onions with Hazelnuts
Zwiebeln mit Haselnüsse

Serves 6

Stuffed Onions:
6 large onions
½ cup (2 oz) dry breadcrumbs
30 g (1 oz) butter
90 g (3 oz) hazelnuts, chopped
salt
freshly ground black pepper

Sauce:
45 g (1½ oz) butter
2 tablespoons flour
1 cup (8 fl oz) hot milk
2 tablespoons brandy
salt
freshly ground black pepper
2 sprigs parsley, chopped
1 tablespoon chopped chives

1. Preheat the oven to 175°C (250°F/Gas ½). **2.** Parboil the onions in salted water for 10 minutes. **3.** Scoop out the centres of the onions leaving the sides approximately 1.25 cm (½ inch) thick. **4.** Finely chop the scooped-out portion of the onions and combine with the breadcrumbs which have been previously fried crisp in the butter. Add half the chopped hazelnuts, season with salt and freshly ground black pepper. **5.** Place the stuffing into the onion shells and arrange them on a buttered baking dish. **6.** To make the sauce, melt the butter, add the flour and cook for a few minutes without colouring it. Gradually add the hot milk. **7.** Add the brandy, salt and pepper. Cook for 5 minutes. **8.** Pour the sauce over the onions and bake them in the preheated oven for 35–40 minutes. **9.** Serve sprinkled with parsley and chives.

Stuffed Cucumbers in Dill-Paprika Sauce
Gefüllte Gurken

Serves 6

Stuffed Cucumbers:
3 eggs, hard-boiled
½ cup (2 oz) dry breadcrumbs
45 g (1½ oz) Parmesan cheese, grated
45 g (1½ oz) almonds, chopped
freshly ground black pepper
salt
½ teaspoon sugar
1 pinch powdered cloves
2 egg yolks, lightly beaten
3 large cucumbers, peeled, cut lengthwise and seeded
60 g (2 oz) butter

Dill-Paprika Sauce:
½ small onion, finely chopped
3 sprigs parsley, finely chopped
45 g (1½ oz) butter
2 tablespoons flour
3 sprigs dill, finely chopped
1–2 cups beef or chicken stock (see p. 328)
1–2 teaspoons paprika
1 tablespoon white wine vinegar
¼ cup (2 fl oz) sour cream

1. Preheat the oven to 175°C (350°F/Gas 4). **2.** Prepare the stuffing: mix the eggs, breadcrumbs, Parmesan cheese, almonds, salt, pepper, sugar and cloves and bind the mixture with the egg yolks. **3.** Blanch the cucumbers in hot salted water for 2–3 minutes. **4.** Place the stuffing into the groove in each of the halves of the cucumbers. **5.** Melt the butter in a heavy-bottomed baking dish and arrange the cucumbers in it. **6.** Bake them in the preheated oven for approximately 10–15 minutes until they are tender. **7.** To make the sauce, fry the onion and parsley in the butter until the onion colours lightly. Add the flour and cook the roux for 2–3 minutes. Add the dill and gradually add the heated stock. **8.** Add the paprika (the quantity will depend on the taste required), the wine vinegar and the sour cream. Gently simmer for 5 minutes. **9.** Serve the cucumbers masked with the sauce.

Right: A fine display of dishes in the gardens of the Berghotel Tulbinger Kogel. Foreground: Saddle of Venison 'Williams' (see page 217); Almond Croquettes (see page 204); Background left: White Bread Dumplings (see page 205); right: Red Cabbage with Apples (see page 209).

POULTRY

Chicken with Seedless Grapes
Huhn mit Trauben

Serves 4

1 × 1.75 kg (3¼ lb) roasting chicken
salt
freshly ground black pepper
1 onion, roughly chopped
60 g (2 oz) melted butter
1½ cups (12 fl oz) dry white wine
1½ cups (12 fl oz) water
1 cup (8 fl oz) chicken stock (see p. 328)
¾ cup (6 fl oz) sour cream
3 sprigs parsley, finely chopped
750 g (1½ lb) seedless grapes

1. Preheat the oven to 175°C (350°F/Gas 4). **2.** Rub the chicken with salt and pepper and place the onion into the cavity. Pour some of the melted butter inside the cavity and brush the rest of it on to the outside of the chicken. **3.** Place the chicken in a roasting pan, add the wine, water and chicken stock. **4.** Cook the chicken in the preheated oven for approximately 1 hour until tender. **5.** Remove the chicken from the oven and keep it hot. **6.** Pour the cooking juices into a saucepan and reduce to 1½ cups (12 fl oz). **7.** Add the cream, parsley and the seedless grapes. Heat the sauce but do not allow it to boil. **8.** Cut the chicken into serving pieces, place them on a platter and mask with the sauce.

Chicken Breasts with Mousseline Sauce
Hühner Brüstchem mit Eiersauce

Serves 6

2 cups (16 fl oz) chicken stock (see p. 328)
1 tablespoon tarragon vinegar
6 egg yolks
salt
freshly ground black pepper
4 tablespoons chopped chives
6 chicken breasts (suprêmes)
60 g (2 oz) butter
juice of 1 lemon
thin lemon slices
2 sprigs parsley, finely chopped

1. Reduce the chicken stock to 1 cup, add the tarragon vinegar. **2.** In the top of a double boiler whisk 6 egg yolks over boiling water, add salt and pepper and continue whisking until the sauce thickens. **3.** Gradually add the reduced chicken stock and continue whisking to thicken the sauce. **4.** Add the chives. **5.** Lightly poach the chicken breasts in the butter for 2–3 minutes, sprinkle them with lemon juice, pepper and salt. **6.** To serve, arrange the chicken breasts on a platter and pour the mousseline sauce over them. Garnish with lemon slices dipped in the finely chopped parsley.

Viennese Crumbed Chicken
Wiener Backhendle

No recipes on Viennese cooking would be complete without the Viennese Crumbed Chicken, despite the fact that it is a very simple and basic recipe.

Serves 4

1 × 1.8 kg (3 lb 10 oz) roasting chicken
1 cup (4 oz) flour
1 teaspoon salt
freshly ground black pepper
2 eggs, lightly beaten with 2 tablespoons water
1 cup (4 oz) dry breadcrumbs
250 g (½ lb) lard
12 sprigs parsley, fried

1. Cut the chicken into quarters. Dip the pieces first in flour, to which salt and pepper has been added, then transfer them to the lightly beaten egg and finally coat them with the breadcrumbs. Make sure they are well coated. **2.** In a deep frying pan, preheat the lard and fry the chicken pieces slowly so that the inside meat is cooked and the outside crust is golden-brown. **3.** Transfer the chicken to the preheated oven and bake for 10–15 minutes. **4.** Serve on a large platter and garnish with the fried parsley. **5.** Traditionally, the dish is served hot with parsley potatoes and cucumber salad but it can also be served cold with potato salad.

MEAT & GAME

Stuffed Beef Fillet
Edler Lungenbraten

Serves 6

1.5 kg (3 lb) fillet or Scotch fillet of
beef
salt
freshly ground pepper
90 g (3 oz) butter
1 onion, finely chopped
125 g (4 oz) mushrooms, chopped
6 stalks parsley, chopped
3 goose, duck or chicken livers, chopped

1. Preheat the oven to 200°C (400°F/Gas 6).
2. Trim the fillet of all fat and cut it deeply length-wise. **3.** Season with salt and pepper. **4.** In a heavy-bottomed frying pan melt the butter, heat it and rapidly brown both sides of the fillet. Remove and keep warm. **5.** In the same frying pan, fry the onions lightly, add the mushrooms and parsley, sauté for 2–3 minutes. **6.** Finally, add the livers and sauté for a further 2 minutes. **7.** When removing the mixture tilt the pan and drain off as much butter as possible. Use the butter to baste the fillet during cooking. **8.** Spread the filling mixture over the fillet, roll it up and tie it with string. **9.** Roast the fillet in the preheated oven, basting occasionally, until rare inside (approximately 20–25 minutes depending on the size of the fillet). **10.** Remove the fillet from the oven, rest it for about 10 to 15 minutes, slice it and serve with Madeira sauce and vegetables.

Styrian Roast Beef in Cider
Steirischer Rostbraten mit Kartoffelknödeln

From the Hotel Erzherzog Johann, Graz.

Serves 4-6

1 kg (2 lb) silverside or topside beef
2–3 frankfurts
¼ cup (2 fl oz) oil
250 g (8 oz) carrots, diced
125 g (4 oz) celery, diced
2 onions, diced
4 cups (1 litre) apple juice
salt
2 bay leaves
pinch sugar
peppercorns
3 sprigs parsley, chopped

1. Preheat oven to 175°C (350°F/Gas 4). **2.** With a sharp knife make small pockets in the meat and insert small pieces of the frankfurt sausage. **3.** Fry the meat in the oil until brown. **4.** Remove the meat and in the same oil fry the carrots, celery and onions until they are light brown. Add the apple juice, salt, bay leaves, sugar and peppercorns. **5.** Transfer the meat and sauce to a casserole. **6.** Cover the casserole and cook the meat in the preheated oven for 2 hours. **7.** Remove the meat from the sauce. **8.** Put the sauce through a blender or food processor and pass it through a sieve. **9.** To serve, slice the meat in 1 cm (⅜ inch) slices and mask it with the sauce. Sprinkle with the chopped parsley. Serve accompanied with Potato Dumplings (see p. 205).

Boiled Beef
Tafelspitz

From the Hotel Sauerhof, Baden bei Wien.

Serves 4

625 g (1¼ lb) rump
6 cups (1.5 litres) water
salt
½ parsnip, sliced
6 sprigs parsley, roughly chopped
4 stalks celery, chopped
1 leek, white part only, sliced

1. In a large saucepan, combine all ingredients and slowly bring to the boil. Simmer the meat for approximately 1½–2 hours, until tender. **2.** Allow the meat to cool slightly in the liquid for about 10 minutes. **3.** Remove the meat from the liquid and serve it sliced thinly. **4.** The Hotel Sauerhof recommends serving Tafelspitz with Apfelkren (Apple Horse-radish Sauce, p. 206), Schnittlauch Sauce (Chive Sauce, p. 206) and hashed brown potatoes fried with bacon.

Roast Leg of Pork

Schweinsstelze

From the Autes Haus, Vienna. This is the traditional way of roasting pork in Vienna.

Serves 8-10

3 kg (6 lb) leg of pork, boned and rolled
salt
1 tablespoon caraway seeds
3-4 cups (0.75-1 litre) beef stock (see p. 328)

1. Preheat the oven to 200°C (400°F/Gas 6).
2. Pour enough hot water into a baking dish to cover the bottom 1 cm (¾ inch). **3.** Place the meat in the baking dish, cover it and place in the preheated oven to steam for 1 hour. **4.** Remove the meat and, using a sharp knife, make incisions 1 cm (¾ inch) apart. **5.** Rub the skin with salt and caraway seeds. **6.** Return the meat to the baking dish with the skin facing upwards. **7.** Pour some of the stock into the bottom of the baking dish. **8.** Place the meat in the preheated oven and roast it for a further 1½-2 hours until it is done. **9.** During the cooking time baste with the stock, adding it gradually. **10.** When the meat is cooked, remove it from the oven and let it stand for 10-15 minutes before carving. **11.** In the meantime remove as much of the fat as possible from the cooking juices. **12.** Pour the cooking juices into a saucepan and reduce by half. Use this as a gravy to serve with the meat. **13.** To serve, cut the meat in slices and serve it masked with the gravy. **14.** Traditionally, roast pork prepared in this way is served with potato dumplings.

Roast Pickled Pork

Surbratl mit Weinkraut und Kartoffelknödel

From the Goldener Adler, Innsbruck.

Serves 6-8

1 × 3 kg boned rolled loin of pickled pork
(boned leg may also be used)
rock or sea salt
1 tablespoon caraway seeds
2-3 cups (16-24 fl oz) beef stock for basting (see p. 328)

1. Preheat the oven to 175°C (350°F/Gas 4).
2. Place the meat in a baking dish and sprinkle the top with rock or sea salt and caraway seeds. **3.** Place the meat in the preheated oven and roast for 2-2½ hours. **4.** During the roasting time baste occasionally with the beef stock. **5.** When the meat is cooked, remove it from the oven and keep it in a warm place for approximately 20 minutes before carving to allow the juices to settle. **6.** Drain the fat from the cooking juices, add more beef stock and cook until it has reduced to a thicker consistency. Serve this gravy with the meat. **7.** Carve the meat into thin slices and serve with Weinkraut (Cabbage cooked in Wine, p. 208) and Kartoffelknödel (Potato Dumplings, p. 205).

Vienna Pork Casserole

Wiener Eintopf

Serves 4-6

1 kg (2 lb) shoulder of pork cut into 4 cm (approx. 1½ inch) cubes
salt
freshly ground black pepper
3 onions, sliced
120 g (4 oz) butter
4 potatoes, peeled and cut into small cubes
2 carrots, cut into julienne strips
½ cabbage, chopped
1 teaspoon caraway seeds
1½-2 cups (12-16 fl oz) beef stock (see p. 328)

1. Preheat the oven to 180°C (350°F/Gas 4).
2. Season the meat. Melt the butter and fry the meat and onions in the butter until the onions are golden-brown. **3.** Drain the butter and reserve it for later use. **4.** Place half the potatoes in a casserole and then arrange in alternate layers the carrots, meat and cabbage, finishing with a layer of potatoes. Sprinkle each layer with caraway seeds. **5.** Pour in sufficient stock to cover the top layer of potatoes. **6.** Cover the casserole and place in the preheated oven. Bake for 1½ hours. **7.** Shortly before the end of the cooking time, take off the lid and let the potatoes brown on top. **8.** Serve the casserole from the dish.

Ham Fritters

Schinkenkrapfen

Serves 4-6

375 g (12 oz) ham, finely chopped
2 sour cucumbers, finely chopped
1 teaspoon mustard
salt
freshly ground black pepper
90 g (3 oz) grated Parmesan cheese
3 cups (12 oz) flour
¾ cup (6 fl oz) beer
enough water to make a stiff batter
1 teaspoon salt
2 egg whites, stiffly beaten
250 g (8 oz) lard

1. In a mixing bowl combine the ham, cucumber, mustard, salt and pepper. **2.** Shape the mixture into small balls the size of a walnut and dip them in the grated Parmesan cheese. **3.** Prepare a batter from the flour, beer and water, making sure that it is fairly stiff. Add the salt and gently fold in the egg whites. **4.** Dip the ham balls in the batter and fry them in hot lard until they are golden-brown.

Right: At the Hotel Erzherzog Johann Graz: Styrian Roast Beef in Cider (see page 213); Potato Dumplings (see page 205).

Stuffed Veal Olives
Gefüllte Kalbs Vögerl

From the Gasthof Auerhahn, Salzburg.

Serves 6

750 g (1½ lb) veal, cut into thin steaks

Stuffing:
100 g (3⅓ oz) veal, minced
100 g (3⅓ oz) pork, minced
2 egg yolks
1 slice bacon or speck, chopped
2 slices white bread, crumbed
2 sprigs parsley, chopped
½ clove garlic, crushed
1 sprig thyme, chopped
½ onion, chopped and lightly fried
salt
pepper
30–60 g (1–2 oz) lard
2 cups (8 fl oz) veal or beef stock (see p. 328)
1–2 tablespoons flour
½ cup (4 fl oz) cream

1. Preheat the oven to 175°C (350°F/Gas 4). **2.** Cut the steak into pieces approximately 12 cm × 10 cm (5 × 4 inches) and lightly beat them with a meat mallet. **3.** In a mixing bowl, combine the veal, pork, egg yolks, bacon, crumbs, parsley, garlic, thyme and onions. Season to taste and mix well together. **4.** Spread out the veal pieces and distribute the stuffing equally between them. **5.** Roll up the veal pieces with the stuffing inside and secure the rolls with toothpicks or tie them with fine thread. **6.** Melt the lard in a frying pan and lightly fry the veal 'birds'. **7.** Pour the stock into an ovenproof dish large enough to hold the veal birds and arrange them next to each other. **8.** Cover the dish with aluminium foil and put it into the preheated oven. **9.** Cook for approximately 30 minutes. **10.** Remove the veal birds and keep them hot. **11.** Transfer the cooking juices into a saucepan and reduce by one-quarter. **12.** Add the cream, pepper and salt to taste. **13.** Serve the veal birds, arranged on a serving platter, masked with the sauce.

Viennese Goulash
Wienersaft Gulyás

Serves 6

1 kg (2 lb) onions, sliced
125 g (4 oz) butter
3 sprigs marjoram, chopped
1 teaspoon caraway seeds
rind of 1 lemon, grated
1 tablespoon tomato paste
1 tablespoon paprika
1 kg (2 lb) shin beef, cut into large chunks
1 cup (4 fl oz) water
salt
pepper
1 red or green pepper (capsicum), cut into slivers

1. In a casserole, sauté the onions in the butter until light brown and add all ingredients except the peppers. **2.** Cover the casserole and simmer for approximately 1½–2 hours or until the meat is tender. If necessary add more water during cooking. **3.** Serve the goulash straight from the casserole, garnished with the slices of pepper. Traditionally, it is served with spetzler noodles or boiled potatoes.

Breast of Veal with Brain Stuffing
Kalbsbrust mit Hirnfüllung

Serves 6

1.5 kg (3 lb) breast of veal (ask the butcher to cut a pocket in the meat)

Stuffing:
350 g (11 oz) calf's brains
60 g (2 oz) butter
2 tablespoons chopped parsley
4 soft bread rolls
1 cup (8 fl oz) milk
4 tablespoons dry breadcrumbs
2 eggs
salt
pepper
water or stock for basting

1. Preheat oven to 175°C (350°F/Gas 4). **2.** Prepare the stuffing by frying the calf's brains in butter for about 4 minutes. **3.** Add the parsley and fry for 1 more minute. **4.** Remove the brains and chop them finely. **5.** Soak the bread rolls in milk for 10 minutes. Squeeze them dry and mash them. **6.** In a bowl combine the brains, bread rolls, dry breadcrumbs and eggs; season with salt and pepper. Mix well together. **7.** Place the stuffing in the pocket of the meat and fasten it with skewers. Season the meat. **8.** Place the meat on a baking dish and roast in the preheated oven, basting frequently with the water or stock, for 1¼–1½ hours. **9.** Remove the veal and keep hot. **10.** Degrease the cooking juices, season, and serve with the veal. **11.** Slice the veal and serve with potatoes (or potato dumplings) and vegetables.

Paprika Veal Cutlets
Paprikaschnitzel

Serves 6

1 kg (2 lb) veal cutlets 1.25 cm (½ inch) thick
(from leg)
2½ tablespoons flour
salt
90 g (3 oz) butter
3 slices bacon or speck, chopped
2 onions, thinly sliced
1 tablespoon flour
1-2 cups beef stock (see p. 328)
salt
freshly ground pepper
1 cup sour cream
1 teaspoon paprika, or more to taste
1 tablespoon tomato purée

1. Dust the cutlets with flour and sprinkle with salt.
2. Fry them in hot butter on both sides for 2-3 minutes, remove and keep hot. 3. Add the bacon or speck to the butter and melt it, add the onions and fry them lightly. 4. Add the flour and the heated beef stock; season. 5. Add the sour cream. 6. Add the paprika and tomato purée. Cook for 5 minutes. 7. Add the fried cutlets and simmer for 30 minutes or until tender.

Crumbed Veal Cutlets
Wiener Schnitzel

Serves 4-6

1 kg (2 lb) veal cut about 1.25 cm (½ inch)
thick (from the leg)
4 tablespoons flour
2 eggs, beaten
125 g (4 oz) fine dry breadcrumbs
salt
freshly ground pepper
155 g (5 oz) butter
lemon wedges

1. Cut the veal into large pieces which, after they have been beaten, would be approximately the size of a small dinner plate. 2. Gently pound each piece with a meat hammer. 3. Dip each piece into flour then into the eggs and then into the breadcrumbs. 4. Shake the loose breadcrumbs off the cutlet and sauté over low heat in the melted butter for approximately 3-4 minutes each side until brown. Do not use too much heat or the breadcrumbs will burn before the meat has cooked. 5. Serve garnished with lemon wedges. Traditionally, Wiener Schnitzel is accompanied by salads and is never served with sauce.

Roast Saddle of Venison 'Williams'
Rehrücken 'Williams'
From the Tulbinger Kogel, Wienerwald.

Serves 4-6

1 saddle of venison (300 g (9½ oz) per
person)
2 slices bacon, cut into strips
salt
freshly ground black pepper
60 g (3 oz) lard
1 parsley root, chopped
2 carrots, chopped
2 stalks celery, chopped
1 onion, chopped
1 cup (8 fl oz) dry red wine
1 cup beef stock (see p. 328)
6 juniper berries, crushed
2 bay leaves
6 peppercorns
2 sprigs thyme, chopped
1 cup (8 fl oz) cream
stewed peaches, halved, filled with cranberries

1. Preheat the oven to 190°C (375°F/Gas 5). 2. Skin the saddle and lard it with the bacon. 3. Brown the saddle on all sides in the lard and season with salt and pepper. 4. Remove the saddle from the frying pan. 5. Lightly sauté the parsley, carrots, celery and onions without allowing them to brown. Add the wine, stock, juniper berries, bay leaves, peppercorns and thyme. 6. Transfer to a roasting dish, place the saddle on top and roast in the preheated oven for 45 minutes. Make sure that the meat is still pink inside otherwise it will be dry and tasteless. 7. Remove the meat from the roasting pan and keep it warm. 8. Pass the cooking liquid through a sieve, pressing hard with a wooden spoon to extract all juices from the ingredients. 9. Add the cream and season. 10. To serve, cut the meat off the bone and slice it. 11. Serve the meat masked with the sauce, together with the peaches and Almond Croquettes (see p. 204).

CAKES & PASTRIES

Apple Strudel

Apfelstrudel

From the Wien Hilton, Vienna.

Makes one large strudel

Dough:
¾ cup (6 oz) flour
1 egg yolk
salt
¼ tablespoon oil
¼ cup (2 fl oz) lukewarm water
juice of ½ lemon
1 cup (8 fl oz) melted butter
1 tablespoon sugar

Filling:
125 g (4 oz) roasted almonds, finely chopped
1½ kg (3 lb) apples, peeled and sliced
155 g (5 oz) raisins
⅓ cup (3 oz) sugar

1. Place the flour in a mound on a pastry board. **2.** Make a hole in the centre and place in it the egg yolk, salt, oil, water and lemon juice. **3.** Mix the ingredients, using a knife. **4.** Knead the dough with your hands until it becomes elastic and leaves the board freely. **5.** Place the dough into a preheated stainless steel bowl, cover and keep it warm for 30 minutes. **6.** Spread a tablecloth on a table and sprinkle the cloth with flour. **7.** Place the dough in the centre of the cloth and sprinkle it with flour. Flatten it slightly with a rolling pin. **8.** Brush the dough with approximately ¼ cup of the melted butter. **9.** Place your hands, palms upward, under the dough and while lifting it, pull and stretch it in all directions until it becomes thin and transparent. If there are any thick edges left, cut them off with a knife. **10.** The sheet of thin dough should be approximately rectangular in shape. **11.** Place the chopped almonds on about two-thirds of the dough. Mix together the rest of the filling ingredients and arrange them over the almonds. Sprinkle with ¼ cup of the melted butter. **12.** To roll the strudel, lift the end of the cloth nearest to you and, starting from the end with the filling, continue lifting the cloth, which will cause the strudel to roll over and over. **13.** Lift the strudel with the cloth and, finally, roll it from the cloth into a greased baking dish. **14.** With a pastry brush, brush the remaining butter on to the surface of the strudel. **15.** Place in the preheated oven and bake for approximately 30–45 minutes or until the outside of the strudel is crisp. **16.** Before serving, sprinkle with sugar.

Sachertorte

Sacher Cake

Makes one 23 cm (9 inch) round cake

250 g (8 oz) butter, softened
175 g (5½ oz) caster (powdered) sugar
10 egg yolks
250 g (8 oz) dark chocolate, melted and cooled
12 egg whites, stiffly beaten
200 g (6½ oz) flour

Apricot Glaze:
¼ cup (3 oz) apricot jam
hot water
1–2 tablespoons apricot brandy (optional)

Chocolate Fondant Icing:
1¾ cups (11 oz) sugar
¼ teaspoon cream of tartar
1 cup (8 fl oz) boiling water
½ cup melted dark chocolate

1. Preheat the oven to 175°C (350°F/Gas 4). **2.** In a mixing bowl, cream the butter and sugar. **3.** Beat in the egg yolks, two at a time, making sure that they are well incorporated before adding the next two. **4.** Add the chocolate and mix well. **5.** Gently fold in the beaten egg whites, at the same time gradually adding the sifted flour. Fold in carefully. **6.** Butter and flour a springform pan and pour the batter into it. **7.** Bake the cake in the preheated oven until it is puffy and dry. (Test by inserting a thin skewer in the centre — it should come out clean and dry.) **8.** Take the cake out of the oven and remove the ring of the springform. Most recipes recommend that the cake is rested for one or two days before it is spread with the apricot glaze and the chocolate fondant icing. **9.** Spread the top and sides of the cake with a thin layer of apricot glaze. Spread the chocolate fondant icing over the glaze. **10.** Traditionally the cake is served with sweetened whipped cream.

To make the apricot glaze: 1. In a double boiler, heat the apricot jam, thinning it down with a little hot water. **2.** Add the apricot brandy if desired.

To make the chocolate fondant icing: 1. Combine the sugar and cream of tartar in a heavy saucepan. **2.** Add the boiling water and stir until the sugar has dissolved. **3.** Cook the syrup, without stirring, until it reaches the thread stage (115°C/240°F on a sugar thermometer). **4.** Remove the fondant from the heat and pour it on to a metal surface. **5.** With a spatula, work it until it cools and knead it into a smooth mass. This should be done as quickly as possible. **6.** Place the fondant in an airtight container and store it in the refrigerator. **7.** To make the fondant icing, heat the fondant in the top of a double boiler over simmering water and add the melted chocolate. **8.** Thin the fondant to a spreadable consistency with boiling water. **9.** To ice the cake, pour the fondant icing on to it and quickly tilt it in all directions to spread the icing. **10.** If the fondant gets too stiff, it can be reheated to the required consistency.

Right: *A selection of the delicious cakes on display at the Hotel Musil, Klagenfurt.*

Linzer Cake

Linzertorte

Makes one 23 cm (9 inch) cake

185 g (6 oz) flour
⅛ teaspoon ground cloves
⅛ teaspoon cinnamon
185 g (6 oz) unblanched almonds, finely ground
125 g (4 oz) sugar
1 teaspoon grated lemon peel
250 g (8 oz) butter, softened
2 egg yolks, lightly beaten
1 teaspoon vanilla essence
2 hard-boiled egg yolks
1¼ cups thick raspberry jam
1 egg, well beaten
2 tablespoons fresh cream
icing (confectioners') sugar

1. Preheat the oven to 180°C (350°F/Gas 4). **2.** In a mixing bowl, combine the flour, cloves, cinnamon, almonds, sugar, lemon peel, butter, egg yolks, vanilla essence and the hard-boiled egg yolks. Mix the ingredients well together. (Alternatively, they may be processed in a food processor.) **3.** Wrap the dough in plastic film and refrigerate for 1 hour until firm. **4.** Take out three-quarters of the dough and return the rest to the refrigerator. **5.** Lightly butter a springform tin and place the dough in. Using your fingers press out the dough to cover the bottom and sides of the tin. **6.** Spread the jam evenly over the bottom of the shell. **7.** Roll out the rest of the dough and cut it into strips 1 cm (½ inch) wide. Cut it into lengths to form diagonal strips spaced 2.5 cm (1 inch) apart and place over the jam. **8.** Loosen the top edge of the shell away from the tin and fold it over the edge of the jam to form a rim. **9.** Lightly beat the egg with the cream and brush over all the pastry parts. **10.** Bake for 45–50 minutes or until light brown. **11.** Slip the rim off the tin and cool the cake for 10–15 minutes. **12.** To serve, sprinkle with icing sugar.

Apple Strudel with Short Crust Pastry

Mürber Apfelstrudel

From the Konditorei Sluka, Vienna.

Short Pastry:
250 g (8 oz) butter
2 cups (8 oz) flour
⅓ cup (3 oz) sugar
pinch of salt
2 egg yolks
2 tablespoons milk
2 tablespoons dry white wine

Filling:
6 apples, peeled, cored and cut into thin slices
⅓ cup (3 oz) sugar
50 g (1¾ oz) raisins
50 g (1¾ oz) blanched slivered almonds
grated rind of 1 lemon
juice of ½ lemon
1 egg white
2 tablespoons sugar

1. Preheat the oven to 200°C (400°F/Gas 6). **2.** To make the pastry, place the butter and flour into a bowl. Cut the chilled butter into small cubes and, with your fingertips, rub it quickly into the flour. Add the sugar and salt and continue working it, but only briefly, until it has the consistency of breadcrumbs. **3.** Working rapidly, beat in the egg yolks together with the 2 tablespoons of milk and the white wine. Chill the dough in the refrigerator for 1 hour. **4.** Roll out the pastry into a rectangle 6 mm (¼ inch) thick. **5.** Spread the apples in a long row along the centre of the rectangle of pastry. **6.** Sprinkle the apples with the sugar, raisins and blanched almonds. Sprinkle the lemon rind and lemon juice evenly over the top. **7.** Fold the pastry over the filling and seal the top with the egg white. **8.** Place the strudel on a buttered dish, bending it into a horseshoe shape. **9.** With a pastry brush paint the top with the remaining egg white. **10.** Place the strudel in the preheated oven for approximately 30 minutes or until it is golden-brown. **11.** Sprinkle with the sugar and serve hot.

Vanilla Crescents
Vanilla Kipferl

Makes 60 crescents

200 g (6½ oz) butter, chilled and cut into cubes
2 cups (8 oz) flour
⅓ cup (3 oz) sugar
60 g (2 oz) almonds, blanched and ground
2 egg yolks
½ teaspoon vanilla essence
vanilla-flavoured icing (confectioners') sugar

1. Preheat the oven to 150°C (300°F/Gas 2).
2. Working rapidly, mix the butter, flour, sugar, almonds, egg yolks and vanilla essence into a smooth dough, making sure that it is worked as quickly as possible. If you are using a food processor, combine all the ingredients except the eggs and the vanilla essence and process to the consistency of breadcrumbs. Add the egg yolks and vanilla essence and process a few more seconds to form a smooth dough. **3.** Wrap the dough in plastic film and refrigerate for 1 hour. **4.** Roll the dough out into thin ribbons the thickness of a finger. **5.** Cut the ribbons into 7.5 cm (3 inch) long pieces and curve them into crescent shapes. **6.** Place them on a buttered baking sheet and bake them in the preheated oven for approximately 20 minutes until they are a light golden colour. **7.** Sprinkle them with the vanilla-flavoured icing sugar. **8.** While still warm, transfer the crescents on to a serving plate and sprinkle with more vanilla icing sugar.

Lightning Biscuits
Blitzgebäck

125 g (4 oz) butter, softened
½ cup (4 oz) sugar
3 eggs
¾ cup (3 oz) flour
½ teaspoon vanilla essence
60 g chopped hazelnuts
vanilla-flavoured icing (confectioners') sugar

1. Preheat the oven to 175°C (350°F/Gas 4).
2. Cream the butter with the sugar. **3.** Add one egg at a time, alternating with 3 tablespoons of flour between each egg. Finally add the vanilla essence. **4.** Spread the mixture approximately 0.75 cm (¼ inch) thick on a well-buttered baking sheet. **5.** Sprinkle with the chopped hazelnuts. **6.** Bake in the preheated oven for approximately 15 minutes or until golden-brown. **7.** While still warm, cut into fingers approximately 2 cm (¾ inch) wide and 7.5 cm (3 inches) long. Dust them with the vanilla-flavoured icing sugar.

Walnut Biscuits
Walnuss Gebäck

185 g (6 oz) butter
⅔ cup (5 oz) + 3 tablespoons sugar
2 cups (8 oz) flour
1 egg yolk
½ teaspoon vanilla extract
½ cup (2 oz) chopped walnuts
½ teaspoon ground cinnamon

1. Preheat oven to 200°C (400°F/Gas 6). **2.** Cream the butter and ⅔ cup of the sugar, and mix in the egg yolk. **3.** While stirring, add the flour and vanilla extract. **4.** Wrap the dough in plastic film and refrigerate until firm. **5.** Put the dough into a cookie (biscuit) press and press the biscuits onto an unbuttered baking sheet through a selected nozzle. **6.** Sprinkle with walnuts and remaining sugar mixed with cinnamon. **7.** Bake the biscuits in the preheated oven for 5–6 minutes or until light golden.

Linzer Biscuits
Linzer Gebäck

250 g (8 oz) butter, softened
⅔ cup (6 oz) sugar
1¾ cups (7 oz) flour
pinch of salt
apricot or raspberry jam
icing (confectioners') sugar

1. Preheat the oven to 190°C (375°F/Gas 5).
2. Cream the butter with the sugar until light, add the flour and salt and make a smooth dough. **3.** Roll it out approximately 0.75 cm (¼ inch) thick. **4.** Using a 7.5 cm (3 inch) fluted biscuit cutter, cut out rounds of dough. Then, with a smaller cutter, cut out the centres of half of the biscuits. **5.** Bake in the preheated oven for 10 minutes until light brown. **6.** Cool the biscuits and spread the rounds with jam. Place the ones with the cut-out centres on top. Add more jam in the hole and sprinkle with icing sugar.

Esterhazy Cake

Esterhazy Torte

From the Konditorei Sluka, Vienna.

Makes one 20 cm (8 inch) cake

Almond Genoese Cake Base:
5 egg yolks
50 g (1¾ oz) sugar
50 g (1¾ oz) ground almonds
2½ tablespoons flour
3 egg whites, stiffly beaten
juice of ½ lemon

Chocolate Butter Cream:
Makes 2½ cups

⅓ cup (3 oz) sugar
⅓ cup (2½ fl oz) water
6 egg yolks, well beaten
315 g (10 oz) softened butter
125 g (4 oz) chocolate, melted and cooled

Apricot Glaze:
¼ cup (3 oz) apricot jam
hot water
1–2 tablespoons apricot brandy (optional)

Fondant Icing:
1¾ cups (11 oz) sugar
¼ teaspoon cream of tartar
1 cup (8 fl oz) boiling water
½ cup melted dark chocolate
4 tablespoons roasted almond flakes

Almond Genoese Cake Base: 1. Preheat the oven to 180°C (350°F/Gas 4). **2.** Cream the egg yolks with the sugar and stir in the ground almonds and flour. **3.** Add the egg whites, folding them into the mixture and then fold in the lemon juice. **4.** Pour the cake mixture into a round buttered 20 cm (8 inch) cake tin and bake in the preheated oven for 30–40 minutes or until cooked. **5.** Allow the cake to cool before removing it from the mould. **6.** When cold, cut into four horizontal slices.

Chocolate Butter Cream: 1. Boil the sugar and water to the thread stage (115°C/240°F on a sugar thermometer). **2.** Pour the sugar mixture over the egg yolks, beating until the mixture is frothy and cold. **3.** Gradually stir in the softened butter and continue stirring until smooth. **4.** If the mixture separates, add more butter. **5.** Stir in the melted chocolate.

Apricot Glaze: 1. In a double boiler, heat the apricot jam, thinning it down with a little hot water. **2.** Add one or two tablespoons of apricot brandy, if you are using it.

Fondant Icing: 1. In a heavy saucepan, combine the sugar and the cream of tartar. **2.** Add the boiling water and stir until dissolved. **3.** Cook the syrup without stirring until it reaches the thread stage (115°C/240°F on a sugar thermometer). **4.** Remove the fondant from the heat and pour it on to a metal surface. **5.** With a spatula, work it until it cools and knead it into a smooth mass. This should be done as quickly as possible. **6.** Place the fondant in an airtight container and store it in the refrigerator. **7.** To make the fondant icing, heat the fondant in the top of a double boiler over simmering water and add the melted chocolate. **8.** Thin the fondant to a spreadable consistency with boiling water. **9.** To ice the cake, pour the fondant icing on to it and quickly tilt it in all directions to spread the icing. **10.** If the fondant gets too stiff, it can be reheated to the required consistency.

To assemble: 1. Cut the Almond Genoese Cake Base into four layers and spread each layer with the chocolate butter cream as they are stacked one on top of the other. **2.** Glaze the top and sides of the cake with a thin layer of the apricot glaze and allow to dry. **3.** Finally cover the cake with the chocolate fondant icing and press the almond flakes into the icing before it sets.

Leaf Cake

Blättertorte

Makes one cake

½ cup (4 oz) sugar
1 cup (4 oz) flour
5 hard-boiled egg yolks, riced
2 egg yolks
4 egg whites
30 g (1 oz) sugar
3 tablespoons raspberry jam, drained
¾ cup (6 fl oz) cream, whipped
1 tablespoon sugar
1 cup fresh raspberries
icing (confectioners') sugar

1. Preheat the oven to 175°C (350°F/Gas 4). **2.** Make a smooth dough from the sugar, flour, hard-boiled egg yolks and fresh egg yolks. **3.** Divide the dough into three parts and roll out as thinly as possible into three rounds. **4.** Place the rounds on a buttered baking sheet and bake in the preheated oven until they are golden-brown. **5.** Beat the egg whites until stiff. Continue beating while gradually adding the sugar. Fold in the raspberry jam. **6.** Cover one round of the cake with half of the meringue, place a second round on top and cover this with the remainder of the meringue. Place the third round on top. **7.** Pipe a circle of whipped cream about 5 cm (2 inches) from the edge. **8.** Fill the inside of the circle with the fresh raspberries. **9.** Just before serving, sprinkle with icing sugar.

Right: A selection of cakes on display at the Konditorei Sluka, Vienna including far right: Esterhazy Cake (above) and far left: Dobosch.

DESSERTS

Chocolate Pudding

Schokoladendunstkoch

Serves 4-6

125 g (4 oz) butter
6 egg yolks
¼ cup (2 oz) sugar
90 g (3 oz) grated chocolate
6 slices stale white bread
2 cups (16 fl oz) milk
125 g (4 oz) almonds, grated
grated rind of ½ lemon
6 egg whites, stiffly beaten
3 tablespoons split almonds

Chocolate Cream Sauce:
45 g (1½ oz) sugar
¼ cup (2 fl oz) water
¼ teaspoon tartaric acid
90 g (3 oz) chocolate, melted
½ cup cream, whipped
extra whipped cream, for decoration

1. Cream the butter, add the egg yolks and sugar and continue beating until the sugar is dissolved. 2. Add the melted chocolate. 3. Remove the crusts from the bread and soak in milk for 15 minutes. 4. Drain and squeeze dry. Mash the bread to a fine pulp. 5. Add the mashed bread to the chocolate mixture. 6. Add the almonds and lemon rind and gently fold in the egg whites. 7. Grease a pudding mould and dust it with flour. Place the split almonds into the bottom of the pudding mould, they will serve as decoration. 8. Pour the chocolate mixture into the pudding mould. 9. Place the pudding mould into a deep dish and pour in hot water till it reaches two-thirds of the height of the pudding mould. 10. Cover the pudding mould and cook it in the hot-water bath for 1 hour. 11. To prepare the chocolate cream sauce, dilute the sugar in the water and add the tartaric acid. Without stirring, cook it to the thin thread stage (115°C/240°F on a sugar thermometer). Add the chocolate, cool the mixture and fold in the whipped cream. 12. To serve, turn the pudding out on to a plate, mask it with the chocolate cream sauce and decorate with whipped cream.

Peaches Stuffed with Almonds

Pfirsiche mit Mandeln

Serves 6

⅓ cup (3 oz) caster (powdered) sugar
90 g (3 oz) almonds, finely chopped
¼ cup (2 fl oz) rum
6 large peaches, peeled, cut in half, stones removed
¼ cup (2 oz) vanilla-flavoured sugar
½ cup sour cream
1 tablespoon rum

1. Heat oven to 175°C (350°F/Gas 4). 2. In a food processor combine the sugar and the almonds and process until they form a thick paste, add the rum. 3. Fill the centres of the peaches with the almond paste and place the two halves of each peach together. 4. Place the peaches in a buttered baking dish and sprinkle with some of the vanilla-flavoured sugar. 5. Place them in the preheated oven and bake for approximately 15 minutes or until they are soft. 6. Combine the rest of the vanilla-flavoured sugar and the sour cream and add 1 tablespoon of rum. 7. Serve the peaches either hot or cold topped with the rum-flavoured sour cream.

Cream Cheese Pancakes

Topfenpalatschinken

From the Gasthof Auerhahn, Salzburg.

Serves 4

8 pancakes (see p. 330)
Filling:
60 g (2 oz) butter
45 g (1½ oz) sugar
2 egg yolks
250 g (8 oz) cottage or cream cheese
3-6 tablespoons sour cream (use only if the cheese is too dry)
4 egg whites, stiffly beaten
2 tablespoons raisins
icing (confectioners') sugar

1. Cream the butter with the sugar and egg yolks. 2. Add the cheese and, if necessary, the sour cream. 3. Fold in the egg whites and raisins. 4. Divide the filling into 8 parts and spread it over the pancakes. 5. Roll the pancakes and serve dusted with a little icing sugar. 6. Another way to serve this dessert is to arrange the pancakes on a buttered baking dish, cover with a mixture of sour cream and egg yolks, to which a little sugar has been added, and bake in an oven for 25-30 minutes. However, this preparation is slightly rich.

Small Doughnuts with Poppy-seed Sauce
Minkelen

From the Goldener Adler, Innsbruck. This is a true South Tyrolean dessert speciality which consists of small doughnuts (the size of an olive) deep fried and served with a sweet poppy-seed sauce.

Dough:
1 cup (8 fl oz) milk
45 g (1½ oz) sugar
vanilla essence
pinch of salt
30 g (1 oz) yeast
¼ cup (2 fl oz) lukewarm water
4 cups (1 lb) flour
45 g (1½ oz) melted butter
2 eggs

Poppy-seed Sauce:
125 g (4 oz) poppy seeds
30 g (1 oz) butter
2–4 tablespoons honey
2 tablespoons brandy or rum
½ cup (4 fl oz) water

Minkelen: 1. Bring the milk to the boil and add the sugar, salt and a few drops of vanilla essence. **2.** Cool it to lukewarm temperature. **3.** Dissolve the yeast in the lukewarm water. **4.** Place the flour in a large mixing bowl and while mixing vigorously, add the milk, yeast, melted butter and eggs. **5.** Beat and stir the dough until it is smooth and comes away from the bowl. **6.** Cover the dough with a warm tea towel and place it in a warm place until it doubles its bulk (approximately 1½ hours). **7.** Punch the dough down and with a teaspoon put pieces of the dough into deep hot fat, 190°C (375°F) and deep fry until golden-brown. **8.** Serve on a hot plate together with the Poppy-seed Sauce.

Poppy-seed Sauce: 1. In a blender or food processor grind the poppy seeds to a smooth mass. **2.** Place the poppy seeds, butter, honey, brandy and water in a saucepan and simmer for approximately 15 minutes. **3.** Serve hot with the Minkelen.

Salzburg Soufflé
Salzburger Nockerl

From the Gasthof Auerhahn, Salzburg.

Serves 6

3 egg yolks
6 drops vanilla essence
grated rind of ½ lemon
2 tablespoons flour
5 egg whites
pinch of salt
2 tablespoons caster sugar
icing (confectioners') sugar

1. Preheat the oven to 175°C (350°F/Gas 4). **2.** Cream the egg yolks with the vanilla essence and lemon peel and then add the flour. **3.** Add a pinch of salt to the egg whites and whip them until stiff peaks form, meanwhile gradually adding the caster sugar. **4.** Gently fold the egg whites into the yolk and flour mixture, just until they are mixed together. **5.** Butter an oval dish approximately 25 × 20 cm (10 × 8 inches) and 5 cm (2 inches) deep. **6.** Place the mixture into the dish and with a spatula make 3 or 4 separate mounds. **7.** Bake in the preheated oven for 10–12 minutes or until light brown on top. **8.** Sprinkle with icing sugar and serve immediately — before it collapses.

225

SPAIN

Spanish cuisine is the sum total of many different parts. It is basically countrymen's fare and at no stage are special skills required to master even the more complex dishes.

I started my journey in Madrid where, in addition to the cooking of its own region (New Castile), one can find food from all parts of the country. Here I tried an authentic version of the already familiar Cochimillo Asado. It was an appropriate beginning for the central regions of Spain, New Castile and Old Castile, are renowned for their roasts.

The brown, dusty landscape of the centre soon changes to the moist, misty and vivid green of Galicia and despite incessant rain Santiago de Compostela, for a thousand years renowned for its shrine of St James the Apostle, lost none of its theatrical impact. This part of Spain has some of the best and most varied supply of seafood and the scallops here are the best I have tasted anywhere.

The Basques have the reputation of being the best cooks in Spain so I was not surprised to find in San Sebastián the best restaurant I came across during my stay in that country. Juan Arzac is a great friend and admirer of Michel Guérard, and in his restaurant he prepares an original Nouvelle Cuisine version of traditional Basque cooking.

The cooking of Navarre and of neighbouring Aragón is best known for its sauces. 'A la Chilindrón' denotes a dish served in a sauce that combines garlic, onions, tomatoes, red or green peppers (capsicums) and ham; these ingredients, and the various meats such as rabbit, lamb, chicken or veal with which they are used, blend into a characteristic flavour. There are also a number of peculiar dishes called Migas in which breadcrumbs are the main ingredient.

I was looking forward to my visit to Barcelona and this time my expectations were not only of a culinary nature. As an architect I had always admired the idiosyncratic buildings of Antonio Gaudí and I was soon to see them in real life. Gastronomically there is a strong French influence, and the pungent Ali-oli, which reappears all along the Mediterranean coast of Spain and France, is of Catalán origin.

From Barcelona I travelled south, past the beaches and holiday resorts which extend along the coast, to Valencia, an important agricultural district in the centre of Spain's rice country.

An all too fleeting visit to Granada and Sevilla, in Andalusia, gave me a tantalising taste of the most romantic of the Spanish regions. The south has hot summers and winters are short. Regional food is light, and the refreshing Gazpacho is a typical example of food adapted to a hot climate. Most food is fried crisp in good quality oil.

The last region I visited was Extremadura which has a severe climate and where living conditions in the past have been hard. Its people make the best of what is available and local dishes reflect a frugal approach to life. But there is good hunting for deer, hare, partridge and even wild boar and local chorizo is well known for its strong taste.

Right: A formal garden nestles between the Parador Raimundo de Borgoña and the mediaeval walls of Avila.

TAPAS & ENTREMESES

Shepherd's Crumbs

Migas a la Pastora

From the El Cachirulo, Zaragoza, Aragón.

Serves 6

750 g (1½ lb) fresh breadcrumbs
water
salt
125 g (4 oz) lard
4 cloves garlic, crushed
125 g (4 oz) button mushroom heads
125 g (4 oz) chorizo (spicy pork sausage), sliced

1. Sprinkle the breadcrumbs with salt and just enough water to moisten them, cover with a damp cloth and refrigerate for 12 hours. **2.** Melt and heat 100 g (3½ oz) of the lard, fry the garlic, add the breadcrumbs and stir continuously over low heat for 10 minutes. **3.** Fry the mushrooms and the chorizo slices. **4.** Reserve 6 mushroom heads and chorizo slices for garnish, and mix the rest with the breadcrumbs. **5.** Serve in an earthenware bowl and garnish with mushrooms and chorizos.

Baby Squid cooked on a Hotplate

Chipirones a la Plancha

From the Restaurant Casa Costa, Barceloneta, Catalonia.

Serves 6

18 baby squid, cleaned
¼ cup (2 fl oz) olive oil
3 sprigs parsley, finely chopped
2 cloves garlic, crushed
1 tablespoon paprika
salt
freshly ground black pepper

1. Place the squid on a hotplate, or over charcoal, or into a heavy frying pan. **2.** Sprinkle with oil and with half of a mixture of parsley, garlic, paprika, salt and pepper. **3.** Keep sprinkling with oil, turn the squid after about 3 minutes and sprinkle with the remaining mixture. **4.** Cook for a further 3 minutes until brown.

Prawns Cooked on a Hotplate

Gambas a la Plancha

From the Restaurant Casa Costa, Barceloneta, Barcelona, Catalonia.

Serves 4

6 tablespoons olive oil
juice of 2 lemons
1 clove garlic, crushed
salt
freshly ground black pepper
12 fresh king prawns, uncooked

1. In a screw-top jar, combine oil, lemon juice, garlic, salt and pepper. Shake well. **2.** Pour the mixture into a bowl and add the prawns. Let them steep for a few minutes. **3.** Place the prawns on a hotplate over an open charcoal fire or into a heavy-bottomed frying pan. Sprinkle with the mixture and cook the prawns on both sides for 4 to 8 minutes, depending on the size of the prawns. Serve hot and eat with fingers.

Deep-fried Squid

Calamares Fritos

Serves 6

1 cup (4 oz) flour
1 teaspoon baking powder
½ teaspoon salt
1 egg, lightly beaten
1 cup (8 fl oz) milk
2 tablespoons olive oil
750 g (1½ lb) small squid, cleaned and cut into rings
a little extra flour
oil for deep frying
salt
freshly ground black pepper
quarters of lemon

1. Make batter by combining flour, baking powder, salt, egg, milk and oil. **2.** Pat the squid dry, sprinkle with flour, dip into batter and deep fry until crisp and light golden-brown. **3.** Serve hot sprinkled with salt, pepper and lemon juice.

SOUPS

Iced Vegetable Salad Soup
Gazpacho Andaluz

From the Restaurant El Burladero, Sevilla, Andalusia.
Most cooks in Spain have their own versions of Gazpacho; pine nuts may be used instead of almonds, and in some parts of the country finely diced meat or chicken is added. In Extremadura, game (especially rabbit meat) is used.

Serves 4–6

Soup:
3 tablespoons stale white breadcrumbs
1–2 cloves garlic, crushed, according to taste
1 tablespoon wine vinegar
1 tablespoon olive oil
1 green or red pepper (capsicum), seeded and chopped
1 onion, chopped
4 tomatoes, peeled and chopped
1 cucumber, peeled, seeded and chopped
8 almonds, finely crushed
iced water
salt
finely ground white pepper

Garnishes:
1 large cucumber, peeled, seeded and diced
1 green and 1 red pepper (capsicum), seeded and cut into small squares
2 tomatoes, peeled and cut into small dice
1 onion, finely chopped
2 hard-boiled eggs, chopped
2 slices stale white bread, cut into small dice

1. Combine all soup ingredients except the almonds, water, salt and pepper. Soak and refrigerate for 1 hour. **2.** Purée in a blender or food processor. **3.** Add almonds, salt, pepper and enough iced water to dilute to desired consistency. **4.** Refrigerate for 3–4 hours before serving. **5.** Arrange each of the garnishes in a separate dish and place these in the centre of the table. **6.** Serve the soup in chilled bowls. Each diner adds garnishes selected according to individual taste.

White Bean, Cabbage and Potato Soup
Caldo Gallego

Serves 6

250 g (8 oz) dried white beans
6–10 cups (1.5–2.5 litres) water
2 chorizo (spicy pork sausage)
1 ham bone or smoked pork ribs
250 g (8 oz) Spanish ham or prosciutto cut into 1.5 cm (½ inch) cubes
500 g (1 lb) potatoes, peeled and chopped
500 g (1 lb) cabbage or turnip tops, roughly chopped
1 onion, roughly chopped
salt
pepper
1 teaspoon paprika

1. Either soak the beans overnight or boil 6 cups (1.5 litres) of water, add the beans and boil them for 2 minutes. Remove the saucepan from the heat and leave the beans to soak for 1 hour. **2.** Bring the beans to the boil again. **3.** Add the whole sausages, the ham bone or pork ribs, and the cubes of ham. Simmer over low heat for 1 hour. **4.** Add the potatoes, cabbage and onion, season with salt and pepper. Cover the saucepan and simmer as slowly as possible for at least 2 hours. **5.** Add paprika and cook for another 10 minutes. **6.** To serve, remove and discard the bone, serve sausages and meat on a side plate, and the soup separately.

Fish and Rice Soup
Sopa de Cádiz

Serves 4

1 large snapper head
4 cups (1 litre) water
salt
6 peppercorns
2 bay leaves
½ cup (3 oz) rice
2 tablespoons olive oil
1 onion, finely chopped
1–3 cloves garlic, according to taste
3 sprigs parsley, chopped
juice of 1 lemon

1. Gently cook the fish head in the salty water, together with the peppercorns and bay leaves, for 30 minutes. **2.** Take off the heat and allow to cool. Strain the stock and save all flesh from the fish head. **3.** In the stock, cook the rice for 15 minutes. **4.** In a frying pan, heat the oil and fry the onion, garlic and parsley until the onion is transparent. **5.** Add the onion to the stock and cook for 10 minutes. **6.** Add the flesh of the fish and lemon juice. Season to taste. **7.** Serve hot with fresh crusty bread.

Cream of Crayfish Soup

Crema de Cangrejos

From the Casa Duque, Segovia, Old Castile.

Serves 6–8

6 tablespoons oil
90 g (3 oz) butter
1 stalk celery, chopped
2 leeks, white part only, sliced
1 turnip, peeled and chopped
2 tomatoes, peeled and chopped
3 sprigs parsley, chopped
3 sprigs fresh herbs (oregano, thyme, marjoram)
2 cloves
6 peppercorns
¼ cup (2 oz) rice
1 cup (8 fl oz) dry white wine
8 cups (2 litres) fish stock or water
500 g (1 lb) uncooked freshwater crayfish or prawns
¼ teaspoon Tabasco sauce (or ¼ teaspoon sliced hot peppers)
1 cup (8 fl oz) cream
salt
½ cup (4 fl oz) brandy

1. In a saucepan heat the oil and butter, add celery, leeks and turnip and sauté until soft and lightly coloured. **2.** Add tomatoes, parsley, the other herbs, cloves, peppercorns, rice, wine and water or fish stock. Bring to the boil and simmer over low heat. **3.** Place the crayfish or prawns on top, cover the saucepan and steam them for 10 minutes. **4.** Set aside 6–8 of the crayfish or prawns (to be used as garnish later). Shell all the other crayfish or prawns and set the tails aside. Return the shells to the saucepan and mix them in. **5.** Continue to simmer for 40 minutes. **6.** Remove from heat, allow to cool and purée in a food processor or rub through a sieve, or crush with a wooden spoon and rub through sieve. **7.** Return the liquid to the saucepan, add Tabasco (or hot peppers), cream and seasoning. Add the crayfish or prawn tails, and heat but do not boil. If necessary add more stock, water or cream. **8.** Heat the brandy, pour it into the saucepan and mix well. **9.** Serve hot, each soup plate garnished with a whole crayfish or prawn.

SAUCES

Garlic Mayonnaise

Ali-oli

A pestle and mortar, a mixer, a rotary hand beater or a food processor may be used. Originally a speciality of Catalonia.

Makes 2 cups (16 fl oz)

4–5 cloves garlic, crushed
2 egg yolks
1½ cups (12 fl oz) olive oil
½ teaspoon salt
pinch of cayenne pepper
juice of 1 lemon
water

1. Mash the garlic to a smooth paste. **2.** Add the egg yolks and beat or process until they are thick and pale yellow. **3.** While continuing to beat, gradually and slowly add the oil. **4.** Season with salt and cayenne pepper and stir in the lemon juice. **5.** Stir in enough cold water to achieve the desired consistency. Serve in a separate bowl, with boiled, grilled or barbecued fish, meat or vegetables.

Caper Sauce

Salsa de Alcaparrado

60 g (2 oz) butter
2 tablespoons flour
1 cup (8 fl oz) hot beef stock (see p. 328)
2 tablespoons vinegar
½ cup (2 oz) capers, chopped
salt
freshly ground black pepper

1. Melt the butter, add the flour and cook until the flour starts to colour. **2.** While stirring, gradually add the hot stock and the vinegar. Cook for 10 minutes until the sauce is smooth. **3.** Add the capers, salt and pepper. Serve with fish or with smoked meats.

Right: The El Cachirulo restaurant in Zaragoza, Aragon calls itself 'the regional monument of gastronomy'. Built in the style of an Aragonese country villa, it has numerous dining rooms, a cellar and the typical local bar. Here hams and tasty sausages hang from the beams, while on the bar counter are tapas to tempt the drinkers. Clockwise from bottom right: Shepherd's Crumbs (see page 228); Cod with Garlic; Eggs in Sauce with Asparagus Tips; Peaches in Wine (see page 252); Roast Baron of Lamb (see page 246); Chicken in Chilindron Sauce (see page 244).

La Picada Catalana

The Picada is not really a sauce in the true sense. It is used to flavour soups, stews, meat and fish dishes and is added half-way through the cooking. There are regional variations and sometimes different ingredients are used, but this is the basic recipe.
A food processor may be used instead of the traditional mortar.

¼ teaspoon saffron
2 cloves garlic, peeled
¼–½ teaspoon salt
30 g (1 oz) toasted, blanched almonds
30 g (1 oz) toasted, blanched hazelnuts
½ teaspoon cinnamon
2 sprigs parsley, chopped
¼ cup (2 fl oz) dry sherry

1. In a mortar, grind all the dry ingredients to a fine paste. **2.** Gradually add enough sherry to dilute to the desired consistency.

Catalán Barbecue Sauce

Salsa Barbacoa Catalana

Traditionally, this sauce is made with a pestle and mortar. However, it may be easily prepared in a food processor.

Serves 4-6

4 cloves garlic
2 sprigs mint
12 toasted almonds
12 toasted hazelnuts
5 ripe tomatoes, peeled, seeded and chopped
salt
freshly ground black pepper
1 teaspoon vinegar
½ cup (4 fl oz) olive oil

1. In a mortar, crush the garlic, mint and nuts to a fine paste. Add tomatoes, salt, pepper and vinegar and continue until all ingredients combine to form a smooth sauce. **2.** While stirring constantly, slowly pour in the oil (as for mayonnaise). Serve with barbecued meats, fish or vegetables.

Catalán Pepper Sauce

Romescu

5 tomatoes
3 cloves garlic, whole but peeled
12 toasted almonds
12 toasted hazelnuts
½–1 teaspoon cayenne pepper, according to hotness desired
salt
1 cup (8 fl oz) olive oil
2 tablespoons vinegar
¼ cup (2 fl oz) sherry
1 sprig parsley, finely chopped

1. Heat the oven to 180°C (350°F/Gas 4). **2.** Bake the tomatoes and garlic for 20 minutes. Cool, peel the tomatoes and remove their seeds. **3.** In a mortar or food processor, make a paste with the nuts. Add tomatoes, garlic and salt and continue until the mixture has a smooth texture. **4.** Slowly and gradually add the oil, thoroughly incorporating it into the sauce before adding more. It should be thick and creamy. **5.** Finally, add the vinegar and enough sherry to achieve the desired consistency. Stir in the parsley. **6.** Refrigerate overnight to allow the flavours to blend. Serve with grilled or boiled meats, fish or other seafood.

Pine Nut Sauce

Salsa de Piñones

From the Restaurant Forn del Nastasi, Lérida, Catalonia.

Serves 4

½ teaspoon cumin seeds, crushed
100 g (3½ oz) pine nuts
1 clove garlic
2 hard-boiled egg yolks
2 cups (16 fl oz) chicken stock (see p. 328)
salt
freshly ground black pepper

1. In a mortar or food processor, make a fine paste from the cumin, pine nuts, garlic and egg yolks. **2.** Gradually add the stock, season, and put it in a saucepan. Bring to the boil and simmer over low heat for 15 minutes. Serve with barbecued or roasted chicken.

EGG DISHES

Omelette with Asparagus

Tortilla con Espárragos

From the Restaurant Sobrino de Botin, Madrid, New Castile.

Serves 1

3 asparagus spears
2 eggs
salt
freshly ground black pepper
2 tablespoons water
15 g (½ oz) butter

1. Cut the asparagus spears into 2.5 cm (1 inch) lengths, put the pieces into boiling salted water for 3 minutes, then drain them. **2.** In a bowl, beat the eggs with salt, pepper and water. **3.** In a small frying pan, heat the butter, pour in the egg mixture and add the asparagus. **4.** Cook until the mixture sets. Fold in half and serve hot.

Hot Pepper Omelette

Tortilla Estilo Badajoz

From the Parador Nacional 'Via de la Prata', Mérida, Extremadura
On my way to Badajoz, which is on the Portuguese border, I came across local farmers turning the red peppers which were spread out to dry on the huge canvas sheets in the warm late autumn sun. The colours were magnificent.

Serves 4

200 g (6½ oz) chorizo (spicy pork sausage), sliced
3–4 tablespoons olive oil
1 small thin hot red or green pepper, seeded, washed and sliced
1 teaspoon paprika
8 eggs
2 tablespoons water
salt

1. In a frying pan, sauté the sausage in 2 tablespoons of oil. **2.** Add the peppers and paprika, lightly sauté over low heat for 10 minutes. **3.** In a bowl, whip the eggs well with water and salt. **4.** If necessary, add more oil to the frying pan, then pour in the eggs, stir with a fork and fry until set. **5.** Fold it over, divide into 4, and serve to those who like it hot!

Baked Eggs with Vegetables, Ham and Sausage

Huevos a la Flamenca

From the Restaurant El Burladero, Sevilla, Andalusia.

Serves 4

1 cup (8 fl oz) olive oil
2 potatoes, peeled and cut into small dice
1 onion, chopped
1 clove garlic, crushed
1 red or green pepper (capsicum), seeded and chopped
2 slices serrano ham, prosciutto or lean smoked ham, chopped
1 chorizo (spicy pork sausage), sliced
200 g (6½ oz) green peas, cooked
200 g (6½ oz) green beans, cooked, cut into small pieces
1 small can asparagus tips (use fresh asparagus, when in season)
4 tomatoes, peeled, juice and seeds squeezed out, chopped
2 tablespoons tomato paste
½–1 cup (4–8 fl oz) water
salt
freshly ground black pepper
4 eggs
an additional ½ red or green pepper (capsicum), seeded and cut into strips
6 small sprigs parsley for garnish

1. Preheat the oven to 200°C (400°F/Gas 6). **2.** Heat the oil in a large frying pan and fry the potatoes until golden. Remove, and set them aside. **3.** In the same pan, fry the onion, garlic, chopped pepper, ham and chorizo (but keep 6 slices for garnish) until the onions are soft and transparent. **4.** Add the peas (keep some for garnish), beans, asparagus tips (keep some for garnish), tomatoes, tomato paste, the potatoes and water. Season, and cook over low heat until most of the liquid has evaporated. Stir occasionally. **5.** Use either a large ovenproof dish or 4 individual dishes (in Spain glazed earthenware dishes are used). Brush the inside with oil and pour in the vegetable mixture. **6.** Make four hollows and break the eggs into them. **7.** Garnish the top with slices of chorizo, peas, asparagus tips and strips of red or green pepper. **8.** Bake in the preheated oven for 15–20 minutes until the egg whites turn opaque. **9.** Serve decorated with sprigs of parsley.

Omelette with Kidneys

Tortilla Madrileña con Riñones

From the Sobrino de Botín, Madrid, New Castile.

Serves 4

4 tablespoons olive oil
90 g (3 oz) butter
2 onions, chopped
3 lamb's kidneys, chopped
3 sprigs parsley, finely chopped
½ cup (4 fl oz) dry sherry
salt
freshly ground black pepper
4 tomatoes, cut in half
125 g (4 oz) Spanish ham
6 eggs, well beaten

1. Heat half of the oil and butter in a frying pan and sauté 1 chopped onion until soft and transparent. Add kidneys and parsley and cook for 5 minutes. **2.** Add the sherry, bring to boiling point and season with salt and pepper. Remove the mixture from the pan, set aside and keep it warm. **3.** Heat the rest of the oil and butter and fry the tomatoes. Remove them from the pan, set aside and keep them warm. **4.** In the same pan, sauté the remaining onion, add the ham, pour in the eggs, and season. Fry on both sides. **5.** Serve the omelette on a heated serving plate, with the kidney heaped in the centre, surrounded by the tomatoes.

Egg Scrambled with Vegetables

Pisto Castellano

From the Mesón de Rastro, Avila, Old Castile.

Serves 4

2 tablespoons olive oil
2 onions, chopped
60 g (2 oz) bacon, chopped
4 potatoes, peeled and cut into small dice
2 zucchini (courgettes), sliced
4 tomatoes, peeled and chopped
3 red or green peppers (capsicums), seeded and chopped
1½ cups (12 fl oz) meat stock (see p. 328)
4 eggs
salt
freshly ground black pepper
4 slices bread, cut into triangles and fried

1. Heat the oil in a large frying pan and sauté the onion and bacon. **2.** Add the potatoes and zucchini, cover, and cook for 5 minutes. **3.** Add the tomatoes, peppers and stock. Simmer over low heat until the liquid is reduced by half. **4.** Whip the eggs with salt and pepper and add to the mixture. Cook until the eggs are set. Stir occasionally. **5.** Serve with the fried bread.

Spanish Potato and Onion Omelette

Tortilla

There are many variations of this basic recipe. Fried chorizo, chopped ham or cooked chicken meat, or cooked vegetables such as chopped red or green pepper (capsicum), beans, spinach, peas or asparagus pieces may be added to the onions and potatoes or, if desired, can replace them.

Serves 4

1 cup (8 fl oz) olive oil (no substitutes)
2-3 potatoes, peeled and sliced or cut into small cubes
2 large onions, chopped
salt
freshly ground black pepper
4 eggs

1. Heat the oil in a medium-sized frying pan, add the potatoes and onions, and season. Cover with a lid and sauté over low heat for 15–20 minutes. **2.** Whip the eggs in a large bowl until frothy. **3.** When the potatoes and onions are tender, remove them from the frying pan and put them into the egg mixture. Mix well together. **4.** Drain off most of the oil from the frying pan, leaving just enough to cover the bottom of the pan. **5.** Reheat the oil and pour in the egg-vegetable mixture. With a fork, distribute the vegetables evenly and flatten the top. Fry over low heat. **6.** When the mixture has set, cover the frying pan with a plate and invert the tortilla on to it. Then slide the tortilla back into the pan and continue frying until it is done. Alternatively, you may place the tortilla under a preheated grill to cook the top. **7.** The tortilla should look like a firm cake. It may be eaten hot or cold and is very tasty with a green salad.

Right: The Restaurant Arzac in San Sebastian in the Basque Provinces has the reputation of being one of the best restaurants in Spain. Chef Juan Arzac is a friend and admirer of Michel Guérard and has been strongly influenced by the light style of Nouvelle Cuisine. He has created his own original and ingenious approach which is a combination of Nouvelle Cuisine, local methods and traditional ingredients. Clockwise from bottom: Stuffed Baby Squid in its Ink; Fish Pâté (see page 241); Baked Crab; Hake with Seaweed.

VEGETABLES & SALADS

Asparagus with Bread Sauce

Espárragos Andaluz

From the Restaurant Sevilla, Granada, Andalusia.

Serves 4

½ cup (4 fl oz) olive oil
2 cloves garlic, chopped
1 slice white bread
500 g (1 lb) asparagus, cut into 1.5 cm (½ inch) pieces
1 cup (8 fl oz) chicken stock (see p. 328)
salt
freshly ground black pepper
2 teaspoons white wine vinegar
8 triangles of fried bread (croûtons)

1. In a saucepan, heat the oil and lightly sauté the garlic. Remove and reserve. **2.** In the same oil, fry the slice of bread until crisp. Remove and reserve. **3.** In a saucepan, simmer the asparagus pieces in the stock over low heat for 12 minutes. Season and add the vinegar. **4.** In a mortar, crush the fried garlic and the bread and use a little of the stock to make a paste. **5.** Add this to the asparagus, making sure it is not too liquid. Stir and cook for 3 minutes. Serve with the croûtons.

Broad Beans with Ham and Chorizo

Habas de Victoria

Serves 4

broad beans from 2 kg of broad bean pods
150 g (5 oz) Spanish ham or prosciutto, in one piece
150 g (5 oz) bacon or speck, in one piece
200 g (6½ oz) chorizo (spicy pork sausage), in one piece
salt

1. Put the beans in a saucepan and cover with water, put the ham, bacon or speck and chorizo on top. Cover and simmer over low heat for 30–40 minutes. **2.** Pour off the liquid and reserve for later use. **3.** Cut the ham, bacon or speck and chorizo into small pieces. **4.** Put the beans in a serving dish, season if necessary, put the meat on top of the beans, and serve as a separate course.

Spanish Corn

Maíz Español

Serves 4

2 tablespoons olive oil
corn stripped from 4 corn cobs, about 2 cups
2 tablespoons flour
salt
cayenne pepper
¼–½ teaspoon chilli powder (optional)
1 cup (4 oz) grated Parmesan-style cheese
1 onion, finely chopped
12 olives, pitted and roughy chopped
1 clove garlic, crushed
4–6 tomatoes, peeled and finely chopped

1. Preheat the oven to 180°C (350°F/Gas 4). **2.** In a saucepan, combine the oil, corn, flour, salt, cayenne and chilli powder (optional) and cook over low heat for 10 minutes, stirring constantly. **3.** Add the cheese, onion, olives, garlic and tomatoes. **4.** Pour it into a small casserole and bake in the preheated oven for 30–40 minutes. Serve as a separate course.

Sevillian Salad

Ensalada Sevillana

From the Restaurant El Burladero, Sevilla, Andalusia.

Serves 8

6 red or green peppers (capsicums), cut in half and seeded
4 cups (20 oz) cooked rice
4 onions, finely sliced
6 tomatoes, peeled and each cut into 8 segments
200 g (6½ oz) green olives, may be pitted if preferred
½ cup (4 fl oz) olive oil
2 tablespoons vinegar
1 clove garlic, crushed
salt
freshly ground black pepper

1. Place the pepper halves (skin side up) under a preheated grill until the skin blackens. Cool and remove the skin. Cut the peppers into strips. **2.** Put the rice on the bottom of a serving dish and on top arrange the pepper strips, onions, tomatoes and olives. **3.** In a screw-top jar, make a dressing from the oil, vinegar, garlic, salt and pepper. Shake well and pour over the salad.

Stuffed Onions

Cebollas Rellenas a la Catalana

From the Restaurant Forn del Nastasi, Lérida, Catalonia.

Serves 4

8 large onions, peeled
½ cup (3 oz) rice
2 cups (16 fl oz) stock or water
2 cloves garlic, crushed
2 red or green peppers (capsicums), chopped
2 tablespoons olive oil
2 hard-boiled eggs, finely chopped
salt
freshly ground black pepper
½ cup (1 oz) fresh breadcrumbs
30 g (1 oz) butter, softened

1. Preheat the oven to 180°C (350°F/Gas 4). **2.** Cut the top off each onion about one-third from the top end. Set the tops to one side. **3.** In a saucepan, boil some water, add the onions and cook for 1 minute. **4.** Take out the centre of each onion, leaving an outer casing of 2 or 3 layers. Set the centres aside. **5.** Boil the rice in 1 cup of stock for 15 minutes. **6.** Finely chop the tops and centres of the onions and, together with the garlic, add to the rice. **7.** Sauté the chopped peppers in the oil for 15 minutes. **8.** Add the peppers to the rice, then add the chopped eggs and season. **9.** Stuff the onion cases, place them in a baking dish. Add the remaining stock, cover the dish and place in the preheated oven. Bake for 45 minutes. **10.** Remove the lid, sprinkle the onions with breadcrumbs, turn the oven up to 200°C (400°F/Gas 6), and bake for a further 15 minutes until the breadcrumbs turn brown.

Spinach with Raisins, Pine Nuts and Anchovies

Espinacas a la Catalana

Serves 4

2 kg (4 lb) spinach
½ cup (4 fl oz) olive oil
1 clove garlic, crushed
4 fillets of anchovy, chopped
½ cup (2 oz) pine nuts
1 tablespoon raisins
salt
freshly ground black pepper

1. In a large saucepan, boil some water and cook the spinach for 3 minutes. Drain, and chop it roughly. **2.** In a frying pan, heat the oil and lightly sauté the garlic, add the anchovies, spinach, pine nuts and raisins, and season. Cook over low heat for 20 minutes. Serve as a separate course or with other dishes.

Mixed Salad 'Sevilla'

Ensalada Especial 'Sevilla'

From the Restaurant Sevilla, Granada, Andalusia.

Serves 4-6

1 tomato, peeled and cut into wedges
¼ of a small firm lettuce, chopped
6 green beans, thinly sliced
1 small carrot, grated
6 asparagus spears (canned)
2 artichoke hearts (canned), cut into pieces
2 pieces of heart of palm, sliced
½ small leek, white part only, thinly sliced
½ cup (4 fl oz) olive oil
2 tablespoons vinegar or lemon juice
salt
freshly ground black pepper
4 hard-boiled eggs, peeled, cut into wedges

1. In a bowl, gently mix the vegetable ingredients. **2.** In a screw-top jar, combine the oil, vinegar or lemon juice, salt and pepper. Shake well. **3.** Pour the dressing over the salad and serve garnished with the egg wedges.

Grilled Vegetables

Escalibades

From the Forn del Nastasi, Lérida, Catalonia. Traditionally the vegetables are grilled over an open fire but hot grill may be used.

Serves 4-6

4 red peppers (capsicums), cut in half and seeded
4 small eggplant (aubergine), whole
4 tomatoes, whole
4 onions, whole
1 cup (8 fl oz) olive oil
1 sprig parsley, finely chopped
1 clove garlic, crushed
salt
freshly ground black pepper

1. Preheat the griller and place the vegetables under. Turn them, keep grilling until they are blackened all round. Allow to cool. **2.** To make the dressing, combine the oil, parsley, garlic, salt and pepper in a screw-top jar and shake well. **3.** Peel the grilled vegetables, cut them into strips, pour the dressing over and serve them with grilled or roasted meats. This can also be served as a first course with Garlic Mayonnaise (Ali-oli Sauce) (see p. 230).

RICE DISHES

Paella Alicantina

The combination of rabbit (or chicken) with mussels and prawns is unusual and delectable. This simple paella is worth trying.

Serves 4-6

3 tablespoons olive oil
salt
freshly ground black pepper
1 rabbit or chicken, cut into small pieces
1 clove garlic, bruised
400 g (13 oz) short grain rice
4 cups (1 litre) salted boiling water in which
2 pinches saffron have been boiled
24 fresh mussels
8-12 fresh uncooked prawns, shelled and deveined
2 red peppers (capsicums), seeded and cut into strips

1. Heat the oil in a paellera or large frying pan. Season the meat and fry until brown but not completely cooked. Remove the meat and keep it warm. **2.** Fry the garlic long enough to flavour the oil. Discard the garlic. **3.** Lower the heat, add the rice to the pan and cook for 2-3 minutes. **4.** Turn up the heat and add boiling saffron water (enough to cover the rice). **5.** Cover the pan and cook over low heat for 20 minutes. **6.** Add the meat and place the mussels and prawns on top. Decorate with the strips of red pepper. **7.** Cover the pan, cook for a few minutes until the mussels open and the prawns are cooked. Serve directly from the pan.

Paella a la Valenciana

There are many types of paella which vary according to the produce available locally. Meat, chicken, even game, together with vegetables and spicy sausages, are used inland; while along the coast around Valencia a combination of seafood, meat, chicken and rice is preferred. Further north, in Barcelona, only fish and shellfish are popular. There are no strict rules and whatever seafood and meat is available goes into the paellera. The addition of sherry will greatly improve the taste.

Serves 6-8

3 tablespoons olive oil
2 cloves garlic, crushed
2 onions, chopped
2 red peppers (capsicums), seeded and cut into strips
1 small chicken, cut into small pieces
250 g (8 oz) pork, ham or beef, diced
4 tomatoes, peeled and quartered
750 g (1½ lb) rice
4-6 cups (1-1.5 litres) chicken stock
(see p. 328), enough to cover
¼ teaspoon saffron
125 g (4 oz) shelled peas
125 g (4 oz) fresh kidney beans
6 artichoke hearts (optional)
500 g (1 lb) cod, whiting or hake, cut into small pieces
1 crayfish, cut into small pieces
250 g (8 oz) raw prawns, shelled and deveined
3 sprigs parsley, chopped
salt
freshly ground black pepper

1. Heat the oil in a paellera or a large frying pan, add the garlic, onions, pepper strips, chicken pieces and meat. Sauté until the meat browns. **2.** Add the tomatoes, stir in the rice and cook over low heat for 5 minutes. **3.** Add the stock, saffron, peas, beans and artichoke hearts (optional). Cook for 10 minutes. **4.** Add the fish and prawns, cook gently for 10-15 minutes, adding more stock if necessary. The rice should be moist but not soggy. **5.** To serve, take out some of the meat, fish, prawns, peas and capsicums and arrange them in a decorative pattern on top. Sprinkle with parsley and set the paellera or pan on the table.

Right: Sevilla is well known for its bullfighting. It is with much pride that the restaurant El Burladera (which means 'refuge in a bullring') displays photographs of famous bullfighters. It also takes pride in serving typical regional dishes. On the menu, as well as a fine Gazpacho, are Huevos a la Flamenca, a tasty dish of eggs, vegetables and meat, and Cocido Andaluz, the local stew. Clockwise from bottom left: Gazpacho (see page 229); Oxtail with Potatoes; Baked Eggs with Vegetables, Ham and Sausage (see page 233).

FISH

Sardines with Tomatoes

Sardinas con Tomate

From the Forn del Nastasi, Lérida, Catalonia.

Serves 4

⅓ cup (2 fl oz) olive oil
8–12 fresh sardines (depending on size),
cleaned
3 tablespoons flour
salt
freshly ground black pepper
2 cloves garlic, crushed
1 kg (2 lb) tomatoes, peeled and chopped
2 sprigs parsley, chopped

1. Heat the oil in a pan, sprinkle the sardines with flour, season with salt and pepper and fry briefly. Take out of the oil and set aside. **2.** In the same oil, sauté the garlic, add the tomatoes and simmer for 10 minutes. **3.** Add the sardines and simmer over low heat for 5 minutes. Season to taste and serve sprinkled with parsley.

Albufera Fish Stew

Lubina 'Llobarro' Albufera

From the Restaurant Viveros, Valencia.

Serves 4

⅓ cup (2 fl oz) olive oil
12 blanched almonds, crushed
2 cloves garlic, crushed
2 sprigs parsley, chopped
1 teaspoon paprika
2 teaspoons flour
4 cups (1 litre) fish stock (see p. 328)
1.5 kg (3 lb) fillet of white-fleshed fish, cut into
pieces
1 small hot chilli, chopped
salt
100 g (3½ oz) fresh shelled peas
strips of cooked red pepper (capsicum) for
garnish

1. Heat the oil in a casserole. Sauté the almonds, garlic and parsley until the almonds lightly change colour. **2.** Add the paprika and flour, stir well and cook for 2–3 minutes without browning the flour. **3.** Mix in the fish stock and, while stirring, cook until the sauce thickens. **4.** Add the fish pieces and chilli, season, and cook for 5 minutes. **5.** Add the peas and cook for a further 5 minutes or until the peas are cooked. Decorate with cooked strips of red pepper (capsicum) and serve from the dish.

Mixed Fish Dish

Zarzuela de Pescado

From the Casa Costa, Barceloneta, Barcelona, Catalonia.
This is a very popular Catalán dish. The ingredients vary according to what is available from the day's catch. It should include at least two types of white fish, prawns, lobster, mussels or squid.

Serves 4

500 g (1 lb) of white fish (buy 250 g (8 oz) each
of two types such as bream, snapper, jewfish
or whiting), cut into pieces
½ cup (2 oz) flour
4 tablespoons olive oil
2 cloves garlic, crushed
3 tomatoes, peeled and chopped
2 sprigs parsley, chopped
½ cup (4 fl oz) dry white wine
¼ cup (2 fl oz) brandy
1 tablespoon paprika
¼ teaspoon saffron
6 blanched almonds, crushed
salt
freshly ground black pepper
1 cup (8 fl oz) fish stock (see p. 328)
1 lobster, deveined and cut into pieces
12 prawns, uncooked
12 mussels, scrubbed

1. Preheat the oven to 230°C (450°F/Gas 8). **2.** Dust the fish pieces with flour, heat the oil in a large pan and brown the fish. Set them aside. **3.** In the same oil, sauté the garlic, tomatoes, and parsley. **4.** Add the white wine, brandy, paprika, saffron, crushed almonds, salt and pepper and fish stock. Cook for 10 minutes. **5.** Add the fish, stir gently and cook for 5 minutes. **6.** Add the lobster pieces, prawns and mussels and cook for about 5 minutes. **7.** Place the dish in the preheated oven. To serve, arrange the lobster pieces, prawns and mussels in a decorative pattern on top and serve without delay.

Fish Pâté

Pastel de Kabrarroca

From the Restaurant Arzac, San Sebastian, Basque Provinces.

Serves 8

**1 onion, chopped
2 stalks celery, chopped
1 carrot, chopped
6 peppercorns
2 bay leaves
salt
500 g (1 lb) white-fleshed fish fillets
8 eggs
1 cup (8 fl oz) cream
½ cup (4 fl oz) tomato purée
freshly ground black pepper
20 g (⅔ oz) butter, softened
2 tablespoons dry breadcrumbs**

1. Preheat the oven to 220°C (425°F/Gas 7). **2.** In a saucepan, cook the onion, celery, carrot, peppercorns and bay leaves in boiling salted water for 20 minutes. **3.** Add the fish and simmer over low heat for 10 minutes. Cool. Drain the stock and save it for future use. **4.** In a bowl, break up the fish and, beating vigorously with a wooden spoon, incorporate the eggs, cream and tomato purée. Season to taste. **5.** Butter a 1.5 litre (6 cup) capacity pâté mould, sprinkle with breadcrumbs and spoon in the pâté mixture. **6.** Cover with foil, place it in a baking dish almost filled with boiling water and bake in the preheated oven for 1¼ hours. **7.** Cool and carefully take it out of the mould, then refrigerate. **8.** Slice the pâté, mask it with pink mayonnaise and serve with slices of fresh hot toast. Pink mayonnaise is made by adding 1–2 tablespoons of tomato paste to 2 cups (16 fl oz) of mayonnaise (see p. 330).

Cod with Olives and Tomatoes

Esqueixada de 'Bacalla'

From the Forn del Nastasi, Lérida, Catalonia. A dish that the farmers from Segarra used to prepare for a midday meal in the fields. Best when served as a cold dish in hot weather.

Serves 4

**¾ cup (6 fl oz) olive oil
2 onions, finely chopped
4 tomatoes, peeled and chopped
salt
400 g (13 oz) dried and salted cod, soaked overnight and rinsed
100 g (3½ oz) black olives, pitted**

1. Heat the oil in a casserole, brown the onions, add the tomatoes and seasoning. Cook for 15 minutes. **2.** Add the cod, simmer for 10 minutes, remove from the heat and let it stand for 1 hour. **3.** Add the olives and refrigerate for 2–3 hours before serving.

Pickled Trout

Truchas en Escabeche

From the Hostería Nacional 'Del Comendador, Cáceres, Extremadura.

Serves 6

**6 small trout
½ cup (2 oz) flour
½ cup (4 fl oz) olive oil**

**Marinade:
1 onion, finely chopped
3 carrots, sliced
3 bay leaves
3 cloves garlic, crushed
1 teaspoon paprika
3 cups (24 fl oz) dry white wine
2 cups (16 fl oz) vinegar
salt**

1. Sprinkle the trout with flour and fry them in oil until they are cooked. **2.** To prepare the marinade, combine all ingredients in a saucepan. **3.** Bring the marinade to the boil and cook for 10 minutes. **4.** Place the trout in a dish deep enough to contain the marinade. Pour the hot marinade over the fish, cool and refrigerate for at least 12 hours before serving. The marinade maybe re-used. Serve the trout on a plate, with a vegetable salad.

Trout with Ham

Truchas Gran Duque

From the Casa Duque, Segovia, Old Castile.

Serves 6

**Sauce:
½ cup (4 fl oz) olive oil
2–3 cloves garlic, crushed
200 g (6½ oz) Spanish ham or prosciutto, finely chopped
3 sprigs parsley, finely chopped
2 bay leaves
salt
freshly ground black pepper**

**6 plate-size trout
¼ cup (1 oz) flour
½ cup (4 fl oz) oil
6 slices Spanish ham or prosciutto**

1. Preheat the oven to 200°C (400°F/Gas 6). **2.** To make the sauce, heat the oil in a saucepan and sauté the garlic. **3.** Add the chopped ham, parsley and bay leaves and sauté until the ham is crisp. Season. **4.** Dust the trout with flour, heat the oil in a frying pan and sauté the trout. **5.** Place the trout in a shallow ovenproof dish, place the ham slices on top of the trout, pour the sauce over and bake in the preheated oven for 10 minutes. Serve hot, directly from the oven dish.

POULTRY & GAME

Chicken Stew with Peas, Mushrooms and Olives
Pepitoria de Gallina

Serves 4

1.5 kg (3 lb) chicken, cut into pieces
salt
freshly ground black pepper
½ cup (2 oz) flour
¼ cup (2 fl oz) olive oil
2 onions, chopped
5 tomatoes, peeled and chopped
1 teaspoon sugar
1 red or green pepper (capsicum), seeded and chopped
water
1 cup green peas
125 g (4 oz) small button mushrooms
1 cup chopped and stoned green or black olives
flour and water for thickening

1. Sprinkle the chicken with salt, ground pepper and half of the flour. **2.** Heat the oil in a casserole and brown the chicken pieces. Remove, and set aside. **3.** In the same oil, sauté the onions, add the tomatoes, sugar, some salt and the chopped pepper, then simmer over low heat for 10 minutes. **4.** Add the chicken pieces and enough water to cover them. Cover the casserole and simmer for 1 hour. **5.** Add the peas, mushrooms, olives and enough flour mixed with a little water to thicken the sauce. Simmer for 15 minutes, check seasoning and serve hot.

Chicken with Olives in Sherry Sauce
Pollo al Jerez

From the Restaurant Sevilla, Granada, Andalusia.

Serves 4

1.5 kg (3 lb) chicken, cut into 8 pieces
2 onions, chopped
2–3 cloves garlic, crushed
3 bay leaves
1 teaspoon dried oregano or 2 sprigs fresh oregano, chopped
salt
¼–½ teaspoon hot chilli powder
20–24 green olives, pitted
1 cup (8 fl oz) dry sherry
1–2 teaspoons cornflour (cornstarch)

1. Put the chicken into a saucepan, cover with water, add onions, garlic, bay leaves, oregano and salt, bring to the boil and simmer over low heat for 50 minutes. **2.** Add chilli powder, olives and sherry, simmer for another 10 minutes. **3.** Dilute the cornflour in some water and add it to the chicken. Simmer for 2–3 minutes until the sauce thickens. Serve with boiled rice.

Right: Lamb in Chilindron Sauce (see page 248) and Casserole of Cod and Lobster as served at Las Pocholas in the Hostal del Rey Noble in Pamplona, Navarre.

Chicken Stew with Chickpeas

Olla Podrida

One of the many versions of Olla Podrida.

Serves 6

2 cups (12 oz) chickpeas, soaked overnight
4 slices of bacon, cut into 4 cm (1½ inch)
pieces
8 cups (2 litres) water
1.5 kg (3 lb) chicken, cut into pieces
125 g (4 oz) chorizo (spicy pork sausage), sliced
1 clove garlic, crushed
1 tablespoon paprika
salt

1. In a saucepan, combine the chickpeas, bacon and water, bring to the boil, cover and simmer over low heat for 2 hours. **2.** Add the rest of the ingredients and simmer for a further hour or until the chicken is tender.

Andalusian Duckling with Olives

Pato con Aceitunas

Serves 4

2 tablespoons olive oil
45 g (1½ oz) butter
3 onions, sliced
2 carrots, sliced
1.5 kg (3 lb) duckling
1 tablespoon flour
1 cup (8 fl oz) hot chicken stock (see p. 328)
salt
freshly ground black pepper
1 cup (8 fl oz) Madeira or dry sherry
3 tablespoons tomato paste
2 sprigs parsley, finely chopped
48 green olives, pitted

1. Use a large, heavy pan with a lid or a casserole deep enough to accommodate the duckling. Heat the oil and butter in the pan, add the onions, carrots and duckling and fry over medium heat until the duckling is light golden-brown. Remove the duckling and vegetables and keep them warm. **2.** Stir the flour into the fat, cook for 2–3 minutes and, while stirring constantly, add the hot stock. Season. **3.** Add the wine, tomato paste and parsley and cook for 5 minutes, stirring constantly. **4.** Put the duckling and vegetables back into the pan, cover, and simmer over low heat for 1¼ hours until duckling is tender. **5.** Put the duckling on a serving plate, remove excess fat from the sauce and strain into a saucepan. Add olives, check the seasoning, and simmer only long enough to heat the olives. To serve, pour the sauce over the duckling.

Chicken in Chilindrón Sauce

Pollo en Chilindrón

From the El Cachirulo, Zaragoza, Aragón.

Serves 4–6

½ cup (4 fl oz) olive oil
1 clove garlic, chopped
1.5 kg (3 lb) chicken, cut into pieces
salt
freshly ground black pepper
1 onion, chopped
2 red or green peppers (capsicums), seeded and chopped
1 tablespoon paprika
¼ teaspoon saffron
200 g (6½ oz) Spanish ham or prosciutto, cut into cubes
250 g (8 oz) tomatoes, peeled and chopped
½ small hot pepper, seeded and chopped

1. Heat the oil in a casserole and sauté the garlic. Remove it when it is cooked. **2.** Add the chicken pieces, season, and brown on all sides. Remove the chicken and set aside. **3.** Sauté the onion and peppers (capsicums) until they are soft. Add paprika, saffron, ham and tomatoes. **4.** Mix the browned chicken pieces and the hot peppers into the sauce, cover and simmer over low heat for about 1 hour or until the chicken is tender. To serve, arrange the chicken pieces on a platter and cover with sauce.

Duck in Almond Sauce

Pato en Salsa de Almendras

Serves 4

90 g (3 oz) lard
1 duck liver or 2 chicken livers, chopped
1 onion, sliced
2 cloves garlic, crushed
1.5 kg (3 lb) duck, cut into 8 pieces
¼ cup (1 oz) flour
salt
freshly ground black pepper
4 tomatoes, peeled and chopped
20 blanched almonds, grilled
½ cup (4 fl oz) dry sherry
2 sprigs parsley, finely chopped

1. Heat the lard in a large frying pan and lightly fry the liver. Remove and set aside. **2.** Sauté the onion and garlic. Remove and set aside with the liver. **3.** Remove most of the fat from the pan, sprinkle the duck pieces with flour, salt and pepper, and fry them in the remaining fat until brown. **4.** Add the tomatoes, cover the pan and simmer over low heat. **5.** In a mortar or food processor, grind the liver, onion and garlic with the almonds into a smooth paste. Mix in the sherry. **6.** Add the mixture to the duck, add the parsley and adjust seasoning. **7.** Cover and simmer over low heat for 1–1¼ hours until the duck is tender. To serve, arrange the duck pieces on a platter and strain the sauce over.

Rice with Rabbit

Arros amb Conill

From Forn del Nastasi, Lérida, Catalonia.

Serves 4

½ cup (4 fl oz) olive oil
1 rabbit, cut into pieces
1 onion, chopped
2 cloves garlic, crushed
1 red or green pepper (capsicum), seeded and chopped
200 g (6½ oz) snails (optional)
2 tomatoes, peeled and chopped
4 cups (1 litre) stock or water
1¼ cups (8 oz) rice

Picada:
3 blanched ground almonds
2 cloves garlic, crushed
¼ teaspoon saffron
2 sprigs parsley, finely chopped for garnish

1. Heat the oil in the casserole, brown the rabbit pieces, add the onion, garlic and chopped pepper and sauté until the onion is soft and transparent. **2.** Add the snails (optional), tomatoes and water or stock, bring to the boil and add the rice. **3.** Cook over high heat for 5 minutes, turn down the heat, add the Picada and simmer for 20 minutes until the rice is cooked. **4.** Let it stand for 10–15 minutes before serving, sprinkle with parsley and serve it directly from the casserole.

Picada: Finely grind the ingredients in a mortar.

Rabbit with Romera Sauce

Conejo de Bosque con Salsa Romera

From the Forn del Nastasi, Lérida, Catalonia.

Serves 4

¾ cup (6 fl oz) olive oil
1–2 rabbits (depending on size), cut into pieces
salt
freshly ground black pepper
1 onion, finely chopped
2 cloves garlic, crushed
400 g potatoes (14 oz), peeled and diced
½ cup (4 fl oz) brandy

Picada:
½ tablespoon olive oil
2 rabbit livers or chicken livers, chopped
1 clove garlic, crushed
½ cup (2 oz) ground almonds
2 sprigs parsley, chopped
2–3 cups (16–24 fl oz) water

1. In a casserole, heat the oil and fry the rabbit pieces until brown. Season with salt and pepper. **2.** Add the onion, garlic and potatoes and fry until the onion is soft and transparent. Add the brandy. **3.** To make the Picada, heat the oil and sauté the rabbit or chicken livers. Chop them and put them in a mortar together with the garlic, almonds and parsley. Pound them thoroughly. This may be done in a food processor. **4.** Add the Picada to the casserole. Cook lightly for a few minutes, add water, cover the casserole and simmer over low heat for 1 hour or until the rabbit is tender.

MEAT

Boiled Lamb Shepherd's Style

Cordero a la Pastoril

From the Restaurant Sevilla, Granada, Andalusia.

Serves 4

1 kg (2 lb) boned leg of lamb, cut into pieces
¼ cup (2 fl oz) olive oil
⅓ cup (2½ fl oz) vinegar
2 cloves garlic, crushed
1 teaspoon dried oregano
1 teaspoon paprika
pinch cayenne pepper
2 cups (16 fl oz) water
salt

1. Sauté the meat in the oil until brown all over.
2. Combine the meat and the remaining ingredients in a casserole and simmer over low heat for 1½ hours.

Lamb Casserole

Caldereta de Cordero

From the Casa Duque, Segovia, Old Castile.

Serves 6

½ cup (4 fl oz) olive oil
1 onion, finely chopped
4 cloves garlic, crushed (use according to taste)
2 kg (4 lb) meat from a shoulder of lamb cut into 5 cm (2 inch) cubes
salt
½ hot pepper, chopped
4 red or green peppers (capsicums), seeded and chopped
4 cloves
1 tablespoon paprika
2 cups (16 fl oz) dry white wine
2 sprigs fresh herbs, chopped
4 cups (1 litre) water or stock

1. In a casserole, heat the oil and sauté the onion and garlic. **2.** Add the meat, salt, hot pepper, red or green peppers (capsicums), cloves, paprika, wine, herbs and water. **3.** Simmer for 1 hour or until the lamb is tender. Adjust seasoning and serve in individual ceramic bowls called 'casuela de barro'.

Roast Baron of Lamb

Ternasco Asado Aragonés

From El Cachirulo, Zaragoza, Aragón.

Serves 4

6 cloves garlic, crushed
salt
30 g (1 oz) lard
1.5 kg (3 lb) baron of baby lamb
1 kg (2 lb) potatoes, peeled and sliced
1 cup (8 fl oz) boiling water
4 tablespoons olive oil
2 sprigs rosemary, chopped
2 sprigs parsley, chopped
2 cups (16 fl oz) dry white wine

1. Preheat the oven to 220°C (425°F/Gas 7). **2.** Mix half of the garlic with the salt and lard and rub it on the lamb. **3.** Put the potatoes in the bottom of a baking dish and place the lamb on top, add the water and bake it in the preheated oven for 20 minutes. **4.** In a mortar, crush the remainder of the garlic with the oil, rosemary, parsley and some salt. Add the wine and mix well. **5.** Pour this mixture over the lamb and potatoes and continue baking for a further 30–40 minutes until the lamb is golden-brown and the potatoes are cooked. To serve, arrange the potatoes on a platter and place the lamb on top. Spoon the cooking juices over the lamb.

Right: Paradors are Spanish government hotels situated throughout Spain. Some are newly built but many of them occupy old castles, convents, monasteries and palaces. One of the most attractive of the renovated and rebuilt old buildings is the Parador Nacional 'Via de la Plata' in Merida. The Parador is proud of its kitchen and features on the menu many regional dishes of Extremadura. In the shady courtyard, on the edge of a well in the courtyard of the Parador Nacional rests a dish of Baby Lamb Stew (see page 248).

Roast Suckling Lamb

Cordero Lechal Asado

From the Casa Duque, Segovia, Old Castile.

Serves 6

½ side of baby lamb, cut into 6 portions
salt
freshly ground black pepper
1½ cups (12 fl oz) water
1½ cups (12 fl oz) dry white wine
2 cloves garlic, crushed
2 sprigs thyme, chopped

1. Preheat the oven to 200°C (400°F/Gas 6). **2.** Place the lamb pieces in a baking dish, sprinkle with salt and pepper and add the water. **3.** Bake in the preheated oven for 30 minutes. **4.** Add the wine, garlic and thyme, turn the meat and continue cooking for 45 minutes. Baste occasionally. **5.** Serve hot with the cooking liquid and with fried potatoes and lettuce salad.

Baby Lamb Stew

Caldereta Extremeña

From the Parador Nacional 'Via de la Plata', Mérida, Extremadura.

Serves 6-8

2 kg (4 lb) baby lamb, cut into pieces
salt
1 tablespoon paprika
3 bay leaves
250 g (8 oz) lamb's liver
2 cups (16 fl oz) dry white wine
2 cloves garlic, crushed
3 slices bread, cut into pieces and fried in oil

1. In a bowl, combine the meat, salt, paprika, bay leaves, liver and wine. Refrigerate for 12 hours. **2.** Transfer to a casserole, bring to the boil, cover and simmer over low heat for 1½ hours. **3.** Take out the liver, cut into small pieces and put it in a mortar or food processor, add the garlic and bread and purée it to a paste. **4.** Add the paste to the lamb, season and cook over low heat for 10 minutes. Serve hot.

Lamb in Chilindrón Sauce

Cordero en Chilindrón

From 'Las Pocholas', Hostal del Rey Noble, Pamplona, Navarre.

Serves 6

1 cup (8 fl oz) olive oil
4 onions, finely chopped
1 clove garlic, crushed
1 kg (2 lb) tomatoes, peeled and chopped
1.5 kg (3 lb) lamb from the forequarter, cut into pieces
3 red or green peppers (capsicums), seeded and chopped
2 cups (16 fl oz) dry white wine
salt
freshly ground black pepper

1. Heat half of the oil in a casserole and sauté 2 of the onions and the garlic until the onions are soft and transparent. **2.** Add the tomatoes and simmer over low heat for 20 minutes. Cool. **3.** Rub through a sieve, set aside. **4.** In the casserole, heat the remaining oil and sauté the remaining onions. **5.** Add the meat and chopped peppers and fry until the meat starts to brown. **6.** Add the wine, the tomato-onion-garlic sauce and seasoning. Cover and simmer over low heat for 1 hour.

Veal Knuckle Stew

Jarrete Guisado

From the Anexo Vilas, Santiago de Compostela, Galicia.

Serves 4

2 veal knuckles, cut into 5 cm (2 inch) pieces
1 cup (8 fl oz) dry white wine
3 cloves garlic, crushed (or less, to taste)
salt
freshly ground black pepper
½ cup (4 fl oz) olive oil
8-12 small, whole onions, peeled
8-12 small, whole new potatoes, peeled

1. Marinate the meat overnight in a mixture of wine, garlic, salt and pepper. **2.** Wipe the meat dry, set the marinade aside. Heat the oil in a casserole, add the meat and brown it on all sides. Add the onions and continue cooking until the onions are soft and transparent. **3.** Preheat the oven to 180°C (350°F/Gas 4). **4.** Add the marinade, cover, and simmer for 45 minutes. **5.** Add the potatoes, cover, and cook in preheated oven for a further 45 minutes.
Serve hot straight out of the casserole.

Pickled Shoulder of Pork with Cabbage

Lacón con Grelos

From the Anexo Vilas, Santiago de Compostela, Galicia.
Cooked pickled shoulder or loin of pickled pork can be bought from delicatessens.

Serves 8

1.5 kg (3 lb) boneless shoulder or loin of pickled pork
8 whole large potatoes, peeled
½ cabbage, roughly chopped (the original recipe called for kale)
4 small chorizo (spicy pork sausage)
freshly ground black pepper
2-3 cups (16-24 fl oz) water

1. Place the meat in a large saucepan, cover with water, bring to the boil and simmer over low heat for 2 hours. This should remove excessive salt. **2.** Discard the water. Add potatoes, cabbage, chorizo, pepper and fresh water. Cover and simmer over low heat for 1 hour. **3.** To serve, cut the meat into slices and arrange them with the cabbage, chorizo and potatoes in the casserole.

Beans, Chorizo and Pig's Trotters

Judías del Barco de Ávila

From the Mesón del Rastro, Ávila, Old Castile.

Serves 4

¼ cup (2 fl oz) olive oil
2 onions, chopped
1 clove garlic, crushed
2 red or green peppers (capsicums), seeded and roughly chopped
2 chorizo (spicy pork sausage), sliced
4 pig's trotters
salt
freshly ground black pepper
4 cups (1 litre) water
375 g (12 oz) dried beans, soaked overnight

1. Heat the oil in a casserole or a saucepan and sauté the onion and garlic until the onions are soft and transparent. **2.** Add the chopped peppers, chorizo slices, pig's trotters, seasoning and cook for 10 minutes, stirring occasionally. **3.** Add the water and beans, cover, and simmer over low heat for 1½-2 hours until the trotters are cooked. **4.** Serve out of the casserole with some of the chorizo slices and the trotters arranged on top.

Tripe and Chickpeas

Callos a la Gallega

From the Anexos Vilas, Santiago de Compostela, Galicia.

Serves 6

30 g (1 oz) lard
2 onions, chopped
1-2 cloves garlic, crushed
1 tablespoon flour
1 tablespoon paprika
½ teaspoon cumin
salt
8 cups (2 litres) water
1 kg (2 lb) tripe, cut into pieces
1 boned shoulder of lamb, cut into pieces
2 chorizo (spicy pork sausage), sliced
500 g (1 lb) chickpeas, soaked overnight

1. In a casserole, heat the lard and sauté the onions and garlic until the onions are soft and transparent. **2.** Add the flour, paprika, cumin, salt and water, stir well and cook for 5 minutes. **3.** Add the tripe, cover and cook for 1½ hours. **4.** Add the lamb and chorizo slices and cook for 30 minutes. **5.** Add the chickpeas and cook for a further hour. Season and serve directly from the casserole.

Sweetbreads in Sauce

Mollejas de Ternera

From the Casa Duque, Segovia, Old Castile.

Serves 6

½ cup (4 fl oz) olive oil
2–3 cloves garlic, crushed
800 g (26 oz) sweetbreads blanched, cleaned
and cut into pieces
1 tablespoon flour
2 tomatoes, peeled and chopped
1 tablespoon tomato paste
¼ cup chopped hot pepper
3 sprigs parsley, chopped
2 bay leaves
½ cup (4 fl oz) dry sherry
1 cup (8 fl oz) water
salt

1. Preheat the oven to 200°C (400°F/Gas 6). **2.** In a frying pan, heat the oil and lightly fry the garlic, add sweetbreads, sprinkle with flour and sauté until light brown. Add tomatoes, tomato paste, hot pepper, parsley, bay leaves, sherry, water and salt to taste. **3.** Transfer to a casserole and cook in the preheated oven for 10 minutes. Serve directly from the dish.

Broad Beans and Meat Stew

Judiones de la Granja Duque

From the Casa Duque, Segovia, Old Castile.

Serves 8

8 cups (2 litres) water
750 g (1½ lb) broad beans, soaked overnight
4 pig's trotters
2 chorizo (spicy pork sausage)
2 blood pudding sausages
100 g (3½ oz) bacon, roughly chopped
1 onion, cut into quarters
1 clove garlic
2 bay leaves
salt

Sofrito:
½ cup (4 fl oz) olive oil
2 onions, finely chopped
2 cloves garlic, crushed
3 tomatoes, peeled and chopped
1 tablespoon paprika

1. In a casserole, combine all ingredients except those for the Sofrito. Cover, bring to the boil, then simmer over very low heat for 2 hours. **2.** To make the Sofrito, heat the oil in a frying pan, add the onions and garlic, cover and sauté over low heat for 15 minutes, stirring occasionally. **3.** Add the tomatoes and paprika and sauté for a further 10 minutes. **4.** Add the Sofrito to the casserole and continue simmering for 1 further hour. **5.** Serve, with the meat arranged on top, straight from the casserole.

Right: At the Casa Duque in Segovia, Old Castile I have eaten some of the best food that I found during my journey through Spain. The Duque family has run the restaurant since 1895, and the son of the present owner is a fourth-generation innkeeper. Here the host of Casa Duque proudly displays some of the traditional local dishes. Clockwise from bottom left: Trout with Ham (see page 241); Lamb Casserole (see page 246); Beans, Chorizo and Pig's Trotters and Castillian Soup.

DESSERTS & CAKES

Peaches in Wine

Melocoton con Vino

From the El Cachirulo, Zaragoza, Aragón.

Serves 4

**4–8 slipstone/freestone peaches, peeled and
halved
2 cups (16 fl oz) dry red wine
¼ cup (2 oz) sugar
1 stick cinnamon, 5 cm (2 inches) long
½ cup (4 fl oz) brandy**

1. Stir the wine, sugar, cinnamon and brandy until
the sugar is dissolved. **2.** Place the peaches in a
bowl, pour the mixture over the peaches, cover the
bowl with plastic film and refrigerate for 4 days.
3. Serve cold in individual dessert bowls.

Tart of St James

Tarta de Santiago

*From the Anexo Vilas, Santiago de Compostela,
Galicia.*

Serves 6–8

**8 eggs
2 cups (1 lb) sugar
2⅓ cups (9½ oz) flour
250 g (8 oz) butter, softened
1 cup (8 fl oz) water
4½ cups (1 lb) ground almonds
1 teaspoon grated lemon peel
icing (confectioners') sugar**

1. Preheat the oven to 180°C (350°F/Gas 4).
2. Cream the eggs with the sugar until pale yellow,
light and fluffy. **3.** Add the flour, butter and water.
Beat with an electric beater for 15 minutes. **4.** Add
almonds and lemon peel. **5.** Pour the mixture into
a round, greased baking tin and bake in the
preheated oven for 30–40 minutes until done.
6. Serve sprinkled with icing sugar and cut into
wedges.

Sweetmeats made from Syrup and Eggs

Tocinillo de Cielo

*From the Hosteria Nacional 'Del Comendador',
Cáceres, Extremadura.*

Serves 6

**1½ cups (12 oz) sugar
½ cup (4 fl oz) water
11 egg yolks
1 whole egg**

1. Preheat the oven to 160°C (325°F/Gas 3).
2. Dissolve all but 3 tablespoons of sugar in the
water. **3.** Bring the dissolved sugar to the boil and
cook until the syrup forms a thread. Cool slightly.
4. Sprinkle the remaining 3 tablespoons of sugar on
the bottom of a large rectangular baking tin at least
3 cm (1¼ inches) deep, place over heat until the
sugar caramelises. Set aside. **5.** Place the yolks and
egg in a bowl and, either by hand or with a mixer,
whip until the eggs start to cream. Keep beating and
slowly incorporate the warm syrup until the mixture
is thick. **6.** Carefully pour the mixture into the baking dish. Cover the dish with foil, place it into another, slightly larger dish filled with boiling water.
Place in the preheated oven and cook until the mixture sets. **7.** Cool and refrigerate. To serve, cut into
slices about 10 × 10 cm (4 × 4 inches), and serve
on individual plates.

French Toast

Torrijas

From the El Cachirulo, Zaragoza, Aragón.

Serves 4

8 slices white bread
1 cup (8 fl oz) milk
½ teaspoon cinnamon
2 eggs, lightly beaten
oil, for frying
3 tablespoons sugar mixed with ½ teaspoon
cinnamon

1. Briefly soak each bread slice in milk mixed with cinnamon, then dip the slice in the beaten egg. **2.** Fry in hot oil until brown. **3.** Serve hot, sprinkled with cinnamon sugar.

Rice Pudding

Arroz con Leche Caldoso

From the Casa Duque, Segovia, Old Castile.

Serves 6

4 cups (1 litre) milk
1 teaspoon grated lemon peel
1 teaspoon grated orange peel
100 g (3⅓ oz) rice
150 g (5 oz) sugar
½ teaspoon cinnamon

1. In a saucepan, heat the milk, lemon peel and orange peel. When it boils, add the rice and, stirring occasionally, cook over low heat for 25 minutes. **2.** Add the sugar and simmer for 10 minutes. **3.** Allow to cool. Serve cold sprinkled with cinnamon.

Galician Cake

Pastel a la Gallega

From the Anexo Vilas, Santiago de Compostela, Galicia.

Makes a 21 × 11 × 6 cm (8½ × 4½ × 2½ inch) loaf

¾ cup (3 oz) flour
1 tablespoon baking powder (or use 100 g
(3½ oz) self-raising flour instead of the plain
flour and baking powder)
⅓ cup (3 oz) sugar
5 tablespoons oil
1 tablespoon milk
2 egg yolks
grated rind of 1 lemon
juice of 1 lemon
2 egg whites, stiffly whipped

1. Preheat the oven to 180°C (350°F/Gas 4). **2.** In a bowl, sieve the flour and the baking powder (or the self-raising flour), add sugar, oil, milk, egg yolks, rind and lemon juice. Mix well together. **3.** Fold in the egg whites. **4.** Butter the cake tin and pour in the mixture. **5.** Bake for 30 minutes in the preheated oven. **6.** Place the cake on a wire rack to cool. Serve sliced.

PORTUGAL

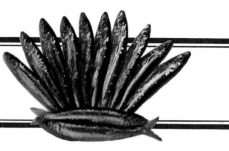

The food of Portugal is the food of farmers and fishermen. It follows the seasons, feast days and other important events. Fresh seafood is available in all but the most remote mountain regions and, in turn, fresh products from the land are offered in the markets of the coastal regions.

Portuguese cooking has been influenced by explorers who travelled to the East Indies, the Far East and the New World. In the south of the country and on the island of Madeira, Moorish and African influence can be detected, while Spanish cooking has also had its influence, especially in the north.

In general, herbs and spices, even curry, are widely used. Salt-dried cod is one of the staples and it is hard to imagine Portuguese cooking without it. Pork and veal are the most popular meats and there are plenty of chickens. Eggs are used extensively, especially the yolks, which can be found in many delicious sweets and desserts — such as the rich yellow custard called Pudim. Fresh and dried figs, nuts and chestnuts as well as rice are part of popular cooking. Olive oil rather than animal fats is used and lemon juice is frequently sprinkled on meat.

In the mountainous inland areas thick soups, stews and heavy dishes are generally prepared. The three northern provinces of Minho, Trás-os-Montes e Alto Douro and Douro Litoral are mostly rugged and poor, but the cooking is good and in many respects similar to the cooking of Galicia to the north. It is also in this part of the country that the grapes are cultivated to produce Portugal's most famous wine, the port of Oporto.

Most representative of coastal cooking is the province of Beira Litoral. The Caldeirada, a rich fish and shellfish stew, is prepared all along the Portuguese coast.

Lisbon is to the south and like most capital cities it offers food from all over the country. Being a fishing port it has a large number of fish specialities, in particular fish soups, such as Lisbon's own version of the Caldeirada.

The narrow winding streets and steep alleys of the Alfama district are a living reminder of the Moorish presence in this part of the country. There you will not find gourmet food, but in the informal and relaxed atmosphere of a tiny restaurant you will enjoy tasty local dishes. In fact, throughout the country better and more authentic cooking can be found in small, modest taverns than in the big restaurants of the larger towns.

Algarve, the southern coastal region of Portugal, is one of Europe's popular summer holiday resorts. Here Sardinhas Assadas, fresh sardines, are popular and Caldeirada, the ever-popular fish chowder of fishermen throughout Portugal, is particularly tasty in this part of the country.

To the north of Algarve is the region of Alentejo, the largest province but not as well known as its southern neighbour. The local bread is very tasty and the famous bread soups, the Açordas, started in this area.

Right: View of the Castle of Bragança from Pousada S. Bartolomeu.

SOUPS

Cabbage and Potato Broth
Caldo Verde

From the Pousada de S. Lourenço, Manteigas, Serra da Estrela.
The most typical of Portugal's soups. It is made with kale or cabbage, shredded as fine as possible.

Serves 4-6

500 g (1 lb) potatoes, peeled and each cut into quarters
4 cups (1 litre) water
salt
4 tablespoons olive oil
1 onion, finely chopped
250 g (8 oz) cabbage leaves, very finely shredded
freshly ground black pepper

1. Boil the potatoes in salted water until they are soft enough to mash. **2.** Transfer the potatoes to a bowl and save the water. **3.** Mash the potatoes and return them to the saucepan with the water. **4.** Add the oil, onion and cabbage and boil for 3-4 minutes. Season and serve hot. Slices of chouriço (a Portuguese spicy pork sausage) may also be cooked in the soup.

Bread and Garlic Soup
Sopa à Alentejana

Serves 4

2 cloves garlic
1 teaspoon coarse salt
4 sprigs fresh coriander, chopped
½ cup (4 fl oz) olive oil
2 cups (16 fl oz) boiling water
4 slices bread, fried in lard
4 poached eggs

1. Grind the garlic, salt and coriander in a mortar, or process to a paste in a food processor, and gradually beat in the oil. **2.** Pour in the water and mix well. **3.** Place a slice of bread in the bottom of each soup bowl, pour the soup over it and put a poached egg on top. In the original recipe, the bread is used fresh.

Alentejo Tomato Soup
Sopa de Tomate à Alentejana

Serves 6

175 g (5½ oz) lard
175 g (5½ oz) chouriço (spicy pork sausage), sliced
2 onions, sliced
500 g (1 lb) tomatoes, peeled, seeded and chopped
6 cups (1.5 litres) stock (see p. 328) or water
2 bay leaves
1 red or green pepper (capsicum), seeded and roughly chopped
salt
6 slices fresh bread

1. Heat the lard in a saucepan and sauté the sausage and onions until the onions are golden-brown. **2.** Add the tomatoes and cook for 5 minutes. **3.** Add stock or water, bay leaves, chopped peppers and salt. Cook for 10 minutes. **4.** To serve, place a slice of bread in each soup bowl and pour the hot soup over the bread.

Fisherman's Stew
Caldeirada à Pescador

Serves 4

4 tablespoons olive oil
2 onions, sliced
3 cloves garlic, finely chopped
3 tomatoes, peeled, seeded and chopped
1 tablespoon paprika
2 sprigs parsley, finely chopped
4 cups (1 litre) fish stock (see p. 328) or water
750 g (1½ lb) mixed fish fillets, cut into pieces
250 g (8 oz) mussels
salt
freshly ground black pepper
4 slices fried bread

1. In a saucepan, heat the oil and sauté the onions and garlic until the onions are soft and transparent. **2.** Add the tomatoes, paprika and parsley and cook for 5 minutes. **3.** Add stock or water, fish, mussels and seasoning. Gently bring to the boil and simmer over low heat for 5 minutes. To serve, place the bread in individual soup bowls and ladle the hot soup over it.

VEGETABLES

Broad Beans with Salami and Ham
Favas à Algarvia

Serves 4

1 tablespoon olive oil
1 onion, finely chopped
125 g (4 oz) salami, finely chopped
125 g (4 oz) prosciutto-style ham, sliced
2½ cups (20 fl oz) chicken stock (see p. 328)
500 g (1 lb) fresh broad beans
125 g (4 oz) carrots, sliced
1 tablespoon tomato purée
salt
freshly ground black pepper

1. Heat the oil in a casserole and sauté the onion, salami and ham for 5 minutes. **2.** Add the stock, beans, carrots, tomato purée and seasoning. **3.** Cover and simmer over low heat for 1 hour or until the beans and carrots are cooked.

Deep-fried French Beans

Serves 6

500 g (1 lb) French (green) beans
125 g (4 oz) self-raising flour
1 egg
salt
⅔ cup (5½ fl oz) dry white wine
flour
oil for deep frying
freshly ground black pepper

1. String the beans and cook them in boiling salted water until they are almost tender. **2.** Make a smooth batter by combining self-raising flour, egg, salt and wine. **3.** Dust the beans with flour, dip them in the batter and fry them for 1–2 minutes until they are crisp and light brown. Serve immediately, sprinkled with salt and pepper.

Mixed Vegetables with Tomatoes and Scrambled Eggs

Serves 4

1 tablespoon olive oil
½ onion, finely chopped
½ clove garlic, crushed
3 tomatoes, peeled, seeded and chopped
salt
freshly ground black pepper
1 potato, peeled and diced
1 carrot, scraped and diced
100 g (3½ oz) green beans, cut into 2.5 cm (1 inch) pieces
100 g (3½ oz) cauliflower, broken up into small flowerets
scrambled eggs made from 8 eggs

1. Heat the oil and sauté the onion and garlic for 5 minutes. **2.** Add the tomatoes, salt and pepper and simmer for 20 minutes. **3.** Add the potato and carrot and cook for 5 minutes. **4.** Add the beans and cauliflower and cook for a further 10 minutes. **5.** If necessary, season to taste. Serve with hot scrambled eggs.

Broad Beans, Bacon and Sausage
Favas à Saloia

Serves 4

75 g (2½ oz) lard
1 onion, finely sliced
1 clove garlic, crushed
1 sprig coriander or parsley, chopped
2 slices bacon, chopped
250 g (8 oz) chouriço (spicy pork sausage), chopped
1 tablespoon sugar
salt
500 g (1 lb) fresh broad beans
1–2cups (8–16 fl oz) stock

1. In a casserole, heat the lard and sauté the onion and garlic until the onion is soft and transparent. **2.** Add the coriander or parsley, bacon, chouriço sausage, sugar, salt, beans and enough stock to cover. Cover the casserole and cook for approximately 1 hour or until the beans are cooked.

FISH

Baked Jewfish

Cherne à Portuguêsa

From the Casa de Leão, Castelo de S. Jorge, Lisbon.

Serves 4

4 onions, sliced
1.5 kg (3 lb) jewfish (or halibut)
salt
freshly ground black pepper
1 clove garlic, crushed
1 cup (8 fl oz) dry white wine
1 tablespoon vinegar
2 tomatoes, peeled and sliced
2 bay leaves
4 cooked, sliced potatoes
3 tablespoons olive oil

1. Preheat the oven to 200°C (400°F/Gas 6).
2. Place half of the onion slices on the bottom of a buttered ovenproof dish. **3.** Put the fish into the dish, sprinkle with salt, pepper, garlic, wine and vinegar. **4.** Cover with the remaining onion slices, the tomatoes and bay leaves. **5.** Arrange the potato slices around the fish. Sprinkle with olive oil and bake in the preheated oven for 45 minutes. Occasionally baste with the cooking juices.

Country-baked Red Porgy

Pargo Assado à Regional

From the Casa Leão, Castelo de S. Jorge, Lisbon.
Traditionally, this dish is prepared in an ovenproof claypot but any ovenproof dish may be used.

Serves 4-6

1 kg (2 lb) redfish fillets
salt
freshly ground black pepper
2 onions, finely chopped
3 tomatoes, peeled and finely chopped
3 sprigs parsley, finely chopped
2 cloves garlic, crushed
1 cup (8 fl oz) dry white wine

1. Preheat the oven to 180°C (350°F/Gas 4).
2. Place the fish in a greased ovenproof dish and add the remaining ingredients. **3.** Bake in the preheated oven for 35-45 minutes. Serve with boiled potatoes.

Baked Fish with Port

Peixe Assado

Serves 4

2 tablespoons olive oil
2 onions, finely chopped
1 clove garlic, crushed
4 tomatoes, peeled, seeded and finely chopped
2 sprigs thyme, finely chopped
½ cup (4 fl oz) port
salt
freshly ground black pepper
4 plate-size snapper or other white-fleshed fish

1. Preheat the oven to 180°C (350°F/Gas 4).
2. Heat the oil and sauté the onions and garlic until the onions are soft. Add tomatoes, thyme, port and seasoning. **3.** Place the fish in a greased baking dish, pour the sauce over and bake in the preheated oven for 30 minutes. Serve the fish masked with the sauce.

Cod with Potatoes, Onions and Black Olives

Bacalhau à Gomes de Sá

Serves 6

750 g (1½ lb) dried salt cod
6 potatoes
1¼ cups (10 fl oz) olive oil
4 onions, sliced
1 clove garlic, crushed
24 black olives
6 hard-boiled eggs, cut into quarters
2 sprigs parsley, finely chopped

1. Soak the cod in cold water for 12 hours, changing the water several times. **2.** Preheat the oven to 180°C (350°F/Gas 4). **3.** Drain the cod and rinse under running water. **4.** Put the cod in a saucepan, cover with water and simmer over low heat for 1 hour. **5.** Drain, remove skin and bones and, with a fork, flake into pieces. Set aside. **6.** Boil the potatoes. **7.** Peel and cut the potatoes into slices. Set aside. **8.** In a frying pan, heat the oil and sauté the onions and garlic. **9.** Grease a casserole and arrange two layers each of potatoes, cod, onions and olives. **10.** Bake in the preheated oven for 20 minutes or until brown. **11.** Serve garnished with eggs and parsley.

Right: Some of the dishes served at Casa de Leão in Lisbon including bottom left: Baked Jewfish (above).

Pickled Fish
Escabeche

Serves 6

1 cup (8 fl oz) olive oil
1 kg (2 lb) white fish fillets
3 onions, sliced and separated into rings
2–4 cloves garlic (according to taste), crushed
3 carrots, coarsely grated
4 sprigs parsley, chopped
3 bay leaves
1 teaspoon paprika
¼ teaspoon chilli powder or dash of Tabasco sauce
1½ teaspoon salt
freshly ground black pepper
1 cup (8 fl oz) white wine vinegar

1. Heat half of the oil and fry the fish fillets. When they are cooked, remove the skin and any bones and break them up with a fork into large flakes. 2. Heat the rest of the oil and sauté the onion rings until soft and transparent. 3. Add the rest of the ingredients and cook for 5 minutes. Check seasoning. 4. Arrange the fish in a glass or glazed dish and pour the hot marinade over it. Cover the dish and refrigerate for 2 days. 5. Serve with sautéed potatoes.

Scampi or Prawn Skewers with Rice and Sauce
Camarão à Portuguêsa

Serves 4

4 tablespoons olive oil
2 onions, finely chopped
3½ cups (21 oz) rice
7 cups (1.75 litres) fish stock (see p. 328)
salt
freshly ground black pepper
1 clove garlic, crushed
500 g (1 lb) tomatoes, peeled and chopped
½ cup (4 fl oz) dry white wine
12 olives, stoned
750 g (1½ lb) scampi or prawns

1. Heat 2 tablespoons of oil in a saucepan and sauté 1 chopped onion and the rice until they start to colour. 2. Add the stock and season. While stirring, bring to the boil, then cover and simmer over low heat for 20 minutes. 3. To make the sauce, heat 1 tablespoon of oil and sauté the remaining onion and garlic until the onion is soft and transparent. Add the tomatoes, wine, and olives and check the seasoning. 4. Put the scampi or prawns on to skewers, brush them with the remaining tablespoon of oil and grill them for approximately 8 minutes. 5. To serve, dish out the rice on individual plates, place the skewers on top, and serve the sauce separately.

Seafood Stew
Caldeirada

Any type and selection of fish and seafood may be used in this dish.

Serves 6

½ cup (4 fl oz) olive oil
4 onions, sliced
2–4 cloves garlic (according to taste), crushed
5 tomatoes, peeled, seeded and chopped
3 sprigs parsley, chopped
2 bay leaves
salt
freshly ground black pepper
¼ teaspoon nutmeg
dash of Tabasco sauce
250 g (8 oz) of 3 types of fish fillets, cut into 2.5 cm (1–2 inch) chunks
250 g (8 oz) squid, cleaned and cut into 5 × 2.5 cm (2 × 1 inch) pieces
18 mussels
½ cup (4 fl oz) dry white wine
2 tablespoons vinegar
30 g (1 oz) melted butter
6 thick slices of bread, without crust

1. Preheat the oven to 180°C (350°F/Gas 4). 2. Heat the oil in a pan and sauté the onions and garlic until the onions are soft and transparent. 3. Add the tomatoes, parsley, bay leaves, salt, pepper, nutmeg and Tabasco and simmer over low heat for 15 minutes. 4. In a heavy casserole, arrange layers of fish, squid and mussels alternating with the sauce. 5. Pour in the wine, vinegar and butter, place the bread on top, cover the casserole and bring it to the boil on top of the stove. 6. Put it in the oven for 20–30 minutes. Serve hot from the casserole.

Tuna Steak with Wine and Bacon
Atum à Algarvia

Serves 4

1 tablespoon olive oil
125 g (4 oz) bacon, roughly chopped
750 g (1½ lb) fresh tuna cut into steaks 3 cm (1¼ inches) thick
2 onions, sliced
1 cup (8 fl oz) dry white wine
salt
freshly ground black pepper

1. Heat the oil in a pan and fry the bacon and onions until the onions are soft and the bacon starts to brown. 2. Add the tuna and lightly fry on both sides. 3. Add the wine and simmer over low heat for 10 minutes. Season and serve with the bacon, onions and cooking juice poured over the tuna.

POULTRY & GAME

Braised Stuffed Partridge with Port Alcantara

Perdiz Convento de Alcantara

Ingredients are for 1 bird which will serve 2 people.

1 cup (2 oz) soft breadcrumbs
2 tablespoons oil
50 g (1¾ oz) liver pâté
2 tablespoons finely chopped pickled cucumbers
salt
freshly ground black pepper
1 partridge
½ cup (4 fl oz) port wine
½ cup (4 fl oz) dry white wine

1. Soak the breadcrumbs in the oil for 10 minutes. **2.** In a bowl, combine breadcrumbs, pâté, pickles, salt and pepper. Mix well and place the stuffing in the bird. Sew up the opening or secure it with skewers. **3.** Place the bird in a bowl with the wines which have been seasoned. Cover and refrigerate for 24 hours, turning the bird occasionally. **4.** Place the bird and the wine marinade in a heavy-lidded casserole, cover, bring to the boil and simmer over low heat for 1½ hours. **5.** Remove the bird and reduce the sauce to half. To serve, cut the bird lengthways into two, making sure that the stuffing stays in the cavities. Arrange on a decorative platter, skin side up, and serve masked with the sauce.

Chicken with Port Wine

Galinha com Vinho do Pôrto

Serves 4

1.5 kg (3 lb) chicken, cut into pieces
3 tablespoons olive oil
2 onions, chopped
2 sprigs parsley, chopped
1 cup (8 fl oz) port wine
water
salt
freshly ground pepper
1 tablespoon flour
triangular croûtons made from 4 slices of bread

1. Sauté the chicken in the oil, add the onions and parsley and fry until the chicken is golden-brown. **2.** Transfer to a saucepan, add port wine and enough water to cover; season. Cover the pan and simmer over low heat until the chicken is cooked, about 30 minutes. **3.** Thicken the cooking liquid with the flour mixed with a little cold water. Serve hot with the sauce and croûtons.

Stewed Pheasant with Brandy, Port and Almonds

Faisão Estufado

Serves 6

2 pheasants
salt
freshly ground black pepper
¾ cup (6 fl oz) brandy
¾ cup (6 fl oz) port
90 g (3 oz) butter
12 blanched almonds
12 small onions
4 sprigs fresh thyme and/or oregano, chopped

1. Season the pheasants and marinate them in brandy and port for 2 days. Turn them occasionally. **2.** In the butter, fry the pheasants with almonds and onions until golden-brown. **3.** Transfer them to a casserole, add the marinade, cover the casserole and simmer over low heat for 1–1½ hours until the pheasants are tender. **4.** Season if necessary. If desired, the cooking juices may be thickened with a little flour. Cut each bird into 6 pieces, arrange on a serving platter and pour the sauce, almonds and onions over. Serve hot.

MEAT

Portuguese Steak

Serves 8

60 g (2 oz) butter
4 onions, sliced
1 clove garlic, crushed
4 tomatoes, peeled, seeded and chopped
1 tablespoon tomato purée
1 tablespoon vinegar
1 sprig parsley, chopped
salt
freshly ground black pepper
8 rump steaks

1. Melt the butter and sauté the onions and garlic until the onions are soft and transparent. **2.** Add the tomatoes, tomato purée, vinegar, parsley, salt and pepper. Simmer for 20 minutes. **3.** Grill the steak to your liking. To serve, pour the sauce over the steaks, garnish with parsley and serve with boiled or fried potatoes.

Roast Veal with Tomatoes and Onions

Vitela Assada

Serves 4

4 slices prosciutto-type ham
4 thick veal chops
6 tomatoes, peeled, seeded and chopped
2 onions, sliced
salt
freshly ground black pepper
1 cup (8 fl oz) port

1. Preheat the oven to 180°C (350°F/Gas 4). **2.** Place a slice of ham on each chop and place them in an oven dish. **3.** Cover the chops with tomatoes and onions, sprinkle with salt and pepper and pour the port over. **4.** Cook in the preheated oven for 1–1¼ hours or until the meat is tender. Serve directly from the oven dish.

Marinated Roast Veal

Posta de Vitela à Transmontana

From Pousada S. Bartolomeu, Bragança.

Serves 6

2 cups (16 fl oz) dry white wine
2 cloves garlic, crushed
1 tablespoon paprika
¼ cup (2 fl oz) olive oil
salt
freshly ground pepper
1.5 kg (3 lb) rolled veal shoulder
1½ cups (12 fl oz) water
2 tablespoons vinegar
3 tablespoons finely chopped mixed pickles

1. Combine the wine, garlic, paprika, oil, salt and pepper and marinate the meat for two days, turning it occasionally. **2.** Preheat the oven to 180°C (350°F/Gas 4). **3.** Place the meat on a rack in a roasting dish and cook for 1½–2 hours. Occasionally baste with the marinade. When cooked, keep the meat warm. **4.** Pour the remaining marinade and cooking juices into a saucepan, add water, vinegar and pickles and boil rapidly to reduce to 2 cups (16 fl oz). Season to taste. **5.** Serve the meat cut into slices with a little of the sauce poured over it. Serve the rest of the sauce separately. Traditionally the veal is served with baked potatoes and a vegetable, especially spinach purée, cooked with garlic and oil.

***Right:** Three of the house specialities of the Pousada de Oliveira in Guimarães including bottom right: Cabbage and Potato Broth (see page 256).*

Stewed Lamb with Onions

Ensopada de Borrego

Serves 4-6

1 kg (2 lb) lamb, cut into cubes
flour
125 g (4 oz) lard
500 g (1 lb) onions, sliced
4 cloves garlic, crushed
2 bay leaves
1 tablespoon crushed peppercorns
salt
pinch of hot chilli
1 tablespoon paprika
2 sprigs parsley, chopped
3 tablespoons vinegar
8-12 slices of stale bread

1. Dust the meat with flour. In a frying pan, fry it in half of the lard until golden. Put the meat in a casserole. **2.** Melt the rest of the lard in the frying pan and sauté the onions, garlic, bay leaves and pepper until the onions are soft and transparent. Add them to the casserole. **3.** Add salt, chilli, paprika, parsley, vinegar and approximately 4 cups (1 litre) water. Cover the casserole, bring to the boil and simmer over low heat for 1½ hours until the lamb is tender. **4.** To serve, place the bread into large soup bowls and pour the hot broth on top. Serve the rest separately.

Roast Loin of Pork

Lombo Assado à Alentejana

Serves 4

1 kg (2 lb) loin of pork
2 cloves garlic, crushed
1 tablespoon green pepper (capsicum) paste
(see p. 264)
salt
freshly ground black pepper
½ cup (4 fl oz) dry white wine
½ cup (4 fl oz) water

1. Preheat the oven to 180°C (350°F/Gas 4). **2.** Mix the garlic, green pepper paste, salt and pepper and spread it over the meat. **3.** Put it in a roasting dish, add wine, water, salt and pepper. Place the dish in the preheated oven and roast it for 1½ hours until the meat is done. If necessary, add more wine or water. **4.** Degrease the cooking juices and serve the meat slices masked with the gravy.

Pork Cutlets with Green Pepper Paste

Costeletas de Porco à Alentejana

Serves 4

8 pork cutlets
2 cloves garlic, crushed
salt
freshly ground black pepper
1 tablespoon green pepper (capsicum) paste
(see below)
3 tablespoons dry white wine
1 egg, lightly beaten with 2 tablespoons water
½ cup (2 oz) dry breadcrumbs
oil for deep frying
16 orange slices

1. Rub the cutlets with a mixture of garlic, salt, pepper and green pepper paste. **2.** Place them in a flat dish and add the wine. Cover with plastic film and refrigerate for 24 hours. Occasionally spoon the liquid over the chops. **3.** Dip the chops in the egg mixture, coat them with the breadcrumbs and deep fry until golden-brown. **4.** Serve hot, garnished with orange slices.

Green Pepper Paste

Capsicum Paste

This is a method of preserving red or green peppers (capsicums) and is used for coating meats.

12 red or green peppers (capsicums), seeded
and cut into pieces
3 thin slices of fresh ginger
2 onions, cut into quarters
salt
2 tablespoons olive oil

1. Combine all the ingredients, except the oil, in a food processor and process until a fine texture. **2.** Place it in a jar, cover with oil and refrigerate for several days before using. It will keep for a long time.

Spicy Loin of Pork
Lombo de Porco de Monção

Serves 4

1 kg (2 lb) loin of pork
½ cup (4 fl oz) dry white wine
4 cloves
¼ teaspoon nutmeg
1 bay leaf
salt
freshly ground black pepper
16-20 roasted, peeled chestnuts (optional)

1. Preheat the oven to 180°C (350°F/Gas 4). **2.** Put the meat in a roasting dish with the wine, cloves, nutmeg, bay leaf, salt and pepper. **3.** Place the dish in the preheated oven and cook for 1½ hours, basting the meat frequently. **4.** Degrease the cooking juices, season and serve with the sliced meat, which can be garnished with chestnuts.

Pork and Mussels
Carne de Porco à Alentejana

Serves 4

500 g (1 lb) lean pork, cut into small pieces
30 g (1 oz) lard
1 tablespoon olive oil
2 onions, chopped
2 tomatoes, peeled and chopped
2 bay leaves
salt
freshly ground black pepper
1 tablespoon paprika
500 g (1 lb) mussels

1. Fry the pork in the lard until the meat is almost cooked. Set aside. **2.** Heat the oil and sauté onions until soft and transparent. Add the tomatoes, bay leaves, salt, pepper and paprika and cook for 10 minutes. **3.** Add the mussels and pork and cook until the mussels open. Serve hot with crusty bread.

Portuguese Meat Stew and Rice
Cozido à Portuguêsa

Serves 6-8

1 kg (2 lb) shin beef
250 g (8 oz) smoked bacon
1 kg (2 lb) potatoes, cut into quarters
500 g (1 lb) carrots, thickly sliced
500 g (1 lb) turnips, thickly sliced
1 large cabbage, cut into quarters
250 g (8 oz) chouriço (spicy pork sausage), sliced
salt
2 cups (12 oz) rice

1. Place the beef and bacon in a large saucepan of boiling water and simmer over low heat for 2 hours. **2.** Add potatoes, carrots, turnips and cabbage. After 15 minutes of cooking add chouriço sausage. **3.** Remove 4 cups (1 litre) of liquid and place in a separate saucepan. In this, cook the rice, under cover, undisturbed for 20 minutes; the rice should absorb most of the liquid. During that time, continue to simmer the meat and vegetables. When cooked, if necessary adjust the seasoning. **4.** Serve the liquid as a soup. In accordance with tradition, serve the meat and vegetables arranged in separate mounds on a very large platter, accompanied by the rice.

Marinated Fried Liver
Iscas à Portuguêsa

Serves 4

500 g (1 lb) calf's liver (can be pig's or lamb's),
thinly sliced
1 cup (8 fl oz) dry white wine
1 clove garlic, crushed
2 cloves
6 crushed peppercorns
2 bay leaves
salt
flour
2 rashers bacon, chopped
2 tablespoons olive oil
3 potatoes, peeled and finely diced

1. Marinate the liver in a mixture of wine, garlic,
cloves, peppercorns, bay leaves and salt. Refrigerate
overnight. **2.** Take the liver out of the marinade.
Boil the marinade to reduce it by half. **3.** Pat the
liver dry, dust it with flour and fry it briefly in the
oil with the bacon and potatoes. Serve it with the
reduced marinade.

Lisbon Tripe with Chickpeas
Dobrada com Grão

Serves 4-6

2 tablespoons olive oil
2 onions, finely chopped
1 clove garlic, crushed
3 tomatoes, peeled, seeded and chopped
2 carrots, scraped and sliced
2 bay leaves
salt
freshly ground black pepper
250 g (8 oz) chouriço (spicy pork sausage),
sliced
500 g (1 lb) tripe, cut into 2 cm (¾ inch)
squares
500 g (1 lb) chickpeas, soaked overnight
1 cup (8 fl oz) water or stock (see p. 328)

1. Heat the oil in a casserole and sauté the onions
and garlic until the onions are soft and transparent.
2. Add remaining ingredients, cover and simmer
over low heat for 2–2½ hours or until the tripe is
cooked (using a crock-pot, cook on low for 8–10
hours).

Oporto Tripe with Veal Shank, Chicken and Sausage
Tripas à Moda do Pôrto

Serves 8

30 g (1 oz) lard
3 onions
750 g (1½ lb) tripe, cut into 2.5 cm (1 inch)
squares
1 veal shank
water
half a chicken, cut into pieces
250 g (8 oz) chouriço (spicy pork sausage), cut
into slices
125 g (4 oz) smoked bacon, cut into pieces
125 g (4 oz) dried beans, soaked overnight
3 carrots, scraped and sliced
3 sprigs parsley, chopped
3 bay leaves
salt
freshly ground black pepper

1. In a casserole, heat the lard and sauté the onions
until soft and transparent. **2.** Add the tripe, veal
shank and enough water to cover. Cover with a lid,
bring to the boil and then simmer over low heat for
2 hours. **3.** Add the remaining ingredients and simmer for a further 1–1½ hours. If necessary, add
more water; the result should be like a stew.

*Right: From the Pousada S. Bartolomeu in Bragança, in
foreground: Marinated Roast Veal (see page 262); top left: Eel
Fricassée with Egg-Lemon Sauce; top right: Orange Roll (see
page 268).*

DESSERTS

Soft Egg Custard

Ovos Moles

Serves 4

1 cup (8 oz) sugar
½ cup (4 fl oz) water
6 egg yolks

1. Boil the sugar and the water to make a light syrup. **2.** Allow it to cool. **3.** Beat the egg yolks until they are creamy and gradually add the syrup. **4.** Pour the mixture into the saucepan and slowly heat, stirring it constantly until it thickens. Do not boil. **5.** Pour it into a bowl, cool it, place it into the refrigerator and serve it when chilled.

Almond Pudding with Port

Serves 4-6

2¼ cups (8 oz) ground almonds
1¼ cups (10 fl oz) milk, boiling
1 cup (8 oz) sugar
½ cup (4 fl oz) port
3 eggs
3 egg whites
3 tablespoons sugar

1. Combine the almonds, boiling milk, sugar and port and let it stand for 10 minutes. **2.** Whip the eggs and egg whites together and gently stir them into the mixture. **3.** Sprinkle the sugar on the bottom of a flameproof mould and place it over heat until the sugar melts and browns. Do not let the sugar burn or it will taste bitter. Cool it until it sets. **4.** Pour the mixture into the mould. Cover the mould and place it in a pan with water. Heat the water and steam the mould until the mixture sets. Leave it to cool and unmould it to serve.

Cinnamon Biscuits

Biscoitos de Coimbra

1 cup (8 fl oz) milk
1 teaspoon baking powder
1 tablespoon cinnamon
100 g (3½ oz) butter
250 g (8 oz) sugar
1½-2 cups (6-8 oz) flour

1. Preheat the oven to 180°C (350°F/Gas 4). **2.** In a bowl, mix milk, baking powder, cinnamon, butter, sugar and enough flour to make a firm dough. **3.** Roll it out on a floured surface and with a biscuit cutter make the biscuits. **4.** Place them on a greased tray and bake in the preheated oven until golden-brown.

Orange Roll

Torta de Laranja

10 eggs
2 cups (1 lb) sugar
2 tablespoons flour
1 cup (8 fl oz) fresh orange juice
orange slices and cherries in syrup for garnish

1. Preheat the oven to 200°C (400°F/Gas 6). **2.** Beat the eggs with the sugar until they are light and the sugar has dissolved. **3.** Mix in the flour and slowly incorporate the orange juice. **4.** Pour the mixture into a shallow greased baking tray, sprinkled with flour. **5.** Bake in the preheated oven for 30 minutes or until the mixture sets. **6.** Let it cool. Form it into a roll, slice it and serve it with orange slices and cherries in syrup.

Strawberries and Oranges with Port

Morangos com Vinho do Pôrto

Serves 4

250 g (8 oz) strawberries, hulled
½ cup (4 fl oz) port wine
2 oranges, peeled and thinly sliced
2 tablespoons sugar
½ cup (4 fl oz) cream, whipped with
1 teaspoon sugar and ½ teaspoon vanilla essence

1. Soak the strawberries with the port for 30 minutes. **2.** Add the orange slices and sugar to taste and refrigerate for 1 hour. **3.** Serve with the cream.

Deep-fried Biscuits

Sonhas

Serves 4

1¼ cups (10 fl oz) water
125 g (4 oz) butter
¼ cup (2 oz) sugar
pinch of salt
1¼ cups (5 oz) flour
4 eggs
oil for deep frying

For sprinkling:
¼ cup (2 oz) sugar
½ teaspoon cinnamon
grated rind of ½ lemon

1. In a saucepan, boil the water with the butter, sugar and a pinch of salt. Add the flour and stir it in quickly. Add more water if the mixture is too thick. Remove from heat and beat until the mixture is cold. **2.** Add the eggs, one at a time and beat in vigorously. Let it stand for 15 minutes. **3.** Heat the oil. With a spoon or piping bag, drop pieces of dough into the oil. Fry until pale brown; drain on kitchen paper. **4.** Mix ¼ cup of sugar with cinnamon and lemon rind; sprinkle it over the sonhas and eat them either hot or cold.

Madeira Pudding

Pudim Madeira

Serves 4

2 tablespoons sugar dissolved in 2 tablespoons water
1 cup (8 oz) sugar
1 tablespoon vinegar
2 eggs
6 egg yolks
1¾ (14 fl oz) milk, hot
¼ cup (2 fl oz) Madeira or port

1. Dissolve the sugar-water mixture over low heat and cook over moderate heat until the mixture turns a light amber colour. Pour this caramel into a pudding mould to coat the bottom and sides. **2.** In a bowl, combine the sugar, vinegar, eggs and egg yolks, and beat with a whisk until the sugar dissolves and the mixture is pale yellow. **3.** Slowly add the hot milk and the Madeira or port. Pour the mixture into the caramel-lined mould. Place the mould in a pan with water, cover it and bake in the preheated oven for 45 minutes to 1 hour, until it sets. **4.** Allow it to cool and then refrigerate it. To serve, unmould it on to a decorative plate.

Portuguese Sweet Rice

Arroz doce

From Pousada de S. Lourenço, Manteigas, Serra da Estrela.

Serves 6

1 cup (6½ oz) rice
salt
2 cups (16 fl oz) water
2 cups (16 fl oz) milk
1 teaspoon vanilla essence
1 teaspoon cinnamon
thin slivers of lemon rind
3 egg yolks
½ cup (4 oz) sugar

1. Cook the rice covered in salted water for 15–20 minutes until all moisture is absorbed and the rice is cooked. **2.** Fluff the rice up with a fork and let it stand for 10 minutes. **3.** Combine the milk, vanilla, cinnamon and lemon rind and simmer it for 10 minutes. **4.** Remove from heat and let it stand for 10 minutes. Remove lemon rind. **5.** Cream the egg yolks with the sugar until the sugar is dissolved and the mixture is pale yellow. Gradually add the spiced milk. **6.** Pour the mixture into a saucepan and stir constantly over low heat until the custard thickens. Do not boil. **7.** Add the rice, leave it over low heat while continuing to stir for 2–3 minutes until it heats up. To serve, pour the rice into a glass serving bowl or individual dessert dishes. Sprinkle the top with cinnamon and serve at room temperature.

GREECE

The island of Corfu was the starting point for my gastronomic tour of Greece. Fish and seafood are of very good quality on Corfu and in fact they form one of the main sources of food throughout Greece and its islands. During my travels along the shores of Greece I would try to glean interesting recipes from the fishermen, like the Fisherman's Wife's Soup (see p. 274) given to me one sunny morning near the Canal of Corinth.

A great deal of Greek cooking is a result of making wholesome and tasty dishes out of modest ingredients. Hearty soups served with salads, fresh bread and wine frequently constitute the entire meal.

Religious festivities and observances strongly influence eating habits. The seven-week Lenten fast is strictly observed in Greece, when all animal products are forbidden. Easter Sunday is celebrated with a spit-roasted lamb, Easter bread and many other dishes, all washed down with generous amounts of retsina.

The taverna is a great Greek institution. It is a type of bar where people spend hours sipping retsina and Ouzo — the anise-flavoured spirit which turns cloudy when mixed with water — choosing from a wide variety of Mezéthes, and talking and gossiping.

Olives are grown extensively throughout Greece and are eaten with every meal, and at many times in between. Famous are the black olives of Kalamata in the southern Peloponnese and the green olives of Itea near Delphi. Feta cheese, eaten daily, is made from goat's, sheep's or cow's milk and its lightly pungent and salty taste is one of the typical flavours of Greece. Grapes have been grown in Greece since ancient times and produce wines of reasonable quality. Retsina, the most popular wine, is best drunk chilled and is a perfect match for the strong flavour of Greek food.

The Greeks' liking for sweets is reflected in the innumerable pastry shops, and a cup of coffee is seldom drunk without an accompanying pastry or sweetmeat. Although a meal usually finishes with fresh fruit, a Greek will not forgo dessert, which usually follows an hour or two after the meal. Baklavá is the best known but others, such as cream puffs, custard cream, fruit tarts, the very Middle Eastern halva, and Loukoumia, universally known as Turkish Delight, are equally popular.

Greece, despite its Western ways, in many respects remains a country orientated towards the East, and a culinary visit to Greece can be an introduction to the food of the Middle East.

Right: One of the many temple sites at Delphi.

FIRST COURSES

Cheese Triangle Puffs

Tiropites

From the Amalia Hotel, Olympia.
In Greece these tasty crisp 'pasties' are served not only as savouries at cocktail parties but also for dinner as small appetisers or as a main course. Using filo pastry, which is readily available in delicatessen shops, they are easily and quickly prepared. While preparing them double the quantity and deep freeze half for future use, when they only have to be reheated to be ready for an unexpected guest.

Depending on their size this recipe will yield between 36 and 48 puffs

250 g (8 oz) feta cheese, finely crumbed
185 g (6 oz) Gruyère or mature Cheddar-style cheese, grated
3 eggs, lightly beaten
4 sprigs parsley, finely chopped
freshly ground black pepper
salt
250 g (8 oz) filo pastry sheets
100 g (3½ oz) butter, melted

1. Preheat the oven to 200°C (400°F/Gas 6). 2. Combine the feta, the Gruyère or Cheddar, the eggs, parsley and pepper. Taste before adding the salt, as the mixture may be sufficiently seasoned. Mix thoroughly until all ingredients are well blended. 3. Cut the leaves of filo pastry lengthways into three equal strips. Cover them with a damp teatowel so that the sheets do not dry out. One strip will be required per puff. 4. Lay out one strip and brush it with melted butter. Fold it in half, brush it again with butter. 5. Place a teaspoon of the mixture on the end of the strip. 6. Fold one corner of pastry over the filling and continue folding as illustrated. 7. Place the triangles on a buttered baking tin, brush tops with melted butter and bake in the preheated oven for 12–15 minutes until they are plump, crisp and golden. Serve hot.

Zucchini Pie

Kolokithópitta

Makes 12 servings

1.5 kg (3 lb) zucchini (courgettes), unpeeled, grated
2 onions, finely chopped
2 tablespoons olive oil
4 sprigs dill, chopped
4 sprigs parsley, chopped
3 eggs, beaten
½ teaspoon grated nutmeg
freshly ground black pepper
salt
500 g (1 lb) feta cheese, cut into 1.5 cm (½ inch) cubes
½ cup (4 oz) butter, melted
12 sheets filo pastry

1. Preheat the oven to 180°C (350°F/Gas 4). 2. Over low heat, sauté the zucchini and onions in the oil for about 30–40 minutes until the moisture evaporates. Stir occasionally. 3. Cool, and in a large bowl, combine all ingredients except the filo pastry and melted butter. 4. With a little of the melted butter, grease a baking dish, approximately 30 × 25 × 7 cm (12 × 10 × 3 inches) in size. 5. On the bottom and up the sides of the dish, place 6 sheets of filo pastry, each sheet generously brushed with melted butter before the next is placed. 6. Spoon the zucchini mixture into the pan and fold the edges of the filo over the mixture. 7. Cover the mixture with the remaining 6 sheets of filo pastry, each in turn well brushed with melted butter. Brush the top with melted butter. 8. Tuck the edges of the covering filo leaves around the inside edges of the pan. 9. Bake in the preheated oven for 45 minutes until golden and crisp. Cool for a few minutes. To serve, cut into squares.

Fried Cheese Cubes

Kasséri Tiganitó

A simple yet appetising cocktail snack.

250 g (8 oz) Kasséri or Kefalotíri cheese (if not available, use Gruyère or Parmesan cheese), cut into 2.5 cm (1 inch) cubes
2 eggs, lightly beaten
125 g (4 oz) dry breadcrumbs
½ cup (4 fl oz) frying oil
juice of 1 lemon
freshly ground black pepper

1. Dip the cheese cubes in the egg and then in the breadcrumbs. 2. Fry them in hot oil, sprinkle with lemon juice and freshly ground black pepper and serve on cocktail sticks.

Rice-stuffed Vine Leaves

Dolmadakia

From the Restaurant Kuyu in Piraeus.

Yields 36

⅔ cup (5 fl oz) olive oil
9 large onions, finely chopped
6 spring onions (scallions), finely chopped
1 teaspoon salt
freshly ground black pepper
2 tablespoons pine nuts
150 g (¾ cup) rice
1 tablespoon finely chopped dill
½ bunch parsley, finely chopped
1 teaspoon finely chopped mint
juice of ½ lemon
1 cup (8 fl oz) water
36 vine leaves
parsley stalks
lemon wedges
parsley sprigs

Preparation of vine leaves: If fresh vine leaves are used, rinse them immediately in cold water, then blanch them in boiling water for 3 minutes, drain, allow to cool and use as described in the recipe.

To preserve, select clean leaves, not larger than 15 cm (6 inches). Wash them in cold water. Cut off the stems and place them in stacks of 15–20 leaves with the dull side facing up. Roll them tightly and tie them with a string. Boil 2 litres (8 cups) of water, add 125 g (4 oz) salt, and place the rolled-up leaves into the water. Boil for 3 minutes. Remove the bundles, cool them slightly and arrange them in 2–3 cup jars. Pour the boiling salt water into the jars, filling them to the top, and seal them tightly. The leaves preserved in this way do not require refrigeration.

Preparation of the Dolmadakia: 1. In half of the olive oil, sauté the onions and spring onions until they are soft and transparent. **2.** Add the salt, pepper, pine nuts and rice. Cook for 10 minutes, stirring from time to time. **3.** Add the dill, parsley, mint, lemon juice and the water. Cover the saucepan and simmer for approximately 10 minutes, until the water is absorbed. Season if necessary. **4.** Spread the vine leaves with the dull side up and on each place a teaspoonful of stuffing. First fold the stalk end of the leaf over the stuffing, then the right-hand side, followed by the left-hand side. Finally, starting with the stalk-end, roll the vine leaf firmly into a cylindrical shape. Squeeze it gently in the palm of your hand to keep it intact. **5.** Place the parsley stalks on the bottom of the saucepan and arrange the stuffed vine leaves in layers on top of them. Weight them down with an inverted plate. **6.** Combine the remaining olive oil, 2 tablespoons of lemon juice and enough water to barely cover the plate. **7.** Cover the saucepan, bring slowly to the boil and simmer for 1½ hours. **8.** Remove from the stove and let the Dolmadakia cool for 2–3 hours or overnight. **9.** To serve, arrange them on a serving platter and present them at room temperature or slightly chilled and garnished with lemon wedges and parsley sprigs.

Spinach Pie

Spanakópitta

Makes 20 pieces in a 35 × 25 × 5 cm (14 × 10 × 2 inch) baking dish

¼ cup (2 fl oz) olive oil
2 onions, finely chopped
6 spring onions (scallions), chopped
1.75 kg (3½ lb) fresh spinach, washed, drained and finely chopped
3 sprigs dill, finely chopped
3 sprigs parsley, finely chopped
½ teaspoon salt
freshly ground black pepper
375 g (12 oz) feta cheese, finely crumbled
4 eggs, lightly beaten
½ cup (4 oz) butter, melted
14 sheets filo pastry

1. Preheat the oven to 180°C (350°F/Gas 4). **2.** In a large saucepan, heat the oil and sauté the onions and spring onions until transparent and soft. **3.** Add the spinach, cover the pan and cook for 5 minutes. **4.** Add dill, parsley, salt and pepper and, while stirring, cook for 10 minutes. **5.** Cool. Then add the cheese and mix in the eggs. If necessary, adjust seasoning. **6.** With some of the melted butter, brush the baking dish. **7.** On the bottom and up the sides of the dish, place 6 sheets of filo pastry, each sheet generously brushed with melted butter before the next is placed. **8.** Spoon the spinach mixture into this, smooth the top, and fold the edges of the filo over the mixture. **9.** Cover the mixture with the remaining 8 sheets of filo pastry, each in turn, as well as the top, well brushed with the melted butter. **10.** Tuck the edges of the covering filo around the inside edges of the pan. **11.** Bake in the preheated oven for 45 minutes until golden and crisp. Cool for a few minutes, and serve cut into squares.

Eggplant Dip

Melitzanosalata

3–4 large eggplants (aubergines)
1 clove garlic, crushed (or ½ onion finely chopped)
juice of ½–1 lemon (depending on taste)
½ cup (4 fl oz) olive oil
salt

1. Preheat the oven to 200°C (400°F/Gas 6). **2.** Bake the eggplants for 30–40 minutes. **3.** Cool, and peel. **4.** On a cutting board, chop the eggplant flesh very finely. Put it in a mixing bowl. **5.** Add the garlic or onion, and the lemon juice, stirring with a wooden spoon, and gradually add the oil (as in preparing mayonnaise). **6.** Season, and refrigerate.

Serve it as a dip, with chunky fresh bread.

SOUPS

Fisherman's Wife's Fish Soup
Kakavia I

On the road winding its way along the shore from the Canal of Corinth to Athens, I stopped to buy some fish from a fisherman whose boat was tied up at a beach. With the help of a woman who was also there to buy fish and who spoke a little English, the fisherman gave me his wife's favourite recipe.

Serves 8–10

2 onions, roughly chopped
2 carrots, sliced
4 stalks celery, sliced
2 potatoes, diced
4 sprigs parsley, chopped
2 cloves garlic, crushed
½ cup (4 fl oz) oil
4 tomatoes, peeled and roughly chopped
12 cups (3 litres) water
1 cup (8 fl oz) dry white wine
salt
12 black peppercorns
4 bay leaves
1 teaspoon oregano
1.5 kg (3 lb) fish, a selection of 3 or 4 types of fish available on the day
juice of 1–2 lemons

1. In a large saucepan, fry the onions, carrots, celery, potatoes, parsley and garlic in the oil, until light brown. **2.** Add the tomatoes, water, wine, a little salt, peppercorns, bay leaves and oregano. Cover and simmer for 30 minutes. **3.** Add the fish. Cover and simmer for 20 minutes. **4.** Cool sufficiently so that you can handle the fish. Carefully remove it from the saucepan and remove the flesh from the bones. **5.** Discard the bones and return the pieces of fish to the pan. **6.** Heat it without boiling, if necessary adjust the seasoning, and serve hot sprinkled with lemon juice, with chunky fresh bread.

Cucumber Yogurt Soup
Tzatziki Soúpa

A healthy, refreshing summer soup.

Serves 6

2 cucumbers, peeled and seeded
4 cups (1 litre) plain yogurt
juice of 1 lemon
freshly ground black pepper
6 mint leaves, chopped
1 tablespoon chopped chives
½ clove garlic, crushed
½ teaspoon sugar
salt
3 sprigs parsley, for garnish

1. Grate or finely chop the cucumber. **2.** Combine all ingredients, except the parsley. Season. **3.** Refrigerate 1–2 hours and serve in chilled bowls sprinkled with parsley. If the soup is too thick, add a little fresh cold milk.

Egg-lemon Soup
Soúpa Avgolémono

Serves 6

6 cups (1.5 litres) chicken stock (see p. 328)
65 g (2¼ oz) short-grain rice
4 eggs, well beaten
juice of 1–2 lemons
salt
pepper
2 tablespoons finely chopped fresh mint

1. Bring the stock to the boil, add the rice and simmer for 15 minutes. **2.** Combine the beaten eggs, lemon juice, salt and pepper. **3.** Add a ladle of the hot stock to the eggs, beating constantly. **4.** Remove the soup from the heat and, while whisking constantly, slowly add the egg mixture to it. Adjust the seasoning. **5.** Serve hot sprinkled with the mint.

Right: Simple, tasty Greek food supplements the international cuisine offered at the Hotel Divani in Kalambaka. Top to bottom: Lamb on Skewers (see page 285); Greek Salad (see page 277); Rice-stuffed Vine Leaves (see page 273).

SAUCES

Tomato Sauce

Sáltsa Domáta

½ cup (4 fl oz) olive oil
2 onions, finely chopped
1–2 garlic cloves, crushed
1 kg (2 lb) tomatoes, peeled and chopped
4 tablespoons tomato paste
2 bay leaves
1 cup (8 fl oz) dry white wine
1 teaspoon dried basil
1 teaspoon dried oregano
1 teaspoon sugar

1. Heat the oil in a saucepan and sauté the onions and garlic until the onions are soft and transparent. **2.** Add the remaining ingredients and simmer over low heat for 1 hour. Serve with meatballs, pasta or sausages.

Garlic Sauce

Skorthaliá

This sauce is a type of mayonnaise and is very popular with fried fish or vegetables. The sauce can be made in a food processor, mixer or blender.

Yields 2 cups (16 fl oz)

3 egg yolks
juice of 1 lemon
2 tablespoons white wine vinegar
2–5 garlic cloves, crushed (according to taste)
1 cup (8 fl oz) olive oil
1 teaspoon salt
90 g (3 oz) blanched almonds, finely chopped

1. Place the egg yolks, lemon juice, vinegar and garlic in the food processor container and process for 30 seconds. **2.** Add the oil in a slow, steady flow and process until thick, smooth and creamy. If too thick, add 1 or 2 tablespoons of water. **3.** Transfer into a serving dish or storage container, and mix in the almonds. **4.** Refrigerate. Serve with fish or vegetables.

Egg and Lemon Sauce

Sáltsa Avgolémono

Almost a universal sauce in Greece, used in soups and stews, with meat, poultry, fish or vegetables.

Yields 1½ cups (12 fl oz)

3 eggs, separated
salt
1 tablespoon cornflour (cornstarch), optional, if thicker sauce is desired
juice 1 lemon
1½ cups (12 fl oz) chicken stock (see p. 328)

1. Beat the egg whites with salt until stiff. **2.** Add the egg yolks and lemon juice and beat together. **3.** Heat the stock. If using cornflour, mix it to a paste with some water and, while stirring constantly, add it to the stock. Simmer for 2–3 minutes. **4.** Take the stock off the heat and cool a little. Then while beating continuously, add it to the eggs. Season if necessary. **5.** Return it to the heat, continue beating until it thickens. Do not boil. **6.** To serve, pour it over the dish for which it is prepared.

Oil and Lemon Sauce

Latholémono

This is a simple lemon-oil dressing which in Greece is used a great deal with cooked and raw vegetables and for the basting of grilled fish, seafood and meat. If made in large quantities it may be stored in the refrigerator for later use.

Yields 1 cup (8 fl oz)

1 cup (8 fl oz) olive oil
juice of 1–2 lemons
2 sprigs parsley, finely chopped
4 mint leaves, chopped (optional)
1 teaspoon dried oregano (optional)
salt
freshly ground black pepper

1. In a screw-top jar, combine all ingredients and shake well. **2.** If not for immediate use, store in refrigerator.

SALADS & VEGETABLES

Braised Eggplant with Onions and Tomatoes

Imám Bayildí

The name means "the Imam fainted" and the dish is known throughout the Middle East and many claim its origin. The legend is that the Imam swooned when he scented its fine fragrance. Served as an appetiser or main course.

Serves 6

3 long eggplants (aubergine), each weighing 500 g (1 lb)
salt
4 onions, cut in half and sliced
2 cloves garlic
½ cup (4 fl oz) olive oil
5 large firm ripe tomatoes, peeled and chopped or 250 g (1 cup) drained canned tomatoes, chopped
4 sprigs parsley, chopped
freshly ground black pepper
juice of 1 lemon
1 teaspoon sugar
½ cup (4 fl oz) water
3 sprigs parsley, chopped, for garnish

1. Cut off the stem and peel each eggplant lengthways, leaving alternate strips of skin about 2.5 cm (1 inch) wide. **2.** Cut each eggplant in half. Into the cut side, make 3 or 4 long incisions. **3.** Sprinkle these sides with salt. Place them, salted side down, in a shallow dish and pour in enough water to cover and let stand for 30 minutes. **4.** Over a low heat, fry the onions and garlic in half of the oil until soft and transparent. **5.** In a bowl, combine the onions and garlic, tomatoes and parsley. Season to taste. **6.** Remove the eggplant from the water, squeeze the pieces gently and dry them with a paper towel. **7.** Using an oven dish or casserole large enough to contain the eggplant in one layer, fry them lightly on both sides in the remaining oil. **8.** Arrange them with the cut side up and force the onion-tomato mixture into the cuts and heap the rest in equal amounts on each. **9.** Sprinkle each with the lemon juice and sugar and spoon some of the oil on top. **10.** Add ½ cup of water to the dish, bring to the boil, then reduce the heat. Cover and simmer for one hour, basting occasionally with the cooking juices. If necessary, add more water. **11.** To serve, spoon the cooking juices over the eggplants and garnish with parsley.

Greek Salad

Saláta

This salad was served to me at the Marmara Restaurant in Mistras and it contains most of the ingredients that Greeks may use in their salads. However, to these ingredients you may add lettuce, tender spinach or dandelion leaves, sliced radishes or celery, capers or zucchini, or any combination of ingredients available at the time.

Serves 6

3 firm ripe tomatoes, cut into wedges
2 cucumbers, peeled and sliced
3 green peppers (capsicums), seeded and cut into strips
2 onions, roughly chopped
6 fillets of anchovies
12 Kalamata olives
250 g (8 oz) feta cheese, cut into 1.5 cm (¾ inch) cubes

Dressing:
½ cup (4 fl oz) olive oil
⅓ cup (3 fl oz) white or red wine vinegar
1 clove garlic, crushed
2 tablespoons finely chopped dill
1 teaspoon fresh (or dried) oregano
½ teaspoon salt
freshly ground black pepper

1. In a salad bowl, combine all the vegetables. **2.** To prepare the dressing, combine the ingredients in a watertight screw-top jar, shake vigorously, taste for seasoning. **3.** Pour the dressing over the salad and toss. **4.** Arrange the anchovies and olives on top and sprinkle with feta.

Orange and Black Olive Salad

Portokália me Eliés

Serves 6

1 small onion, thinly sliced
3 large oranges, peeled and thinly sliced, seeds discarded
24 large black olives, pitted
3 tablespoons olive oil
juice of ½ lemon
salt
freshly ground black pepper
6 lettuce leaves
3 sprigs parsley, finely chopped

1. Blanch the sliced onion in boiling water for 1 minute. **2.** In a bowl, combine the blanched onion, oranges and olives. **3.** In a screw-top jar, combine oil, lemon juice, salt and pepper. Shake well and pour it over the oranges. **4.** Refrigerate for 6 hours. Serve on lettuce leaves and garnish with chopped parsley.

Marinated Vegetables à la Grecque

Lahana Marináta

Any one or any combination of vegetables may be used. Note, the different vegetables require different cooking times and should be cooked separately. Recommended cooking times are given in brackets.

Serves 6

Marinade:
1 cup (8 fl oz) dry white wine
8 cups (2 litres) water
¾ cup (6 fl oz) olive oil
juice of 3 lemons
3 teaspoons salt
1 garlic clove, crushed
10 sprigs parsley, roughly chopped
1 stalk celery, chopped
1 stalk fennel, chopped
2 sprigs fresh thyme, chopped
10 peppercorns
10 coriander seeds, cracked

Vegetables (1 kg serves 6):
pickling-type onions, peeled (20 min)
green peppers (capsicums), seeded, cut into strips (10 min)
button mushrooms, caps only (5 min)
cucumbers, peeled, seeded, cut into strips (5 min)
zucchini, cut into 4 lengthways (10 min)
cauliflower, broken up into flowerets (8 min)
carrots, cut lengthways into strips (15 min)

1. In a large saucepan combine all marinade ingredients, bring to the boil and simmer for 1 hour. **2.** Strain through a sieve and mash the solids to extract all the flavour. **3.** Prepare vegetables and simmer each vegetable separately in marinade until tender. If 'al dente' texture is desired, use shorter cooking times. **4.** Remove with slotted spoon and arrange on a china or glass serving dish. **5.** Boil marinade until reduced to 1 cup (8 fl oz). Taste, and season if necessary. **6.** Pour over vegetables, cool and refrigerate for 12 hours. Serve at room temperature.

Plain Rice Pilaf

Rízi Piláfi

Serves 4

45 g (1½ oz) butter
1½ cups (8 oz) long-grain rice
1 onion, finely chopped
3 cups (24 fl oz) chicken stock (see p. 328) or water
salt
⅛ teaspoon saffron (optional)

1. In the butter, lightly sauté the rice and onions for 5 minutes. **2.** Add stock or water, and salt (and saffron, if desired). Bring to the boil and under cover, undisturbed, simmer over low heat for 20–25 minutes.

Artichokes with Egg-lemon Sauce

Angináres me Avgolémono

Serves 6

12 large artichokes
½ cup (2 oz) cornflour (cornstarch)
salt
juice of 2 lemons
1½ cups (12 fl oz) egg-lemon sauce (see p. 276)
3 sprigs dill, finely chopped

1. Wash the artichokes and trim each one by breaking off all the coarse outer leaves. **2.** Cut the stalk at a point where it breaks easily. Leave the remainder of the stalk on the artichoke as it will be tender and edible. **3.** Lay the artichoke on its side and cut 2.5–4 cm (1–1½ inches) off the tips of the leaves. Rub the cut surfaces with some of the lemon juice. **4.** Dissolve the cornflour in 4 cups (1 litre) of water, add the remaining lemon juice and place the artichokes in this as soon as they are trimmed. This will prevent discolouration. **5.** Strain the artichokes and put the liquid into a large saucepan. Add enough fresh water to cover the artichokes; bring to the boil. Add the artichokes, cover them with a teatowel and place a lid on the pan. **6.** Boil for approximately 25 minutes or until tender. Remove them from the pan with a slotted spoon and rinse under cold water. **7.** Gently part the leaves and remove and discard the choke. **8.** Place them on a serving platter. **9.** Prepare the egg-lemon sauce, using chicken stock, in accordance with the recipe on p. 276. **10.** To serve, pour the sauce over the artichokes and sprinkle with dill.

***Right:** The Gerofinikas in Athens is an old, elegant and fashionable restaurant. The present owner has been running it since 1967 and during that time its reputation for serving true Greek dishes has grown to the extent that a meal there is a must when visiting Athens. The Greek custom of showing the dishes that are offered is strictly observed. The guests are first taken to a long counter where the food is displayed in a most appetising and tempting manner. Clockwise from bottom left: Lamb Shanks with Artichokes and Egg-Lemon Sauce (see page 285); Swordfish and Prawns Wrapped in Bacon on Skewers; Greek Salad (see page 277); Moussaka and Stuffed Eggplant (in centre foreground).*

FISH

Prawns with Feta Cheese
Garíthes me Fétta

At the Kuyu Restaurant along the Mikro-limana at Piraeus, this dish goes under the modest name of Shrimp Casserole. It is simple but delicious. I have tried my own version of this dish in which I substituted the prawns with pieces of fish. I have also used oysters and scallops, added at the last moment. Any seafood, such as mussels or crayfish pieces, could be used. I have also tried retsina instead of dry white wine and achieved an added flavour.

Serves 4 as a main course or 6 as a first course.

1 onion, chopped
1 garlic clove, crushed
3 tablespoons olive oil
8 large ripe peeled tomatoes, fresh or canned, roughly chopped (if using canned tomatoes, use the liquid as well)
2 tablespoons tomato paste
½ cup (4 fl oz) dry white wine (or retsina)
1 teaspoon dried oregano
4 sprigs parsley, chopped
salt
freshly ground black pepper
125 g (4 oz) feta cheese, cut into 2.5 cm (1 inch) cubes
16-20 king prawns, green, shelled and deveined

1. Lightly fry the onion and garlic in the oil until the onion is transparent and soft. **2.** Add the tomatoes (and liquid, if using canned tomatoes), tomato paste, wine and oregano. **3.** Simmer for 20–30 minutes until some of the liquid has evaporated and the mixture has the texture of a thick sauce. **4.** Add the parsley and season to taste. **5.** Add the feta and the prawns, and continue cooking for 2–3 minutes — long enough to cook the prawns and heat the feta. If cooked too long, the prawns will be tough and the feta will melt too much. **6.** Serve hot, with chunky pieces of fresh white bread, and wash down with a glass of chilled retsina.

Prawn Pilaf
Garíthes Piláfi

This is an adaptation of the Greek recipe, as I do not agree with the method that requires the precooking of prawns (which only need the barest of heat).

Serves 4

16-24 uncooked prawns, depending on size
8 cups (2 litres) water
1 stalk celery, chopped
1 carrot, chopped
2 onions, chopped
6 peppercorns
3 bay leaves
½ teaspoon chopped oregano
2 tablespoons olive oil
½ clove garlic, crushed
3 ripe tomatoes, peeled and chopped
2 tablespoons tomato purée
1 green pepper (capsicum), seeded and roughly chopped
1 cup (5 oz) long-grain rice
4 cups (1 litre) prawn stock (from steps 1–6, below)
salt
freshly ground black pepper
12 olives for garnish
grated Kefalotíri or Parmesan cheese (optional)

1. In a large saucepan, using all the water, simmer the celery, carrot, 1 of the chopped onions, peppercorns, bay leaves and oregano for 30 minutes. **2.** In the meantime, peel the uncooked prawns, putting the shells and heads aside. **3.** With a sharp knife, make an incision in the back of the prawns and devein them. **4.** Rinse the prawns under cold water and cut each into 2–3 pieces. Set these aside. **5.** To the vegetables in the saucepan, add the prawn shells and heads, mix well together. Cover and simmer gently for 20 minutes. **6.** Remove from heat and let it cool for 20–30 minutes. Then strain the prawn stock. (Four cups of this stock will need to be heated for use in step 9.) **7.** Heat the oil and sauté the second chopped onion and the garlic until the onion is soft and transparent. **8.** Add the tomatoes, tomato purée and green pepper. Cook for 5 minutes. **9.** Stir in the rice. Add the strained, heated prawn stock. Season. **10.** Cover the saucepan, lower the heat, and simmer for 20 minutes without taking off the lid. **11.** Stir in the chopped prawns, cover the saucepan and continue to simmer for 5 minutes. **12.** Take off the heat and let stand for 10 minutes. Taste and season if necessary. Serve garnished with black olives and if desired sprinkled with grated Kefalotíri or Parmesan cheese.

Fish with Prawns and Mayonnaise
Athenaiki

Serves 4

1 kg (2 lb) fish fillets, steamed and allowed to
cool
250 g (8 oz) small prawns, cooked, shelled and
cooled
1 small onion, finely chopped
1 tablespoon capers
1½ cups (12 fl oz) mayonnaise, (see p. 330)
salt
freshly ground black pepper
2 sprigs parsley, finely chopped
12 black olives

1. With the back of a fork, flake the fish fillets.
2. In a bowl, combine fish, prawns, onion, capers,
½ cup (4 fl oz) of the mayonnaise, salt and pepper.
Mix well together. 3. On a decorative round serving
platter, form the fish mixture into a mound, coat it
with the remainder of the mayonnaise, sprinkle with
parsley and garnish with olives. Refrigerate for
1 hour before serving.

Fish with Tomatoes, Wine and Oregano
Psári Ladorigano

From the Metaftsis Restaurant, Volos.

Serves 6

6 fish cutlets, 2.5 cm (1 inch) thick (use jewfish,
snapper or any firm white-fleshed fish)
salt
freshly ground black pepper
juice of 1 lemon
250 g (1 cup) canned peeled tomatoes, chopped
3 tablespoons tomato purée
½ cup (4 fl oz) dry white wine
½ cup (4 fl oz) olive oil
1 clove garlic, chopped
2 teaspoons dried oregano
3 fresh tomatoes, peeled and sliced
3 sprigs parsley, chopped

1. Preheat the oven to 200°C (400°F/Gas 6).
2. Arrange the fish cutlets in a baking dish 5 cm (2
inches) deep. Sprinkle with salt, pepper and lemon
juice. 3. In a saucepan, combine the rest of the ingredients, except the fresh tomato slices and parsley.
Simmer on low heat for 30 minutes. 4. Pour the
sauce over the fish, arrange the fresh tomato slices
on top, and sprinkle with parsley. 5. Place the baking dish in the preheated oven and cook for 30
minutes. Serve hot.

Grilled Marinated Snapper
Psári tis Skaras

Serves 6

6 "plate-size" (approximately 500–600 g)
snapper or bream, cleaned and scaled
¼ cup (2 fl oz) olive oil
¼ cup (2 fl oz) dry white wine
1 clove garlic, crushed
4 sprigs parsley, finely chopped
3 sprigs mint, finely chopped
salt
freshly ground black pepper
juice of 1 lemon

1. Place the fish in a deep baking dish. 2. Prepare
the marinade by mixing the remaining ingredients,
except the lemon juice. Pour it over the fish and
cover with plastic film. 3. Refrigerate for at least 3
hours, turning the fish occasionally. 4. Preheat the
griller. 5. Drain the fish and reserve the marinade.
6. Place the fish under the griller, baste frequently
with the marinade and grill for 5–8 minutes on each
side. 7. Serve sprinkled with the pan juices and
lemon juice.

Marinated Fried Fish
Psári Marinato

Serves 4

4 large fish fillets
salt
freshly ground black pepper
flour
½ cup (4 fl oz) olive oil
1 clove garlic
4 bay leaves
2 sprigs fresh rosemary, chopped
⅓ cup (2½ fl oz) wine vinegar
1½ cups (12 fl oz) water

1. Sprinkle the fish with salt and pepper and dust
with flour. 2. Heat the oil and fry the fish until crisp
and brown. 3. Place the fish in a glass or china dish.
4. To the oil in the pan, add the garlic, bay leaves
and rosemary, and sauté lightly until the garlic
browns. 5. Add the vinegar and water, simmer for
20 minutes. Taste for seasoning. 6. Pour the marinade over the fish and refrigerate overnight, turning
the fish occasionally. 7. Serve at room temperature
with a fresh salad and crusty bread.

POULTRY

Grilled Chicken Breasts Oregano
Kotopoulo Riganato tis Skáras

Serves 4

6 chicken breasts
½ cup (4 fl oz) olive oil
juice of 2 lemons
**2 tablespoons dried oregano or 3 tablespoons
fresh oregano, chopped**
**1 tablespoon dried thyme or 2 tablespoons
fresh thyme, chopped**
salt
freshly ground black pepper

1. Place the chicken breasts in a baking dish. **2.** To prepare the marinade, combine the remaining ingredients in a screw-top jar and shake well. **3.** Pour the marinade over the chicken breasts and refrigerate overnight. **4.** Preheat the griller and place the dish containing the chicken and the marinade under the griller. **5.** Baste frequently and grill the breasts 5 minutes each side. If they are grilled too long they will be tough and dry. **6.** Serve hot on a platter together with the remaining marinade.

Baked Chicken Pilaf
Kota Piláfi

Serves 4

1 clove garlic, crushed
2 tablespoons tomato paste
2 tablespoons olive oil
1 teaspoon oregano
salt
freshly ground black pepper
8 chicken pieces, such as breasts, legs, thighs
1 cup (5 oz) long-grain rice
**2½ cups (20 fl oz) boiling chicken stock
(see p. 328) or water**

1. Preheat the oven to 180°C (350°F/Gas 4). **2.** Mix the garlic, tomato paste, oil, oregano, salt and pepper. **3.** Coat the chicken pieces with this mixture and place them in a deep baking dish or casserole. **4.** Bake in preheated oven for 35 minutes, turning the pieces at least once. **5.** Add the rice and stock or water. **6.** Cover with lid or foil and cook for a further 30 minutes. **7.** Take it out of the oven, let it stand for 10 minutes and serve with a green salad.

Chicken Pie in Filo Pastry
Bourekakia Kotopoulo

Serves 8

100 g (3½ oz) butter
3 onions, chopped
3 stalks celery, chopped
1 clove garlic, crushed
1 kg (2 lb) coarsely chopped raw chicken meat
½ cup (2 oz) flour
2 cups (16 fl oz) hot chicken stock (see p. 328)
6 eggs, whisked
4 sprigs parsley, chopped
4 sprigs dill, chopped
juice of 2 lemons
⅛ teaspoon nutmeg
salt
freshly ground black pepper
½ cup (4 oz) butter, melted
12 sheets filo pastry

1. Preheat the oven to 200°C (400°F/Gas 6). **2.** Heat the butter in a large frying pan and sauté the onion, celery and garlic for 5 minutes. **3.** Add the chicken meat and flour, and fry for a further 5 minutes, stirring constantly. **4.** Reduce heat and add the hot chicken stock, cook on low heat for 3 minutes. **5.** Take off the heat and, while stirring constantly, add the whisked eggs. **6.** Stir in the parsley, dill, lemon juice, nutmeg, salt and pepper. **7.** With a little of the melted butter, grease a baking dish approximately 30 × 25 × 7 cm (12 × 10 × 3 inches). **8.** On the bottom and up the sides of the dish, place 6 sheets of filo pastry, each sheet generously brushed with melted butter before the next is placed. **9.** Spoon the chicken mixture into this and fold the edges of the filo over the mixture. **10.** Cover the mixture with the remaining 6 sheets of filo pastry, each in turn, as well as the top, well brushed with the melted butter. **11.** Tuck the edges of the covering filo sheets around the inside edges of the baking dish. **12.** Bake in the preheated oven for 30 minutes until golden. Serve hot.

Right: The Pileas Restaurant in Hania, Mt Pelion serves hearty local dishes which, especially in winter after a day's skiing, is the perfect food. Foreground: Dried White Bean Soup; Sausages with Green Peppers, Onions and Tomatoes; Greek Feta with Yogurt.

Chicken with Egg-lemon Sauce

Kotopoulo Avgolémono

Serves 4

8 chicken pieces, such as breasts, legs, thighs
juice of 2 lemons
1 teaspoon dried oregano
salt
freshly ground black pepper
60 g (2 oz) butter
1 cup (8 fl oz) dry white wine
1 cup (8 fl oz) chicken stock (see p. 328)
3 eggs, separated
1 tablespoon cornflour (cornstarch)
2 sprigs dill, chopped

1. Preheat the oven to 180°C (350°F/Gas 4). **2.** Sprinkle the chicken pieces with lemon juice, oregano, salt and pepper and let them stand for 2 hours. **3.** In a casserole, heat the butter and fry the chicken pieces until light brown but not cooked. **4.** Add wine and chicken stock. Cover, bring to the boil and braise in the oven for 1 hour. **5.** Beat the egg whites with some salt until stiff. **6.** Add the egg yolks and beat together. **7.** Take the chicken pieces out of the casserole and arrange them on a serving platter. **8.** Take out 1 cup (8 fl oz) of the cooking juice and mix it with the cornflour (optional, if a thicker sauce is required). **9.** Pour it back into the casserole and heat it until it thickens. **10.** While beating constantly, add a cup of the thickened cooking juice to the egg mixture. Then, while continuing to beat vigorously, pour the egg mixture into the casserole. **11.** Heat until it thickens but do not boil. Taste, and if necessary, add more lemon juice, salt or pepper. **12.** To serve, pour the sauce over the chicken pieces and serve sprinkled with the dill.

Traditionally served with rice.

Stuffed Roast Turkey

Gallos Yemistós

In Greece the most popular stuffing for turkey — which traditionally is served at Christmas and New Year — is rice. An unusual flavour is added by the use of feta cheese.

Serves 8–10

1 turkey 4–5 kg (8–10 lb), prebasted
juice of 2 lemons
1 teaspoon grated lemon rind
salt
freshly ground black pepper

Stuffing:
2 onions, finely chopped
3 stalks celery, finely chopped
2 tablespoons oil
375 g (¾ lb) minced veal-pork mixture
turkey liver, chopped
2 cups (12 oz) cooked rice
1 cup (8 fl oz) red wine
½ cup (2 oz) pine nuts or chopped almonds
½ cup (2½ oz) currants
½ teaspoon nutmeg
1 teaspoon dried oregano
4 sprigs parsley, finely chopped
½ teaspoon cinnamon
125 g (4 oz) feta cheese, crumbled

1. Preheat the oven to 180°C (350°F/Gas 4). **2.** Rub the cavity of the turkey with half of a mixture of lemon juice, lemon rind, salt and pepper. Let it stand while preparing the stuffing. **3.** To make the stuffing, sauté the onions and celery in the oil. **4.** Add the minced meat and the liver, and fry for 5–8 minutes. **5.** Add the rice and wine, cook for 10 minutes. **6.** Add the rest of the ingredients, mix well together, and if necessary adjust seasoning. **7.** Stuff the mixture into the turkey body and neck cavities and secure the openings with skewers. **8.** Rub the skin with the rest of the seasoned lemon juice. Cover the bird with foil. **9.** Place the turkey in the preheated oven and roast for 2½ hours. Remove the foil and continue cooking so as to brown the skin, for 1 more hour or until done. **10.** When cooked, remove the turkey from the oven and let it stand for 10–15 minutes before carving. **11.** Arrange the carved pieces in the middle of a serving platter and place the stuffing around it. Do not worry if some parts of the turkey are undercooked. After carving, and while preparing a gravy from the cooking juices, put the platter in the turned-off oven to keep warm. The underdone parts will set during that time. An overcooked turkey would be dry and tasteless.

MEAT

Lamb on Skewers
Souvlákia

From the Restaurant Marmara, Mistras. Souvlákia is marinated meat, grilled on a skewer. The most popular meat is lamb, though beef and poultry are also used. The meat can be skewered plain or it may be skewered with tomatoes, mushrooms, onions and green peppers. At the Marmara, meat and vegetables are combined.

Serves 6

1 cup (8 fl oz) olive oil
juice of 2 lemons
½ cup (4 fl oz) dry red wine
1 clove garlic, crushed
2 bay leaves
½ teaspoon salt
freshly ground black pepper
1½ tablespoons dried oregano
1.5 kg (3 lb) lamb from a leg, cut into 4 cm
(1½ inch) cubes
3 green peppers (capsicums)
2 onions, each cut into 6 wedges
12-18 small button mushrooms
3-4 tomatoes, cut into quarters

1. In a large bowl combine oil, lemon juice, wine, garlic, bay leaves, salt, pepper and oregano. **2.** Mix well and add the meat. **3.** Halve the green peppers, remove and discard the seeds, cut the peppers into 2.5 cm (1 inch) squares. **4.** Boil some salted water and plunge in the peppers and onions. Boil them for 5 minutes. Rinse them in cold water and add them to the marinade. **5.** Marinate for 24 hours. **6.** Two hours before grilling the meat, add the mushrooms and the tomatoes to the marinade. **7.** Allow 1 skewer per person. Divide all the ingredients equally between the six skewers and thread a piece of lamb, pepper, onion, mushroom, tomato and then repeat. **8.** At each end allow some of the skewer to project for easy turning. **9.** Grill either over an open charcoal fire or under a griller for some 15 minutes until cooked to taste. While grilling, frequently baste with the marinade. Occasionally, Souvlákia is served on a bed of rice pilaf.

Lamb Shanks and Artichokes with Egg-lemon Sauce
Arni me Anginéres Avgolémono
From: Gerofinikas, Athens.

Serves 6

6 large or 12 small artichokes
½ cup (2 oz) cornflour (cornstarch)
salt
juice and rind of 2 lemons
12 small lamb shanks
12 peppercorns
4 bay leaves
1 carrot, chopped
2 stalks celery, chopped
1 onion, chopped
3 eggs, separated
salt
juice of 3 lemons
freshly ground black pepper
3 sprigs parsley, finely chopped

1. Wash the artichokes and trim each by breaking off all coarse outer leaves. **2.** Cut the stalk at a point where it breaks easily. Leave the remainder of the stalk on the artichoke as it will be tender and edible. **3.** Lay the artichoke on its side and cut 2.5-4 cm (1-1½ inches) off the tips of the leaves. **4.** Dissolve the cornflour in 4 cups (1 litre) of water, add the lemon juice and the rind and place the artichokes in this as soon as they are trimmed. This will prevent discolouration. **5.** Strain the artichokes and put the liquid into a large saucepan. Add enough fresh water to cover the artichokes and bring to the boil. Add the artichokes, cover them with a teatowel and place a lid on the pan. **6.** Boil for 15-20 minutes depending on their size. Remove with a slotted spoon, gently part the leaves and remove and discard the choke. Keep them warm. **7.** To cook the lamb shanks, in a saucepan with enough water to cover the shanks add salt, peppercorns, bay leaves, carrot, celery and onion. On low heat, simmer the lamb shanks for 1½ hours. Take off the heat and let them stand until the sauce is prepared. (1½ cups of the stock will be used in step 11.) **8.** To prepare egg and lemon sauce, beat the egg whites with a pinch of salt until stiff. **9.** Continue beating and add the egg yolks and the juice of 3 lemons. **10.** While beating continuously, add 1½ cups (12 fl oz) of the hot lamb stock to the egg-lemon mixture. **11.** Heat for 2-3 minutes until the sauce thickens but do not boil. Season to taste. **12.** To serve, arrange the hot lamb shanks and artichokes on a serving dish, pour the sauce over and garnish with the parsley. Serve immediately.

Stuffed Peppers and Tomatoes

Pipperiés ke Domátes Yemistés

From the Restaurant Kuyu, Piraeus.
This dish is very popular in Greece and can be found, at one time or another, in all Greek homes as well as in most restaurants. Not only peppers and tomatoes are prepared in this way but also zucchini and eggplant. It is important to note that the different vegetables require varying baking times.

Serves 4

4 large firm tomatoes
1 teaspoon sugar
4 large green peppers (capsicums)
¾ cup (4 oz) long-grain rice
4 tablespoons olive oil
1 onion, chopped
¼ bunch parsley, finely chopped
500 g (1 lb) minced beef or lamb
500 g (1 lb) peeled, chopped tomatoes
2 tablespoons tomato paste
salt
freshly ground black pepper
6 mint leaves, finely chopped
½ cup (4 fl oz) dry red wine

1. Preheat the oven to 180°C (350°F/Gas 4). **2.** Cut a thin "lid" off the top of each tomato. With a teaspoon, scoop out the pulp, chop it and set it aside for the stuffing. **3.** Sprinkle the inside of the tomatoes with the sugar and place them upside down to drain. **4.** Cut the top off each pepper, scoop out and discard the seeds. **5.** Plunge the peppers and their lids into boiling water and cook for 5 minutes. Drain and place them into some cold water. **6.** In ½ cup of water, parboil the rice. **7.** In 2 tablespoons of the oil, sauté the chopped onion until it is soft and transparent, then add the parsley. **8.** Add the reserved tomato pulp, the peeled and chopped tomatoes, and the tomato paste, salt and pepper, mint and wine. **9.** Mix well and simmer over low heat for 20 minutes, stirring occasionally. If the mixture dries out, add some water. **10.** Separately, in the remaining 2 tablespoons of oil, fry the meat until brown, stirring constantly. **11.** To the meat add the parboiled rice and two-thirds of the tomato sauce. **12.** On low heat, cook this stuffing for 10 minutes, stirring occasionally. If necessary add some water to keep the mixture moist. Remove from heat and cool. **13.** Stand the peppers and the tomatoes in two separate baking dishes and with a teaspoon fill each loosely with some stuffing. **14.** Replace the lids, pour the remaining tomato sauce into the dishes, cover them with foil and cook them in the preheated oven, the peppers for 35 minutes and the tomatoes for 15 minutes. **15.** Remove the foil and cook both for a further 10 minutes, basting them with the lids removed. Serve hot with the remaining tomato sauce.

Roast Leg of Lamb Greek Style, with Potatoes

Arní Bóuti tou Foúrnou me Patátes

The lamb in this recipe is roasted and partly braised for a long time which gives it the characteristic succulent texture and flavour.

Serves 6

3 kg (7 lb) leg of lamb
juice of 2 lemons
salt
freshly ground black pepper
3 tablespoons dried oregano
1 clove garlic, cut into slivers
1 cup (8 fl oz) dry white wine or water
1 onion, sliced
1 stalk celery, chopped
6 large potatoes, peeled and cut into quarters

1. Preheat the oven to 200°C (400°F/Gas 6). **2.** Rub the leg of lamb with half of the lemon juice. Sprinkle it with salt, pepper and some of the oregano. **3.** With a sharp knife, make deep cuts in the leg and insert the garlic slivers. **4.** Place the meat, fat side up, in a baking dish without lid. Cook in the preheated oven for 1 hour. **5.** Add the wine or water (or a mixture of both), the onion and the celery. Reduce the heat to 160°C (325°C/Gas 3) and cook for 2 hours. Check occasionally and add more wine or water if necessary. **6.** Add the potatoes to the pan, sprinkle them with the remaining lemon juice, salt, pepper and oregano. **7.** Continue roasting for 20 minutes. Turn the potatoes and roast for another 30 minutes or until potatoes are brown and cooked. **8.** To serve, cut the meat into chunks, place them on a serving platter and arrange the potatoes around it. Skim the fat off the cooking juices, season and pour it over the meat and potatoes.

Lamb Fricassée with Lettuce

Arní Fricassée me Maroúlia

From the Costoyanis Taverna, Athens.

Serves 6

1.25 kg (2½ lb) breast or shoulder of lamb, cut
into 2.5 cm (1 inch) cubes
2 onions, sliced
6 spring onions (scallions), sliced
125 g (4 oz) butter
2 tablespoons flour
2 small lettuces, shredded
4 cups (1 litre) water
1 tablespoon salt
freshly ground black pepper
4 sprigs parsley, chopped
3 sprigs dill, chopped
3 egg yolks
2 tablespoons water
juice of 1½–2 lemons

1. Sauté the meat, onions, and spring onions in the
butter for 5 minutes. **2.** Sprinkle with flour and,
while stirring, fry for 2 minutes. **3.** Add the lettuce,
water, salt, pepper, parsley and dill. **4.** Simmer
covered for 1 hour. Remove from heat. **5.** Beat the
egg yolks, water and lemon juice together. Continue
beating and add ¼ cup (2 fl oz) of the lamb cooking
juice. **6.** Return the lamb to the heat and while stirring constantly add the egg mixture to the juices. Do
not boil. Serve hot.

Beef Stew with Onions and Red Wine

Stifátho

Serves 4

½ cup (4 fl oz) olive oil
1 onion, chopped
1 clove garlic, crushed
750 g (1½ lb) shin beef, cut into 2.5 cm (1 inch)
cubes
4 ripe tomatoes, peeled and chopped
2 tablepoons tomato paste
1½ cups (12 fl oz) dry red wine
1 tablespoon red wine vinegar
water
2 bay leaves
⅛ teaspoon cumin
⅛ teaspoon cinnamon
salt
freshly ground black pepper
12–16 small pickling-type onions

1. In a heavy-bottomed casserole, heat three-quarters
of the oil and fry the onions, garlic and meat until
the meat is brown on all sides. **2.** Add the tomatoes,
tomato paste, wine and vinegar, and enough water
to cover the meat. **3.** Add the rest of the ingredients,
except the onions. **4.** Cover the casserole, bring to
the boil. Reduce heat and simmer for 1½ hours.
5. In a frying pan, brown the onions in the remainder of the oil. **6.** Add them to the meat and continue
simmering for a further 30–45 minutes. **7.** Before
serving, season to taste. Serve hot with rice pilaf (see
p. 278).

Home-made Smyrna Sausages in Tomato Sauce

Souzoukákia apo tin Smyŕnie

Serves 6

Tomato Sauce:
2 tablespoons olive oil
2 onions, finely chopped
1.3 kg (3 lb) fresh ripe tomatoes, peeled and
chopped
185 g (6 oz) tomato paste
4 basil leaves, chopped
1 clove garlic, crushed
1 bay leaf
½ teaspoon salt
6 peppercorns
1 tablespoon honey

Sausages:
500 g (1 lb) minced beef
½ cup (2 oz) dry breadcrumbs
1 teaspoon salt
½ teaspoon powdered cumin
¼ teaspoon cinnamon
1 clove garlic, crushed
90 g (3 oz) butter

1. In a large saucepan, heat the oil and sauté the onions until soft and transparent. **2.** Add the other ingredients, cover, bring to the boil. Reduce heat and simmer for 1 hour. **3.** To make the sausages, in a bowl mix meat, breadcrumbs, salt, cumin, cinnamon and garlic. Knead for 10 minutes until the mixture is the consistency of paste. This can be done in a food processor, one cupful at a time, approximately 20–30 seconds each load. **4.** Shape the mixture into small sausages 12 cm (4¾ inches) long. **5.** In a frying pan, heat the butter and brown the sausages. **6.** Place them in a casserole, cover with tomato sauce, cover the dish and simmer for 30 minutes. Serve with rice or pasta (sprinkled with grated cheese), and a dry red wine.

Greek Meatballs

Keftéthes

From the Amalia Hotel, Olympia.

Yields 48 egg-sized meatballs

1 onion, finely chopped
1 tablespoon olive oil
1 kg (2 lb) finely minced lamb, beef or veal
4¼ cups (8 oz) soft breadcrumbs
2 teaspoons finely chopped mint
3 sprigs parsley, finely chopped
2 teaspoons salt
freshly ground black pepper
juice of 1 lemon
2–3 tablespoons Ouzo, or ½ cup (4 fl oz) dry
red wine
2 eggs, lightly beaten
½ cup (2 oz) flour
⅔ cup (5 fl oz) olive oil for frying

1. Lightly fry the onion in 1 tablespoon of oil until golden. **2.** Combine all ingredients except the flour and the oil for frying. Knead well until the mixture is blended and smooth. **3.** Shape it into balls. The size may vary, depending on whether they are to be small, walnut-sized balls for cocktails or large-sized balls for a main course dish. **4.** Roll the balls in flour. **5.** Cook them in hot oil, rolling them until they are brown on all sides.

DESSERTS

Plaited Sweet Almond Bread

Tsouréki

Makes 2 loaves

1 packet active dry yeast
½ cup (4 fl oz) lukewarm water
½ cup (4 fl oz) water
1 tablespoon Ouzo
½ teaspoon ground cinnamon
½ teaspoon aniseed
½ teaspoon grated orange peel
½ cup (4 fl oz) milk
125 g (4 oz) butter
200 g (6½ oz) sugar
¼ teaspoon salt
750 g (1½ lb) flour
1 egg, lightly beaten in 2 tablespoons water
60 g (2 oz) slivered almonds

1. Dissolve the yeast in the lukewarm water and leave to activate for 20 minutes. **2.** In a saucepan, bring to the boil the water, Ouzo, cinnamon, aniseed, orange peel, milk, butter, sugar and salt. Stir until the sugar dissolves, and cool. **3.** Add the yeast to this mixture. **4.** Place the flour in a large mixing bowl and stir the liquid into the flour until the dough leaves the sides of the bowl easily. If necessary, adjust consistency by adding more flour or more water. **5.** On a floured surface, knead the dough for about 10 minutes until it is smooth and elastic. **6.** Grease the bowl and return the dough to it. Cover with a teatowel and stand it in a warm, draught-free place to rise until double, approximately 2 hours. **7.** Punch down the dough and knead lightly. **8.** Divide the dough into two parts and each, in turn, into three. Roll out each into a strand 35 cm (14 inches) long. Plait three strands together and, using some water, press the ends together. Plait the other three strands to make the second loaf. **9.** Place the two loaves on a greased baking dish 5 cm (2 inches) apart, cover with a teatowel and let the dough rise for a further 2 hours. **10.** Preheat the oven to 180°C (350°F/Gas 4). **11.** Brush the loaves with the egg-water mixture and sprinkle the tops with the almonds. **12.** In the bottom of the oven, place a bowl with boiling water; this will help to produce a crisp crust. **13.** Bake for 45 minutes until brown and the loaves sound hollow when tapped. **14.** Cool on a wire rack.

Baklavá

Yields 30 pieces in a 33 × 23 × 5 cm (13 × 9 × 2 inch) baking tin

1 cup (8 oz) unsalted butter, melted
500 g (1 lb) walnuts, finely chopped
250 g (8 oz) almonds, blanched and finely chopped
¼ cup (2 oz) sugar
2 teaspoons cinnamon
¼ teaspoon ground cloves
500 g (1 lb) filo pastry

Syrup:
220 g (7 oz) sugar
1 cup (12 oz) honey
2 cups (16 fl oz) water
juice of 1 lemon
2 whole cloves
1 sliver of lemon rind

1. Preheat the oven to 160°C (325°F/Gas 3). **2.** With a little of the melted butter, brush the inside of the baking tin. **3.** In a bowl, mix well together the nuts, sugar, cinnamon and cloves. **4.** Over the bottom of the tin, place 10 sheets of filo pastry, each sheet generously brushed with butter before the next is placed. Sprinkle the top sheet with some of the nut-sugar mixture. **5.** Place 2 buttered sheets of filo pastry on top and sprinkle with the nut mixture. Repeat this process until all the nut mixture is used up. There should be 15–20 layers. **6.** Trim along the edges and brush the top with the remaining butter. **7.** Score the top layer diagonally with parallel lines. **8.** Place in the preheated oven and bake for 30 minutes. **9.** Move the tin to the top of the oven for a further 30 minutes. If the top browns too quickly, cover with aluminium foil. **10.** While the Baklavá is baking, prepare the syrup. Combine all ingredients, heat and stir to dissolve the sugar. **11.** Bring to the boil and boil briskly for 10 minutes. **12.** Strain, cool and pour half of the syrup over the hot Baklavá. **13.** Let it stand for 30 minutes, then pour over the remainder of the syrup. **14.** Leave overnight before cutting.

***Right:** A selection of dishes offered at the Hotel Amalia in Olympia. From bottom: Triangle Cheese Puffs (see page 272); Greek Salad (see page 277); Greek Meat Balls (see page 289); Beans à la Piaz. Also in picture are dishes of cold meats and a display of Greek wines.*

Custard Semolina Pie

Ghalatoboureko

Makes a pie 30 × 23 × 5 cm (12 × 9 × 2 inches)

6 eggs
185 g (6 oz) sugar
1½ cups (8 oz) semolina
7 cups (1.75 litres) milk
1 teaspoon grated lemon peel
60 g (2 oz) butter
¾ cup (6 oz) butter, melted
16 filo pastry sheets

Syrup:
500 g (1 lb) sugar
1 cup (8 fl oz) water
juice of 1 lemon

1. Preheat the oven to 180°C (350°F/Gas 4).
2. Cream the eggs and sugar together until thick.
3. Add semolina, milk and lemon peel. **4.** Cook over low heat, stirring continuously, until the mixture thickens. **5.** Remove from heat and stir in 60 g butter. **6.** With some of the melted butter, brush the inside of the baking tin. **7.** On the bottom and up the sides of the dish, place 8 sheets of filo pastry, each sheet generously brushed with melted butter before the next is placed. **8.** Spoon the mixture into this and fold the edges of the filo pastry over at the top. **9.** Cover the mixture with the remaining 8 sheets of filo pastry, each in turn, as well as the top, well brushed with melted butter. **10.** Tuck the edges of the covering filo sheets around the inside edges of the pan. **11.** With a sharp knife, cut through the top 3 sheets in parallel lines forming 7.5 cm (3 inch) squares. **12.** Bake in the preheated oven for 45 minutes. Allow to cool. **13.** To prepare the syrup, combine all the ingredients, heat, and stir to dissolve the sugar. **14.** Bring to the boil and boil for 5–8 minutes. **15.** Cool and pour lukewarm syrup over the pie. **16.** Serve cold, cut into squares.

Almond 'Pears'

Amigthalotá

This recipe originates from the island of Hydra.

500 g (1 lb) ground almond meal, available in nut speciality shops (if not, whole blanched nuts may be ground in a food processor or blender)
1 cup (8 oz) sugar
75 g (2½ oz) semolina
1½ cups (12 fl oz) orange flower water
1 cup (6 oz) icing (confectioners') sugar
cloves

1. Preheat the oven to 200°C (400°F/Gas 6). **2.** Mix the ground almonds and 2 tablespoons of the sugar in a mortar and grind them finely. A food processor is very handy for this purpose, in which case using 1 cupful of almond meal and some of the sugar at a time. Process until the mixture is very fine. **3.** Add semolina, and some orange flower water. The texture of the mixture should be such as to keep its shape when formed into pear-shaped balls. If necessary, add more orange flower water or more semolina. **4.** Form the mixture into walnut-sized 'pears' and insert a clove to form the 'stalk'. **5.** Arrange 'pears' on a buttered and floured baking tray and bake in the preheated oven for 20 minutes. **6.** Cool, dip them into orange flower water and sprinkle them with icing sugar. Before serving, coat them with icing sugar again.

Halvás

Halvás

Serves 6

1 cup (8 fl oz) milk
1 cup (8 fl oz) water
1 cup (8 oz) sugar
1½ teaspoons vanilla extract
125 g (4 oz) unsalted butter
½ cup (2 oz) pine nuts or unsalted pistachios
1 cup (5 oz) coarse semolina
1 teaspoon cinnamon

1. Gently boil the milk, water and sugar for 15 minutes. Add vanilla extract and take off the heat. **2.** Melt the butter in a frying pan and lightly sauté the nuts. **3.** Add semolina to the frying pan and cook over low heat for 15 minutes. Do not allow it to become too brown. **4.** Take off the heat and slowly add the milk mixture. Be careful, as it may spatter. **5.** Simmer over low heat for 5 minutes or until the mixture is very thick and comes away from the sides of the pan. **6.** Spread the mixture about 2.5–4 cm (1–1½ inches) thick in a buttered dish. Allow to cool for about 1½ hours. **7.** To serve, unmould on to a decorative plate, cut into small squares and sprinkle with cinnamon.

Fritters with Honey Syrup

Loukoumathes

Makes 36 fritters

Syrup:
1 cup (8 oz) sugar
½ cup (6 oz) honey
½ cup (4 fl oz) water
juice of 1 lemon

Fritters:
1 tablespoon dried yeast
1¼ cups (10 fl oz) lukewarm water
3 cups (12 oz) flour
½ teaspoon salt
½ cup (4 fl oz) lukewarm milk
1 egg
oil for frying
1 tablespoon cinnamon

1. To make the syrup, combine the ingredients in a saucepan and, while stirring constantly, cook until the syrup thickens sufficiently to coat a spoon. 2. Pour the hot syrup into a heatproof container (a jug would be best) and set aside. 3. To make the fritters, mix the yeast with 3–4 tablespoons of the lukewarm water and let it stand to rise until the mixture doubles in volume. 4. Put the flour and salt in a large mixing bowl. 5. In a separate bowl, mix together the yeast, the rest of the lukewarm water, the milk and egg. Gradually incorporate it into the flour, then beat vigorously until the dough is smooth and just firm enough to hold its shape. If necessary, adjust its consistency by adding either more lukewarm water or more flour. 6. Cover the bowl with a teatowel and stand it in a warm draught-free place for about 45 minutes to 1 hour until the dough doubles in volume. 7. Preheat 8–10 cm (3–4 inches) of oil in a saucepan. 8. Dip a tablespoon in cold water, pick up a level spoonful of the dough and push it with another spoon into the hot oil. Do up to 6 fritters at a time. Fry for 2–3 minutes until golden-brown. 9. Keep them warm in a preheated oven. 10. To serve, heap the fritters on a serving dish, pour the syrup over them and sprinkle with cinnamon. The syrup may be served separately.

Deep-fried Sweet Pastry

Thiples

Makes about 50

3 eggs, separated, at room temperature
1 teaspoon baking powder
juice of ¼ orange
¼ cup (2 fl oz) vegetable oil
2 cups (8 oz) flour
4 cups (1 litre) oil for frying
2 cups (1½ lb) honey
1 cup (8 fl oz) water
1½ cups (6 oz) finely chopped walnuts or almonds
cinnamon for sprinkling

1. Whip the egg whites with the baking powder until they hold their peaks. 2. Beat the egg yolks and mix them with the egg whites. 3. Add orange juice, oil and flour, mix well, and transfer to a lightly floured board. Knead for 15 minutes. The dough will be sticky. 4. Divide it into 6 or 8 parts. Wrap in plastic film and refrigerate for 1 to 2 hours. 5. Take out one ball at a time and roll it out paper-thin on a floured board. 6. With a sharp knife, cut into rectangles 7.5 cm (3 inches) long and 5 cm (2 inches) wide. Fold them into triangles. 7. Heat the frying oil until very hot, drop the Thiples, one at a time, into the oil and fry for about 1 minute until golden-brown. Keep the oil free of crumbs. 8. Carefully remove with slotted spoon on to some paper towelling. 9. Stack them between layers of paper towels. 10. Boil the honey and water for 5 minutes and set aside. 11. Place the Thiples in layers on a serving plate, pour some honey over each and sprinkle with nuts and cinnamon. 12. Carefully spoon the Thiples on to individual serving plates and spoon any excess syrup on to them.

BENELUX

Benelux comprises Belgium, Netherlands and Luxembourg. While each country has its own distinctive cooking style, they do have elements in common.

The Belgians have an unashamed approach to eating. At home they use the best of ingredients in putting together dishes which are somewhat akin to those of their French neighbours. When eating out, they set high standards. Restaurants in Belgium enjoy the highest of reputations and places like Comme chez Soi in Brussels are among the best in the world. They have to be: the eating public spends lavishly on their food but in return, they expect the best.

Belgian cooking is well-known for its seafood: mussels, oysters, shrimp, eel and many varieties of sea fish are of exceptional quality and freshness.

The mediaeval town of Ghent offers what has now become one of the best-known Belgian specialities: Waterzooi, made either with fish or with chicken. It's a soup which is substantial enough to serve as a main course.

The Flemish north shares many of its dishes with the Dutch while in the south the French-speaking Walloons have a style of cooking related to that of their French neighbours. Here the forests of the Ardenne mountains produce excellent game. In the mountain streams and rivers one can find trout, pike and freshwater crayfish. All of these play an important part in local cooking.

The Belgians share the Ardenne mountains with their south-eastern neighbour of Luxembourg where the main attraction in their cooking is also the furred and feathered game from its extensive forests. Here too the rivers yield a rich and tasty harvest of trout, pike, crayfish and many other freshwater fish.

Vegetables are of exceptional quality and extensive orchards render a wide variety of fresh fruit. Plums are popular and especially delicious when used in the well-loved local plum tart. Pork is the most often-used meat and is eaten pickled or smoked, together with lots of aromatic sauerkraut.

Holland evokes well-known images: windmills standing in a lush green landscape, criss-crossed by many waterways; black and white cows; wooden clogs, tulips and Dutch cheese.

Until not so long ago, the Dutch were a nation of farmers and fishermen leading a hard struggle against nature. They were homely people and their food was nourishing and simple. Today they are still hearty eaters with a liking for substantial and filling food.

Dutch fishermen bring home a rich harvest from the sea. Herrings are most popular and the whole nation celebrates the season's new catch. Holland's best-known export is undoubtedly its cheese. The famous light yellow Gouda and orange-yellow Edam are quite unmistakable. Today produced on a large scale they were once made by individuals.

In recent years there has been a concentrated effort to revive old eating styles and an increasing number of restaurants serve traditional dishes which while quite simple have an appealing quality of their own.

Right: One of Belgium's finest restaurants, Le Moulin Hideux reflected in the Mill Pond.

SOUPS

Dutch Vegetable Soup with Meatballs
Netherlands

From De Drentse Heerlijkheid, Meppel.

Serves 6

6 cups (1.5 litres) beef stock (see p. 328)
2 leeks, white part only, sliced
3 small carrots, sliced
100 g (3–4 oz) green beans, cut into 2.5 cm (1 inch) lengths
1 bulb of fennel, chopped
3 stalks celery, cut into 2.5 cm (1 inch) pieces
100 g (3½ oz) vermicelli
30 small meatballs (see p. 304)
salt and pepper

1. Combine all ingredients, bring to the boil and simmer for 3 minutes. **2.** Season to taste and serve hot with meatballs (see p. 304).

Green Pea Soup 'Port van Cleve'
Erwtensoep
Netherlands

From Die Port Van Cleve Restaurant, Amsterdam.

Serves 6

1 kg (2 lb) split green peas, soaked overnight
6 cups (1.5 litres) water
4 leeks, white part only, washed and finely sliced
1 bunch celery, chopped
4 onions, chopped
4 pigs' trotters
1 oxtail, cut into pieces
500 g (1 lb) smoked sausage, approximately 2.5 cm (1 inch) in diameter
salt
freshly ground pepper

1. Combine all the ingredients except the salt and pepper. Bring them to the boil and simmer for 2 hours or until the meat is cooked. **2.** Add salt and pepper to taste and serve hot with the trotters, oxtail and sausage cut into thick slices.

Leek Soup
Porrettenzopp
Luxembourg

From the Hotel du Commerce, Wiltz.

Serves 4

2 leeks, white parts only, chopped
30 g (1 oz) butter
3 medium potatoes, chopped
6 cups (1.5 litres) water
salt and pepper
1 egg
4 tablespoons fresh cream

1. Lightly sauté the leeks in the butter. **2.** Add the potatoes and the water; season. **3.** Bring to the boil and simmer for 45 minutes. **4.** Beat the egg and combine it with the cream. **5.** Stir it into the soup and heat it without allowing it to boil. **6.** Serve hot with Grompere Kichelcher (Potato Fritters) p. 297.

Hotchpotch Ghent Style
Hochepot à la Gantoise
Belgium

This dish may be served either as a soup or as a 'one pot' meal.

Serves 8–10

500 g (1 lb) of each of the following meat: sirloin, breast of lamb (without fat), veal shoulder, pickled pork
3 pigs' trotters
4 stalks of celery, cut into 1.5 cm (½ inch) pieces
2 carrots, chopped
2 leeks, white part only, sliced
1 onion, chopped
1 teaspoon chopped thyme
1 teaspoon chopped marjoram
6 peppercorns
2 bay leaves
250 g (8 oz) chipolata sausages
4–5 potatoes, peeled and quartered
salt and pepper

1. Cut the meat into approximately 5 cm (1 inch) cubes and place in a large saucepan. Cover the meat with water and bring slowly to the boil. Simmer for 15 minutes, skim off any scum that appears on the surface. **2.** Add the rest of the ingredients except the chipolatas and potatoes and simmer over low heat for 1½ hours. **3.** Add the sausages and potatoes and simmer for a further 30 minutes or until all ingredients are cooked. **4.** Season to taste. Serve as a soup or as a main course dish.

VEGETABLES

Red Cabbage
Netherlands

Serves 4

1–1.25 kg (2–2½ lb) red cabbage,
finely chopped
¼ cup (2 fl oz) water
2 large cooking apples, peeled, cored and cut
into cubes
2 bay leaves
3 cloves
salt
freshly ground pepper
30 g (1 oz) butter
2–3 tablespoons herb vinegar

1. In a saucepan combine the cabbage, water, apples, bay leaves, cloves, salt and pepper. **2.** Cook, covered, for 30 minutes. **3.** Add the butter and vinegar and serve hot as a vegetable.

Potato Fritters
Grompere Kichelcher
Luxembourg

From the Hotel du Commerce, Wiltz.

Serves 6–8

1.5 kg (3 lb) potatoes, peeled and grated
2 onions, finely chopped
2 eggs, lightly beaten
salt
freshly ground pepper
4 sprigs parsley, finely chopped
oil for frying

1. In a bowl, combine potatoes, onions, eggs, salt and pepper. **2.** Heat the oil in a frying pan and place tablespoonfuls of the mixture into the pan. Flatten them with the back of the spoon and fry them until they are light brown and crisp on both sides. These Potato Fritters are traditionally served with Leek Soup (see p. 296).

Chicory of Brussels
Belgium

No list of Belgian vegetables would be complete without chicory, wrongly called Belgian endive. Light green and almost white in parts, its crisp leaves are eaten raw in salads and cooked in many ways as a vegetable. In cooking chicory two ingredients are essential — a sprinkling of sugar to neutralise a slight bitterness and a few drops of lemon juice to prevent discolouring. The simplest way to cook it is to braise the whole chicory in butter and eat it lightly seasoned.

Chicory with Mornay Sauce

Serves 4

2 cups (16 fl oz) milk
½ onion, chopped
6 peppercorns
4 sprigs parsley, chopped
2 sprigs thyme, chopped
1 bay leaf
45 g (1½ oz) butter
50 g (1¾ oz) flour
½ cup (4 fl oz) meat or fish stock (see p. 328)
½ cup (2 oz) grated Parmesan cheese
½ cup (2 oz) grated Gruyère cheese
20 g (⅔ oz) butter
salt and pepper
1 teaspoon sugar
juice of ½ lemon
6–8 chicory

1. Simmer the milk with the onion, peppercorns and herbs for 10 minutes. **2.** Strain the milk. **3.** Melt the butter in a saucepan, add the flour and cook it for 2–3 minutes. **4.** Add the hot milk all at once and whisk vigorously to obtain a smooth sauce. **5.** Add the stock and simmer for 30 minutes, stirring from time to time. **6.** Add the cheese, heat and stir until the cheese dissolves. Season to taste. **7.** Preheat the oven to 200°C (400°F/Gas 6). **8.** In a saucepan, boil some water, add the sugar and lemon juice, drop in the chicory and boil for 2–3 minutes. **9.** Cut the chicory into slices 1.25 cm (½ inch) thick and arrange them on the bottom of an ovenproof dish. **10.** Pour the sauce over the chicory and bake in the oven until the top browns.

FISH

Gratin Fish Casserole
Netherlands

Serves 6

1.5 kg (3 lb) haddock fillets
1¾ cups (11 oz) rice
1.5 kg (3 lb) potatoes, peeled and cut into large pieces
90 g (3 oz) butter
2 large onions, cut into rings
2 cups (16 fl oz) milk
salt
freshly ground pepper
½ cup (2 oz) breadcrumbs
½ teaspoon nutmeg
1 tablespoon French mustard

1. Preheat the oven to 200°C (400°F/Gas 6). **2.** Simmer the fish for 6–8 minutes until cooked. Remove the skin and any remaining bones and cut the fish into pieces. Set aside. **3.** Cook the rice to your liking. **4.** Boil the potatoes until they are soft enough to mash. **5.** Mash them with half the butter, add salt, pepper and nutmeg. **6.** Fry the onions in one tablespoon of the butter until golden. **7.** In an ovenproof dish place a layer of rice and spread it with mustard. Place the onions on top. **8.** Arrange the fish over it and cover with the mashed potatoes. **9.** Sprinkle the surface with breadcrumbs and put dabs of the remaining butter over it. **10.** Place the dish in the preheated oven, or under the griller until the crust is brown. Serve hot accompanied by lots of frothing Dutch beer.

Riesling Trout
Truit au Riesling
Luxembourg

Serves 4

50 g (1½ oz) butter
3 spring onions (scallions), chopped
4 cleaned trout
1¼ cups (10 fl oz) dry white wine
salt
freshly ground pepper
1½ cups (12 fl oz) cream
1 tablespoon beurre manié (flour and water paste)
2 tablespoons chopped chives

1. Preheat the oven to 160°C (325°F/Gas 3). **2.** In a roasting dish, melt the butter and lightly sauté the spring onions. **3.** Arrange the trout on top, add the wine and sprinkle with salt and pepper. **4.** Tightly cover with aluminium foil and bake in the oven for 15–20 minutes. **5.** Arrange the trout on a preheated platter and keep it warm. **6.** Add the cream to the cooking juices and cook for 10 minutes to reduce the amount. **7.** Thicken with the beurre manié and pour the sauce over the trout. Serve garnished with chopped chives.

Green Eel
Anguilles au Vert
Belgium

From the Restaurant 'T Bourgoensche Cruyce' Brugge.

Serves 4

1 kg (2 lb) eel, skinned and cut into 5 cm (2 inch) pieces
60 g (2 oz) butter
salt
freshly ground pepper
60 g (2 oz) chervil, chopped
100 g (3⅓ oz) sorrel, chopped
1 teaspoon dried tarragon or 1 tablespoon fresh tarragon, chopped
juice of 1 lemon
2 egg yolks, lightly beaten

1. In a frying pan sauté the eel in the butter and season it. Take it out of the pan and set aside. **2.** Put the chervil, sorrel and tarragon into the pan and cook them briefly. Return the eel to the pan, cover, and stew it slowly for approximately 10–15 minutes or until the eel is tender. **3.** Add the lemon juice mixed with the eggs and heat it long enough to thicken the sauce. Do not boil it. Serve either hot or cold.

Right: Dutch Vegetable Soup with Meatballs (see page 296) and Plaice with Hollandaise Sauce as served at De Drentse Heerlijkheid restaurant at Meppel in Holland.

Marinated Fish Montaise Style

Poissons à la Montaise
Belgium

Serves 6

1 kg any fish fillets (in the original recipe
small freshwater fish are used)
salt and pepper
flour
oil
12 small pickling-type onions
1 cup (8 fl oz) vinegar
4 cups (1 litre) water (in which the onions were
boiled)
6 spring onions (scallions), chopped
2 cloves
2 teaspoons fresh chopped thyme or
1 teaspoon dried thyme
2 bay leaves
2 sprigs tarragon, chopped, or 1 teaspoon
dried tarragon
6 peppercorns, crushed
25 g (1⅔ oz) butter
25 g (1⅔ oz) flour
2 lemons, peeled and sliced

1. Cut the fish fillets into 7.5 cm (3 inch) pieces,
season them, dip them in flour and briefly fry them
in the oil until they are golden-brown. **2.** Boil the
onions in some water until they are tender. **3.** In a
saucepan mix the vinegar and 4 cups of the water in
which the onions were boiled. Add the spring
onions, cloves, herbs and pepper and boil for 5 minutes. (The amount of vinegar may be varied according to taste.) **4.** Melt the butter in another saucepan
and add the flour to make a roux. Cook for 5 minutes. **5.** Add the strained vinegar water and mix it
into a smooth light sauce. Cook it slowly for 10
minutes. **6.** In a glass or earthenware dish arrange
alternate layers of fish pieces, onions and lemon
slices. **7.** Pour the hot sauce over it. Cool and refrigerate for 12 hours. Serve cold with a tossed salad
and chunks of fresh bread.

Mussels with Mayonnaise

Netherlands

Serves 4

32 mussels, cooked
½ cup home-made mayonnaise (see p. 330)
1 Granny Smith apple, peeled, cored and
finely cubed
1 tablespoon finely chopped, mixed pickles
1 small onion, finely chopped
2 sprigs dill, finely chopped
1 sprig tarragon, or oregano, finely chopped
freshly ground pepper
finely chopped chives for garnish

1. Open the mussels and arrange in portions on individual plates. **2.** Mix the remaining ingredients
and if the sauce is too thick, thin it down with a little
fresh cream. **3.** Put a dob of the sauce on each
mussel and serve sprinkled with the chives.

POULTRY

Roast Chicken
Netherlands

Serves 4

1.5 kg (3 lb) chicken
salt
freshly ground pepper
100 g (3⅓ oz) butter
1½ cups (12 fl oz) concentrated chicken stock (see p. 328), or 4 chicken cubes dissolved in water
1 tablespoon tomato paste

1. Preheat the oven to 180°C (350°F/Gas 4). **2.** Rub the chicken inside and outside with salt and pepper. Heat the butter in a roasting dish and brown the chicken all over. Add the stock. **3.** Place the chicken in the oven and roast it for 1 hour, basting it from time to time. **4.** Remove the chicken from the dish and skim off any excess fat. **5.** Add the tomato paste and mix it with the cooking juice. Season to taste. **6.** Carve the chicken and serve it with the sauce, boiled potatoes, apple sauce and a tossed green salad.

Chicken Oscar
Netherlands

From the Ruitercentrunn Edda Huzid, Voorthuizen.

Serves 4

1.5 kg (3 lb) chicken
50 g (1½ oz) butter
⅔ cup (5 fl oz) cream
½ cup (4 fl oz) dry white wine
1 large onion, chopped
1 teaspoon dried tarragon
1 red pepper (capsicum), cut into thin strips
1 tablespoon chopped fresh rosemary
1 tablespoon tomato purée
4 slices cooked ox tongue

1. In a heavy casserole, sauté the chicken until brown. **2.** Cut the chicken in half lengthwise, remove the back and breast bones and return it to the casserole. **3.** Add the cream, white wine, onions, tarragon, red pepper, rosemary and the tomato purée and season to taste. **4.** Cover and simmer over low heat for 1 hour or until the chicken is tender. **5.** Arrange the two chicken halves on a platter and pour the sauce and vegetables over them. Serve garnished with slivers of ox tongue together with French beans, cauliflowers and sautéed potatoes.

Flemish Chicken Soup with Asparagus
Waterzooie de Volaille aux Asperges de Malines
Belgium

From the Comme chez Soi Restaurant, Brussels. The Comme chez Soi is owned by the famous chef, Wynants, and is the highest rated restaurant in Brussels. With emphasis on Nouvelle Cuisine, here is the chef's version of the famous Belgian dish presented as a main course rather than a soup.

Serves 4

2 × 1.2 kg (2 lb 6 oz) chickens
8 cups (2 litres) strong aromatic chicken stock (see p. 328)
90 g (3 oz) carrots, cut into julienne strips
90 g (3 oz) leeks, white part only, cut into julienne strips
1 kg (2 lb) asparagus, peeled and cut into 3 cm (1¼ inch) pieces
⅔ cup (5 fl oz) cream
salt and pepper
juice of ½ lemon
3 egg yolks, lightly beaten, with 2 tablespoons of cream
chopped parsley

1. Simmer the chickens in the stock for 20 minutes. When cooked, halve each chicken, take out the breast bones and cut each half into 3 or 4 pieces. **2.** Quickly blanch the carrots and leeks in boiling salted water, set aside the vegetables and use the water to cook the asparagus. **3.** Cook the asparagus pieces for about 5 minutes so that they are still firm. **4.** Combine 2 cups (16 fl oz) of the chicken stock and 2 cups (16 fl oz) of the vegetable cooking water and cook briskly to reduce by half. **5.** Add the cream and then the vegetables, season and add the lemon juice. **6.** Add the chicken and heat it. **7.** Just before serving, thicken the liquid with the egg yolks. **8.** Arrange the chicken pieces and vegetables on a plate, mask with the sauce and sprinkle with parsley.

Chicken in White Wine

Coq au Riesling
Luxembourg

From the Hotel Nobilis, Luxembourg.

Serves 4

1 kg (2 lb) chicken, cut into 4
60 g (2 oz) butter
1 carrot, chopped
8 small spring onions (scallions)
2 twigs thyme, finely chopped
2 bay leaves
1 cup (8 fl oz) dry white wine (Riesling)
salt
freshly ground pepper
125 g (4 oz) button mushrooms, sliced
1 cup (8 fl oz) cream
finely chopped parsley

1. In an enamelled cast iron casserole, brown the chicken pieces in the butter. **2.** Add the carrot, onions, thyme, bay leaves and wine. Season to taste. **3.** Cover, bring to the boil, lower the heat and simmer for 35–40 minutes. **4.** Add the mushrooms 15 minutes before the chicken is cooked. **5.** Before serving add the cream and cook for 5 minutes. **6.** Sprinkle with parsley and serve hot.

Spatchcocks Brussels Style

Belgium

Serves 4

4 × 500 g (1 lb) spatchcocks
salt and pepper
4 chicken livers, finely chopped
2 onions, finely chopped
100 g (3⅓ oz) butter
1 kg (2 lb) chicory (witloof) cut into slices
pinch of nutmeg

1. Season the insides of the birds. **2.** Mix the livers with half of the onions and stuff the spatchcocks. **3.** Heat half of the butter in a pan and brown the spatchcocks. **4.** Transfer them to another dish and keep them warm. **5.** Add the remaining butter to the pan and sauté the remaining onions. Add the chicory and the nutmeg. Season to taste and cook the vegetables for 5 minutes. **6.** Place the spatchcocks on top of the vegetables, cover, and cook for 20–30 minutes or until they are tender. While they are cooking occasionally add a little water. **7.** To serve, arrange the vegetables on a preheated platter and place the spatchcocks on top. Boiled, parslied potatoes are traditionally served with this dish.

Duckling with Green Peppercorns

Canette au Poivre Vert
Belgium

From the Restaurant le Vieux Liège, Liège.

Serves 2

1 duckling
1 cup (8 fl oz) water
⅓ cup (2½ fl oz) lime juice
½ cup (4 oz) sugar
1 tablespoon cornflour (cornstarch), optional
salt and pepper
pinch of saffron
1 tablespoon of green peppercorns, rinsed
2 tablespoons fine juliennes of lemon zest, blanched
6 slices of lime
¼ cup (2 fl oz) gin

1. Preheat the oven to 200°C (400°F/Gas 6) and roast the duckling for 1½ hours or until cooked. Set aside and keep hot. Strain the fat off the cooking juices and set them aside. **2.** While the duckling is roasting, prepare the sauce. **3.** Over high heat cook the water, lime juice and sugar until it is lightly caramelised. **4.** Pass it through a fine sieve or tammy. If desired thicken it with the cornflour. Season to taste and colour it with saffron. Add the peppercorns and a tablespoon of the lemon zest. **5.** Arrange the duckling on a serving platter, pour the sauce over it and garnish with the zest of lemon and the lime slices. Just before serving, heat the gin, ignite it and pour it over the duckling. Serve it flaming.

Right: From the finest restaurant in Belgium, Comme chez Soi, Flemish Chicken Soup with Asparagus (see page 301) and Fruit Salad with Meringue.

MEAT

Hotchpotch with Bacon and Vegetables

Hutspot met Klapstuk
Netherlands

From Die Port Van Cleve Restaurant, Amsterdam.

Serves 4

500 g (1 lb) bacon, in one piece
3 cups (24 fl oz) water
2 onions, cut into rings
6 carrots, chopped
1 kg (2 lb) potatoes, peeled and cut into cubes
90 g (3 oz) butter
salt
freshly ground pepper

1. Slowly boil the bacon in the water for 1½ hours. **2.** Add the onions, carrots and potatoes and cook for a further 30 minutes or until the vegetables are cooked. **3.** Remove the bacon and mash the vegetables, add the butter and salt and pepper to taste. **4.** Slice the bacon and serve it on top of the vegetables.

Meatballs

Netherlands

From De Drentse Heerlijkheid, Meppel.

Serves 6

2 slices of bread
300 g (9½ oz) minced beef
salt
freshly ground pepper
pinch of nutmeg

1. Soak the bread in water for a few minutes, squeeze out and mix it thoroughly with the remaining ingredients. **2.** Roll the mixture into 2 cm (¾ inch) balls. **3.** To cook, add them to the Vegetable Soup (p. 296) and simmer them for 10 minutes.

Riesling Pies

Paté au Riesling — Rieslings paste'tchen
Luxembourg

From the Auberge De Coq, Wormeldange.

Serves 4

Filling:
300 g (9½ oz) lean minced pork
350 g (11 oz) veal, cut into small cubes
100 g (3⅓ oz) bacon, diced
150 g (5 oz) cooked ham, diced
4 cups (1 litre) any white wine

Pastry:
2 cups (8 oz) flour
pinch of salt
3 tablespoons lard
20 g (¾ oz) butter
1 egg yolk
water
1 egg mixed with some water
1 tablespoon gelatine

1. Mix all the filling ingredients and marinate for 48 hours. **2.** To make the pastry, rub together the flour, salt, lard and butter, until it has the texture of breadcrumbs. Add a little water to make a firm dough. Cover with a damp cloth and refrigerate for 2 hours. **3.** Preheat the oven to 180°C (350°F/Gas 4). **4.** Roll out the pastry 3 mm (⅛ inch) thick and cut it into rectangles 7.5 × 5 cm (3 × 2 inches). **5.** Place some of the filling lengthwise onto each rectangle, moisten the edges with the egg-water mixture and seal them. Make a hole in the top, brush the pies with the egg wash and bake them in the preheated oven for 15–20 minutes or until the pastry is golden-brown. Let them cool. **6.** In the meantime bring the wine to the boil and reduce it by one-third. **7.** Dissolve the gelatine in some warm water and add it to the reduced wine. **8.** Let it cool and pour it into the pies through the holes on top. Refrigerate until the wine sets to jelly. Serve cold as a snack or with a tossed green salad.

Flemish Meat Stew

Carbonnades Flamandes
Belgium

Serves 4

500 g (1 lb) neck or shin of beef, cut into flat pieces
50 g (1²/₃ oz) lard
3 large onions, thinly sliced
1 tablespoon flour
2 cups (16 fl oz) beer
2 bay leaves
2 sprigs thyme, chopped
3 sprigs parsley, chopped
1 root parsley, sliced (if available)
1 tablespoon sugar
1 tablespoon vinegar
salt
freshly ground pepper
1 slice of bread thickly spread with French mustard

1. In a heavy-bottomed casserole, fry the meat in the lard until sealed and brown. **2.** Remove the meat and set aside. **3.** Put the onions in the casserole and brown them lightly. **4.** Sprinkle them with the flour, stir well. **5.** Add the beer, bay leaves, thyme, parsley and root parsley and cook gently. **6.** Add the sugar, vinegar, salt, pepper and the meat. **7.** Cover and cook slowly for 30 minutes. Add the bread. **8.** Continue cooking for 1 hour or until the meat is tender. **9.** Serve the stew hot with boiled new potatoes.

Pork St Hubert Style

Belgium

Marinating the pork gives it a gamey flavour, hence its dedication to the patron saint of huntsmen.

Serves 4

8 pork chops
½ teaspoon thyme
2 bay leaves
2 sprigs parsley, chopped
½ teaspoon freshly ground pepper
pinch of nutmeg
1 clove garlic, crushed
2 cups (16 fl oz) dry red wine
1 tablespoon olive oil
60 g (2 oz) butter
1 tablespoon French mustard (or to taste)
1 tablespoon redcurrant jelly
1 tablespoon tarragon vinegar
1 tablespoon cornflour (cornstarch)

1. Place the chops in an earthenware or glass dish. **2.** Combine the thyme, bay leaves, pepper, nutmeg, garlic, red wine and olive oil and pour it over the meat. **3.** Marinate it in the refrigerator for 2 days. **4.** Take out the chops, dry and season them, then fry them in half of the butter. Keep them warm. **5.** Pour the marinade into a saucepan and boil it until it reduces by half. **6.** Add the mustard, redcurrant jelly and the desired amount of vinegar. **7.** Dissolve the cornflour in some water and add enough to thicken the sauce. Season to taste and finish it off by adding the remaining butter. **8.** Arrange the chops on a heated serving platter, pour the sauce over and serve the meat with chestnut purée or buttered lentils.

Sirloin with Gin and White Wine

Netherlands

From the Restaurant Edda Huzid, Voorthuizen.

Serves 4

salt
freshly ground pepper
4 slices of sirloin steak approximately 3.75 cm (1½ inches) thick
45 g (1½ oz) butter
1 onion, finely chopped
1 teaspoon tarragon
1 green pepper (capsicum), seeded and chopped
1 leek, white part only, chopped
¼ cup (2 fl oz) gin
¼ cup (2 fl oz) dry white wine

1. Season the meat and sauté it in the butter to your liking. Set aside and keep warm. **2.** To the pan add the onion, tarragon, green pepper and the leek. Sauté briefly until the onions are transparent. **3.** Add the gin and wine and reduce over high heat. Adjust the seasoning. **4.** Serve the meat on preheated plates with the vegetable and cooking juices poured over the meat. At the Edda Huzid this dish is served with fresh broad beans, green beans, cooked pears and sautéed potatoes.

Liver Pâté

Liewerpaté
Luxembourg

Serves 8-10

500 g (1 lb) calf's liver
500 g (1 lb) pork meat
salt
freshly ground pepper
3 sprigs parsley, finely chopped
2 onions, finely chopped
90 g (3 oz) stale bread, soaked in milk
pinch of nutmeg
3 eggs, lightly beaten
3 tablespoons cream
4-6 slices bacon

1. Preheat the oven to 180°C (375°F/Gas 4). **2.** Finely mince the liver and the meat together. **3.** Season, add parsley, onions, the bread squeezed dry, the nutmeg, eggs and cream. Mix everything together thoroughly. **4.** Line a pâté or terrine mould with the bacon, leaving enough to cover the top. **5.** Fill the mould with the mixture and press it firmly down. Cover the top with the remaining bacon. Cover with a lid or aluminium foil and stand the mould in a baking dish filled with water. **6.** Put it into the oven and bake for 1½ hours. Let the pâté cool in the mould and refrigerate for 12-24 hours before serving. Cut the pâté into slices and serve. with a tossed salad and fresh chunky bread.

Sweetbreads in Beer

Ris de Veau à la Bièr
Belgium

Serves 4

4 small sweetbreads
1 tablespoon white wine vinegar
salt
3 sprigs parsley, chopped
150 g (5 oz) button mushrooms, finely chopped
3 shallots, finely chopped
100 g (3⅓ oz) butter
½ cup (2 oz) dry breadcrumbs
freshly ground pepper
2 cups (16 fl oz) beer

1. Soak the sweetbreads for about 4 hours in cold water to which the vinegar has been added. **2.** Boil some water with 1 teaspoon of salt, plunge the sweetbreads in it and simmer for 10 minutes. **3.** Take them out with a slotted spoon and rinse them under cold running water. **4.** Remove all the skin and cut them into large chunks. **5.** Make a stuffing by combining the parsley, mushrooms, shallots, a tablespoon of the butter, the breadcrumbs, salt and pepper. **6.** Place half of the sweetbreads on the bottom of a buttered casserole, cover them with the stuffing and pour half of the beer on top. Put the rest of the sweetbreads on top and add the rest of the beer. **7.** Bring to the boil, cover the casserole and simmer over low heat for 30 minutes. **8.** Just before serving, put the rest of the butter on top of the sweetbreads, cover again and let the butter melt. **9.** Serve hot, straight from the casserole.

Right: Set in the beautiful forests of the Ardenne mountains the Hôtel du Commerce at Wiltz, Luxembourg serves local specialities. Bottom: Apple Cake, left: Pickled Pork, right: Ardenne Ham.

Rabbit with Prunes and Raisins Flemish Style
Belgium

Serves 4

10 prunes with stones removed
100 g (3⅓ oz) raisins
4 tablespoons brandy
4 slices bacon, chopped
flour
2 rabbits, each cut into 6 parts
8 small, pickling-type onions
1 tablespoon flour
1¼ cups (10 fl oz) meat stock (see p. 328)
2 sprigs thyme, chopped
2 teaspoons sugar
1 tablespoon wine vinegar

1. Soak the prunes and raisins in the brandy for 2–3 hours. **2.** Fry the bacon until the fat has melted. Pour off the bacon fat and keep it for frying. Set aside the crisp bacon pieces. **3.** Dip the rabbit pieces in flour. Pour some of the fat into a casserole, heat it and fry the rabbit pieces, a few at a time, until they are brown. **4.** Put the browned rabbit pieces aside. **5.** In the same fat, fry the onions, set them aside. **6.** Sprinkle the flour into the casserole and cook it for 5 minutes without burning it. **7.** Pour in the stock, bring it to the boil and stir it until it is smooth. Add the crisp bacon pieces and the thyme. **8.** Put the rabbit pieces into the casserole, cover with a lid and simmer over low heat for 1 hour. **9.** Add the onions, raisins and prunes, together with the brandy. Cover and cook for a further hour or until the rabbit is tender. **10.** Over high heat, boil the sugar with ¼ cup of water, stirring until the sugar starts to caramelise. Add the vinegar and then pour in the liquid from the casserole. Mix well, season and pour it back into the casserole. Heat it for 2–3 minutes. Serve the rabbit straight from the casserole.

DESSERTS

Farmer Boy's Ice Cream with Eggnog
Netherlands

From the Amsterdam Sonesta Hotel, Amsterdam.

Serves 8–10

1 litre vanilla ice cream, slightly softened
½ cup (3 oz) raisins
4 tablespoons cognac or brandy
6 egg yolks
1½ tablespoons sugar
juice of ½ lemon
wafer biscuits

1. Mix together the ice cream, three-quarters of the raisins (leaving the rest for garnish) and the cognac or brandy. Return the mixture to the freezer for 1 hour. **2.** Before serving the ice cream, cream the yolks and sugar until the sugar has dissolved. Mix in the lemon juice. **3.** Serve the ice cream in dessert glasses and pour some of the eggnog over each portion. Sprinkle with the remaining raisins and decorate with a triangular-shaped wafer biscuit.

Wine Mousse
Mousse au Vin
Netherlands

From the Auberge du Coq, Wormeldange.

Serves 4

2 eggs
4 tablespoons sugar
1 tablespoon cornflour (cornstarch)
¾ cup (6 fl oz) dry white wine

1. Using a whisk or an electric beater, mix together the eggs, sugar and cornflour and beat until the mixture is frothy. **2.** Add the wine and pour the mixture into a saucepan (preferably stainless steel, enamel or glass). **3.** Place it over low heat and continue beating until it is frothy and light. Serve immediately in glass dessert dishes.

Pear Liqueur Soufflé

Soufflé à la Poire William

Belgium

From the Restaurant 'la Fermette', Warre, Durbuy.

Serves 6

2½ cups (20 fl oz) cream
¼ cup (2 oz) icing (confectioners') sugar
8 egg yolks
1 cup (8 oz) sugar
2 tablespoons eau de vie de Poire William (Pear liqueur)
3 pears, halved and poached
½ cup candied almonds

1. Whip the cream with the icing sugar until it thickens. **2.** Cream the yolks with the sugar until they are pale yellow and frothy. **3.** Gradually combine the cream and the yolks. **4.** Add the liqueur. **5.** Pour the mixture into glass dessert bowls and put them in the freezer for 2–3 hours or until frozen firm. **6.** Garnish with the pears, sprinkle with crushed candied almonds and serve with a wafer.

Honey Ice Cream with a Coulis of Blackcurrants

Belgium

From Arno Pankert at the Hotel Zur Post, St. Vith.

Serves 4

4 egg yolks
½ cup (4 oz) sugar
2 cups (16 fl oz) milk
½ vanilla pod or ½ teaspoon vanilla essence
½ teaspoon grated orange or lemon rind
2 tablespoons cream
3 tablespoons honey
½ cup blackcurrants (raspberries or strawberries may be used)
1 tablespoon sugar dissolved in ¼ cup (2 fl oz) boiling water
4 mint leaves

1. Using an electric mixer, cream the egg yolks and sugar until pale yellow and frothy. **2.** Boil the milk with the vanilla pod and let it stand for 10 minutes. **3.** Remove the pod and while whisking the egg yolks pour the hot milk into them. **4.** Return the milk-egg mixture to the saucepan and cook over low heat, stirring constantly, until the mixture is thick enough to coat the back of the spoon. **5.** Add the orange or lemon peel, the cream and honey, cool the mixture and then refrigerate it until it is chilled. **6.** If you have an ice cream churn make the ice cream according to the instructions. If not, the mixture may be frozen, then returned to the mixer or blender, whipped and again returned to the freezer. **7.** To make the coulis, rub the berries through a sieve and add the sugar syrup. Refrigerate. **8.** To serve, float the coulis on the bottom of the plate and put a scoop of ice cream on top. Garnish with the mint leaves.

SCANDINAVIA

I first tried Scandinavian food and enjoyed Scandinavian hospitality some 17 years ago in Copenhagen. Appropriately my first meal was a Smorgasbord prepared at home by the parents of a university friend.

Of Swedish origin, the Smorgasbord can vary from a modest few items served as a first course at home, to an elaborate affair comprising dozens of items and including almost all ingredients of the Scandinavian cooking repertoire.

In my travels through Denmark, Sweden, Norway and Finland, I had the opportunity of tasting many a Smorgasbord which in each place was proudly presented as the 'local speciality'.

I started my tour of Scandinavia in distant Finland, the country of lakes and forests. Helsinki, its capital has a splendid market by the harbourside where most of the ingredients which make up Finnish cooking can be bought: fish of all kinds, from the royal salmon to the modest herring, all types of shellfish and a vast range of lake and river fish. Fresh fruit is abundant, especially berries like raspberries, blueberries and cloudberries. There are crisp, garden-fresh vegetables and bunches of aromatic herbs, especially dill, so popular in local cooking. Finnish cooks make good use of these first class ingredients and put them together enthusiastically in a simple but wholesome cuisine.

Traditional Swedish cooking, despite the sophistication of its people is good, wholesome country cooking. In the past it followed the seasons and special methods were devised to preserve the food for the winter. This is why marinated, pickled, smoked and dried fish and meat form such an important part of Swedish cooking.

The Danish reputation of producing the finest dairy and meat products is well founded. Danish cooks transform them into a wide range of fine dishes. Since earliest days there has been a strong influence of French and German cooking styles. Modern Danish cooking is a happy blending of these influences and traditional farm-house cooking. All parts of the country are close to the sea and there is a fresh supply of fish and seafood available every day.

Among Denmark's most important culinary contributions are the Smorrebrod and Danish Pastry. The Danes love baking and their pastries are eaten throughout the world. The Danish Smorrebrod is a cross between a sandwich and a salad. Designed to be visually pleasing and tantalising to the palate, these open-faced sandwiches are quick, practical, thrifty and of infinite variety.

Of all the Scandinavians, the Norwegians have had the hardest life and have relied to a great extent on the sea for a major part of their nourishment. Here fish and seafood are some of the best that can be found. In the past, farms were self-sufficient and produced a modest but ample supply of seasonal ingredients for a simple country style of cooking. Food had to be stored, and traditional methods of preserving were developed. During autumn and winter, ample game is available including even mouse. Trout and salmon from mountain streams is of exceptional quality. Cod, eaten fresh in season and dried in winter has been part of the Norwegian diet for a thousand years.

Right: Sunrise over one of the many lakes of Finland.

SMORGASBORD

Smoked Eel and Salmon Terrine
Sweden

Chef Torsten Friborg's recipe, as served at Fem Sma Hus in Stockholm.

Makes 1 terrine 10 × 29 × 10 cm (4 × 11½ × 4 inches)

1 kg (2 lb) fillets of pike or snapper
6 egg whites
salt and pepper
juice of 1 lemon
1 tablespoon finely chopped chives
1 onion, finely chopped
30 g (1 oz) butter
100 g (3½ oz) cooked, finely chopped spinach
smoked eel, the length of the terrine dish
10 thin slices smoked salmon
watercress for garnish

1. Preheat the oven to 220°C (425°F/Gas 7). **2.** Using either a food processor, blender or meat grinder, finely grind the fish. **3.** Place the finely minced fish in a bowl and, using a wooden spoon, beat in the egg whites, season and add lemon juice and chives. This can also be done in a food processor. **4.** Melt the butter and sauté the onions until they are soft; add the spinach, season and cook for 8–10 minutes, stirring continuously. If necessary add more butter. **5.** Bone the eel and remove the skin. **6.** Line the terrine with the smoked salmon, keeping some slices for the top. **7.** Place half of the fish stuffing into the dish. **8.** Stuff the eel with the spinach and place it on top, then add the rest of the fish stuffing and cover the top with the salmon slices. **9.** Cover the dish with aluminium foil, place it in a baking dish with hot water and bake it in the preheated oven for 40–50 minutes or until the terrine is cooked. **10.** Cool it and refrigerate for 12 hours. Unmould the terrine carefully on to a platter, slice it and serve with a sauce made of half mayonnaise and half cream. Garnish with watercress.

SOUPS

Cauliflower Soup with Danish Blue Cheese
Denmark

Serves 4–6

1 medium-sized cauliflower
2 onions, finely chopped
2 stalks celery, chopped
4 cups (1 litre) chicken stock (see p. 328)
45 g (1½ oz) butter
2 tablespoons flour
1 cup (8 fl oz) cream
60 g (2 oz) grated Danish blue cheese
salt and freshly ground pepper
chopped parsley
croûtons

1. Trim the cauliflower, break it up into flowerettes and put it in a saucepan. **2.** Add the onions, celery and chicken stock and cook it for 15 minutes. **3.** Save some of the flowerettes for garnish. **4.** Purée the vegetables and liquid in a blender or food processor. **5.** Melt the butter, add the flour and cook the roux for 2–3 minutes without browning it. **6.** Stir in the purée and cream; if too thick add some stock. **7.** Stir in the cheese and adjust seasoning. **8.** Sprinkle with parsley and serve hot with the croûtons.

Spinach Soup
Sweden

Serves 4–6

60 g (2 oz) butter
1 bunch spinach, trimmed and chopped
3¾ cups (30 fl oz) beef or chicken stock (see p. 328)
1 egg yolk
⅓ cup (2½ fl oz) cream
salt and pepper
finely chopped parsley

1. In a large saucepan, heat the butter and sauté the spinach for 8–10 minutes. **2.** Add the stock and simmer for 5 minutes. **3.** Mix the yolk with the cream and stir it into the soup; heat without boiling. **4.** Season to taste and serve sprinkled with parsley.

Cream of Mushroom Soup
Sweden

Serves 4

60 g (2 oz) butter
375 g (12 oz) mushrooms, finely chopped
2 onions, finely chopped
2 tablespoons flour
1¼ cups (10 fl oz) beef or chicken stock (see p. 328)
2½ cups (20 fl oz) milk
3 tablespoons cream
salt and pepper
chopped parsley or dill for garnish

1. In a large saucepan, melt the butter and sauté the mushrooms and onions for 5–8 minutes. **2.** Blend in the flour and gradually add the stock, stirring until smooth. **3.** Add the milk and cream and season to taste. **4.** Simmer for 10 minutes and serve sprinkled with parsley or dill.

Swedish Summer Soup
Sweden

Any vegetables in season may be used, e.g. celery, leeks, parsnips, onions, beans, broccoli etc.

Serves 4

2 carrots, chopped
2 cups (16 fl oz) water
2 cups (16 fl oz) milk
1 teaspoon salt
¼ cauliflower, cut into flowerettes
250 g (8 oz) shelled peas (buy 500 g (1 lb) fresh peas)
100 g (3½ oz) fresh spinach, chopped
1 tablespoon flour
1 egg yolk
3 tablespoons cream
4 sprigs parsley, finely chopped

1. Place the carrots in a saucepan with the water and milk, bring it to the boil, add the salt and simmer for 10 minutes. **2.** Add the cauliflower and peas and simmer for 5 minutes; add the spinach and continue simmering for a further 5 minutes. **3.** Mix the flour, cream and egg yolk together and while stirring gently, add it to the soup. Heat it without boiling. **4.** Serve the soup hot, sprinkled with parsley.

Norwegian Fish Soup
Norway

From Lillehammer Hotel, Lillehammer.

Serves 4-6

Soup
2 tablespoons butter
1 tablespoon flour
6 cups (1.5 litres) hot fish stock
2 tablespoons sour cream
1 carrot, cut into julienne strips
1 leek, white part only, cut into julienne strips
½ onion, finely sliced
1 tablespoon finely chopped chives

Fish Pudding
500 g (1 lb) cod, finely puréed
2 eggs, lightly beaten
2 tablespoons cornflour (cornstarch)
¾ cup (6 fl oz) milk
salt
white pepper
a pinch of nutmeg

1. To make the soup, melt the butter, stir in the flour and cook for 5 minutes without colouring. **2.** Slowly add the stock and cook for a further 5 minutes. **3.** Take it off the heat and stir in the sour cream, add the carrot, leek and onion and cook for 2–3 minutes. **4.** Serve it with 3–4 slices of the Fish Pudding cut into julienne strips, and sprinkled with chives. **5.** To make the Fish Pudding, put the fish purée into a bowl and add the eggs and cornflour, mixing well. Stir in the milk, season and add the nutmeg. **6.** Pour the mixture into a terrine or pâté mould. Cover with foil. Place it in a baking dish half filled with water and bake it in the preheated oven for 1½ hours. Let it cool in the dish before unmoulding it. Slice it and cut it into thin julienne strips. Use the rest sliced as an entrée served with a salad and mayonnaise.

Pea Soup
Finland

From the Hotel Polar, Lamenranta.

Serves 6-8

1½ cups (10 oz) dried peas, soaked
8 cups (2 litres) water
500 g (1 lb) shoulder of pork
salt and freshly ground pepper
2-3 teaspoons mustard

1. In a large saucepan, combine peas, water, pork, salt and pepper. Bring to the boil and simmer over low heat for about 3 hours. **2.** When the meat is cooked, take it out, cut it into small cubes and put it back into the soup. Flavour the soup with mustard according to taste. Serve hot with chunks of fresh rye bread.

VEGETABLES & SALADS

Fredrikshavner Salad
Denmark

From the Hyttefad I and II, Fish Bistro, Trindelen, Fiskerihavnen, Fredrikshavn.

Serves 6–8

250 g (8 oz) cooked mussels
250 g (8 oz) prawns, cooked, shelled and deveined
250 g (8 oz) peas, shelled and lightly cooked
100 g (3½ oz) button mushrooms, sliced
½ small lettuce, shredded
1 cup (8 fl oz) salad oil
¼ cup (2 fl oz) white vinegar
1 teaspoon French mustard
salt
freshly ground pepper
1 clove garlic, crushed
2 hard-boiled eggs, sliced
2 tomatoes, peeled and sliced
chopped chives

1. In a large salad bowl, gently mix the mussels, prawns, peas, mushrooms and lettuce. **2.** To make the dressing, combine the oil, vinegar, mustard, salt, pepper and garlic. Shake well together. **3.** Pour the dressing over the salad and toss gently. **4.** Serve decorated with egg and tomato slices and sprinkled with chives.

Pickled Mushrooms
Finland

500 g (1 lb) button mushrooms, tops only
3 cups (24 fl oz) water
⅓ cup (2 fl oz) white wine vinegar
1⅔ cups (12 oz) caster (powdered) sugar (or to taste)
1 teaspoon salt
20 cloves
20 whole allspice
3 bay leaves
1 piece of ginger (about 2.5 cm (1 inch) long)

1. Put the mushrooms into the water, bring to the boil and simmer for 3 minutes. **2.** Place them in a jar, mix the remaining ingredients with water and pour them into the jar. **3.** Seal the jar and refrigerate for 48 hours before using the mushrooms. **4.** Serve as a relish with meats or as a cocktail snack.

Smoked Fish Salad
Finland

From the Haikko Manor Restaurant.

Serves 4–6

1 cooking apple, peeled, cored and diced
1 fresh cucumber, peeled, seeded and diced
1 salted dill cucumber, diced
125 g (4 oz) shelled cooked peas (250 g (8 oz) in the pod)
125 g (4 oz) button mushrooms, finely sliced
4 fillets smoked fish, cut into pieces
½ cup (4 fl oz) mayonnaise or ½ cup (4 fl oz) French dressing made with lemon juice
3 sprigs dill, finely chopped (for garnish)

1. Mix all the ingredients, garnish with the dill and serve in a salad bowl.

Hasselback Potatoes
Sweden

Serves 4

12 small new potatoes, peeled
salt
freshly ground pepper
60 g (2 oz) butter or margarine
2 tablespoons fresh dry breadcrumbs
4 tablespoons grated cheese

1. Preheat the oven to 230°C (450°F/Gas 8). **2.** Make cuts in each potato about 3 mm (⅛ inch) apart without slicing them right through. **3.** Arrange them cut side up in a buttered baking dish. Sprinkle them with salt and pepper and dot them with butter or margarine. **4.** Bake the potatoes in the preheated oven for 30 minutes. Sprinkle them with a mixture of breadcrumbs and cheese and return them to the oven for a further 30 minutes, or until they are soft and cooked.

Right: Reindeer Stew served with dill cucumbers, mashed potatoes and cranberries at the Hotel Revontuli at Sala, Finland.

SAUCES

Sauces for Marinated Herrings
Denmark

From the Skagen Fiske Restaurant, Skagen, North Jutland.

Makes 1 cup (8 fl oz)

Basic Sauce:
⅔ cup (5 fl oz) sour cream
½–1 teaspoon white wine vinegar
pinch of salt
½ teaspoon sugar
1 teaspoon French mustard
½ small onion, grated

1. Combine all the ingredients. **2.** For variation add to the basic sauce:
Horse-radish Sauce — add 1 tablespoon preserved horse-radish and ½–1 teaspoon sugar.
Dill Sauce — add 1½–2 tablespoons finely chopped dill.
Curry Sauce — add 1–1½ teaspoons curry powder and ½ teaspoon sugar.

Parsley Sauce
Denmark

Makes 2 cups (16 fl oz)

45 g (1½ oz) butter
2 tablespoons flour
1¼ cups (10 fl oz) chicken stock (see p. 328)
2 tablespoons cream
4 sprigs parsley, finely chopped
juice of 1 lemon
salt
freshly ground pepper

1. In a saucepan, melt the butter, add the flour and cook without browning for 2 minutes. **2.** Add the stock and stir until the sauce is smooth. Simmer for 5 minutes, stir in the cream, parsley, lemon juice and season to taste.

Mustard Sauce with Whipped Cream
Denmark

For a less rich sauce, use half whipped cream and half yoghurt.

Makes 1½ cups (12 fl oz)

1 cup (8 fl oz) cream, whipped
1 hard-boiled egg, finely chopped
1 tablespoon French mustard
1 raw egg yolk
juice of 1 lemon
2 sprigs dill, finely chopped
salt
freshly ground pepper

1. Fold all ingredients into the whipped cream.

Mustard Sauce
Sweden

From the Hooks Herrgård, Hok.

Makes 1 cup (8 fl oz)

2 tablespoons French mustard
1 tablespoon caster (powdered) sugar
1½ tablespoons white wine vinegar
pinch of salt
freshly ground pepper or a pinch of white pepper
3 tablespoons vegetable oil
3 tablespoons finely chopped dill

1. Combine all the ingredients except oil and dill. **2.** Stir as for mayonnaise, gradually incorporating the oil. **3.** Mix in the dill and serve with Dill-cured Salmon (Gravlax) (see p. 320).

Finnish Lemon Sauce
Finland

From the Kartanohotelli, Messilä.

Makes 2½ cups (20 fl oz)

90 g (3 oz) butter
2 tablespoons cornflour (cornstarch)
grated rind of 1 lemon
juice of 1 lemon
1¼ cups (10 fl oz) heated fish stock (see p. 328)
1 teaspoon sugar
salt and white pepper
3 egg yolks, lightly beaten

1. In a saucepan, melt the butter, add the cornflour, lemon rind and juice. Cook for 5 minutes, stirring constantly. **2.** Add the fish stock and simmer over low heat for 15 minutes. Season. **3.** Beat in the egg yolks, stir constantly; heat but do not boil. Serve with fish dishes especially Fish Mousse (see p. 318).

Lemon Sauce
Sweden

(for fish dishes)

Serves 6–8

30 g (1 oz) butter
2 tablespoons flour
1¾ cups (15 oz) heated fish stock (see p. 328)
1 cup (8 fl oz) cream
juice of 1 lemon
1 egg yolk, lightly beaten with 2 tablespoons of fish stock
salt and pepper

1. In a saucepan, melt the butter, add the flour and cook it for 2 minutes without browning it. **2.** Gradually whisk in the stock, stir the sauce until it thickens and cook it for 5 minutes. **3.** Mix in the cream and lemon juice. **4.** Stir in the egg yolk mixture, heat the sauce but do not boil it. If too thick add more stock, season to taste. Garnish with chopped dill (optional).

Onion Sauce
Sweden

(for meat and vegetables)

Serves 4–6

45 g (1½ oz) lard or 2 tablespoons melted bacon fat
3 onions, finely chopped
2 tablespoons flour
1¾ cups (14 fl oz) heated meat stock (see p. 328)
⅔ cup (5 fl oz) dry white wine
¼ teaspoon nutmeg
salt and pepper

1. In a saucepan, heat the fat, add the onions and sauté them over low heat until they are soft and transparent. **2.** Add the flour and cook for another 2 minutes. **3.** Add the stock and stir until the sauce is smooth and thick. **4.** Add the wine and nutmeg and season to taste. Simmer for 10 minutes. The sauce may be served as it is or it can be puréed in a blender or food processor or rubbed through a fine sieve.

Piquant Sauce
Sweden

(for pork and veal)

Serves 4

45 g (1½ oz) dripping or lard
½ onion, finely chopped
2 tablespoons flour
1¾ cups (14 fl oz) heated meat stock (see p. 328)
4 tablespoons vinegar
2 sprigs parsley, finely chopped
1 gherkin, finely chopped
1 tablespoon capers
pinch cayenne pepper
salt
1 teaspoon sugar (optional)

1. In a saucepan, melt the fat and sauté the onions until soft and transparent. **2.** Add the flour and cook for 2 minutes without browning. **3.** Gradually stir in the stock, cook for 5 minutes. **4.** Add the vinegar, parsley, gherkin, capers and cayenne pepper. Season to taste and, if desired, add sugar.

Vanilla Sauce
Sweden

Makes 2 cups (16 fl oz)

2–3 egg yolks, lightly beaten
2 cups (16 fl oz) cream
¼ cup (2 oz) caster (powdered) sugar
1 tablespoon cornflour (cornstarch) mixed with 2 tablespoons milk
1 teaspoon vanilla essence

1. In a saucepan, mix 2 or 3 egg yolks (depending on the thickness of sauce required) with the cream. Add sugar and cornflour and whisk it over low heat until the sauce thickens. Do not boil. **2.** Remove from the heat, mix in the vanilla essence. Cool, place plastic wrap over the surface and refrigerate. Serve with desserts or Apple Cake (see p. 325).

FISH

Smoked Fish Pâté
Finland
From the Restaurant Lahden, Seurahuone.

Serves 6

500 g (1 lb) smoked fish fillets
125 g (4 oz) softened butter
2 hard-boiled egg yolks
juice of 1 lemon
pepper
salt (optional)
lemon wedges and sprigs of dill for garnish

1. Purée the fillets in a blender or food processor or put it twice through a fine meat mincer. **2.** With a wooden spoon, whip in the egg yolks, lemon juice and pepper to make a smooth paste. Taste before adding the salt as the smoked fish may be sufficiently salty. **3.** Spoon the mixture into an oiled mould and refrigerate overnight. **4.** Turn out onto a platter, garnish with lemon wedges and dill. Serve with an apple and celery salad and some toast.

Fish Mousse
Finland
From the Kartanohotelli, Messilä.

Serves 6–8

400 g (12½ oz) white fish fillets — snapper,
bream or gemfish
4 egg yolks
60 g (2 oz) white bread, crusts removed
¾ cup (6 fl oz) cream
2 teaspoons salt
½ teaspoon white pepper
4 egg whites, stiffly beaten
2 tablespoons melted butter
dill sprigs and lemon slices for garnish
Lemon Sauce (see p. 317)

1. Preheat the oven to 180°C (350°F/Gas 4). **2.** Pass the fish several times through a mincer or purée it in a food processor. **3.** Beat in the yolks. **4.** Soak the bread in the cream and add salt and pepper. **5.** Add it to the fish and beat until the mixture is well blended. **6.** Gently fold in the egg whites. **7.** Spoon the mixture into a buttered mould, cover it with foil and place it in a baking dish with hot water. (The water should come to two-thirds the height of the mould.) Bake in the preheated oven for 45–55 minutes or until just set. **8.** Cool for 5–10 minutes, loosen the mousse with a spatula and invert on to a serving plate. Garnish with dill sprigs and lemon slices and serve with Lemon Sauce (see p. 317).

Marinated Salmon
Gravlax
Norway
From Hotel Norge, Bergen.

Serves 4–5

2 kg (4 lb) salmon or trout
½ bunch dill, coarsely chopped
1 cup (8 oz) coarse salt
½ cup (4 oz) caster (powdered) sugar
2 tablespoons crushed white peppercorns
¼ cup (2 fl oz) brandy
¼ cup (2 fl oz) vegetable oil

Mustard Sauce:
1 cup (8 fl oz) mayonnaise
1 teaspoon hot mustard
1–2 tablespoons marinade from the fish
2 tablespoons finely chopped dill

1. Fillet the fish, removing all bones. Place one fillet, skin side down in a glass or glazed earthenware dish. **2.** Sprinkle the fillet with the dill. **3.** Mix the salt and sugar together and sprinkle it over the fish. Finally pour over the brandy mixed with the oil. **4.** Place the second fillet on top. Cover with aluminium foil and a rectangular flat board or plate. Put some weights on top, such as cans of food, and refrigerate for 2 to 3 days. **5.** Wipe the fillets clean, carve them into thin slices and serve with the mustard sauce. **6.** To make the mustard sauce, mix the ingredients together and put the sauce into a bowl or sauce boat. **7.** In Norway it is either served as part of a smorgasbord or as a main course dish with dill potatoes, Norwegian flat bread, butter and mustard sauce.

Right: *Well-known Swedish food writer Åke Söderqvist at his restaurant, the Strand at Vaxholm. Clockwise from bottom centre: smoked herrings; caviar-marinated herrings; marinated fried herrings; onion-marinated herrings; marinated smoked herrings; home-made bread; crayfish-marinated herrings; mustard-marinated herrings, spice-anchovy marinated herrings.*

Dill-cured Salmon

Gravlax
Sweden

From the Hooks Herrgård, Hok.

1–1.5 kg (2–3 lb) salmon or large trout, middle cut
¼ cup (2 oz) coarse salt
¼ cup (2 oz) caster (powdered) sugar
1 tablespoon white pepper, coarsely chopped
1 large bunch dill, coarsely chopped

1. Cut the fish into two lengthwise and remove the backbone and all other bones. Cut it across into approximately 10 cm (4 inch) pieces. **2.** In a bowl, mix together the salt, sugar and pepper. **3.** Rub the fish with this mixture. **4.** Place half of the pieces of fish, skin side down, in a glass or enamelled dish and sprinkle on top any of the remaining salt mixture. **5.** Cover the fish with the dill and place the other half of the fish pieces on top, skin side up. **6.** Cover with aluminium foil and weight it down evenly (use a chopping board and tins of food as weights). **7.** Refrigerate for 24 hours, turning the fish over several times. **8.** To serve, remove the dill, shake off excess salt etc. and cut the fish into slices; reserve the skin. Arrange the slices on a platter. **9.** Sauté the skin in hot butter, roll it up and serve it with the fish. Garnish with fresh dill and lemon wedges and serve with Mustard Sauce (see p. 316).

Freshwater Crayfish with Dill

Sweden

Serves 4

10 cups (2.5 litres) water
1 large bunch dill
¼ cup (2 oz) coarse salt
1 tablespoon sugar
about 30 live crayfish (yabbies)
fresh dill for garnish

1. In a large saucepan, combine the water, dill, salt and sugar and boil it for 10 minutes. **2.** Drop the crayfish into the boiling water, cover the pot, bring to the boil again and cook for 7 minutes. **3.** Cool the crayfish in the water, leave them in the water and refrigerate them overnight. **4.** To serve, take the crayfish out of the water, arrange them on a serving platter and decorate them with sprigs of dill. **5.** Traditionally, this dish is served with hot buttered toast and copious amounts of chilled aquavit and beer chasers!

Slethvar Fillets au Gratin

Denmark

(Any flat fish such as sole or flounder may be used)
From the Hyttefad I and II, Fish Bistro, Trindelen, Fiskerihavnen, Fredrikshavn.

Serves 4–6

24 asparagus spears
½ cup (4 fl oz) water
8–12 flat fish fillets
1 onion, finely chopped
¼ cup (2 fl oz) dry white wine
salt
freshly ground pepper
15 g (½ oz) butter
2 teaspoons flour
½ cup (4 fl oz) hot fish stock (see p. 328)
¼ cup (1 oz) grated cheese

1. Preheat the oven to 200°C (400°F/Gas 6). **2.** Boil the asparagus spears in approximately ½ cup of water. Set the asparagus aside and save the water. **3.** Place the fillets in a greased ovenproof dish. **4.** Add the onion, wine, salt and pepper. **5.** Melt the butter, add the flour and cook it without browning. Add enough stock and asparagus water to make a medium thick sauce. **6.** Pour half of the sauce over the fish. **7.** Cover the dish with aluminium foil and cook it in the oven for 8 minutes. **8.** Remove from the oven, arrange the asparagus on top of the fish, cover it with the remaining sauce and sprinkle the cheese on top. **9.** Return to the oven to brown the cheese. **10.** Serve with boiled new potatoes.

Oda's Fish Rissoles

Denmark

From the Hyttefad I and II, Fish Bistro, Trindelen Fiskerihavnen, Fredrikshavn.

Serves 6

1 kg (2 lb) cod fillets, minced
1 onion, finely chopped
250 g (8 oz) pork fat, minced
4 eggs, lightly beaten
1¼ cups (5 oz) potato flour
salt
freshly ground pepper
milk
butter for frying

1. In a bowl, thoroughly combine all ingredients, except the butter, to make a mixture of firm consistency. **2.** Shape it into small flat rissoles, dust them with flour and fry them in the butter until golden-brown all over.

POULTRY & GAME BIRDS

Boiled Chicken with Horse-radish Sauce
Denmark

Serves 4–6

Chicken:
1 × 1.5 kg (3 lb) chicken
8 cups (4 litres) water
1 onion, chopped
3 stalks celery, chopped
2 carrots, sliced
6 peppercorns
2 bay leaves
1 tablespoon chopped fresh herbs
3 sprigs parsley, chopped

Sauce:
30 g (1 oz) butter
1½ tablespoons flour
1¾ cups (14 fl oz) hot chicken stock (see p. 328)
⅔ cup (5 fl oz) cream
4 tablespoons preserved grated horse-radish
salt
freshly ground pepper
4 sprigs parsley, finely chopped

Boiled Chicken: 1. Place the chicken, water and the remaining ingredients in a saucepan and simmer over low heat for 1 hour. Cool the chicken in the stock. **2.** Carve the chicken and set aside, strain the liquid from the stock and save it for the sauce. Refrigerate or deep freeze the rest for future use.

Sauce: 1. Melt the butter, add the flour and cook the roux for 2 minutes without browning it. **2.** Gradually add the stock and simmer for 5 minutes. **3.** Add the cream and cook for a further 5 minutes. **4.** Add the horse-radish, salt and pepper to taste. **5.** Add the chicken to the sauce and serve hot, sprinkled with parsley.

Duckling with 'Brown' Cabbage
Finland

From the 71 Nyhavn Hotel, Copenhagen.

Serves 4

2 ducklings
30 g (1 oz) butter
salt
freshly ground pepper
250 g (8 oz) stoneless prunes
4 Granny Smith apples, peeled, cored and cut into 8 segments
½ cup (4 oz) brown sugar
1 small cabbage, roughly chopped

1. Preheat the oven to 180°C (350°F/Gas 4). **2.** Brown the ducklings in the butter and season them inside and out. **3.** Stuff the ducklings with a mixture of prunes and apples. **4.** Place them on a rack in a baking dish and cook in the oven for about 1½–2 hours, or according to taste. **5.** After the first 30–45 minutes of cooking, remove 1 cup (8 fl oz) of the duck fat. **6.** Heat the fat in a saucepan and add the sugar and cabbage. Season it, cover with a lid and cook gently over low heat for 1 hour, stirring from time to time. **7.** To serve, carve the birds, arrange the meat on a serving platter and surround with the stuffing. Serve the cabbage separately. Wash it all down with Danish beer and icy cold aquavit.

Wood Pigeon à la Rebild
Denmark

From the Rold Stor Kro, Rebild National Park.

Serves 4

4 young pigeons
30 g (1 oz) butter
6 juniper berries, crushed
2 cooking apples, peeled, cored and chopped
1 onion, chopped
salt
freshly ground pepper
4 cups (1 litre) stock or water
1 cup (8 fl oz) cream
1 tablespoon redcurrant jelly

1. In a heavy casserole, brown the pigeons, add the juniper berries, apples, onions, salt and pepper and sauté until the onions are soft and transparent. **2.** Add stock or water, cover the casserole and gently braise over low heat for 1 hour. **3.** Remove the pigeons and keep them warm. **4.** Rub all the cooking juices (including the solids) through a fine sieve. **5.** Add the cream and reduce to 2–3 cups (16–24 oz) by boiling rapidly. **6.** Add and dissolve the jelly and if necessary adjust the seasoning. **7.** Pour some of the sauce over the birds and the rest in a sauce-boat. Serve with Waldorf salad and halved apples, blanched and topped with redcurrant jelly.

MEAT

Fillet of Beef Ataman
Finland

From the Restaurant Lahden, Seurahuone.

Serves 6

1 kg (2 lb) fillet of beef
30 g (1 oz) butter
salt
white pepper
200 g (6½ oz) salted dill cucumbers, cut in julienne strips
200 g (6½ oz) green peppers (capsicums), cut in julienne strips
2 cups (16 fl oz) sour cream
1 clove garlic, crushed

1. Preheat the oven to 220°C (425°F/Gas 7). **2.** Brown the fillet in hot butter, season it and bake it in the preheated oven for 10 minutes. **3.** Take the meat out of the oven and allow it to cool. **4.** Turn the oven temperature up to 250°C (500°F/Gas 10). **5.** Cut the fillet into thick slices and put them back into the baking dish. **6.** Place the cucumbers and peppers on top of the meat. **7.** Mix the cream with the garlic and season it with salt and pepper. **8.** Pour the cream over the meat and return it to the oven for 5–6 minutes. **9.** Serve with paprika flavoured rice and a green salad.

Biff à la Lindström
Sweden

From the Hotel Witt, Kalmar.

Serves 4

2 onions, finely chopped
15 g (½ oz) butter
2 boiled potatoes, mashed
3 slices pickled beetroot, chopped
400 g (13 oz) finely minced lean beef
2 eggs
1 tablespoon chopped capers
salt
freshly ground pepper
butter for frying

1. Sauté the onions in the butter until soft. **2.** Combine all ingredients and work them into a smooth mixture. **3.** Shape it into rissoles and fry them in plenty of butter. **4.** Serve with boiled potatoes and a salad.

Karelian Style Lamb
Ruokolahden Särä
Finland

From the Valtionhotelli, Imatra.
A särä is a dish carved from aspen (poplar) wood, which is soaked in salt water and the meat is cooked in it. If a särä is not available the meat may be placed directly onto the wire shelf of the oven, with a baking dish on the shelf below in which the vegetables are cooked. The meat juices baste the vegetables. Traditionally, Potato Bread (see p. 326), swede pies and home-made beer (kalja) in juniper mugs are served with the dish.

Serves 6

1.5 kg (3 lb) boned leg or shoulder of lamb
salt and white pepper
1–2 cloves garlic, crushed
6 turnips, sliced
6–8 potatoes, unpeeled
2 cups (16 fl oz) meat stock (see p. 328)

1. Preheat the oven to 150°C (300°F/Gas 2). **2.** Season the meat with salt and pepper and rub it with garlic. Roll it up and tie it with string. **3.** Place the meat on the upper wire shelf of the preheated oven. **4.** Place the turnips and potatoes in a baking dish on the shelf below. **5.** Roast the meat for 1½–2 hours or until it is done but not overcooked. **6.** Take the meat out of the oven and let it stand for 10 minutes before carving it in slices. **7.** Arrange the meat on a wooden platter, pour the cooking juices over it and surround it with the vegetables. **8.** Serve with Potato Bread (see p. 326) and swede pies.

Lamb Hotpot
Finland

From the Wanha Laamanni, Porvoo.

Serves 8

2 kg (4 lb) shoulder of lamb, cut into large cubes
750 g (1½ lb) neck of pork, cut into large cubes
1 cup (4 oz) flour
90 g (3 oz) margarine
1–2 cloves garlic, crushed
salt
freshly ground pepper
1 teaspoon crushed mint leaves
1 tablespoon chopped chervil or 4 sprigs parsley, chopped
2 tablespoons tomato purée
6 cups (1.5 litres) water

1. Dust the meat in the flour, heat the margarine in a large casserole and brown the meat. **2.** Add garlic, salt and pepper, mint, chervil or parsley, tomato purée and water. **3.** Cover, bring slowly to the boil and simmer for about 1½–2 hours or until the meat is tender. Season to taste and serve with country style cheese, boiled rice and a seasonal salad.

Mutton and Cabbage Stew
Norway

From Restaurant Ullensvang, Loftus.

Serves 6

1 kg (2 lb) mutton or lamb (from the leg)
1 kg (2 lb) cabbage
1 small head Savoy cabbage, sliced
3 cups (24 fl oz) water
2 teaspoons salt
12 black peppercorns, wrapped in a piece of cheese cloth
3 sprigs parsley, chopped

1. Cut the meat into cubes. **2.** Parboil the cabbage, quarter it, cut out the core and slice it. **3.** In a lidded casserole arrange layers of meat and cabbage and lightly season each layer. Place the peppercorns in the casserole, cover it tightly and simmer over low heat for 2 hours. **4.** Add the Savoy cabbage and cook for a further 30 minutes. Sprinkle with parsley and serve hot. To obtain the best flavour, reheat this three times before serving it.

Veal in Dill Sauce
Denmark

Serves 6

1.5 kg (3 lb) rolled shoulder of veal
30 g (1 oz) butter
3 bay leaves
10 peppercorns
1 tablespoon dried dill
salt
water

Sauce:
45 g (1½ oz) butter
2¼ tablespoons flour
1 cup (8 fl oz) stock (from cooking the veal)
1 cup (8 fl oz) sour cream
1 bunch dill, finely chopped, or 1 tablespoon dried dill
freshly ground pepper

1. In a lidded, heavy casserole brown the veal on all sides in the butter. **2.** Add the bay leaves, peppercorns, dill, salt and enough water to just cover the meat. **3.** Cover the casserole and simmer it over low heat for 1½ hours. Leave the meat in the stock until ready to carve. **4.** To make the sauce, melt the butter, add the flour and cook without browning for 2 minutes. **5.** Add the stock and stir it until smooth. Add the cream, dill (keeping some for garnish), salt and pepper. Cook for 5 minutes; if too thick add more stock. **6.** Carve the meat into slices, arrange them on a platter and pour the sauce over. **7.** Serve with boiled potatoes sprinkled with dill.

Swedish Meat Balls
Sweden

From the Hooks Herrgård, Hok.

Serves 4

15 g (½ oz) butter
1 onion, finely chopped or grated
1½ tablespoons breadcrumbs
1 teaspoon cornflour (cornstarch)
½ cup (4 fl oz) cream
¼ cup (2 fl oz) milk or water
250 g (8 oz) finely minced lean beef
60 g (2 oz) finely minced shoulder of pork
salt
freshly ground pepper
butter for frying

1. Melt the butter and sauté the onion until it is soft and transparent. **2.** In a bowl, mix together the onions, breadcrumbs, cornflour, cream and milk or water. Let it stand for 1 hour. **3.** Add the meat and season to taste. Beat the mixture with a wooden spoon until all ingredients are well combined and the mixture is smooth and light. **4.** Shape it into 2½ cm (1 inch) balls. **5.** Fry them in plenty of butter until golden-brown. Set them aside. **6.** To make the sauce, pour off any excess fat, add the flour, cook for 2 minutes and stir in the cream; season. **7.** Return the meat balls to the pan, cover with a lid and gently simmer for 10 minutes.

Swedish Hash
Sweden

From the Hooks Herrgård, Hok.

Serves 4–6

6 potatoes, cooked in their jackets, peeled and cut into small dice
60 g (2 oz) butter
2 cups diced, fried or boiled leftover meat
3 onions, chopped
1 cup diced ham
salt
freshly ground pepper
4 sprigs parsley, chopped
sliced pickled beetroot
4–6 egg yolks or fried eggs

1. Fry the potatoes in the butter until golden-brown. Put them in a casserole and keep them warm. **2.** In the same butter, fry the meat, add it to the potatoes. **3.** If necessary add more butter, sauté the onions and put them in the casserole. **4.** Add the ham, salt and pepper. Mix all the ingredients together and heat for a few minutes. **5.** Transfer to a heated serving platter and sprinkle with parsley. **6.** Serve with pickled beetroot and either raw egg yolks (which each person mixes into their portion) or fried eggs.

DESSERTS

Red Fruit Pudding
Denmark

From the 71 Nyhavn Hotel, Copenhagen.

Serves 6–8

750 g (1½ lb) (fresh or thawed) one or a
mixture of the following: raspberries,
strawberries, rhubarb, redcurrants
water
1 cup (8 oz) plus 2 tablespoons sugar
1–2 tablespoons cornflour (cornstarch) to each
2½ cups (20 fl oz) juice
¼ cup (1 oz) slivered almonds
cream

1. Place the fruit in a saucepan and add enough
water to cover. **2.** Bring slowly to the boil and simmer over low heat for 5–8 minutes. **3.** Purée the
fruit and juice through a sieve. **4.** Dissolve 1 cup
(8 oz) sugar in the juice without boiling it.
5. Measure the juice, dissolve the appropriate
amount of cornflour in a little water and stir it into
the juice. **6.** Return it to the pan and simmer it for
2 minutes, stirring constantly. Do not boil it and do
not make it too thick. **7.** Pour the jelly into a glass
serving dish or into individual bowls. Sprinkle the
top with the almonds and the remaining sugar.
8. Serve cold with the cream.

June Dessert with Rhubarb
Norway

Serves 6–8

5½ cups (1 lb) ground almonds
2½ cups (1 lb 2 oz) caster (powdered) sugar
3 egg whites
500 g (1 lb) peeled and cubed rhubarb
½ cup (4 oz) sugar
3 tablespoons water
4 bananas, sliced
½ cup (4 fl oz) cream, whipped

1. Preheat the oven to 140°C (275°F/Gas 1). **2.** Mix
the almonds, caster sugar, and egg whites until
smooth. **3.** Pour the mixture into a greased round
baking dish and bake for 45 minutes or until the
cake is cooked. **4.** Stew the rhubarb, sugar and water
over low heat. **5.** Cover the cake with rhubarb and
garnish with the banana slices and the whipped
cream.

Creamed Rice Pudding
Denmark

Serves 6–8

2½ cups (20 fl oz) milk
2 tablespoons caster (powdered) sugar
¾ cup (4 oz) long grain rice
½ cup (2 oz) blanched, chopped almonds
½ cup (4 fl oz) dry sherry
1½ teaspoons vanilla essence
¾ cup (6 fl oz) cream, whipped

1. In a large saucepan, bring the milk to the boil,
add the sugar and rice, stir, reduce heat to low and
cook uncovered for 25 minutes. The rice should be
soft but not mushy. **2.** Transfer the rice to a bowl
and when cold, add the sherry and vanilla essence
and fold in the cream. Serve chilled, either plain or
with a cold cherry or raspberry sauce.

Danish Apple Cake Dessert
Denmark

Serves 4

750 g (1½ lb) cooking apples, peeled, cored
and diced
75 g (2½ oz) butter
2 cups (6 oz) crumbed biscuits or macaroons
¼ cup (2 fl oz) sweet sherry
¾ cup (6 fl oz) cream, whipped with some
sugar and a few drops of your favourite
liqueur
redcurrant jelly

1. Cook the apples in a saucepan with a tablespoon
of water until they are soft. Purée the apples and
leave them to cool. If desired, the purée may be
sweetened; however, if sweet crumbs are used it is
best to leave the apples tart. **2.** To serve, arrange
alternate layers of apple purée and crumbs, which
have been sprinkled with sherry, and top it off with
whipped cream and spoonfuls of redcurrant jelly.

Note: Any fresh berries in season, such as
strawberries, raspberries or blackberries, may be
used instead of apples.

Swedish Apple Cake
Sweden

Serves 6

100 g (3½ oz) butter
½ cup (4 oz) sugar
2 egg yolks, lightly beaten
¾ cup (3 oz) ground almonds
grated rind of ½ lemon
juice of ½ lemon
3 egg whites, stiffly beaten
6 apples, peeled and thinly sliced

1. Preheat the oven to 200°C (400°F/Gas 6). 2. Cream the butter and the sugar until pale yellow and the sugar is dissolved. 3. Stir in the yolks, almonds, lemon rind and juice. 4. Fold in the egg whites. 5. Place the apples on a well-buttered shallow baking dish and spread the batter over. 6. Bake in the preheated oven for 15–20 minutes. Serve warm as dessert with Vanilla Sauce (see p. 317).

Frozen Strawberry Cream
Sweden

Serves 4-6

½ cup (4 oz) sugar
4 tablespoons water
3 egg yolks, lightly beaten
500 g (1 lb) strawberries
juice of ½ lemon
1¼ cups (10 fl oz) cream, stiffly beaten

1. In a saucepan, combine the sugar and water and cook over medium heat for 5 minutes. 2. Put the yolks in a bowl and while beating with a whisk add the sugar syrup. 3. Place the bowl in a saucepan with simmering water and whisk until the mixture thickens. Do not boil. Remove from the heat and continue beating until it cools. 4. Set aside a few strawberries for garnish, purée the rest and mix them into the custard. Add lemon juice and fold in the cream. 5. Pour the mixture into ice cube trays and freeze. 6. Remove from the freezer a few minutes before serving, turn it out on to a chilled platter, cut it into portions and serve garnished with strawberries.

Blackcurrant Dessert
Sweden

Serves 4-6

3 egg yolks
½ cup (4 oz) caster (powdered) sugar
2 cups (4 oz) blackcurrants, fresh, or frozen and defrosted
4 teaspoons gelatine, dissolved in ¼ cup (2 fl oz) hot water
3 egg whites, stiffly beaten

1. Cream the yolks and the sugar until light yellow and the sugar is dissolved. 2. Crush half of the berries and keep the rest whole. Set aside 2 tablespoons of the whole berries for garnish. Mix the rest into the yolks. 3. Cool the gelatine to room temperature and stir it into the berry mixture. 4. Fold in the egg whites, spoon it into glass serving bowls and refrigerate. 5. Serve chilled, garnished with some berries.

Berry Juice Pudding
Kissel
Finland

Serves 6-8

4 cups (1 litre) berry or fruit juice
sugar to taste
4 tablespoons cornflour (cornstarch)

1. Mix the juice and sugar, bring to the boil. 2. Take off the heat. Mix the cornflour with a little water. 3. Stir it into the juice, heat until the mixture thickens and when it comes to the boil take it off the heat. 4. Pour it into one large glass serving dish or into individual bowls. Sprinkle with sugar and allow it to cool. 5. The pudding may be chilled and served with either milk, fresh or whipped cream.

Berry Foam
Finland

From the Wahna Laamanni, Porvoo.

Serves 4-6

½ cup (4 fl oz) lightly sweetened cream, whipped
2 cups (8 fl oz) crushed mixture of berries in season
½ cup (2 oz) crushed biscuit crumbs
8 scoops vanilla ice cream
16-24 whole berries for garnish

1. Mix the cream, crushed berries and crumbs. 2. Place the ice cream in individual bowls, cover with the cream mixture and serve garnished with the berries.

CAKES & PASTRY

Tosca Cake

Denmark

Makes one 20–25 cm (8–10 inch) round cake

Cake:
125 g (4 oz) soft butter
½ cup (4 oz) caster (powdered) sugar
grated rind of 1 lemon
2 eggs, lightly beaten
¾ cup (3 oz) flour
½ teaspoon baking powder

Topping:
90 g (3 oz) butter
⅓ cup (3 oz) sugar
½ cup (2 oz) chopped almonds
1 tablespoon flour
1 tablespoon cream

1. Preheat the oven to 160°C (325°F/Gas 3). **2.** Cream the butter and sugar until light and fluffy. **3.** Add lemon rind and gradually incorporate the eggs. **4.** Mix in the flour and baking powder. **5.** Pour the mixture into a greased springform tin and bake in the preheated oven for 20 minutes or until the mixture sets. **6.** To prepare the topping, melt the butter, stir in the rest of the ingredients and bring it to the boil. **7.** Pour the topping over the cake and return it to the oven for 15–20 minutes or until golden-brown. **8.** Serve lukewarm with fresh cream.

Potato Bread

Finland

From the Valtionhotelli, Imatra.

Makes 8–12 loaves

1 kg (2 lb) mashed potatoes
1¾ cups (7 oz) flour
90 g (3 oz) softened butter
salt
2 tablespoons melted butter

1. Preheat the oven to 200°C (400°F/Gas 6). **2.** Mix the potatoes, flour, butter and salt and knead into a smooth dough. **3.** Shape the dough into loaves about 0.5 cm (¼ inch) thick and 15 cm (6 inches) wide. **4.** Place them on buttered baking sheets and bake them in the preheated oven for about 20 minutes. **5.** Brush with melted butter before serving them.

Cinnamon Layer Cake

Denmark ·

Layer cakes with a variety of fillings are very popular in Denmark. The contrast between the crisp, brittle layers of pastry and the creamy filling is very appealing.

Makes six 20 cm (8 inch) diameter layers

500 g (8 oz) soft butter
1 cup (7 oz) caster (powdered) sugar
2 cups (8 oz) flour
2 teaspoons cinnamon
100 g (3½ oz) dark chocolate
2 teaspoons butter
1¼ cups (10 fl oz) cream, whipped and refrigerated
1 cup (4 oz) slivered almonds

1. Preheat the oven to 220°C (425°F/Gas 7). **2.** To make the pastry, cream the butter and sugar until the sugar is dissolved and the mixture is light and fluffy. **3.** Mix the flour and cinnamon together and incorporate it into the mixture. Knead the dough into a ball. **4.** Divide it into 6 parts. **5.** Roll each between two layers of waxed paper into 20 cm (8 inch) rounds. **6.** Remove the top layer of paper, prick the surface of the rounds with a fork and bake on a baking sheet for 6–8 minutes or until golden-brown. Allow the layers to cool and remove the paper when assembling the cake. **7.** In a double boiler, melt the chocolate and stir in the butter. **8.** Mix ½ cup of the almonds into the whipped cream. **9.** Assemble the cake with alternate layers of pastry and cream. **10.** Coat the outside of the cake with the melted chocolate and sprinkle the top and sides with the remaining almonds. Serve immediately.

Almond Tarts

Sweden

Makes 36

½ cup (4 oz) sugar
200 g (6½ oz) butter or margarine
1 cup (3½ oz) ground almonds
a few drops bitter almond essence
1¾ cups (7 oz) flour
2 tablespoons cornflour
cream, whipped and sweetened
berries in season

1. Preheat the oven to 200°C (400°F/Gas 6). **2.** Cream the sugar and butter or margarine until the sugar is dissolved. **3.** Mix in the remaining ingredients and refrigerate the dough for 1–2 hours. **4.** Roll it out and line small straight-sided or fluted tart moulds with a thin layer of the dough. **5.** Bake in the preheated oven for 10–15 minutes. **6.** Let the cases cool and remove them from the moulds. **7.** Serve them filled with sweetened whipped cream and fruit or berries in season.

Right: *Strawberry Shortcake from the Hotel Lahti in Seurabone, Finland.*

BASIC RECIPES

Beef Stock

Meat stock is very useful in the preparation of soups and sauces; the quantity given here may seem excessive, but it can be deep frozen and kept at hand for future use.

Makes 16 cups (4 litres)

2 kg (4 lb) shin beef on the bone
2 kg (4 lb) veal knuckle (cut into 5 cm (2 in) pieces)
4 pigs trotters
2 kg (4 lb) veal and beef bones (preferably marrow bones, sawn into pieces)
60 g (2 oz) dripping
2 cups carrots, chopped
2 cups onions, chopped
1½ cups celery, chopped
1 bouquet garni of parsley, thyme, marjoram
4 bay leaves
12 black peppercorns
24 cups (6 litres) water

1. In a large saucepan, place all ingredients, except the bouquet garni, peppercorns and water and cook gently, stirring occasionally, until the meat, bones and vegetables have browned slightly. **2.** Add the bouquet garni and peppercorns. **3.** Add the water and slowly bring to the boil. **4.** Simmer 6–8 hours until the liquid is reduced to 16 cups (4 litres). **5.** Cool and strain through muslin. Skim off the fat by refrigerating the liquid overnight and removing the congealed fat the next day.

Brown Roux

Makes 1 cup (8 fl oz)

125 g (4 oz) butter
¾ cup (3 oz) flour

1. Melt the butter in a heavy-bottomed saucepan. **2.** Take it off the heat and, stirring with a wooden spoon or whisk, add the sifted flour. Stir until the mixture is smooth. **3.** Return to the heat and, stirring constantly, cook until the roux has a light brown colour.

Chicken Stock

Makes 10 cups (2.5 litres)

1.5 kg (3 lb) boiling chicken with giblets
8–12 cups (2–3 litres) water
2 carrots, sliced
1 turnip, sliced
3 stalks celery, sliced
2 onions, unpeeled and halved
½ bunch parsley, roughly chopped
1 sprig thyme, chopped
6 peppercorns
3 bay leaves

1. In a large saucepan combine all the ingredients, making certain that the heart, stomach and liver have been properly cleaned. **2.** Bring slowly to the boil and continue to simmer over low heat for 2–2½ hours. **3.** Let all the ingredients cool in the stock, then strain, refrigerate and degrease it. **4.** Discard the vegetables but keep the chicken. Remove the meat from the bones. It can be either chopped and used in a chicken soup or minced and made into chicken croquettes. **5.** Use the stock in the preparation of soups and sauces. It may be refrigerated and will keep for 3–4 days or frozen when it may be kept for months.

Fish Stock

Makes approximately 1¾ cups (14 fl oz)

1 kg (2 lb) fish trimmings, such as fish heads, bones, fresh or cooked shellfish leftovers
1 onion, thinly sliced
6–8 parsley stems (not the leaves; they will darken the stock)
1 teaspoon lemon juice
¼ teaspoon salt
1 cup (8 fl oz) dry white wine
cold water to cover

1. Place all the ingredients in a large heavy saucepan. **2.** Bring it to the boil, skim, and simmer gently for 30 minutes. **3.** Strain the stock through a fine sieve and correct the seasoning. **4.** Fish stock may be refrigerated or deep frozen.

Brown Sauce

This is the basis for many other sauces and it can be refrigerated and deep-frozen for future use.

½ cup bacon, chopped
½ cup carrots, chopped
½ cup onions, chopped
½ cup celery, chopped
1 tablespoon chopped thyme
2 bay leaves
¾ cup (6 fl oz) dry white wine
1 cup (8 fl oz) brown roux
1 cup (8 fl oz) concentrated tomato purée
16 cups (4 litres) hot beef stock

1. In a large saucepan, fry the bacon, add the vegetables and cook them gently until lightly coloured. **2.** Add the thyme and bay leaves. **3.** Add the wine, then the roux and stir. **4.** Add the tomato purée and gradually stir in the stock, making sure there are no lumps. **5.** Stir frequently, while bringing the sauce to the boil, so that it does not stick to the bottom of the saucepan. **6.** Place the saucepan on the flame in such a way that it is just under one edge of the saucepan. **7.** Simmer 3–4 hours, stirring frequently and occasionally removing the spume which accumulates on the surface on the opposite edge to the flame. **8.** The sauce should be completed when it reduces to 8 cups (2 litres) of liquid. **9.** Sieve and cover the surface with plastic to prevent formation of a skin.

Béchamel Sauce

White sauce

Makes 2 cups (16 fl oz)

2 cups (16 fl oz) milk
½ bay leaf
sprig of thyme
1 small onion, peeled
pinch of nutmeg
60 g (2 oz) butter
½ cup (2 oz) flour
salt and pepper

1. Bring the milk to the boil with the bay leaf, thyme, onion and nutmeg. **2.** Remove the mixture from the heat and leave it to infuse for 15 minutes. **3.** In a clean saucepan melt the butter, add the flour and stir well to make a roux. **4.** Strain the milk into the roux, whisking well all the time until it is thick and creamy. **5.** Allow to simmer gently for 3 minutes, stirring constantly, to dissipate any taste of flour. **6.** Add salt and pepper to taste.

Velouté Sauce

Makes 2½ cups (20 fl oz)

60 g (2 oz) butter
½ cup (2 oz) flour
2½ cups (20 fl oz) white stock (may be chicken, veal, or fish for a fish Velouté)
salt and white pepper
4 small mushrooms, wiped clean and thinly sliced (optional)

1. Melt the butter in a heavy saucepan. **2.** Add the flour and cook, stirring constantly, for a few minutes to form a roux. **3.** Add the boiling stock, salt and pepper, and cook for 2 minutes, stirring constantly with a wire whisk. **4.** Add the mushrooms, and cook slowly, stirring occasionally. **5.** When the sauce is sthick, yet light and creamy, it is ready. **6.** Strain through a fine sieve.

Sauce Béarnaise

Makes approximately 1½ cups (12 fl oz)

1 teaspoon dried tarragon
2 teaspoons dried chervil
1 tablespoon chopped spring onions (scallions)
2 peppercorns, crushed
2 tablespoons white wine vinegar
⅔ cup (5 fl oz) dry white wine
3 egg yolks
1 tablespoon water
250 g (8 oz) soft butter, cut into small pieces
salt and pepper

1. Combine the tarragon, chervil, spring onions, peppercorns, vinegar and white wine in a saucepan. **2.** Cook the liquid over a high heat until it is reduced to half its original quantity. **3.** Place the egg yolks, herb and wine mixture and water in the top of a double saucepan over hot but not boiling water, and stir briskly with a wire whisk until it is light and fluffy. **4.** Never let the water in the bottom of the saucepan boil or the sauce will curdle. **5.** Add the butter, piece by piece, to the egg mixture, stirring briskly all the time as the sauce begins to thicken. **6.** Season to taste with salt and pepper. **7.** Strain through a fine sieve and serve.

Demi-glace

Used as a basis for many sauces or to give added body to some sauces.

Makes 2 cups (16 fl oz)

2 cups (16 fl oz) beef stock
2 cups (16 fl oz) sauce Espagnole

1. Add the stock to the Espagnole and simmer, frequently skimming off the spume. **2.** Cook until it reduces to 2 cups. **3.** Strain through a fine cloth or sieve. Store in sealed container until ready to use.

Sauce Espagnole

This is the basis for many other sauces and it can be refrigerated and deep-frozen for future use.

½ cup bacon, chopped
½ cup carrots, chopped
½ cup onions, chopped
½ cup celery, chopped
1 tablespoon chopped thyme
2 bay leaves
¾ cup (6 fl oz) dry white wine
1 cup (8 fl oz) brown roux
1 cup (8 fl oz) concentrated tomato purée
16 cups (4 litres) hot beef stock

1. In a large saucepan, fry the bacon, add the vegetables and cook them gently until lightly coloured. **2.** Add the thyme and bay leaves. **3.** Add the wine, then the roux and stir. **4.** Add the tomato purée and gradually stir in the stock, making sure there are no lumps. **5.** Stir frequently, while bringing the sauce to the boil, so that it does not stick to the bottom of the saucepan. **6.** Place the saucepan on the flame in such a way that it is just under one edge of the saucepan. **7.** Simmer 3–4 hours, stirring frequently and occasionally removing the spume which accumulates on the surface on the opposite edge to the flame. **8.** The sauce should be completed when it reduces to 8 cups (2 litres) of liquid. **9.** Sieve and cover the surface with plastic to prevent formation of a skin.

Kartoffelpuffer

Potato Pancakes

Potato pancakes may be either savoury or sweet. If sweet pancakes are desired, omit the optional ingredients.

Serves 4–6

2 eggs
⅓ cup (1½ oz) flour
1 onion, finely chopped (optional)
½ cup chopped parsley (optional)
½ teaspoon salt
freshly ground black pepper (optional)
¼ teaspoon nutmeg
1 kg (2 lb) potatoes, peeled
125 g (4 oz) lard

1. In a large bowl, lightly beat the eggs. Add the flour and onion, together with the parsley, salt, pepper and nutmeg. **2.** Grate the potatoes and squeeze them so that very little moisture remains. Add them to the egg mixture. **3.** Heat the lard in a frying pan. Drop in sufficient mixture to form pancakes approximately 7.5 cm (3 in) in diameter. Fry them until they are crisp on both sides. **4.** The savoury pancakes may be served instead of potatoes as a vegetable with a main course. If they are served sweet, sprinkle them with sugar and apple sauce.

Madeira sauce

Sauce Madère

Makes 1 cup (8 fl oz)

3 tablespoons Madeira
1 cup (8 fl oz) beef stock
30 g (1 lb) butter
¼ cup (1 oz) flour

1. Add 1 tablespoon of Madeira to the beef stock and bring it to the boil in a saucepan. **2.** In a clean saucepan, melt the butter and add the flour to make a roux. **3.** Add the beef stock and Madeira mixture, stirring well with a wire whisk to make a thickened sauce. **4.** Simmer gently for a few minutes. **5.** Finish the sauce with the remaining 2 tablespoons of Madeira and strain.

Mayonnaise

Makes 1½ cups

2 egg yolks
1¼ cups (10 fl oz) olive oil
1 tablespoon French mustard
juice of 1 lemon
salt
freshly ground black pepper

1. Place the egg yolks and mustard into a bowl and beat with a wire whisk until well blended. **2.** Add the oil, drop by drop at first, then in a thin stream as the mayonnaise thickens. **3.** Add the lemon juice, salt and pepper.

Pancake Batter

Makes 20–24 pancakes

2 cups (8 oz) flour
1 tablespoon sugar (for sweet pancakes)
salt
1¾ cups (14 fl oz) milk
3 eggs, beaten
1½ tablespoons melted butter or oil

1. Sift together the flour, sugar and salt. **2.** Mix in the milk, eggs and melted butter gradually to avoid lumps. **3.** Blend well, then leave to stand for at least 2 hours before cooking. **4.** The batter should be as thin as cream. If it looks too thick, add a little water. **5.** Grease the pan lightly with butter. **6.** For each pancake, spoon about 2 tablespoons of the batter into the heated pan, swirling the pan to allow the batter to thinly coat the entire surface. **7.** Brush a piece of butter around the edge of the hot pan with the point of a knife. **8.** Cook over a medium heat until just golden but not brown (about 1 minute each side). **9.** Repeat until all the pancakes are cooked, stacking them on a plate as they are ready.

10. Cover them with foil to prevent drying out.

Spätzle

Swabian Noodles

Spätzle are closely related to Italian pasta and can be made in various shapes and sizes. Like Italian pasta they should be cooked al dente. They are served either as an accompaniment to main courses or as noodles in soup.

2½ cups (10 oz) flour
½ teaspoon salt
2 eggs, beaten
½ cup (4 fl oz) water (approximately)

1. In a bowl combine the flour and salt. Add the eggs and ¼ cup of the water. Mix until the dough is stiff. Continue adding water until it has the correct consistency, that is, until it comes away easily from the sides of the bowl. **2.** Knead the dough for several minutes until it is smooth, then let it stand for 30 minutes. **3.** Flour a pastry board and roll out to the desired thickness, approximately 3–4 mm (⅛ inch).**4.** With a sharp knife, cut the dough into thin slivers and place them into a saucepan with boiling salted water. Do not put too many slivers in the saucepan at one time because they will stick. **5.** Cook them for approximately 5 minutes until they rise to the surface. Remove them with a slotted spoon or drain them in a colander.

Basic Sweet Pastry

This is a very popular pastry for making fruit flans.

Makes one 25 cm (10 in) flan

1½ cups (6½ oz) self-raising flour
pinch salt
¼ cup (2 oz) caster (powdered) sugar
grated lemon rind or a few drops vanilla essence
125–155 g (4–5 oz) butter or margarine, refrigerated
2 egg yolks or 1 whole egg
1-2 tablespoons cream, wine, rum, milk or water

1. Preheat the oven to 200°C (400°F/Gas 6) for blind baking, or 220° (425°F/Gas 7) with filling. **2.** Combine the flour, salt, sugar, and rind or essence. **3.** With a knife, chop in the butter until it is very fine. If necessary, break it up by hand, keeping the butter as cold and hard as possible. **4.** Form a mound with a hollow on top. **5.** Break the eggs into the hollow, add the liquid and mix with a fork to form a dough. As quickly as possible, knead it with your hands. Prolonged kneading makes the dough soft and difficult to handle. **6.** Press evenly into a cold flan mould. **7.** Bake in the oven until it is a light yellow colour. If underbaked it will taste dull; if overbaked, bitter. Approximate baking time is 20 to 25 minutes for a blind flan, and 30 to 45 minutes with a filling. When baking an unfilled flan, lightly pierce the bottom with a fork.

Savoury Suet Pastry

---

500 g (1 lb) flour
2 tablespoons baking powder (optional)
1½ teaspoons salt
250 g (8 oz) suet, finely chopped
1¼ cups (10 fl oz) water

1. Mix all ingredients, adding enough water to make a pastry of stiff elastic consistency.

Short Crust Pastry

Makes 250 g (8 oz)

2 cups (8 oz) flour
pinch of salt
pinch of sugar
185 g (6 oz) cold butter
a little cold milk

1. Place the flour, salt, sugar and butter in a mixing bowl. **2.** Rub the flour and butter together rapidly between the tips of your fingers until the butter is broken into small crumbs. **3.** Add the milk and blend quickly with your hand, gathering the dough into a mass. **4.** Press the dough into a roughly shaped ball — it should just hold together and be pliable, not damp and sticky. **5.** Place the dough on a lightly floured pastry board and knead it gently to ensure a thorough blend of ingredients. **6.** Gather it again into a ball, sprinkle it lightly with flour and wrap it in greaseproof paper. **7.** Place it in the refrigerator to chill slightly before using.

Puff Pastry

Makes 250 g (8 oz)

2 cups (8 oz) flour
salt
cold water
few drops of lemon juice
220 g (7 oz) butter or margarine

1. Sift the flour and salt together. **2.** Mix to a smooth dough with cold water and a few drops of lemon juice. **3.** Roll out on a floured board into an oblong shape. **4.** Make the butter or margarine into a neat block, and place it in the centre of the pastry. **5.** Fold first the bottom section of the pastry over the butter, and then the top section, so that it is quite covered. **6.** Turn the dough at right angles, press the edges together and depress it with a rolling pin at intervals, to give a corrugated effect and to equalise the pressure of air. **7.** Roll it out to an oblong shape again. **8.** Fold the dough into an envelope, turn it, seal it and repeat the above process. **9.** Repeat this process five times, making seven rollings and seven foldings in all. **10.** Put the pastry in a cold place to prevent it from becoming sticky and soft. **11.** Always chill it before rolling it for the last time, and before baking.

INDEX

Illustrations marked by italic page numbers.

INDEX